Relevant Impact

Organizations operate in environments shaped by volatility, interconnected systems, and rapid technological change. Traditional resilience models cannot keep pace with this level of disruption. *Relevant Impact: A Field Guide to Integrated Assurance* presents a practical path forward. It shows leaders how to strengthen resilience by building capability that functions in real conditions rather than relying on documents and audit scores that often fail under stress.

The field guide expands the Integrated Assurance model introduced in *Integrated Assurance: Unified Risk Strategy* and demonstrates how it works inside real organizations. It explains how governance, operations, security, compliance, and business functions align to create a unified capability that moves with clarity and confidence during uncertainty. The book provides a detailed view of the Integrated Assurance Maturity Model (IAMM) and teaches leaders how to measure trust velocity, control integrity, and recovery performance in ways that influence executive decisions.

This is not a theoretical framework. It is a practical guide that shows organizations how to embed assurance into daily work. It explains how to sense risk as it emerges, strengthen cross-functional coordination, and build teams that act with discipline during high-pressure events. Real examples illustrate how enterprises respond to incidents, manage transformation, and sustain performance while conditions shift around them.

Relevant Impact equips leaders with the structure, language, and metrics needed to convert resilience into a strategic advantage. It offers a clear path for organizations that want to operate with maturity and protect growth in a world defined by constant disruption.

Patrick M. Hayes is a certified enterprise security architect, technology executive, and creator of the Integrated Assurance: Unified Risk Strategy and Integrated Assurance Maturity Model (IAMM). With over two decades of leadership experience, he has launched and scaled multiple startups, led global cybersecurity programs for Fortune 500 and multinational companies, and built award-winning software-as-a-service (SaaS) platforms in risk management and security operations. Patrick is a recognized authority in aligning cybersecurity with business strategy. He is a frequent speaker, published author, and advisor to emerging tech firms and is currently serving as the chief strategy officer and field chief information security officer (CISO) at Third Wave.

Security, Audit and Leadership Series

Series Editor: Dan Swanson, Dan Swanson and Associates, Ltd., Winnipeg, Manitoba, Canada.

The scope and mandate for internal audit continue to evolve each year, as does the complexity of the business environment and speed of the changing risk landscape in which it must operate. The fundamental goal of this exciting series is to produce leading-edge books on critical subjects facing security and audit executives and practitioners. Key topics addressed include Leadership, Cybersecurity, Security Leadership, Privacy, Strategic Risk Management, Auditing IT, Audit Management and Leadership, and Operational Auditing.

Cumulative Effect
Cyber Security Guide for Directors and CEOs
Vladas Leonas

Digital Momentum
Building Real Change-Ready Enterprises
Brice Ominski

Redefining Auditing in the Digital Era
Global Perspectives on Technology, Security, and Leadership
Edited by Abdelmounim Bouziane

Fire Brigades to Firewalls
A Public Safety Guide to Cybersecurity
John Kuforiji

Bridging the Gap
Strengthening the Bond between Audit Committee and Internal Audit
Denise Cicchella

CISO: Evolution of a Vocation
Confessions of a Recovering CISO
Ron Baklarz

Dark Faces in Cyber Places
Shattering Stereotypes and Leading with Legacy in Cybersecurity
Devon Bryan

Logic Before Language
Rethinking AI in the Age of Illusion, Bertrand Russell and the Future of Real AI
Martin Milani

Relevant Impact
A Field Guide to Integrated Assurance
Patrick M. Hayes

For more information about this series, please visit: https://www.routledge.com/Security-Audit-and-Leadership-Series/book-series/CRCINTAUDITA

Relevant Impact

A Field Guide to Integrated Assurance

Patrick M. Hayes

CRC Press
Taylor & Francis Group
Boca Raton London New York

CRC Press is an imprint of the
Taylor & Francis Group, an **informa** business

Designed cover image: Shutterstock ID: 2700678619

First edition published 2027
by CRC Press
2385 NW Executive Center Drive, Suite 320, Boca Raton FL 33431

and by CRC Press
4 Park Square, Milton Park, Abingdon, Oxon, OX14 4RN

CRC Press is an imprint of Taylor & Francis Group, LLC

ISBN: 978-1-041-16700-6 (hbk)
ISBN: 978-1-041-16701-3 (pbk)
ISBN: 978-1-003-68598-2 (ebk)

DOI: 10.1201/9781003685982

Typeset in Sabon
by Apex CoVantage, LLC

To my wife, Yvonne. Your love is a gift from God and the steady grace that carried this work into being. Every chapter is touched by your patience, your quiet strength, and the faith we share. To our children, Olivia, Tadeus, and Adam. You are living reminders of God's promise that hope is found in every new beginning. May you always trust that resilience is born from faith, shaped through trials, and sustained by love.

Lord Jesus, I offer this book to You, the source of all wisdom. Holy Mary, I entrust it to your care and intercession. May every page bring light, strength, and hope to those who read it. Amen.

Contents

About the Book

Relevant Impact: A Field Guide to Integrated Assurance continues the journey that began with *Integrated Assurance: Unified Risk Strategy*. The original work introduced a unified model that connected cybersecurity, IT operations, governance, and business performance. It defined the principles, structures, and maturity model that organizations could use to move from fragmented control toward integrated capability. This second volume builds upon that foundation and presents the model in action. It is a guide for leaders who must translate assurance theory into measurable, repeatable practice.

The purpose of this field guide is to show how Integrated Assurance operates inside modern enterprises. The framework has matured beyond concept. It has become a method for transforming resilience into a core business competency. The focus now rests on how organizations develop assurance as an active capability rather than a static framework. It addresses the cultural, behavioral, and operational realities that shape how trust is earned, sustained, and proven during disruption.

The book's structure reflects this intent.

- **Part I**, "The Shift from Control to Capability," explains how assurance moves from documentation to daily execution and how capability replaces compliance as the measure of readiness.
- **Part II**, "Organizational Change in Motion," explores how this transformation extends beyond security and into human resources, finance, procurement, and engineering.
- **Part III**, "Resilience in the Wild: Use Cases and Outcomes," applies Integrated Assurance to real incidents, showing how enterprises recover stronger through unified operations and shared governance.
- **Part IV**, "Designing for Endurance," looks ahead to the future of federated assurance, adaptive leadership, and the convergence of trust, AI, and resilience at global scale.

The book introduces a new approach to measuring resilience. Traditional indicators such as uptime and policy compliance remain necessary but incomplete. The field guide expands the view with additional performance metrics that include control integrity under stress, trust velocity, adaptation speed, and recovery return on investment (ROI). These measures reflect how resilience performs in motion. They give leaders tangible evidence of readiness and a way to quantify trust as a business asset.

A central theme throughout the field guide is the shift in how risk is perceived and managed. Risk is no longer treated as an external threat to avoid but as contextual intelligence that guides decisions and informs timing, investment, and innovation. When understood through this lens, risk becomes a strategic asset that enables the organization to act decisively amid uncertainty. It serves as both a learning signal and a source of competitive advantage.

The intended audience for this book includes enterprise security architects, transformation leaders, technology executives, and senior decision-makers who seek to connect resilience with performance. It also serves educators and students studying enterprise risk, assurance, and systems thinking. The field guide complements the first book by providing operational guidance and practical examples that demonstrate how Integrated Assurance functions under real conditions.

This work reflects the ongoing evolution of assurance as an enterprise discipline. Integrated Assurance has grown from a unifying cybersecurity framework into a broader organizational model that aligns governance, risk, and performance. It provides a structure for distributed accountability, continuous adaptation, and shared trust across every level of the organization. It turns the concept of resilience into an operational reality.

Relevant Impact: A Field Guide to Integrated Assurance is written for those who must build capability, not just describe it. It is for leaders who believe that assurance belongs inside the rhythm of daily work and that trust should be measured as precisely as any financial outcome. The chapters that follow are both practical and forward-looking, designed to help organizations convert resilience from a recovery plan into a performance advantage.

Author

Patrick M. Hayes is a recognized strategy and operations leader, certified enterprise security architect, and technology executive with over two decades of experience driving innovation, growth, and resilience in the IT and cybersecurity sectors. Throughout his career, he has founded or scaled multiple startups and has spearheaded global expansion strategies across North America, Latin America, and Europe.

Patrick has served in senior executive roles, including chief strategy officer, chief product officer, and chief information security officer, where he architected and launched award-winning software-as-a-service (SaaS) platforms in risk management and security operations. As a certified enterprise security architect, he has led several large-scale security transformation programs for Fortune 500 companies, delivering trusted results in complex and highly regulated environments.

A trusted advisor to emerging tech companies and an active contributor to the cybersecurity community, Patrick blends technical depth with strategic insight. He is a frequent speaker and published author in business and security journals and holds multiple industry certifications.

Patrick is the creator of the Integrated Assurance: Unified Risk Strategy and the Integrated Assurance Maturity Model (IAMM), frameworks that have helped modernize cybersecurity, governance, and operational assurance across global enterprises. Patrick is also the registered trademark holder of Integrated Assurance®, reinforcing his leadership and thought ownership in this evolving field.

Foreword

Looking past hype, fluff, and cluelessness, the most important question any leadership team needs to ask itself is painfully simple:

When the next disruption hits, are we ready, or are we just documented?

I've spent my career of more than 30 years straddling the line between offense and adversary-informed defense and board-level accountability. I've sat in rooms where executives were convinced they were resilient because they had documented plans, clean audit reports, and a screen of logos from compliance frameworks. I've also sat with those same teams during a crisis, watching them realize that none of that paper translated into the ability to seamlessly continue business operations.

That gap, the chasm between assurance on paper and real-world capability in motion, is exactly where this book lives. And that's why it profoundly matters.

Patrick M. Hayes has been quietly building a language and operating system to address that gap. In his first book, *Integrated Assurance: Unified Risk Strategy*, he laid out a foundational model that pulled governance, security, risk, operations, and performance out of their fragmented silos and forced them into one unified conversation. It gave the industry a much-needed framework, the Integrated Assurance Maturity Model (IAMM). This represents a way to talk about resilience as something more than "did we pass the audit?"

Relevant Impact: A Field Guide to Integrated Assurance is where the IAMM grows up and gets to work.

This is not another framework book. It's a book about turning slideware into survivability. Moreover, it's a book about building muscles that the adversaries already assume you lack.

FROM CONTROL THEATER TO REAL CAPABILITY

So many enterprises are extremely good at what I'd call "control theater." They know how to stand up a policy library, pass some audits, assemble responsible, accountable, consulted, informed (RACI) matrices, and deliver decks that make the board and the C-suite feel like things are protected. What they are far less good at is answering the questions that only show up when reality punches back:

- Who actually owns the decisions made in the first 30 minutes of a live incident?
- How fast can we reroute, recover, and communicate without creating more chaos?
- Do our metrics prove resilience and faster containment and recovery, or do they represent clean reports that show what a great group we are?

Patrick's central argument in Part I, "The Shift from Control to Capability," is that resilience has to move from conceptual to operational, from "things we say" to "things we do automatically under stress." He calls out the false comfort of documentation and forces us to confront a hard truth: Compliance coverage is not security capability. Passing an audit is not the same as performing during an attack or an outage.

As a chief information security officer (CISO)-turned-CEO, that distinction is not academic for me. It shows up regularly as protected revenue, avoided churn, reputational durability, and ultimately whether the business emerges from disruption weaker, the same, or stronger.

Integrated Assurance, as Patrick frames it, is the connective tissue that makes this shift possible. Governance stops being a ceremonial exercise and becomes a living authority system. Risk stops being a quarterly heatmap or presentation and becomes a continuous set of signals that informs timing, investment, and innovation. Assurance stops being a bureaucratic department and becomes a capability embedded in how work actually happens.

RISK AS SIGNAL, NOT A CURSE WORD

One of the reasons I resonate with this work is Patrick's refusal to treat risk as a sharply spit-out four-letter word.

In "Risk as a Strategic Asset" and "Opportunity-Focused Risk Culture," he pushes leaders to graduate from a defensive, fear-based risk mindset to one where risk is treated as a source of decision advantage. Risk becomes contextual intelligence:

- It exposes where your operating model is fragile.
- It surfaces where business growth is out of sync with security controls.
- It exposes where organizational culture is either amplifying resilience or eroding it.

That's a step forward from the traditional pattern where risk sits in some corner while innovation sits in another, where there is actual business value. That fragmentation only benefits certain individuals within an enterprise. In the real world, adversaries, market shifts, AI-driven disruption, and identity abuse don't care about that fragmentation. They exploit it.

This book, in its role as a field guide, refuses to let those separations flourish. It insists that risk be democratized and embedded into the tools and workflows where decisions are actually made.

When that happens:

- Risk stops being a bureaucratic slowdown and starts being a speed enabler.
- Resilience stops being a "security project" and becomes a benefit to the whole enterprise.

THE CULTURE WORK

I've long argued that resilience cannot be purchased. It has to be built and embedded in organizational culture.

Patrick dedicates significant space in Part II, "Organizational Change in Motion," to exactly this. The chapters "Breaking the Culture of Siloed Defense," "Operating at the Speed of Trust," and "Boardroom to Break Room" hit on typically avoided topics:

- The psychology of risk.
- The reality of incentives.
- The messiness of human behavior under pressure.

The messages are blunt:

- If governance doesn't reach the teams that ship products, sign contracts, and talk to customers, it's governance theater.
- If trust is not observable in how decisions are made, it's just a word.
- If resilience is not rehearsed in realistic simulations, it will not automagically appear during a crisis.

I appreciate that Patrick doesn't romanticize culture. He treats it as design work. He walks through how to embed cross-functional risk literacy, how to distribute ownership without dissolving accountability, and how to architect telemetry so that executives, operators, and engineers are all looking at the same operational truth and not three incompatible versions of it.

That last point is critical. There is no Integrated Assurance without integrated visibility.

Part III, "Resilience in the Wild: Use Cases and Outcomes," is where many readers will get the "aha" moments. Strategy is important; field cases are where it gets real.

Here, Patrick moves through high-stakes incidents, transformation programs, and recovery scenarios. He uses the IAMM lens to show what differentiated the organizations that merely survived from those that used disruption to be ready. The pattern is consistent:

- Integrated governance moves at the speed of operations.
- Shared playbooks connect security, legal, finance, and business leaders.
- Metrics that focus on recovery, ROI, and adaptation speed, rather than vanity counts of controls or tickets.

CISOs, chief revenue officers (CROs), chief operating officers (COOs), and board members will see mirrored versions of their reality in these stories. These cover the failure patterns and the success paths.

ENDURANCE

Part IV, "Designing for Endurance," speaks directly to where many of us are headed:

- AI-powered adversaries.
- Federated, global enterprises where assurance must work across jurisdictions, cultures, and regulatory regimes.
- A world where trust is a primary currency.

Patrick doesn't treat AI, or any emerging technology, as black magic. He treats them as domains that must be pulled into the assurance fabric. Embedded assurance has to become a reality, as does treating trust as a measurable entity rather than a marketing slogan.

HOW TO READ THIS BOOK

This field guide is not meant to sit on a shelf. It is meant to be used.

My suggestions:

- If you are a security leader, start with Parts 1 and 3. Use the maturity and metric discussions to reframe how you brief your board and executive team. Then pull in your peers in finance, legal, HR, and operations to walk through the incident-driven chapters together.

- If you are a COO, CRO, or business leader, dive into Parts 2 and 4. This is where you'll find the patterns for turning resilience into an organizational competency.
- If you sit on a board or audit/risk committee, treat this as a translation layer. It will give you much better questions to ask than "Are we compliant?" It should also give you a clearer sense of what "good" assurance looks like in an enterprise.

The power of this work is in the shared language it creates. The more disciplines that adopt that language, the faster things move from isolated initiatives to integrated capability.

FINAL THOUGHTS

In my own writing, I've argued that the job of modern security and risk leadership is to become an engine of decision advantage. That requires us to see the enterprise the way an adversary would, but also to act in a way that builds trust, protects revenue, and unlocks innovation.

Relevant Impact: A Field Guide to Integrated Assurance gives leaders a practical, battle-tested way to work toward decision advantage. It replaces static comfort with dynamic capability. It connects boardroom intent to frontline behavior. It treats resilience as a measurable, improvable asset, not a buzzword.

If you are serious about building an organization that can survive disruption and lead through it, read this carefully. Mark it up. Challenge it with your team. Then use it to redesign how assurance works in the messy, high-velocity, high-stakes reality of daily operations.

This book is about performing when it counts, when everything is on the line.

Andres Andreu
Author, The CISO Playbook series

Acknowledgments

I am deeply grateful for the support, feedback, and encouragement.

- Devin Jones—your continued friendship and support and editing of this second book have been invaluable.
- Andres Andreu—from executive insights to the no-nonsense conversations we have daily, you have been a great friend and an inspiration for my cybersecurity work.
- Kevin Austin—my longtime friend and real-world collaborator on how IAMM takes hold in large enterprises.
- A special thanks to Randal Asay and the leadership at Third Wave Innovations for the continued support in my vision of unified security.
- To all my current and past clients, without whom I would not have had the opportunity to develop and refine my skills as an enterprise security architect. This book was born from all these great experiences.

AI Usage Statement

Several artificial intelligence (AI) tools were used in the preparation of this manuscript, each applied with careful oversight and final authorial review. ChatGPT v5.1 assisted in the development of the List of Abbreviations, the Glossary of Terms, the book summary, the chapter abstracts, and the alt-text image descriptions. All figures in this book were generated using Gamma 3.0. Google Gemini v2.5 and v3.0 were employed during later drafting stages to support spelling, grammar, and editorial revisions. Microsoft Copilot in Windows provided spelling and grammar support during initial drafting and early chapter development. All substantive ideas, arguments, interpretations, and conclusions remain entirely the work of the author.

Abbreviations

AI	Artificial Intelligence
AIAMM	AI Integrated Assurance Maturity Model
AICPA	American Institute of Certified Public Accountants
API	Application Programming Interface
AWS	Amazon Web Services
BCM	Business Continuity Management
BIA	Business Impact Analysis
BIOS	Basic Input/Output System
BOM	Bill of Materials
BYOD	Bring Your Own Device
CAIQ	Consensus Assessments Initiative Questionnaire
CFO	Chief Financial Officer
CIO	Chief Information Officer
CIS	Center for Internet Security
CISA	Cybersecurity and Infrastructure Security Agency
CISO	Chief Information Security Officer
CISSP	Certified Information Systems Security Professional
COBIT	Control Objectives for Information and Related Technologies
CPG	Cybersecurity Performance Goals
CSA	Cloud Security Alliance
CSF	Cybersecurity Framework
CSIRT	Computer Security Incident Response Team
CTI	Cyber Threat Intelligence
CXO	Chief Experience Officer/Senior Executive Role
DDoS	Distributed Denial of Service
DLP	Data Loss Prevention
DNS	Domain Name System
DoD	Department of Defense
DR	Disaster Recovery
DRP	Disaster Recovery Plan
EDR	Endpoint Detection and Response
ERP	Enterprise Resource Planning
FBI	Federal Bureau of Investigation
FEMA	Federal Emergency Management Agency
GRC	Governance, Risk, and Compliance
HIPAA	Health Insurance Portability and Accountability Act
HR	Human Resources

IAM	Identity and Access Management
IAMM	Integrated Assurance Maturity Model
ICS	Industrial Control Systems
IoT	Internet of Things
IR	Incident Response
ISAC	Information Sharing and Analysis Center
ISO	International Organization for Standardization
IT	Information Technology
ITIL	Information Technology Infrastructure Library
ITSM	IT Service Management
KPI	Key Performance Indicator
MDR	Managed Detection and Response
MFA	Multifactor Authentication
ML	Machine Learning
MSP	Managed Service Provider
NDA	Non-Disclosure Agreement
NDR	Network Detection and Response
NERC	North American Electric Reliability Corporation
NIST	National Institute of Standards and Technology
NOC	Network Operations Center
OODA	Observe, Orient, Decide, Act
OT	Operational Technology
PaaS	Platform as a Service
PCI DSS	Payment Card Industry Data Security Standard
PII	Personally Identifiable Information
PKI	Public Key Infrastructure
PoC	Proof of Concept
QoS	Quality of Service
RACI	Responsible, Accountable, Consulted, Informed
RAG	Retrieval-Augmented Generation
RFI	Request for Information
RFP	Request for Proposal
ROI	Return on Investment
RPO	Recovery Point Objective
RTO	Recovery Time Objective
SaaS	Software as a Service
SABSA	Sherwood Applied Business Security Architecture
SCADA	Supervisory Control and Data Acquisition
SDLC	Software Development Life Cycle
SIEM	Security Information and Event Management
SLAs	Service Level Agreements
SLOs	Service Level Objectives
SMB	Small and Medium Business
SOC	Security Operations Center
SOW	Statement of Work
SOX	Sarbanes–Oxley Act
SQL	Structured Query Language
SSH	Secure Shell
SSL	Secure Sockets Layer
SWOT	Strengths, Weaknesses, Opportunities, Threats

TCO	Total Cost of Ownership
TOGAF	The Open Group Architecture Framework
TPRM	Third-Party Risk Management
URL	Uniform Resource Locator
USB	Universal Serial Bus
VPN	Virtual Private Network
VPS	Virtual Private Server
WAF	Web Application Firewall
XDR	Extended Detection and Response

Part I

The Shift from Control to Capability

Chapter 1

Beyond Frameworks

1.1 WHY RESILIENCE MUST EVOLVE

Resilience has become a central focus in boardrooms for good reason. Leaders are acutely aware that modern disruptions now occur with greater frequency, velocity, and impact. A supply chain disruption can erode brand trust. A single cyberattack can halt growth. A misinformation campaign can dismantle public confidence within hours. Despite this awareness, many organizations still rely on outdated resilience models designed for a slower, more predictable era. This disconnect introduces unacceptable levels of operational risk.

There is a pattern that repeats itself across industries. After every major disruption, executives will wonder why the company didn't see this coming and why the team wasn't better prepared. More importantly, they will want to know how to ensure it doesn't happen again. The organization's response is often a tactical adjustment—patching procedures, addressing compliance gaps, and layering new controls. What rarely occurs is a foundational shift in how resilience is understood, owned, and executed across the business.

Most of what is considered organizational resilience strategies are conceptual rather than operational. They live in documents rather than in daily decisions. They perform well under ideal conditions but falter in volatility. Too often, control coverage is mistaken for actual capability. Compliance metrics serve as proxies for readiness, giving leaders a false sense of security.

Resilience must now be reframed as an integrated enterprise capability. It is no longer sufficient to treat it as an initiative or a response plan. It must become a defining competency of the organization, embedded across every function, influencing every decision, and shaping every system. This requires more than incremental improvement. It calls for a deliberate transformation from static planning to dynamic execution.

Many organizations continue to approach resilience as an event-driven function. They create continuity plans, run tabletop exercises, and assign accountability to discrete domains. Yet when disruption strikes, confusion dominates. Teams scramble. Responsibilities blur. Decision rights are unclear. Systems are disconnected. Despite best intentions, leaders must often act without real-time insight or coordination.

This is a procedural as well as a structural failure. When resilience is confined to documentation and occasional drills, organizations remain brittle, and plans are purely theoretical. Effective response under stress requires deeply ingrained skills, not loosely affiliated policies. It requires operational muscle, not theoretical knowledge. Consider a basic analogy like preparing for a marathon. Reading about running or occasionally sprinting in isolation will not build the necessary endurance. True readiness comes from repeated conditioning, running under stress, and increased endurance exercises. The same holds for resilience. Integrated performance matters more than individual controls.

DOI: 10.1201/9781003685982-2

Most operating environments only amplify the need for this shift. Distributed workforces, cloud native architectures, and globally interdependent ecosystems increase the complexity and interconnectivity of risk. These conditions demand resilience that functions in real time, across boundaries, with contextual awareness. Evolving resilience begins by redefining its purpose. The objective is not to eliminate disruption. That is unrealistic. The real goal is to build systems that detect anomalies early, absorb impacts without cascading failure, adapt to changing conditions, and recover stronger. Resilience is about elasticity.

This redefinition must extend to the boardroom. Executives should shift their questions from audit compliance to operational responsiveness. Instead of inquiring as to whether systems meet minimum standards, they should ask how quickly the organization can detect, respond, and restore during a critical event. Recovery time should be measured by impact on customers and revenue, not just infrastructure uptime.

Equally important is a change in ownership. Resilience must not reside solely with IT, risk, or compliance teams. That structure creates silos and blind spots. Business units must be equipped with the authority, data, and tools to manage risk in alignment with enterprise strategy. This distributes capability across the organization, improving agility and reducing single points of failure. Resilient teams act instinctively because resilience is embedded in their operating rhythm. Marketing teams adjust campaigns without delay when data breaches occur. Finance ensures liquidity during market volatility. Engineering teams design for graceful degradation and automated restoration. These teams do not need to wait for instructions. Their practices reflect resilience by design, not exception.

Real readiness is measured through live testing. Traditional tabletop exercises often fail to capture the complexity and ambiguity of real incidents. Instead, simulations should reflect authentic business scenarios, where variables are unknown, decisions are unstructured, and teams are tested under pressure. This validates not only systems but also cultural factors such as psychological safety, trust, and leadership under stress.

Technology can enhance assurance, but should not be confused with resilience itself. Monitoring tools, communication platforms, and automation systems add value only when integrated into well-defined workflows with clear accountability. No technology can compensate for organizational misalignment or governance gaps.

At the core of true resilience is trust. Trust within teams. Trust across business functions. Trust in data, in leadership, and in the systems we depend on. Trust accelerates decisions, reduces friction, and enables coordination. It cannot be codified through policy alone. It must be earned through behavior and sustained through shared experience.

This is what it means to build organizational muscle. Not perfection, but preparation. Not documentation, but execution. Not an insurance policy, but a strategic advantage. Organizations that lead in moments of crisis do so because resilience is part of their DNA. Their mission is clear. Incentives are aligned. Teams train together and respond with precision when it matters most.

The objective of *Relevant Impact* is to articulate how organizations can move from theory to capability. It is a call to action to operationalize resilience as a lived discipline and not a theoretical construct. Integrated Assurance provides the blueprint. It connects existing frameworks, embeds accountability into operations, and makes resilience tangible across the organization. Organizations that act on this now will not just survive the next disruption. They will lead through it. See Figure 1.1*:* Integrated Assurance Maturity Model.

1.2 DOCUMENTATION VERSUS REAL CAPABILITY

In many organizations, assurance is perceived as a checkbox exercise. There's an audit checklist, a policy library, and a beautifully formatted disaster recovery plan, all curated and

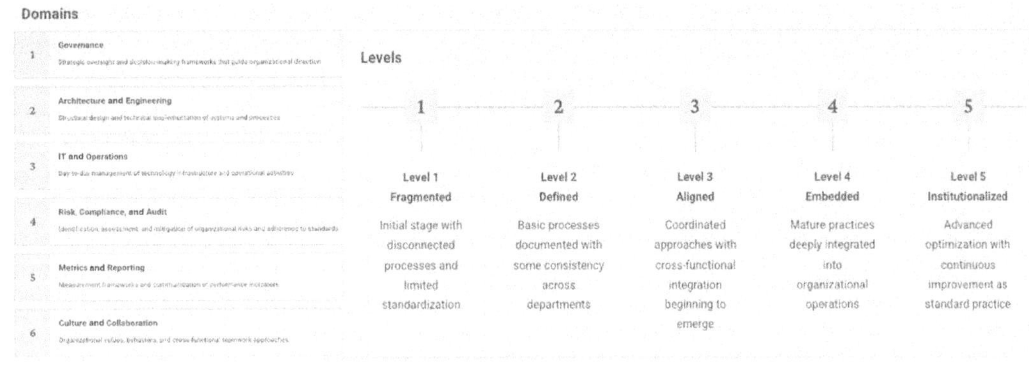

Figure 1.1 Integrated Assurance Maturity Model.
Image created by the author using Gamma.

cataloged to demonstrate due diligence. But when a real crisis strikes, these assets often fail to deliver value in their ability to help respond, recover, and resume operations with confidence.

The allure of documentation is understandable. It offers structure, the appearance of control, and something tangible to show regulators, auditors, and stakeholders. After all, no executive wants to sit in front of a board or oversight committee without a formal plan. But the problem isn't the existence of documentation itself; rather, it's the overreliance on documentation as the primary indicator of readiness.

Frameworks and controls, together with plans, maintain their specific use in operations. These elements serve their purpose in defining expectations while outlining processes and establishing accountability. Documentation serves as a separate entity from actual execution capability. Under stress situations, real capability emerges when people work in concert with processes, technology, and culture to function harmoniously, while a signed-off document provides only passive assurance on its own.

Consider the disaster recovery plan that lists team roles and recovery time objectives. It looks good on paper. But if the named individuals have moved on, the contact numbers are outdated, and the recovery procedures haven't been rehearsed, then the plan becomes nothing more than an artifact. It's a shell of assurance, offering no real help in the moment of truth. During actual disruptions, the most valuable assets are not the plans but the situational awareness, institutional knowledge, and interpersonal trust that enable rapid coordination. Teams that regularly rehearse together, who know each other's roles intuitively, and who operate with shared mental models, are far more effective than those with the most robust documentation.

Many organizations will pass audits but experience failure during real-world emergencies. The established controls remained intact but didn't really align with the operational framework. Although the documentation stayed up to date, the employees lacked proper training. The recorded metrics showed positive results even though they did not accurately represent actual performance. One of the core reasons this illusion persists is the fragmentation of responsibilities. Risk, compliance, cybersecurity, and business continuity are often siloed functions, each maintaining its own version of "the plan." In some cases, these plans even contradict one another. When teams are not working from a single source of operational truth, confusion is inevitable.

The illusion deepens when success is measured by the volume of documentation rather than its effectiveness, even in exercises. All too often, organizations celebrate the completion of compliance frameworks without knowing whether they can actually execute under pressure. This dynamic is especially dangerous in industries such as healthcare, finance, energy, and public infrastructure. In these domains, failure can be life-threatening or financially catastrophic. Yet even here, there's still a dangerous reliance on documented intent over tested performance.

True resilience requires organizations to demonstrate capability beyond creating passive documents. Plans become operational through a combination of drills, walkthroughs, and integrated exercises. Plans need to be accessible to all personnel and not restricted to SharePoint folders, which are difficult to navigate. Every incident, near-miss, and red flag needs to serve as a capability-enhancement opportunity instead of a mere documentation update.

The fundamental principle should be that plans function as hypothetical documents until organizations perform validation tests. The actual execution process allows you to check your assumptions while uncovering dependencies and showing potential bottlenecks. The approach change enables resilience to evolve from a compliance tool into an active learning system.

Documentation is typically accompanied by dashboards and key performance indicators (KPIs) that appear impressive in reports but do not provide any insight into real readiness. A report stating that 100 percent of systems have recovery plans does not convey anything about the effectiveness of these plans or whether they are practiced or if recovery even meets business requirements. A more useful metric would be the percentage of critical systems that have successfully been restored within the recovery time objective during a live exercise. This problem isn't just internal. It affects how organizations communicate resilience to stakeholders. Regulators, investors, and customers increasingly want assurance that goes beyond checklists. They want to know how resilience is tested, if testing includes third parties, and if there's cross-functional coordination under stress.

The good news is that organizations can break this illusion. It begins with the definition of success. Instead of rewarding documentation volume, reward response velocity. Instead of celebrating policy adherence, celebrate the time to containment. This reframing aligns incentives around outcomes, not artifacts. It also involves greater integration. Plans must be developed collaboratively, with input from frontline staff, middle management, and executive leadership. The best resilience plans are not those written by a small team in isolation, but those stress-tested and iterated upon by those who will actually use them.

Technology can support this shift, but only if it's designed for operational use. Plans should be searchable, accessible, and embedded into platforms where work actually occurs. Integration with communication tools, incident management systems, and monitoring dashboards ensures that documentation supports real-time decision-making.

Finally, culture plays a decisive role. In resilient organizations, documentation is treated not as a finish line but as a starting point. Plans are living documents, constantly revised based on lessons learned and changes in the operating environment. Leaders ask tough questions, encourage dissent, and foster psychological safety so that issues are surfaced early. The illusion of documentation will persist until we collectively raise the standard of what preparedness truly means. In this new model, resilience is what you can execute when it matters most. It's not about what you promise regulators. It's about what you deliver to customers. And it's not how clean your documentation looks, but how well your organization functions in chaos. See Figure 1.2*:* Case In Point.

1.3 GOVERNANCE WITHIN IAMM

Governance is the first domain of IAMM, and often the least understood. Many organizations reduce it to a compliance ritual intended to satisfy auditors or demonstrate alignment with regulations. Committees meet, minutes are taken, and policies are approved, yet these structures rarely influence real decisions or operational behavior. When disruption occurs,

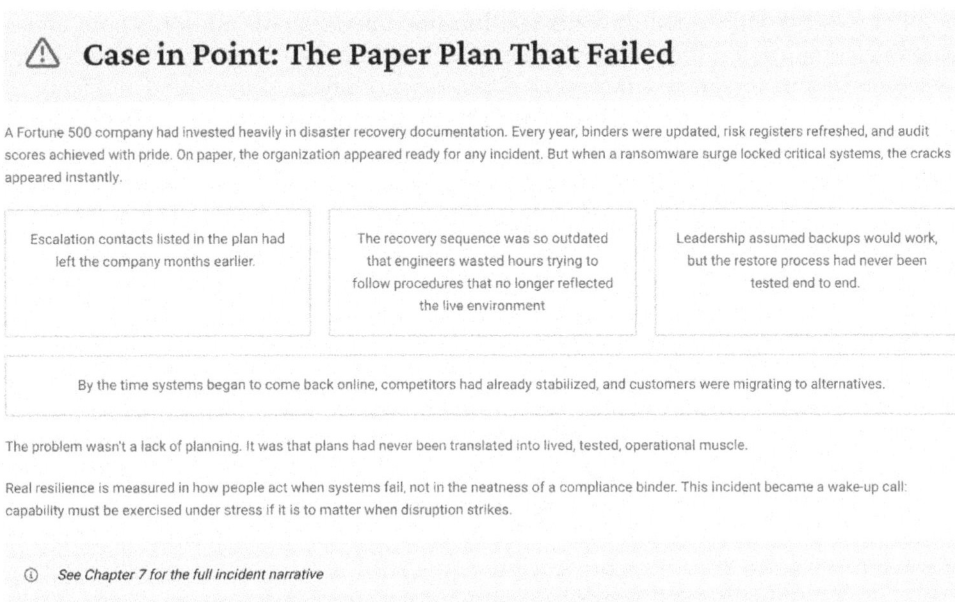

Figure 1.2 Case in Point.

Image created by the author using Gamma.

the weakness becomes visible. Oversight exists on paper, but it does not direct the pace or quality of response. IAMM reframes governance as the anchor of resilience, showing how it must mature to create measurable authority and operational trust.

At Level 1, governance is fragmented or nonexistent. Risk decisions occur in isolation, driven by technical teams without awareness of business priorities. A network engineer might block or permit activity without understanding the financial consequences. A compliance officer may write a control without involving operations. Meetings are infrequent, and decisions are poorly documented. No consistent forum links business, technology, and security. When incidents arise, responses depend on individuals rather than a process. Accountability is unclear, and leadership receives conflicting information or no information at all. This stage reflects fragility built on personalities instead of structure.

Level 2 introduces a definition but remains limited in reach. Governance bodies take form, often as risk committees or steering groups. Policies are written and audits scheduled, creating the appearance of order. The influence of these groups, however, is minimal. They meet quarterly, review sanitized audit reports, and discuss whether controls are documented rather than effective. Operational voices are quiet, and their insight seldom shapes daily work. The organization meets regulatory expectations but gains little in true resilience.

By Level 3, coordination begins to replace formality. Cross-functional forums begin to form and representatives from business, which are the operational parts that can be affected and need to participate in events that affect the company's strategic operations. It could be supply chain, legal, marketing, or even engineering that begins to share ownership of decisions. Records are kept and tracked, though enforcement is inconsistent. Governance becomes a venue for trade-off discussions and risk prioritization. A vulnerability report may be weighed against uptime or customer experience, leading to joint decisions that reflect both risk and value. This stage marks the first point of alignment between oversight and operations, yet it remains dependent on continued executive sponsorship. Without visible support, these structures can lose influence, and decisions may not cascade across the enterprise.

Level 4 represents embedded governance. Forums operate with authority and consistent cadence. Decisions are binding and documented with clear mandates. Business leaders, technology executives, compliance officers, and security architects share equal influence at the table. Governance outcomes feed directly into budgets, product roadmaps, and performance objectives. Exceptions are tracked transparently, and accountability is enforced at the business unit level. Governance now functions as an operational backbone. The organization can demonstrate to boards, regulators, and customers that risk decisions are timely, evidence-based, and authoritative. Oversight transitions from theory to practice.

At Level 5, governance becomes institutionalized. Assurance is not treated as an obligation but as a strategic capability. Governance forums influence innovation, acquisitions, and growth planning. Principles extend into vendor selection, investment portfolios, and customer commitments. Risk ownership is distributed across departments and embedded in performance reviews and operational metrics. Governance becomes part of the enterprise identity. The structure is durable, and its influence is visible in every major decision. Investors recognize stability, customers see reliability, and regulators find consistent trustworthiness.

A real-world example shows this progression clearly. A global manufacturer considers investment in a new digital platform. At Level 2, IT leadership makes the decision alone, treating assurance as an afterthought. Security issues surface late, forcing reactive mitigation. At Level 3, a cross-functional forum reviews the project and identifies risk trade-offs before deployment, creating better visibility but limited enforcement. At Level 4, governance ensures the platform follows secure design patterns, with recovery standards built in and approvals tied to readiness. At Level 5, the decision aligns fully with strategic resilience objectives, satisfies regulatory expectations, and strengthens brand reputation. The maturity of governance defines how effectively strategy becomes reality.

The distinction between Levels 2 and 4 is often measured by timing. When incidents occur, immature organizations learn about risk after the fact. Committees convene after impact. Mature organizations act in near-real time because their governance structures are empowered, informed, and distributed. The difference between compliance and capability determines recovery speed and credibility under pressure. These kinds of controls are typically misinterpreted as cumbersome and bureaucratic. This kind of activity should not be overly onerous, but they do take a moment to understand the overall impact. This is not creating a "department of no," but giving a path to long-term success without unintended consequences. It needs to be an enabler when done right.

IAMM also exposes the barriers that slow progress. Business units often view governance as administrative. Executives delegate authority without visible sponsorship. Finance cycles exclude assurance from planning discussions, limiting influence over priorities. These barriers can be overcome through visible leadership support, integration with budgeting and planning, and clear articulation of value. When governance decisions shape funding and strategy, relevance is no longer in question.

The strategic value of governance maturity lies in its ability to generate trust. Stakeholders increasingly evaluate organizations based on how they make decisions under pressure, not merely on audit results. Level 4 and Level 5 governance provide defensibility. Decisions are documented, traceable, and accountable. This maturity builds confidence among regulators, partners, and customers. It shows that resilience is not reactive but institutional.

Governance is not static or ceremonial. It determines whether assurance is procedural or lived. IAMM transforms governance from oversight to influence, from documentation to direction. Through maturity, enterprises replace fragile coordination with structured authority. In volatile environments, governance maturity becomes the defining factor between organizations that manage disruption and those that are defined by it.

1.4 FROM COMPLIANCE TO CAPABILITY

Organizations don't deliberately choose compliance over capability. Instead, they inherit a system that rewards documentation, enforces regulatory alignment, and emphasizes audit readiness over real-time adaptability. It's a system that was built for a slower, more predictable world. But today's environment requires something far more dynamic, like resilience as a capability.

Compliance, as traditionally practiced, is backward-looking. It answers the question, "Did we do what we said we would do?" Capability, by contrast, is forward-facing and asks, "Can we respond effectively when things go wrong?" The difference between these two mindsets is more than semantics. It defines whether an organization can merely pass an audit or survive a disruption. To be clear, compliance has its place. Regulatory frameworks exist for a reason. They establish minimum standards, enforce accountability, and help ensure uniformity across industries. But minimum standards are just that—necessary but often insufficient. And as we've seen repeatedly, meeting the baseline is not the same as being ready. The most capable organizations recognize that compliance should be a side effect of good operational design, not the primary goal. When systems are designed with resilience in mind, they naturally satisfy compliance requirements. But when systems are designed only to meet audit checklists, they often miss the mark when pressure is applied and miss the point of compliance requirements entirely.

Consider a cybersecurity control that mandates regular vulnerability scans. A compliant organization might run these scans quarterly and store the results for audit purposes. A capable organization, on the other hand, runs scans continuously, correlates findings with threat intelligence, and coordinates with operations to prioritize and remediate critical issues quickly. Both organizations meet the control requirement, but only one derives real operational value.

This concept extends across all domains of enterprise risk. In business continuity, for example, a compliant organization may maintain documented recovery plans and perform annual tabletop exercises. A capable organization goes further. They are conducting frequent simulations with cross-functional teams, integrating resilience into change management, and adjusting plans based on shifting operational priorities and real incidents.

Capability requires investment. It requires buy-in from leadership and a willingness to challenge the status quo. But most of all, it requires a different way of thinking. Instead of asking, "What is required of us to meet compliance?" the capable organization asks, "What is necessary to protect our customers and our brand?" This change in thinking often begins with metrics. Traditional compliance programs measure things like control coverage, policy adherence, and the number of incidents reported. These metrics can create a false sense of security. Capability-oriented organizations, by contrast, measure outcomes, such as mean time to detect, mean time to recover, loss avoided, service impact, and customer satisfaction during disruption.

Another differentiator is how organizations learn. Compliance systems are designed to avoid failure. Capability systems are designed to learn from it. Post-incident reviews, retrospectives, and continuous feedback loops are foundational to building resilience. Mistakes are not hidden. Instead, they are analyzed, shared, and used to inform improvements across the organization. Culture plays a role in this shift. In compliance-driven cultures, employees are often reluctant to speak up about gaps for fear of nonconformance. In capability-driven cultures, identifying gaps is encouraged, even rewarded, because it strengthens the organization.

Integrated Assurance provides the structure to make this shift. It connects compliance activities with operational practices, enabling organizations to fulfill regulatory mandates while also building real resilience. It harmonizes risk, security, and performance goals into a single capability framework. In doing so, it transforms compliance from a standalone

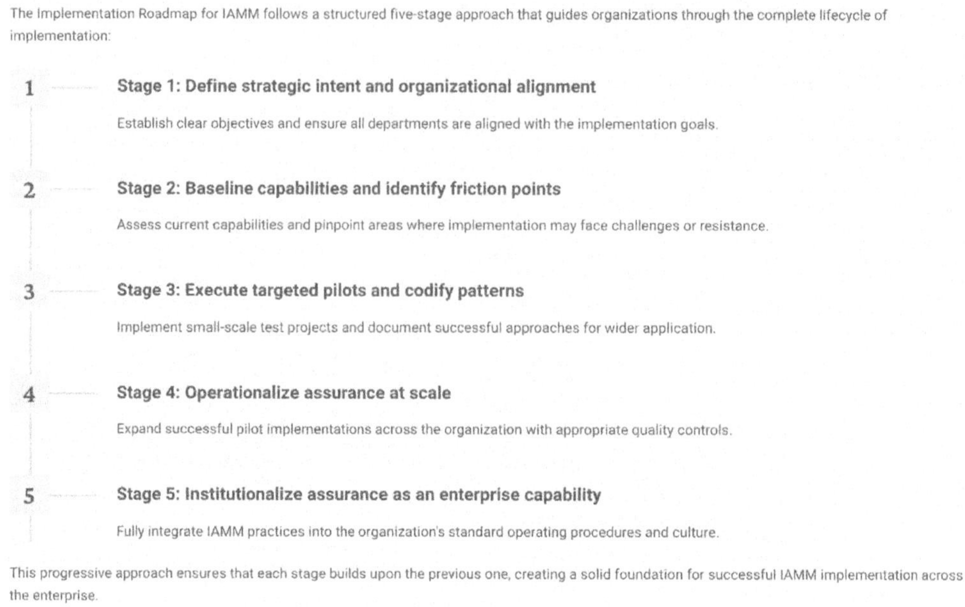

Figure 1.3 Implementation Roadmap for IAMM.
Image created by the author using Gamma.

objective into a natural byproduct of operational excellence. It helps business units see the value of assurance not just in avoiding penalties, but in reducing uncertainty and enabling faster, more confident decision-making.

Moving from compliance to capability doesn't mean abandoning frameworks. It means activating them. It means translating abstract principles into daily habits, relevant metrics, and muscle memory. When that happens, resilience stops being a burden and starts becoming a differentiator. See Figure 1.3*:* Implementation Roadmap for IAMM.

1.5 EMBEDDING ASSURANCE INTO DAILY WORKFLOWS

Assurance cannot be something that only emerges during crisis simulations or audit cycles. To be truly resilient, assurance must be present in the day-to-day operations of the business. That means weaving assurance practices, insights, and decisions directly into the workflows of every team—from engineering to procurement, finance to HR. This is the essence of operationalizing resilience. It should be routine, expected, and consequential. People need to know why they're doing it and how critical it is

Embedding assurance requires more than good intent. It demands redesigning how work is done. In most organizations, assurance lives inside processes. It's in checklists outside of the main systems of record, in risk registers that few people understand, or in documents owned by specialized teams. To change this, assurance needs to be repositioned as a value driver that helps people do their jobs better, not a bureaucratic obstacle.

Start by documenting where the most critical operational decisions are made. These are often the moments where risk is introduced or mitigated, such as vendor selection, system changes, customer onboarding, product releases, or during mergers and acquisitions. At each of these junctures, assurance should be present to inform, constrain, or accelerate decisions. For example, in DevOps workflows, integrating threat modeling into sprint planning ensures that security is not retrofitted after deployment. In procurement, bringing supplier risk scoring into the contract approval process means that risk is visible before commitments are made. In customer support, empowering agents with real-time guidance on privacy policies ensures that responses are consistent with regulatory obligations.

Embedding assurance also requires systems that support it. Assurance inputs, like control effectiveness scores, residual risk levels, and threat intelligence feeds, must be available in the systems where decisions happen. This often means integrating assurance data into enterprise resource planning, customer relationship management, human resources information management, and cloud management platforms. Without integration, assurance becomes an afterthought. With integration, it becomes a natural part of the business rhythm.

Another essential element is workflow ownership. Assurance does not belong solely to second-line functions like risk and compliance. It must be distributed. That means product owners take responsibility for the security implications of their features. Operations managers take ownership of disaster recovery readiness. Finance teams manage fraud risk proactively. This distributed ownership must be backed by support, training, and incentives.

Measurement is key. When assurance is embedded in workflows, new metrics become available. You can now measure things like:

- Percentage of product features that passed privacy review during sprints.
- Time from control failure detection to remediation.
- Supplier onboarding cycle time adjusted for risk score.
- Percentage of service tickets closed with compliance guidance.

These operational metrics are far more valuable than static control checklists. They reflect how resilience is being built and maintained in motion.

Culturally, embedding assurance transforms how teams think about risk, or whether they think of risks at all. It forces them to anticipate the consequences of decisions and makes them responsible for those consequences. Instead of being something managed elsewhere, risk becomes part of how decisions are framed. Instead of avoiding risk, teams learn to navigate it deliberately. This creates a more mature, confident, and accountable organization. The benefits of embedded assurance are substantial. Speed increases because decision-makers have the data they need. Redundancies decrease because assurance is applied once, not in parallel tracks. Trust grows because stakeholders can see that risk is being managed continuously, not periodically.

Embedding assurance can be challenging as it requires cross-functional collaboration. It may challenge existing processes, technology stacks, and governance models. It will likely require investments in tooling, integration, and change management. But it pays dividends in long-term adaptability and confidence. One method for embedding assurance is to create assurance liaisons in each business function. These are individuals who act as translators between central assurance functions and local operations. They understand both worlds and help adapt central principles to local workflows. Over time, this builds embedded capability without creating duplication.

Another key strategy is workflow instrumentation. Embedding doesn't mean inserting assurance steps; it means capturing data. When assurance checkpoints generate data about behavior, performance, or risk posture, that data can be analyzed to drive improvements. Automation plays a growing role here. Risk-aware workflows can trigger automated alerts, route approvals, or initiate remediations. For instance, if a high-risk vendor is selected in a sourcing platform, the workflow can automatically notify legal, flag the issue for a risk analyst, or pause a contract approval until review is complete.

Over time, the goal is to make assurance invisible—not absent—but so well-integrated that it feels like part of the environment. Like good user experience design, embedded assurance supports rather than interrupts. In organizations where this is done well, you see clear patterns. Employees talk about risk naturally. Trade-offs are made with awareness. There are fewer surprises during crises because everyone knows their role, their tools, and their thresholds. The future of resilience is not centralized command-and-control. It is a decentralized capability empowered by shared principles and embedded tools. It is the assurance model in action.

1.6 THE ROLE OF INTEGRATED ASSURANCE

The increasing complexity of risk has outpaced traditional approaches to resilience. Organizations that still rely on siloed risk management, fragmented governance, and isolated operational practices are discovering the painful truth that disjointed assurance leads to disjointed response. Organizations used to be able to get away with ineffectual checklists and binders of outdated processes, but now it's costing real money to not have a plan. The assurance model provides a transformative solution and a unifying operating model that connects governance, risk, security, operations, and performance into a coherent, real-time capability.

At its core, Integrated Assurance is the connective tissue that binds the assurance ecosystem together. It enables organizations to treat risk not as a compliance burden, but as a strategic lever for operational excellence. By aligning assurance functions under a shared vision and shared data model, Integrated Assurance helps the organization respond faster, act smarter, and recover stronger.

What makes the assurance model so powerful is its holistic view. Rather than treating risk management, cybersecurity, compliance, and operational resilience as separate silos, it merges them into an interconnected system that reflects how the business actually runs. This allows for shared situational awareness, better prioritization of risk treatments, and more effective resource allocation.

The traditional problem is that no one sees the full picture. Risk teams see control failures. Security teams see threats. Compliance teams see regulations. Business leaders see disruption. But they all lack a shared view. The assurance model creates that picture by stitching together insights across the assurance lifecycle.

Imagine a scenario in which network operations identifies latency issues affecting a critical customer-facing application. To ensure business continuity, they quickly reroute traffic through a secondary data center and update domain name system (DNS) failover rules. In a fragmented model, operations restores service availability, but security teams may be unaware that the rerouted traffic now bypasses web application firewalls, audit teams may not realize logging has been disrupted, and compliance teams may not know that data is now crossing geographic boundaries in violation of privacy regulations. With Integrated Assurance, the routing change automatically triggers security validation checks, alerts compliance of the data residency shift, initiates audit log verification, and coordinates with all stakeholders to implement compensating controls before the change is finalized. This coordination is what moves organizations from reactive to proactive. It eliminates duplication. It removes friction. It aligns accountability.

But coordination alone is not enough. The assurance model also brings a shift in posture, from defensive compliance to active readiness. Instead of waiting for audits to surface gaps, it continuously monitors performance. Instead of relying on quarterly reviews, it drives daily visibility. Instead of assessing maturity once a year, it cultivates it continuously. This requires a different kind of data architecture. The assurance model is built on shared taxonomies, interoperable tooling, and unified reporting. When a vulnerability appears in a security information and event management (SIEM) dashboard, the business impact should be immediately visible. When a supplier breach occurs, affected business processes should be automatically identified. When a control fails, escalation should be triggered based on impact, not just severity.

That visibility enables smarter decision-making. Risk is no longer abstract. It is tied to revenue, brand, and operational continuity. It's tied to an impact relevant to the business. Leaders can make informed trade-offs, such as accelerating innovation while still protecting the organization.

For the board and executive teams, Integrated Assurance provides something they've long lacked—meaningful assurance that goes beyond static reports. With real-time dashboards, scenario-driven metrics, and integrated response plans, executives can understand where the organization stands and how prepared it is to move forward.

It also empowers frontline teams. The goal of the assurance model is to decentralize capability and give business units access to the same assurance insights as central teams, allowing them to manage their own risk exposure in alignment with organizational objectives.

The cultural impact of Integrated Assurance is significant. It encourages shared ownership. When risk is visible to all, accountability becomes collective. When resilience is part of every team's mission, silos break down. And when assurance functions collaborate instead of competing, the organization becomes more agile.

Successful implementation requires leadership, not just architecture. Organizations must define a vision for Integrated Assurance and align it with strategic priorities. They must empower cross-functional governance bodies to oversee integration efforts. And they must invest in change management to embed new behaviors.

To bring Integrated Assurance to life across the organization, five guiding principles should shape the journey. First, design for interoperability by connecting systems, data, and workflows across risk, compliance, security, and operations. The assurance model depends on a shared ecosystem rather than isolated tools. Second, start with what matters most by focusing on the most critical processes and systems. Integration efforts should tie directly to enterprise value, not generic maturity models. Third, drive with metrics that measure outcomes, not just activity. KPIs should reflect real resilience, such as recovery time, containment speed, or service continuity under stress, rather than compliance coverage alone. Fourth, make it visible by developing dashboards that align executive, operational, and technical views. When everyone is working from the same source of truth, trust and coordination improve. Finally, enable and empower business units to take ownership. This means equipping teams with the right tools, playbooks, and context to manage assurance responsibilities without waiting for central approval. Together, these principles form the foundation of an Integrated Assurance model that is not only scalable but also embedded across the daily rhythms of the organization. See Figure 1.4: Five Principles of Integrated Assurance.

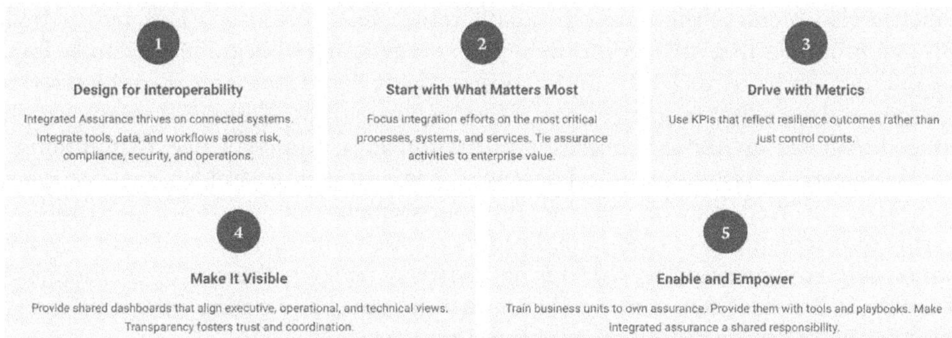

Figure 1.4 Five Principles of Integrated Assurance.

Image created by the author using Gamma.

It's important to recognize that Integrated Assurance is not a programmatic evolution. It is not a new layer on top of existing systems. It is the connective logic that allows those systems to work together.

1.7 DEVELOPING RESILIENCE AS AN ORGANIZATIONAL COMPETENCY

Developing resilience as an organizational competency is not a checkbox exercise. It is a deliberate, enterprise-wide journey that transforms resilience from an abstract goal into a cultural norm and operational strength. When resilience is fully embedded, it becomes as much a part of the organization as its brand, values, or strategic goals. It becomes how the business thinks, how it operates, and how it competes.

True resilience cannot be outsourced, delegated to a single function, or relegated to a disaster recovery binder. It must live in the muscle memory of every team, reflected in the decisions they make, the tools they use, and the trade-offs they evaluate. It is learned over time, through intentional practice and collective reflection.

The first step in developing resilience is recognition. An honest assessment that current models may be insufficient. This means moving beyond the comfort of legacy practices and asking difficult questions like, "When was the last time we tested our readiness?" and "Do people know what to do in a real crisis?" These questions reveal maturity gaps that point the way forward. Mature organizations approach resilience through structured training, scenario-based practice, and continuous feedback. They run realistic simulations that reflect not only technical disruptions but also business-level consequences. They rehearse leadership decision-making under stress. They test interdepartmental coordination, crisis communications, and the ability to operate with incomplete information.

What sets these organizations apart is not perfection. It's preparation. It's not that they avoid disruption, because no organization can. It's that they handle it better, faster, and with more clarity than their peers. They turn resilience into a competitive advantage, reducing downtime, preserving stakeholder trust, and accelerating recovery.

One key trait of resilient organizations is role clarity. In a crisis, ambiguity is the enemy of speed. Everyone must know their role, escalation paths, and decision rights. This clarity is cultivated through repeated training and refinement. Another trait is cross-functional coordination. Too many organizations still respond to disruption within silos. Security handles the breach, operations handle the outage, and PR handles the message. But resilient organizations integrate these functions into a single response engine. They use common playbooks, unified communication protocols, and shared decision frameworks.

Resilience also requires the ability to adapt rather than just react. This means building systems and processes that are flexible, modular, and designed to degrade gracefully. It means having multiple paths to recovery, and choosing them based on context, not prescription. Most importantly, resilient organizations foster a culture of psychological safety. People are encouraged to speak up about concerns, report anomalies, and challenge assumptions. This culture of openness is foundational to learning. When mistakes are hidden, they are repeated. When they are surfaced, they become fuel for improvement.

The role of leadership is critical here. Leaders set the tone for how resilience is valued. If executives only pay attention to risk during quarterly reviews, the rest of the organization will follow suit. But if leaders make resilience part of strategic planning, operational reviews, and performance assessments, it becomes institutionalized.

To truly build resilience as a competency, organizations must also invest in learning infrastructure. This means maintaining a library of incident reviews, capturing lessons learned, and turning them into actionable insights. It means using data to analyze response patterns and improve coordination. And it means celebrating not just success but learning from failure.

Integrated Assurance enables this competency-building by providing the connective framework. It ties resilience to everyday work. It aligns strategy with execution. It ensures that learning loops are closed, that coordination is systematic, and that capability is always maturing. Over time, as resilience becomes a core competency, its effects ripple outward. Teams become more agile. Customers become more confident. Investors become more trusting. And the organization becomes not just more secure, but also more competitive.

This is what *Relevant Impact* is all about. It is not just about managing risk. It is about operationalizing trust, accelerating readiness, and unlocking strategic advantage. Because in a world defined by disruption, resilience isn't just how you survive. It's how you lead.

1.8 CONCLUSION

Organizational resilience has transitioned from being a theoretical concept or compliance requirement to an operational necessity that organizations must prove through their real-time responses and their ability to adapt under stress and recover quickly with assurance. The evidence shows that authentic resilience requires active practice rather than declarations in stressful situations, executed with precision. The development of this strength requires systematic training during the building process because it creates both strength and automatic performance abilities rather than relying solely on strategic documents and audit checklist compliance.

The legacy method, which bases its operations on frameworks and policy verification, creates an inaccurate belief that resilience can be proven through documentation. But disruption doesn't care about your documentation. Your organization's success depends on people's knowledge of procedures and systems, graceful degradation abilities, and the organization's capacity to recover quickly, independent of authorization. The false sense of readiness has led to the loss of trust while enabling weaknesses throughout sectors, which equate regulatory compliance with actual operational ability.

Integrated Assurance provides the necessary paradigm shift. The system integrates existing frameworks to create dynamic operational components that guide daily activities. The assurance process gets integrated into business decisions and goes beyond policy implementation. The system unifies risk management with performance optimization and operational functions to create a unified platform that stays aware and accountable while maintaining readiness. This is not a technological problem. Leaders must overcome this challenge through their ability to transform assurance thinking beyond implementation methods.

Each section of this chapter establishes the fact that resilience needs to become part of organizational structures instead of remaining outside them. It must be an integral element for engineers writing code, as well as procurement choosing vendors and marketing, handling reputation issues, and finance managing market volatility. A complete integration needs organizations to develop trust, which extends from systems to functions and teams and throughout all leadership levels. Trust is required for resilience just as muscles require oxygen to function properly. Such systems appear robust until they face persistent stress, which makes them fail.

The move toward capability-based assurance changes our fundamental organizational values. Organizations should begin rewarding teams for their time-to-containment performance instead of focusing on achieving perfect audit scores. Organizations should shift their focus away from creating recovery documents and toward assessing the effectiveness of their recovery processes. Organizations that demonstrate resilience master rapid learning, respond

This checklist helps leaders determine whether resilience in their enterprise is documented on paper or demonstrated in practice. The goal is to test capability under stress—not just compliance with frameworks.

1

Real-Time Readiness

- ☐ Has every critical business function participated in a live simulation or red-team exercise in the past 12 months?
- ☐ Are incident response roles and decision rights clearly defined, rehearsed, and understood by staff at all levels?
- ☐ Can frontline teams act without waiting for executive approval when disruption strikes?

2

Muscle Memory in Practice

- ☐ Do teams regularly rehearse together across silos (e.g., finance, engineering, communications, legal) instead of isolated tabletop drills?
- ☐ Are recovery playbooks tested under conditions of stress (e.g., missing data, key leaders unavailable, simultaneous crises)?
- ☐ Do employees report they feel psychological safety to surface gaps or concerns during exercises?

3

Capability Over Documentation

- ☐ Do you measure success by time to containment, recovery speed, and stakeholder impact rather than "audit completion" or "policy updates"?
- ☐ Are recovery metrics validated by live drills (e.g., restoring systems within RTO) rather than self-reported compliance?
- ☐ Does leadership regularly review real-world performance metrics instead of checklist status reports?

4

Assurance in Daily Operations

- ☐ Is assurance embedded into workflows such as procurement, product release, HR onboarding, and vendor onboarding?
- ☐ Are assurance tools and data integrated into the systems people already use (ERP, CRM, DevOps pipelines)?
- ☐ Do business unit leaders take ownership of their own resilience posture rather than relying solely on central risk or IT?

5

Trust as the Core Indicator

- ☐ Is there a shared telemetry system providing real-time visibility across functions?
- ☐ Do employees and executives trust the data and dashboards enough to make time-critical decisions?
- ☐ Can leadership demonstrate that customers, regulators, and partners trust the enterprise because of consistent, transparent handling of disruptions?

Key Takeaway: Passing an audit shows compliance. Passing this checklist shows capability under fire. Real resilience is demonstrated when your organization can absorb shocks, act decisively, and recover stronger – without waiting for the manual.

Figure 1.5 Practical Checklist: How to Test If Your Organization Has Operational Muscle.
Image created by the author using Gamma.

fastest, and coordinate most effectively during high-pressure situations. We need to develop this essential strength. Real resilience emerges from developing this capability.

Operationalizing resilience also means decentralizing ownership. Every business unit should possess the power to act, even though central teams provide guidance through governance. Such decentralization enables faster decision-making and better situational awareness, along with effortless response scalability. People in resilient organizations start taking action without permission because they have rehearsed and experienced the procedures and feel a strong sense of ownership.

Leaders play a significant role in determining this outcome. A resilient organization develops from executive decisions that model resilience alongside their commitment to capability development and their funding of Integrated Assurance systems. Leadership behavior regarding resilience determines how the rest of the organization will approach it. When resilience becomes integrated into performance reviews, product planning, and operational reviews, it transforms into cultural behavior, which becomes expected and practiced, leading to repeatable results.

This chapter presented a new approach for determining success. The current dashboard structure requires transformation. The KPIs must measure detection velocity along with recovery success rates and impact on stakeholders while eliminating control metrics. The main objective focuses on precise risk management coupled with confident outcomes. Operational truth-based metrics replace audit convenience to function as improvement tools rather than blocking inaction.

Resilience functions as a unified team effort between different groups. Integrated Assurance establishes a common risk-readiness-recovery terminology that connects all personnel—from executive offices to frontline workers. The system unites people with processes, technology, and culture to create an enhanced response system that surpasses disruption. The transformation of resilience into a core competency enables organizations to build competitive advantage through its development as a fundamental business competency.

Operational domains will be examined in the following chapters to explain how assurance integration affects workflow operations and risk alignment with business objectives and daily resilience practice development. Organizations that endure in a volatile world will be those that view resilience as a dynamic strength rather than a static goal. See Figure 1.5: Practical Checklist: How to Test If Your Organization Has Operational Muscle.

Chapter 2

Risk as a Strategic Asset

2.1 REDEFINING RISK IN A MODERN ENTERPRISE

Risk has long carried a negative association across most industries. In boardrooms and executive strategy sessions, the mention of risk typically triggers a defensive reflex. For many years, it was synonymous with liability, exposure, or the threat of failure. It was something to avoid, mitigate, or transfer as quickly and quietly as possible. This mindset, while understandable, was built for a different time. In a business environment shaped by linear growth and predictable change, it made sense to treat risk as something external to progress. But the world has changed. Speed, interconnectivity, and uncertainty are now defining features of how organizations operate. And in this new reality, risk must be redefined.

Risk is no longer just a threat to be mitigated. It is a vital input that informs strategy, strengthens operational design, and enables innovation. Forward-looking organizations understand that risk can illuminate blind spots, identify emerging pressure points, and provide early signals of opportunity. The key is to move risk out of its reactive position and into a more central role within the business operating model.

Historically, risk has been viewed through narrow lenses. Financial exposure, regulatory compliance, and insurance liability have shaped how organizations define and manage it. Enterprise risk management (ERM) programs evolved around static methodologies such as periodic assessments, control checklists, and heatmaps. Risk was quantified in spreadsheets and reviewed in quarterly governance meetings. These mechanisms made sense in slower environments, where decisions could wait for committee approval and where major shifts happened gradually. Today, those same mechanisms introduce delay, misalignment, and missed opportunities.

Organizations now need to be built on agility. Global supply chains shift daily. Digital systems interact across cloud environments and third-party platforms. Data flows are continuous, and customer expectations change at the speed of influence. In this operating context, a snapshot view of risk is insufficient. Organizations need a live feed. They require risk sensing that is dynamic, integrated, and able to influence decisions in real time.

Risk must now be seen as a signal. It should be treated as part of the organization's sensory nervous system, able to detect fragility, change, and imbalance before damage occurs. It can indicate where assumptions may no longer hold, where dependencies are shifting, or where adversaries may gain advantage. Properly integrated, risk becomes a key part of how the organization learns, adapts, and moves forward.

This redefinition does not call for the elimination of traditional risk functions. Instead, it demands that they evolve. The compliance officer, internal auditor, and risk manager are no longer gatekeepers at the end of the decision chain. They must become embedded partners in product development, business planning, customer experience, and merger and acquisition strategy. Their role is to guide it with insight and foresight. Organizations that treat risk as

DOI: 10.1201/9781003685982-3

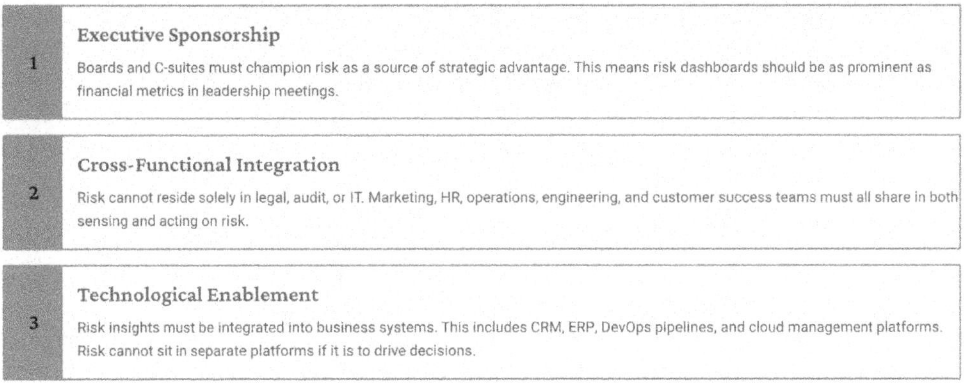

Figure 2.1 Redefining Risk in a Modern Enterprise.
Image created by the author using Gamma.

a growth-enabling function are better positioned to act with speed, scale new offerings, and respond to market shifts confidently.

One of the most visible changes in this new approach is how risk integrates with agile delivery models. Agile methodologies have become the default for product development, transformation programs, and innovation labs. In these environments, work is delivered in short sprints, and priorities are updated frequently. Traditional risk management, which depends on formal reviews and static documentation, simply cannot keep up. Instead, risk must become continuous. It must be embedded into each planning cycle, each sprint review, and each feedback loop.

This is where the concept of Integrated Assurance becomes critical. Integrated Assurance unifies governance, risk, security, and operations within a shared model. It allows risk intelligence to flow across systems and teams. When done right, it ensures that product teams can raise and respond to risk in real time, that operations leaders can make informed trade-offs, and that executives can rely on live dashboards rather than historical summaries. The result is better decisions, faster execution, and greater alignment between enterprise strategy and day-to-day activity. For risk to play this expanded role, three foundational shifts must occur. See Figure 2.1: Redefining Risk in a Modern Enterprise.

First, risk must be championed at the top. Boards of directors and executive leadership must position risk not as a cost of doing business, but as a common skillset required for shaping it. Risk dashboards should sit alongside revenue metrics and customer data in leadership meetings. Risk appetite should be tied to growth objectives, and executives should be fluent in discussing exposure in the context of innovation and transformation. This level of sponsorship signals that risk has a seat at the strategic table, not just in the audit committee.

Second, risk must be democratized across the organization. It cannot be confined to the legal department, compliance office, or cybersecurity team. Risk insights must be available to marketing teams planning a campaign, to procurement teams onboarding a new vendor, and to product teams building new services. When risk is everyone's job, it becomes part of how the organization thinks, designs, and moves. This does not mean creating risk specialists in every role. It means giving each function visibility into the risks that affect their work and empowering them to act.

Third, risk intelligence must be embedded into the systems people use every day. Platforms like CRM, ERP, DevOps toolchains, and cloud orchestration environments must all surface relevant risk insights. These insights must be contextual and actionable. A product team should see privacy risk scores when designing a new feature. A supply chain manager should receive risk alerts tied to geopolitical disruptions. An executive reviewing a strategic initiative should be shown resilience metrics alongside financial forecasts. When risk is integrated into these operational systems, it becomes part of the workflow rather than an external process.

By redefining risk through this operational lens, organizations gain a new capability. They gain the ability to make decisions with greater speed and confidence. They can align action across business units more effectively. And they can pivot more quickly when the environment shifts. Risk ceases to be a compliance overhead. It becomes a source of momentum.

Consider how this plays out in a real-world context. A healthcare provider planning to launch a new patient-facing mobile app will face regulatory, reputational, and operational risk. In the traditional model, risk reviews would happen at the end of the development process, likely as a gating function before deployment. Any issues discovered late would trigger delays, rework, or risk acceptance forms. In a redefined model, risk signals are embedded into the app's development pipeline from the beginning. Privacy controls are reviewed during initial design. Threat modeling is conducted during sprint planning. Risk acceptance thresholds are calibrated to patient trust metrics. As issues emerge, they are addressed immediately, rather than being accumulated for later review. The result is faster delivery with higher confidence and a user experience designed with trust in mind from day one.

Another example involves supply chain risk. A global manufacturing firm may rely on hundreds of third-party vendors across multiple continents. Traditional risk models assess these relationships annually or after a disruption has already occurred. A modern risk approach uses live data to sense delays, monitor geopolitical factors, and analyze vendor performance in real time. With these insights embedded into procurement workflows, the organization can respond to weak signals early. It can switch suppliers, renegotiate contracts, or adjust delivery timelines proactively. This not only reduces disruption but builds strategic agility.

When risk is redefined, it also opens the door to new forms of innovation. Organizations that understand their risk tolerance can take calculated risks. They can experiment with new technologies, enter new markets, or test new business models without waiting for perfect certainty. Risk becomes a boundary condition for innovation, not a blocker. It guides decisions and sets parameters, but it does not prevent progress. In fact, risk can accelerate progress by providing clarity and confidence.

Organizations that embrace this new risk mindset often report stronger cultural alignment. Teams become more comfortable discussing uncertainty. Leadership encourages transparency. Failure is viewed as a learning opportunity rather than a career hazard. This creates a healthier, more adaptive environment where people are empowered to surface concerns early and act decisively.

To truly redefine risk, the organization must move beyond reactive habits. This is not about rebranding risk management. It is about reengineering how risk influences behavior, decisions, and systems. Integrated Assurance plays a central role in this transformation. It serves as the connective architecture that allows risk to flow, to be sensed, and to be acted upon across the business. In doing so, the organization moves from managing risk to harnessing it. Risk becomes an advantage, because it is understood, integrated, and used as a driver of action. The result is an organization that not only survives in uncertainty but thrives within it. This is the hallmark of modern leadership.

2.2 OPPORTUNITY-FOCUSED RISK CULTURE

A cultural shift is underway in how high-performing organizations approach risk. The old model treated risk as a threat to be feared, minimized, and locked away in specialized departments. In this worldview, risk was a liability to be managed quietly and contained aggressively. It was something to survive. Today, the most resilient organizations are embracing a new perspective that sees risk as a resource, while it remains a potential hazard. These organizations are evolving toward opportunity-focused risk cultures, where uncertainty is used as a strategic input rather than a compliance burden.

This transformation is not a surface-level change. It requires deep cultural realignment. It challenges assumptions that have been built over decades. Organizations must reexamine the role risk plays in decision-making, performance measurement, and innovation. The key understanding is whether organizations view risk as something to suppress, or whether they treat it as something to learn from.

Defensive risk cultures are grounded in fear. Their primary instinct is protection, containment, and avoidance. Risk is managed reactively, often in the background. It is handled by a limited group of experts who are expected to monitor compliance, generate reports, and flag issues to satisfy audit committees or regulators. In these environments, risk conversations are often viewed with skepticism. Individuals who raise concerns may be labeled as blockers or pessimists. The cultural undertone is that risk is a distraction from growth, not a tool for it.

Opportunity-focused risk cultures are built on a different foundation. These organizations treat risk as a strategic signal. They ask better questions. Instead of "How do we eliminate this risk?," they ask "What is this risk telling us about our design, our assumptions, our timing, or our approach?" This reframing allows risk to be used as a feedback loop. It becomes a directional input, helping the organization see where innovation is needed, where resilience must be reinforced, and where transformation could accelerate.

Changing the culture starts with language. The words used to describe risk shape how people feel about it. When risk is consistently described using terms like failure, liability, or exposure, the human instinct is to avoid the topic altogether. People fear blame. They worry about reputational damage. In such climates, issues are buried until they explode. But when risk is framed as insight, signal, or foresight, it becomes something people are willing to surface and discuss. A small change in phrasing can unlock a big change in behavior. Instead of identifying a project as too risky, consider reframing it to show that the project highlights several exposure points that can be addressed early, giving you an edge. That simple shift reframes risk as something valuable.

The ability to have open risk conversations depends on psychological safety. Without it, risk intelligence remains hidden. Employees who sense that something is off will stay silent if they fear retaliation or ridicule. In a blame culture, the cost of speaking up feels too high. Risk signals are lost, and systems degrade in silence. Conversely, in a culture built on trust and transparency, raising a concern is seen as a responsible act. Teams share what they see, leaders listen, and the organization grows smarter.

As an example, what if a software firm introduced risk-reflection checkpoints into every development sprint? Alongside standard tasks, such as feature completion and testing, teams were asked to reflect on potential risks that emerged, how they responded, and what they should monitor post-deployment. These questions would become routine. Over time, the exercise could normalize risk discussions. Engineers would begin to flag design issues earlier, identify customer experience trade-offs, and raise architectural concerns proactively. Risk could stop being a red flag and instead be used as a tool for improvement.

An opportunity-focused risk culture also decentralizes ownership. In traditional models, risk is seen as the job of the legal team, compliance function, or information security department. Everyone else assumes they are just users or recipients of rules. This siloed model creates blind spots. It fosters a false sense of safety. But when risk ownership is distributed, the organization gains agility. Each department becomes responsible for the risks it encounters. Marketing teams own reputational risk. Procurement owns third-party risk. Engineering owns technical debt. Everyone is accountable for surfacing, managing, and responding to the risks relevant to their domain.

This distributed model requires strong connective tissue. Integrated Assurance becomes essential. It ensures that different parts of the organization can speak a shared language about risk. It connects the dots between operational insight, compliance requirements, and strategic planning. It ensures risk is not fragmented or duplicated. Instead, it becomes an aligned and enabling function.

Metrics also need to evolve. Defensive cultures often use lagging indicators such as incident counts, audit scores, or policy violations to measure performance. While these are useful, they can be misleading. A team with zero reported risks is not necessarily a high-performing team. They might simply be disengaged or afraid to speak up. A more meaningful indicator is the number of risk signals submitted, the response time to new exposures, and the quality of decision-making under pressure. These leading indicators reflect a more proactive and responsive culture. They show how well the organization is sensing and learning, not just how well it is hiding problems.

Training is another cornerstone. Many employees have never been taught how to identify or communicate risk effectively. They may recognize a concern but struggle to frame it in terms that will be taken seriously. Risk fluency must be built into onboarding, leadership development, and function-specific training. Different teams need different capabilities. Finance teams need to understand regulatory risk. Product teams need to understand ethical risk. Customer service teams need to understand privacy risks. Tailored training builds confidence, which drives participation.

None of this happens without leadership. Executives must model the behavior they want to see. That means asking risk-related questions in meetings. It means acknowledging those who raise concerns. It means reacting with curiosity rather than frustration when an issue is surfaced. The tone from the top defines the temperature of the culture. If senior leaders treat risk conversations as strategic dialogue, others will follow. If they treat risk as a nuisance, it will go underground.

Leaders must also elevate risk to the same level as customer satisfaction, performance metrics, and growth forecasts. Risk data should be reviewed routinely—not just during crisis events or compliance audits, but during quarterly reviews, strategy planning sessions, and product launch assessments. Making risk visible communicates its value. It reinforces that it belongs at the center of decisions, not at the margins.

The shift also requires a systems view. Risks rarely emerge in isolation. They develop across silos and propagate through dependencies. A small vendor failure can trigger a major outage. A lack of clarity in product messaging can evolve into a reputational scandal. Organizations that map interdependencies and encourage cross-functional awareness are better positioned to detect these compound risks before they escalate. They build structural resilience through shared visibility.

Ultimately, organizations that operate with an opportunity-focused risk culture recognize that risk-taking is not inherently negative. Some of the greatest business breakthroughs in history have occurred because someone took a well-informed risk. For example, in 2007, Netflix made a shift to online streaming, despite the wildly successful mail-to-order DVD business it had built. Market investments, product innovation, and digital transformations involve navigating uncertainty. The goal is not to eliminate risk. That is neither realistic nor desirable. The goal is to develop the capacity to engage with risk intelligently, quickly, and transparently.

The transformation from defensive to opportunity-focused risk culture is both necessary and achievable. It requires four core elements. First, leadership modeling that treats risk as a strategic concern. Second, a system design that embeds risk into daily workflows. Third, cultural norms that foster openness, accountability, and trust. Fourth, education and incentives that promote risk fluency and timely response.

Organizations that embrace this shift position themselves to thrive in volatility. They use risk not just to protect the enterprise but to shape its future. They make better decisions, move with confidence, and build stronger relationships with customers, employees, and partners. Risk becomes a force for growth. It becomes a capability and not a constraint.

2.3 IAMM AND RISK MATURITY

Risk is almost always treated as a compliance requirement rather than a strategic discipline. Heatmaps, registers, and quarterly reports dominate executive discussions, yet they seldom reveal how risks influence growth, reputation, or resilience. The Integrated Assurance Maturity Model (IAMM) reframes this view by tracing how risk maturity evolves from fragmented documentation to strategic integration.

At Level 1, risk management is incomplete and inconsistent. Each department maintains its own spreadsheets, and information rarely aligns. The compliance team records control failures while operations tracks downtime. Executives receive conflicting data, and accountability remains unclear. Evidence for regulators is assembled in haste, reflecting symptoms rather than structure. The organization cannot link risk to strategy because it lacks a unified system for identifying or ranking exposures.

Level 2 reflects procedural maturity without strategic depth. Policies exist, and committees review risks on a set schedule. Reports are archived, and auditors find sufficient documentation. Yet the process remains static. Heatmaps describe past assessments and fail to show how risk is changing now. Leadership uses this information defensively, focusing on proving that risks are cataloged rather than managed. Compliance is achieved, but preparedness is not. The organization appears disciplined but remains vulnerable to surprise, and risk has yet to be incorporated into its future-looking decisions strategically.

Level 3 introduces coordination. Shared registers bring together compliance, operations, security, and business leadership. Dialogue replaces isolation. Risk owners debate priorities and recognize the interdependence of issues once considered separate. A system outage is seen not only as a technical problem but also as a financial, regulatory, and reputational one. This collaboration builds coherence, yet the system still depends on manual updates and retrospective reviews. Awareness grows, but agility is limited.

At Level 4, risk becomes part of how the enterprise makes choices. Risk intelligence is present when products are designed, markets are analyzed, and budgets are approved. The board examines exposure alongside performance. When evaluating an acquisition, leadership weighs not only cost and market potential but also resilience, continuity, and regulatory posture. Risk no longer blocks innovation. It provides context that guides investment, development, and governance. The organization begins to treat risk as information, not inhibition.

Level 5 represents full institutionalization. Risk intelligence operates as a strategic asset measured by velocity, mitigation effectiveness, and return on risk investment. Appetite is expressed through behavior rather than paperwork. Decisions are shaped by shared understanding rather than directives. Executives discuss risk in the same frame as revenue and innovation. Investors see disciplined resilience, regulators recognize credibility, and customers trust reliability. At this level, risk maturity defines competitive strength.

The difference becomes visible in practice. A global bank evaluating expansion into a new region demonstrates this progression. At Level 2, it might rely on a compliance checklist and limited local analysis. At Level 3, legal, technology, and operations teams coordinate to assess exposure. At Level 4, risk data feeds into financial modeling, aligning capital decisions with operational realities. At Level 5, continuous telemetry and scenario modeling inform how resilience can serve as an advantage once operations begin. It becomes part of the organization's decision-making model. The shift from reactive review to predictive insight transforms both confidence and performance.

Organizations that stop at Level 2 often discover too late that their records describe the past rather than the present. They are aware of documented risks but are blind to those emerging in real time. Enterprises operating at Levels 4 and 5 adapt faster because risk is integrated into every choice. Their decisions already account for what others must rediscover after disruption.

Progress toward maturity is hindered by perception and structure. Many enterprises view risk management as administrative overhead. Others isolate it within compliance or audit functions. IAMM provides a route beyond these limits. It connects risk to finance, performance, and governance, emphasizing integration, accountability, and visibility as continuous states rather than periodic efforts.

Advancement begins with alignment. Risks must be captured in a shared register, prioritized by both business and technical leadership, and linked to investment and product outcomes. Executives must treat risk reporting as a decision instrument rather than a ceremonial deliverable. Once that alignment takes hold, risk ceases to be a static measure and becomes an operational guide.

IAMM defines risk maturity as a capability that shapes the enterprise itself. The purpose is not to populate forms or color charts but to make exposure visible where decisions occur. When risk intelligence moves with the speed of business, assurance becomes proactive, and resilience becomes measurable. This is the point at which risk evolves from oversight to advantage.

2.4 LEVERAGING RISK FOR COMPETITIVE ADVANTAGE

How organizations manage risk can be viewed as a differentiator. When risk is properly understood, embedded, and aligned with strategy, it becomes a source of advantage that competitors struggle to match. This shift in mindset marks a departure from the traditional notion of risk as something to avoid. Instead, organizations recognize that risk, when harnessed effectively, can accelerate decision-making, sharpen innovation, and build trust with customers and stakeholders.

The organizations that excel are not those that avoid risk entirely. Rather, they are the ones that understand their risks best. They are equipped to navigate uncertainty with agility and to convert disruption into opportunity. These organizations possess the capacity to sense early signals, interpret them in context, and move swiftly, while others hesitate. Risk fluency becomes their advantage. It allows them to respond with clarity when others are still gathering information. It allows them to take informed risks that create value while competitors retreat.

One of the most significant benefits of leveraging risk lies in visibility. Organizations that invest in risk intelligence develop superior awareness of conditions across their ecosystems. They see what others miss. This visibility is not limited to formal audits or compliance reviews. It comes from real-time data, behavioral analytics, ecosystem signals, and continuous sensing across internal and external environments. The ability to detect patterns early and forecast consequences accurately becomes a core operational capability.

Consider a global logistics company that uses its risk telemetry to anticipate the ripple effects of regional political unrest. While competitors wait for delayed shipments and reactive updates, this organization reroutes its cargo, negotiates proactive terms with suppliers, and communicates confidently with clients. Its preparedness comes from an intentional investment in risk visibility. That awareness preserves operational continuity and deepens customer trust. Both outcomes contribute to its market leadership.

Speed is another critical element in turning risk into a competitive advantage. Organizations that internalize risk intelligence move faster. They make decisions without unnecessary hesitation because they have already mapped their exposures, defined their tolerances, and rehearsed their responses. Speed in this context is not about recklessness. It is about readiness. Organizations that embed Integrated Assurance into their operations reduce decision lag. They eliminate blind spots and streamline approvals by aligning risk with business priorities.

A company that knows its risk thresholds does not need to pause for cross-functional debate when action is required. It has already outlined escalation paths, automated decision criteria, and embedded risk checkpoints into daily workflows. This agility translates into strategic flexibility. Whether entering a new market, launching a new product, or responding to an unexpected event, the organization moves with clarity and coordination. Its confidence is earned, not assumed.

This ability to act decisively is especially important in the innovation cycle. All innovation carries risk. Without appropriate boundaries, that risk becomes dangerous. But when those boundaries are known and respected, risk becomes a guide rather than a threat. Organizations that understand their risk tolerance are better positioned to explore new ideas without paralyzing oversight. They can say an informed "yes" more often to experimentation, while still protecting what matters most.

In product development, for instance, this becomes a powerful advantage. Consider a fintech company that implements a system that automatically evaluates proposed features for data privacy, fraud exposure, and regulatory fit. Developers could receive feedback in real time without waiting for a post-sprint audit or compliance review. This process would not inhibit creativity. It empowers it. Teams are able to innovate quickly while maintaining confidence that their solutions are aligned with customer trust and legal obligations. The result would be faster release cycles, fewer security incidents, and increased brand credibility.

This dynamic creates a resilient innovation culture. Risk becomes the structural integrity of forward motion. It allows for acceleration without collapse. The organization becomes both bold and grounded. Customers recognize this discipline. They see it in how organizations handle issues, communicate during setbacks, and prepare for the unexpected. In an era of rising customer skepticism, transparency builds trust, which may be the most undervalued form of capital in the modern economy. In a world flooded with misinformation, regulatory uncertainty, and cyber threats, trust is scarce and powerful. Customers, partners, and regulators gravitate toward organizations that demonstrate maturity in how they handle risk. Trust built on integrity, visibility, and responsiveness is not a soft asset. It is one of the most durable forms of differentiation available today.

The way organizations respond to incidents often determines the lasting impact more than the incident itself. Organizations that try to conceal breaches, delay public statements, or shift blame often suffer long-term reputational harm. On the other hand, those that respond swiftly, share clear information, and provide meaningful remediation retain customer loyalty and often earn new business. The ability to act with integrity and competence in moments of disruption signals operational integrity and organizational strength.

Risk maturity also influences investor perception. Public companies with strong governance and Integrated Assurance structures tend to experience less volatility after crises and recover more quickly. Analysts and investors recognize the value of systems that prevent surprises and support transparent leadership. This plays into valuations, merger decisions, and strategic partnerships. Risk competence becomes a critical aspect of leadership competence.

At the heart of competitive advantage is the ability to take calculated risks. The highest-performing organizations are not risk-averse. They are risk-informed and empowered. They know their limits, but they also know their capacity. They understand their ability to absorb shocks, maintain operations, and recover from failure. This clarity allows them to make bold moves that others are unwilling to consider.

During the COVID-19 pandemic, organizations that pivoted to digital quickly were often those with robust risk governance. These companies already had scenario plans, decision frameworks, and continuity strategies in place. They were able to scale remote operations, protect customer data, and launch new digital products while others were still mobilizing crisis response teams. Their performance was not accidental. It was the result of a risk-aware operating model that had been built deliberately over time.

To enable this kind of confident action, several elements must be in place. First, governance structures must be flexible enough to support rapid, informed decisions. Second, frontline teams must be empowered with the information and authority to act without waiting for top-down instruction. Third, scenario playbooks must be designed in advance to provide decision support when time is limited and the stakes are high.

These mechanisms give the organization the ability to say yes more often to opportunities. They allow organizations to participate in new partnerships, enter unfamiliar markets, and launch innovative offerings without exposing themselves to unmanaged threats. Risk does not disappear, but it is brought under control and used to navigate rather than resist change.

Another overlooked asset is the economic value of risk intelligence. When risk data is structured, contextualized, and shareable, it becomes a product in itself. Organizations can offer their insights as a service, whether to regulators, clients, or partners. A clear risk posture becomes part of the sales process. Strong compliance records open the door to new partnerships. Demonstrated business continuity strengthens procurement positioning. Assurance becomes a commercial capability.

For example, an energy company that faces extreme weather conditions could develop an internal telemetry platform to monitor and respond to environmental threats. Over time, that system could evolve into a client-facing service that delivers real-time alerts to industrial customers. What began as a resilience solution could become a new revenue stream, and risk awareness can be monetized. As ecosystems grow more interdependent, organizations must also take responsibility for the risk posture of their partners. Organizations that invest in helping suppliers and distributors mature their assurance capabilities increase the integrity of the entire value chain. This becomes another form of differentiation and a requirement for cybersecurity maturity model certification.

In another example, a pharmaceutical company could establish third-party risk training to educate its upstream suppliers on cybersecurity, regulatory expectations, and quality standards. This initiative would not only reduce its own exposure but also position it as a partner of choice for hospitals and global distributors. By lifting others, it could ultimately lift itself. The result would be better contract terms, improved delivery performance, and a stronger reputation in a highly regulated industry.

Leadership in risk also improves deal flow. Organizations that can demonstrate resilience, transparency, and control become more attractive in mergers, acquisitions, and joint ventures. Trust becomes the gating factor for collaboration, and due diligence can be radically accelerated because of demonstrable compliance(s). Organizations that articulate their risk capabilities as part of their brand message earn attention from investors, partners, and regulators alike.

Sophisticated companies now embed risk language into their brand narrative. They communicate not only their values but also their control posture. They talk about privacy, security, and resilience with clarity and purpose. These are not just compliance checkboxes. They are part of the brand promise. When customers hear a company talk about trust and see it reflected in operations, it creates a lasting connection. It signals seriousness. It signals maturity.

Organizations like Apple, IBM, and Microsoft do this intentionally. Their communication around data privacy and resilience is designed to establish trust with customers and regulators. That positioning becomes part of the brand's gravitational pull. It attracts talent. It retains customers. And it sets a standard that competitors struggle to match. To fully realize this advantage, organizations must stop treating risk as an afterthought. Risk must become an operating capability. That capability depends on continuous sensing, integrated response systems, well-defined action thresholds, and transparent communication practices. It also depends on a culture that encourages smart risk-taking. Organizations that celebrate intelligent decisions in ambiguous situations build a workforce that is ready to lead through uncertainty.

When risk is operationalized in this way, it enables faster, better, and bolder choices. It creates differentiation that competitors cannot replicate easily. Risk becomes a lever. It becomes a compass. And ultimately, it becomes one of the most powerful strategic assets an enterprise can develop.

2.5 RISK SENSING AND SIGNAL AMPLIFICATION

Risk sensing now separates organizations that anticipate from those that scramble to react. As disruption cycles tighten, the ability to detect, interpret, and act on early signals of emerging risk becomes more than a technical upgrade. It becomes a business necessity. Traditional risk models are too slow. Metrics are reviewed monthly, compliance updates arrive quarterly, and audits happen once a year. By the time a threat appears on these dashboards, the damage has often already occurred. In contrast, modern organizations need continuous sensing capabilities that work across every layer of the organization. These systems must pull from structured and unstructured data, interpret human behavior, and scan external environments. The goal is to move beyond awareness and toward foresight that is both actionable and timely.

The legacy approach to risk is built on static assessment. Frameworks rely on predefined threats and past incidents, offering only a retrospective view. These models can highlight basic exposure but fail to detect shifts in velocity, impact, or dependencies. Modern sensing relies on dynamic inputs. It pulls real-time data, applies behavioral analytics and machine learning, and models future exposure based on present anomalies. Rather than asking what the risks are, organizations begin to ask what signals might indicate tomorrow's threats.

This shift is not only about better tools. It is about creating adaptive intelligence that functions like an organizational nervous system. Most organizations do not lack signals. They lack signal integration. Operational data, HR anomalies, customer complaints, audit findings, and performance metrics all contain insight, but when siloed, they remain weak. Integrated Assurance acts as a signal amplifier. It connects these disparate sources using shared governance, interoperable tools, and consistent taxonomies. That integration allows small signals in one area to be recognized in another. This approach creates a much deeper understanding of the risks and that understanding yields more relevant measurements closer to decision points. The result is not just more information, but higher-quality insight that guides timely action.

Consider a typical pattern, such as a system that begins to slow down by 12 percent. At the same time, call center volume increases with complaints about delays. A vendor notifies the team about an upcoming software patch. Any one of these might go unnoticed. Together, they point to a problem in progress. Integrated Assurance makes that correlation possible and helps the organization act before impact spreads.

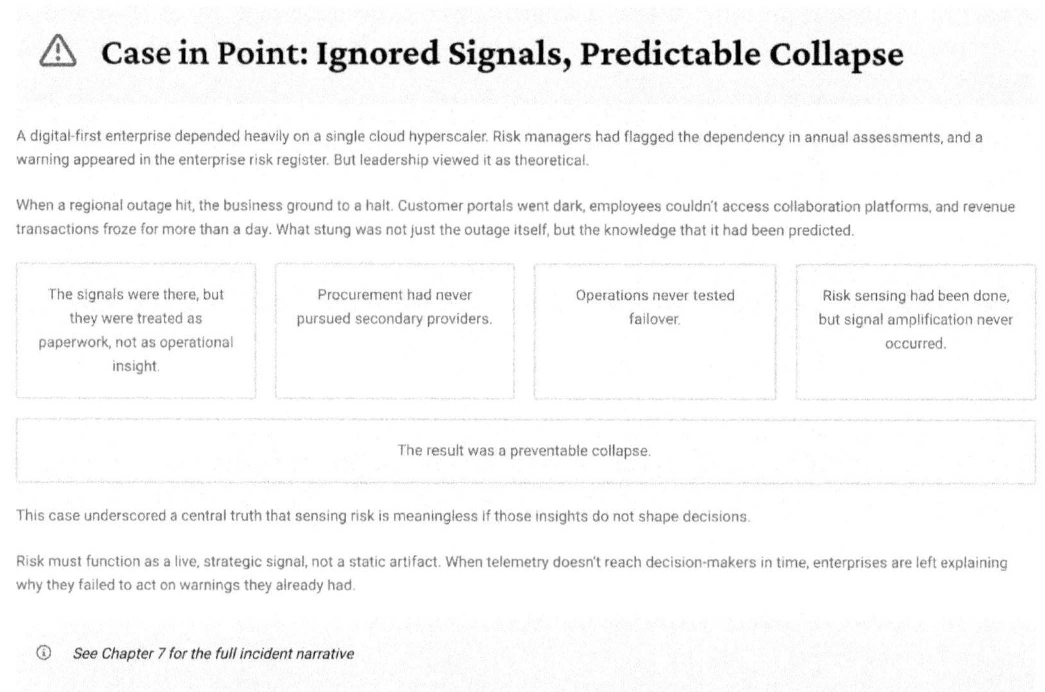

Figure 2.2 Case in Point.

Image created by the author using Gamma.

Building this capability takes more than technology. It also requires a shift in organizational behavior. On the technical side, data pipelines must capture real-time internal and external signals. Analytics platforms need to identify trends and patterns, while dashboards deliver visibility to both technical teams and executives. Automated workflows help ensure signals translate into timely alerts and responses.

Culturally, employees must be encouraged to surface concerns early without fear of blame. Frontline teams need training to recognize signals, even when they seem small. 7Organizations should reward early detection, not just post-incident cleanup. Most importantly, everyone must speak a shared language about what risk signals look like and how to respond to them.

Risk sensing should not be confined to security or compliance. In human resources, unexpected attrition may signal burnout or ethical issues. In procurement, small but repeated supplier delays might reveal deeper instability. In finance, sudden cost deviations could suggest mismanagement or fraud. Early signs often surface in unexpected places, and only a connected sensing model can piece them together before escalation. See Figure 2.2: Case in Point.

A common concern is signal overload. With more data flowing in, many worry about false positives or alert fatigue. The answer lies in context. Sensing systems must prioritize signals based on their relevance to core business objectives. They must baseline expected behavior to detect anomalies and model potential impact so that decision-makers can triage effectively. AI can help reduce noise, but only when fed with the right feedback and framing. Avoiding AI hallucination is nontrivial. The guardrails must be concrete and should include a frequent periodic validation mechanism.

Organizations that mature in risk sensing treat every incident, near miss, and disruption as a learning opportunity. They conduct retrospectives to uncover missed signals, calibrate

Figure 2.3 Case in Point.

Image created by the author using Gamma.

models using real-world input, and evolve playbooks and training. These feedback loops help turn sensing from a tool into an embedded reflex. Over time, sensing becomes not just something the system does, but something the organization is capable of at every level.

As the pace of disruption accelerates, signal strength becomes strategic strength. Organizations that can detect, amplify, and act on weak signals hold the advantage. They see change before it arrives. They respond with clarity instead of chaos. And they recover with speed that competitors cannot match. Integrated Assurance provides the architecture for this capability. It ensures that sensing is not just decentralized but fully connected. Organizations that master this approach do more than survive disruption. They shape it with confidence, speed, and precision. See Figure 2.3: Case in Point.

2.6 AI AND THE DUAL-EDGED SIGNAL

AI models, particularly those trained on vast and diverse datasets, extend the organization's ability to perceive weak indicators long before they appear on traditional dashboards. Properly applied, AI enhances risk sensing by filtering noise, identifying subtle correlations, and surfacing anomalies that human analysts would overlook. Yet the same technology that strengthens foresight also introduces new classes of risk that leaders must actively manage.

Traditional risk sensing systems rely on rule-based triggers and predefined thresholds. These approaches often fail in dynamic environments where new patterns emerge faster than rules can be updated. AI models overcome this limitation by learning from history while adapting to new data in real time. For example:

- Supply chain monitoring: AI models analyze geopolitical events, weather patterns, shipping manifests, and social sentiment simultaneously to predict disruptions weeks before they appear in vendor reports.

- Cybersecurity telemetry: Machine learning detects micro-shifts in traffic, login behavior, or device activity that may indicate insider threats or adversarial reconnaissance before an actual attack occurs.
- Financial exposure: Predictive analytics scan regulatory changes, currency fluctuations, and credit markets to highlight liquidity or compliance risks before they mature into losses.

In these contexts, AI functions as an organizational nervous system amplifier. It detects faint signals, contextualizes them across interdependent systems, and delivers actionable foresight. When embedded into Integrated Assurance, these insights allow executives to move from reactive postures to proactive positioning.

The power of AI does not arrive without complications. While it strengthens detection, it simultaneously introduces vulnerabilities that require vigilance. Key new vectors include:

- Model drift and bias: AI systems evolve as they process new data. Without constant oversight, their outputs can degrade, leading to false positives, blind spots, or discriminatory outcomes that skew decision-making.
- Shadow AI: Employees may deploy unsanctioned AI tools that process sensitive data outside official governance. These tools can create hidden exposure similar to shadow IT—only faster and more difficult to detect.
- Adversarial AI: Threat actors exploit AI by injecting poisoned data, crafting adversarial inputs, or even deploying their own agentic AI systems to bypass detection and overwhelm defenses.
- Opaque decisioning: Black-box AI models may deliver risk scores without transparent reasoning, leaving executives uncertain about how to trust or act on the results.
- AI hallucination: AI hallucination is a significant risk if the model(s) aren't carefully constructed. They require a balance of well-crafted prompts, data-validation sources, and parallel-validation AI models. Without all of these, AI wants to provide a definitive answer but will make up an answer without the proper controls.

These factors demonstrate that AI is not simply an accelerator of risk awareness. It is also a new risk landscape that can undermine assurance if left unmanaged.

To harness AI as a source of strategic advantage, organizations must build assurance into the AI lifecycle and its architecture. This means:

- Continuous validation: Regular stress-testing of models against evolving data to ensure integrity and accuracy.
- Governed integration: Ensuring AI systems operate within Integrated Assurance frameworks so that insights feed into board-level dashboards with context and accountability.
- Human oversight: Empowering skilled analysts to validate AI outputs, interpret edge cases, and prevent blind reliance on algorithmic signals. The most likely comment after a crucial risk-based AI hallucination is "you're fired."
- Resilience design: Treating AI not only as a sensing layer but also as a potential failure point, with contingency plans in case models malfunction or are compromised.

In this balanced approach, AI amplifies the organization's ability to sense risk while Integrated Assurance ensures that its contributions are reliable, explainable, and strategically aligned. This creates an advantage over competitors who either dismiss AI as hype or adopt it recklessly without proper controls.

2.7 EMBEDDING RISK AWARENESS

In many organizations, risk awareness remains abstract until it actively shapes decisions. Despite significant investments in risk management platforms and governance structures, the actual integration of risk intelligence into day-to-day decisions often remains elusive. This gap between insight and execution is a structural vulnerability that inhibits agility, increases exposure, and limits the strategic value of risk functions.

To truly embed risk awareness, organizations must move beyond centralized control and elevate risk from a siloed advisory role to a shared, operational capability. This shift means making risk visible, accessible, and actionable at all layers of the business. When risk becomes a consistent input into decisions, from strategic planning in the boardroom to operational actions on the front lines, the organization becomes not only more secure but also faster, smarter, and better aligned with its objectives.

One of the biggest myths in ERM is that effective control must be centralized. Legal, compliance, IT, cybersecurity, and enterprise risk teams often function in isolated review cycles, issuing guidance after the fact or too late to meaningfully influence direction. This not only reduces risk to a compliance obligation but also ensures that critical decisions are made without timely context. Governance is about enabling better decisions. Decentralizing risk awareness equips all decision-makers with the guidance, context, and tools to act confidently in the moment without sacrificing oversight.

Operationalizing risk awareness requires embedding it directly into the workflows where decisions are made. In product development, for example, privacy and security considerations should be factored in during design reviews and sprint planning and not retrofitted after release. Procurement processes should include real-time vendor risk evaluations before contracts are signed. Marketing teams should review campaign plans for reputational, regulatory, and geopolitical exposure. In finance, automated fraud detection and policy enforcement must be baked into approval flows and close cycles. Operations must align maintenance and supply chain tasks with continuity and safety thresholds. These embedded touchpoints bring risk insight directly to decision-makers, thereby reducing blind spots, rework, and delays.

The principle of decision-making at the edge is especially critical in fast-moving functions like logistics, field operations, or customer support. Centralized governance often lags behind the speed at which action is needed. Empowering edge teams with playbooks, clear escalation paths, and access to real-time policy guidance enables timely, informed responses. A customer support agent, for instance, can confidently handle sensitive data if they have access to privacy guidance and know the thresholds for escalation. This reduces the need for constant oversight, accelerates service delivery, and strengthens compliance in real time.

Not all roles require the same risk insight. A software engineer needs to understand code-level risks and secure development practices during deployment, while a procurement officer benefits more from supplier risk heatmaps and geopolitical exposure data. A regional operations manager may need to assess transportation routes through a lens of political instability or supply chain fragility. Delivering role-specific, contextualized risk information ensures that what employees see is both actionable and relevant, which enables risk-aware decisions without overwhelming them with noise.

Cultural reinforcement is as important as technical integration. Organizations with strong risk cultures normalize risk conversations across all levels. Leaders model transparent discussions of risk and trade-offs, reinforcing that surfacing risks early is a strength and not a liability. Celebrating transparency and holding decision-makers accountable for both their outcomes and their process builds a culture where risk is not just managed but also embraced as a catalyst for better thinking.

Technology plays a key role in making risk data usable and timely. Decision support tools must move beyond static dashboards or end-of-quarter risk reports. Instead, they should integrate directly into core systems, surfacing real-time thresholds, embedded risk scores, and visualizations that illuminate cascading impacts. These tools should not only inform but also interrupt, pausing actions when risks exceed tolerances or triggering alerts when deviations from policy arise. The closer this data is to the point of decision, the more likely it is to guide behavior in meaningful ways.

Training is essential to ensure employees recognize and respond to risk effectively. Onboarding should explain the organization's philosophy on both risk and its rules. Role-specific training can highlight typical risks faced in everyday scenarios and offer practical responses. Simulation exercises and scenario planning foster muscle memory and build confidence. These investments transform risk from an abstract concept into a living capability, understood and applied at every level.

To measure progress, organizations must move beyond compliance metrics and incident counts. Metrics should track the extent to which risk influences decision-making behavior. Are high-impact business decisions incorporating documented risk analysis? How many operational workflows contain embedded risk checkpoints? Are employees confident in their ability to handle risk? What is the speed from signal detection to decision execution? These metrics assess whether risk intelligence is flowing through the organization as intended and whether it's making an impact.

Ultimately, the payoff for embedding risk into decision-making layers is strategic. Organizations gain speed by eliminating delays caused by disconnected risk review processes. They gain alignment by ensuring strategy and execution reflect a shared understanding of risk. And they gain resilience through confident, well-informed responses when disruptions occur. These organizations also learn faster. When risk data is embedded in decisions, every action generates feedback that sharpens future choices. The result is a self-improving system where risk intelligence drives continuous evolution.

Embedding risk awareness is fundamentally about accelerating sound decisions. It transforms risk from a governance artifact into a decision-making asset. When every employee can act with confidence and context, risk becomes a force multiplier, not a constraint.

2.8 TRUST, SPEED, AND PRECISION UNDER UNCERTAINTY

The business environment today remains in a state of ongoing uncertainty. Markets shift overnight. Emerging technologies disrupt entire industries. Geopolitical instability can suddenly redefine supply chain dynamics, regulatory expectations, and investor sentiment. In this environment, volatility is no longer an outlier event. It is the operating norm. The question for senior leaders is no longer how to avoid disruption, but how to consistently outperform within it. That advantage lies in the triad of high-performance traits of trust, speed, and precision. See Figure 2.4: Trust, Speed, and Precision under Uncertainty.

Each of these elements offers standalone value. Trust strengthens internal cohesion and external loyalty. Speed enables agile responses that match the tempo of change. Precision allows for smarter use of resources and sharper execution under pressure. But when trust, speed, and precision are reinforced together through Integrated Assurance, they form a strategic edge. Together, they give the organization the ability to make bold decisions, take calculated risks, and respond with confidence in any context. This is not a theoretical model. It is a practical operating posture that separates the resilient from the fragile.

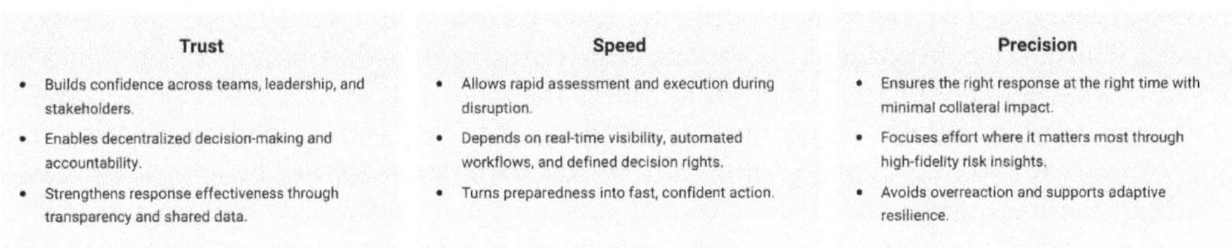

Figure 2.4 Trust, Speed, and Precision under Uncertainty.
Image created by the author using Gamma.

2.8.1 Trust

Trust forms the foundation of all resilient systems. Without it, even the most advanced risk models or automation frameworks are rendered ineffective. Trust is not just a cultural value. It is a strategic resource. It is the confidence employees have in leadership and processes, the belief teams have in one another, and the assurance that external stakeholders hold in the organization's ability to deliver under pressure. It shapes how people interpret risk, how quickly they act, and how confidently they share information.

In organizations where risk is operationalized through Integrated Assurance, trust is not assumed. It is actively built through transparency, consistency, and accountability. Teams do not operate on blind faith. They have visibility into why decisions are made, how risks are managed, and what information underpins their priorities. This shared understanding creates alignment across functions and makes decentralization possible. It also accelerates reflexes. When people trust the data, they move quickly. When leaders trust their teams, they push decision-making closer to the edge. And when customers trust the brand, they stay loyal even during times of failure or disruption.

Trust also determines the organization's ability to respond during moments of crisis. In a breach scenario, for example, the difference between recovery and collapse often comes down to internal confidence and external credibility. A trusted organization can communicate openly, act decisively, and recover faster. Not because it avoids risk altogether, but because its systems and people are aligned and prepared.

2.8.2 Speed

Speed is the second pillar. In an environment where threats move in real time, delayed decisions are as risky as poor ones. The ability to assess, decide, and execute quickly is no longer a competitive advantage. It is a survival requirement. But speed alone can be dangerous. Rapid action without context creates chaos. What makes speed strategic is risk intelligence. When Integrated Assurance delivers real-time signals and embedded controls, organizations can accelerate with clarity. They are not reacting blindly. They are executing with foresight.

Organizations that operate with embedded risk capabilities do not wait for impact before responding. They know where exposure exists, what thresholds matter, and what responses have been premodeled. This enables confidence in the face of ambiguity. A digital channel can be shut down and rerouted without hesitation because the implications are known and rehearsed. Customers can be notified quickly because communications are ready and aligned to severity. Escalation paths are mapped, and ownership is clear.

Strategic speed is driven by four practical enablers. First, decision authority must be clearly defined and linked to risk thresholds. Teams need to know who has the authority to act when tolerances are breached. Second, automated workflows should be used to eliminate unnecessary delay. The more a process depends on manual intervention, the slower it becomes. Third, cross-functional playbooks ensure consistency during disruption. These are not static documents but living guides that reflect the latest lessons and context. And fourth, visibility must be real-time. You cannot respond to what you cannot see. Monitoring must provide clarity on what is changing and how those changes impact key business objectives.

Without these elements, speed becomes panic. With them, speed becomes orchestration. It becomes a strategic rhythm that allows the organization to respond at the pace of its environment without losing control or oversight.

2.8.3 Precision

Precision is the third trait in this model. It is the discipline of acting on the right issue, at the right time, with the right response. Many organizations fail not because they ignore risk, but because their responses are too blunt. They shut down entire systems when only one function is affected. They issue sweeping policy changes in response to isolated failures. These reactions may feel decisive, but they often create unintended consequences. They drain resources, frustrate teams, and damage credibility.

Precision avoids these outcomes. It allows organizations to respond in a measured, effective, and context-specific way. This is only possible when the organization understands its critical assets, models interdependencies, and maintains high-resolution telemetry. Risk sensing must be granular enough to differentiate between localized noise and systemic threat. Escalation protocols must scale with severity. And leadership must reinforce the importance of nuance. Precision is not about avoiding action. It is about making the right call with the appropriate force.

Leadership plays a central role in enabling precision. The behavior that gets rewarded is the behavior that becomes normalized. If leaders only recognize dramatic interventions or crisis heroics, those will become the dominant mode of action. But if they celebrate foresight, measured responses, and early containment, these practices will take hold. Precision is not an accident. It is a product of expectations, incentives, and infrastructure.

These three capabilities work best in combination. Trust enables distributed decision-making. Speed ensures decisions are made in time. Precision ensures they are made effectively. Together, they allow an organization to outmaneuver disruption rather than become paralyzed by it.

To make this concrete, consider a common scenario. A zero-day vulnerability is discovered in a widely used enterprise software platform. Within minutes, an organization using an Integrated Assurance model identifies the exposure through its telemetry. It maps the impacted systems, prioritizes patching based on business process criticality, and begins mitigation. At the same time, communication plans are activated with messaging tailored to severity and stakeholder. Nothing about this response is improvised. It is the product of rehearsed coordination, trusted systems, and high-fidelity intelligence. It reflects the maturity of an organization that acts rather than guesses.

What sets these organizations apart is not luck or budget. It is a commitment to building capability. Trust, speed, and precision are not aspirational. They are measurable. Trust can be tracked through engagement metrics, policy adherence rates, and cross-functional collaboration scores. Speed can be quantified through time-to-detection, time-to-decision, and time-to-response. Precision can be evaluated through containment ratios, false positive rates, and the alignment of response actions to business impact.

When these are treated as operational metrics, they become part of the enterprise maturity model. Leaders can monitor, refine, and scale them over time. They can set targets, benchmark progress, and identify areas of improvement. More importantly, they can link these traits to outcomes, such as revenue protection, customer retention, regulatory posture, and market confidence.

Risk will never be eliminated. That is not the goal. But uncertainty does not have to equal fragility. The strongest organizations do not wait for clarity. They build systems that function under pressure. They embed trust in their people. They act with speed through informed structures. They deliver precision through discipline and design. These traits are not the product of chance. They are the return on strategic investment in Integrated Assurance.

2.9 CONCLUSION

Risk has always existed at the edge of every enterprise decision. What has changed is not the presence of risk, but the speed, interdependence, and visibility required to respond to it. This chapter began with a simple but profound idea: That risk is no longer just something to manage, contain, or survive. It is a resource and a driver. And in today's organization, it is one of the most important capabilities a leadership team can develop.

Throughout this chapter, the role of risk was redefined as a lever and not a liability. We examined how organizations can harness risk as both a warning signal and a directional guide. We explored the shift from static risk management toward continuous risk sensing. And we saw how Integrated Assurance provides the architecture to align governance, security, and operations in a way that allows risk to flow through the business as insight rather than obstruction.

This transformation is not conceptual. It is tangible and measurable. When risk is integrated into daily decision-making, it accelerates execution and improves confidence. When leaders treat risk intelligence as an input rather than an output, decisions become sharper, and alignment becomes easier. When teams at all levels are empowered to see and respond to risk, organizational speed no longer comes at the cost of control. Precision becomes possible even under pressure.

The cultural dimension of this shift cannot be overstated. In organizations where risk is siloed, centralized, or treated as taboo, information moves slowly, trust erodes, and blind spots widen. In contrast, when risk is everyone's responsibility, it becomes a shared language. Risk ceases to be the domain of auditors and compliance professionals alone. It becomes part of how engineers build, how marketers plan, how strategists allocate capital, and how customer service teams respond. That level of integration signals maturity. It signals resilience.

Enterprise success is increasingly defined by the ability to operate in ambiguity without losing clarity. The Integrated Assurance model recognizes this. It does not attempt to eliminate uncertainty. It teaches organizations to engage with it. Through continuous sensing, embedded metrics, and cross-functional collaboration, Integrated Assurance turns risk into a living capability. It ensures that insights are not delayed until the next audit but are made available in the very moment they matter.

The most successful companies of the next decade will not be the ones that avoid risk entirely. They will be the ones that understand it best. They will detect disruption early, amplify weak signals, and respond with speed and discipline. These organizations will treat risk as both an operating input and a competitive edge. They will act decisively when others hesitate. And they will build trust with employees, customers, and regulators through transparency, reliability, and readiness.

Risk becomes strategic when it is aligned with purpose. This alignment requires more than dashboards or frameworks. It demands leadership that speaks the language of risk fluently, technology that supports real-time visibility, and culture that values foresight over blame.

It also requires clear governance that defines thresholds, clarifies ownership, and supports decision-making at every level.

The value of this capability is visible not only in moments of crisis but also in everyday execution. A marketing team that knows how to evaluate geopolitical risk before launching a campaign moves faster and with more confidence. A product team that sees privacy exposure in real time builds with higher trust. A procurement team that understands supplier risk during contract negotiations protects continuity and cost. These actions, repeated daily, create structural integrity and strategic advantage.

The operational benefits of embedding risk as a capability are clear. Less rework. Faster delivery. Fewer surprises. Tighter alignment between intention and impact. However, the strategic benefits are even more compelling. Risk-aware organizations navigate disruption

Use this checklist to translate the ideas in Chapter 2 into tangible actions across your enterprise:

1

Leadership Alignment

- ☐ Do we place risk metrics alongside financial and customer data in board and executive reviews?
- ☐ Do we tie risk appetite directly to growth and innovation objectives?
- ☐ Do we model transparent risk conversations at the top?

2

Cultural Shifts

- ☐ Do we reframe risk language from "failure" and "exposure" to "signal" and "foresight"?
- ☐ Do we foster psychological safety so employees can raise risks without fear?
- ☐ Do we recognize and reward proactive risk identification?

3

Operational Integration

- ☐ Do we embed risk intelligence into core platforms (CRM, ERP, DevOps, and supply chain tools)?
- ☐ Do we create role-specific risk touch points for marketing, procurement, product, and operations?
- ☐ Do we incorporate risk-reflection checkpoints into agile sprints and planning cycles.?

4

Measurement and Metrics

- ☐ Do we track leading indicators (risk signals raised, time-to-response, and quality of decision-making under pressure)?
- ☐ Do we balance these with lagging indicators (incidents, audit findings, and policy violations)?
- ☐ Are these tied to monitoring for trust, speed, and precision as operational metrics are tied to resilience?

5

Capability Development

- ☐ Do we deliver training to build risk fluency in every function?
- ☐ Are these aligned with Integrated Assurance principles to connect signals across silos for early detection?
- ☐ Do we regularly conduct retrospectives after near misses to strengthen sensing and response?

☐ **Executive Action:** Embed risk into leadership, culture, and daily operations by reframing it as foresight, integrating it into core systems, distributing ownership across functions, and measuring trust, speed, and precision as drivers of resilience and growth.

Figure 2.5 Practical Checklist: Making Risk a Strategic Asset.

Image created by the author using Gamma.

with composure. They are more attractive to investors, customers, and partners. They are better positioned to innovate because they have clarity on what they can absorb and where they must protect. They can say yes to opportunity with full awareness of its implications.

In these organizations, trust is not a soft value. It is a performance asset. Speed is about knowing sooner and acting smarter. Precision is about being intentional. Together, these attributes shape the way a modern enterprise competes, adapts, and grows. Risk sits at the heart of that equation—not as a constraint, but as a catalyst.

This chapter has offered a new lens through which to view risk. No longer confined to oversight committees or compliance checklists, risk must be reframed as an asset to be activated. Risk intelligence belongs in planning cycles, sprint reviews, executive dashboards, and frontline workflows. The organizations that realize this are already outperforming their peers because they are structured to thrive within uncertainty.

The model of Integrated Assurance is what enables this outcome. It connects governance to execution. It ensures that signals do not die in silos. It equips every layer of the enterprise to respond with clarity and coordination. And it elevates risk from something to be reported on to something that shapes the path forward.

There is no resilience without risk fluency. No agility without embedded intelligence. And no trust without the discipline to act consistently under pressure. Risk is the proving ground for all three. It is where strategy meets reality and where leadership proves itself. The question is no longer whether risk should have a seat at the table. It is whether your organization knows how to use it.

To make risk a strategic asset, start where it matters most. Integrate insights into your most critical decisions. Equip teams with tools they will actually use. Tie risk outcomes to business value. And most importantly, treat risk as a capability that must be developed, not a function to be feared. Those who do will not just survive disruption. They will shape it. They will lead with confidence. And they will earn the trust that defines enduring success. Risk, used wisely, becomes the engine of informed action. And when embedded across the organization through Integrated Assurance, it becomes one of the most powerful assets a business can have. See Figure 2.5: Practical Checklist: Making Risk a Strategic Asset.

Chapter 3

Resilience Metrics That Matter

3.1 WHY TRADITIONAL METRICS MISLEAD

For a long time, enterprises have leaned on metrics such as uptime percentages, service-level agreement (SLA) compliance, and audit completion rates to demonstrate control and stability. These indicators were convenient because they were simple to collect, easy to report, and widely accepted by executives and boards. They became shorthand for reliability. Yet in today's operating environment, these measures no longer reflect the reality of resilience. At best, they confirm the absence of a visible failure. At worst, they create a false sense of security and lead decision-makers to believe their organizations are more resilient than they truly are.

Resilience cannot be summarized by a green dashboard or a quarterly compliance score. Modern enterprises exist in interconnected ecosystems where disruptions ripple quickly across suppliers, partners, and customers. Cyberattacks, cloud outages, and geopolitical instability rarely respect contractual boundaries. What matters is not how reliably systems ran last month, but whether the organization can pivot, absorb shocks, and preserve trust in the face of disruption. Legacy metrics provide comfort, but not capability. That comfort has become one of the most dangerous risks to survival.

The appeal of uptime percentages and SLA compliance lies in their clarity. A system with 99.99 percent availability appears exceptional, just as flawless SLA adherence suggests operational discipline. These figures are attractive because they compress the complexity of global systems into a single chart that executives and boards can understand at a glance. But simplicity often conceals fragility. They are excellent measurements that define what the norm is, but they only show part of the story, and not even half. They are an incomplete picture that oversimplifies the landscape.

A system can be technically "up" yet functionally broken. Latency may render applications unusable. Transactions may fail silently. Customers may abandon services due to poor experiences. None of these realities appear in an uptime report. Likewise, SLA compliance only shows whether a vendor met a contractual obligation. It does not reveal whether the dependent business function retained integrity or whether customer trust held firm. A metric that signals success while users experience failure is misleading.

These measures were fit for another era, and even then, they were incomplete. When infrastructure was centralized and applications were monolithic, knowing whether systems stayed online was enough. In that world, uptime and SLA compliance were meaningful indicators. Today, enterprises operate across hybrid clouds, distributed architectures, and fragile supply chains. A disruption in one vendor's service can cascade through dozens of business processes. Compliance thresholds offer little insight when customer expectations, regulatory scrutiny, and competitive pressures continue to intensify. Using yesterday's measures to manage today's volatility is like steering with outdated maps.

DOI: 10.1201/9781003685982-4

Another flaw in legacy metrics is that they are retrospective. SLA reports summarize the past. Uptime percentages reflect historical performance. Audit completions confirm that policies were reviewed at a point in time. None of these indicators reveals readiness for the disruption that will arrive tomorrow. An enterprise can celebrate a perfect compliance record, only to collapse when confronted with a partner outage or an unanticipated exploit. By the time the numbers are tallied, the risk environment has already shifted.

These measures are also fragmented across silos. IT reports uptime. Service desks report incident counts. Marketing tracks customer churn. Compliance systems log risk indicators. Rarely are these signals brought together into a unified view. The result is confusion at the very moment when clarity is most needed. A dashboard may show systems available, yet support tickets may surge. A compliance report may declare controls effective, yet staff may hesitate under stress. Fragmented metrics create blind spots that multiply during a crisis.

Legacy dashboards often confuse activity with results. They count incidents, patch cycles, and SLA breaches, but they do not show whether resilience was preserved. Ten minor alerts may hide the one event that matters. A rapid system reboot may restore availability, yet the underlying business process may remain broken.

Measuring activities without outcomes distorts behavior. Teams learn to optimize for closing tickets quickly rather than solving root causes. They meet SLA thresholds while customer experience deteriorates. They pass audits while operational readiness erodes. When the wrong things are measured, the wrong behaviors are reinforced.

Audits and checklists create another layer of false assurance. On paper, controls exist, training has been delivered, and policies are current. In practice, controls degrade, turnover erodes knowledge, and exceptions pile up. Plans that satisfy regulators may fail under the chaos of a real disruption. Too often, compliance is celebrated as evidence of resilience when, in reality, it masks brittleness.

Traditional measures also neglect the human dimension. Yet people decide outcomes. Leadership clarity, team adaptability, and cross-functional trust determine whether a disruption becomes a crisis or a controlled event. Metrics that ignore this dimension strip away the very qualities that matter most under pressure.

By the time metrics reach executives, they are often smoothed, averaged, and sanitized. What remains is a neat but shallow picture. Green lights and upward trends give the impression of resilience when, in truth, brittleness may lie just beneath the surface. Instead of drawing attention to urgent risks, legacy dashboards often conceal them.

This false confidence is the most dangerous outcome of traditional metrics. Executives may assume resilience is assured and make bold strategic moves on the basis of flawed signals. When disruption strikes, the reality surfaces, controls fail, teams hesitate, and customers lose trust. The enterprise that appeared prepared proves fragile.

Traditional measures still have value as context, but they cannot define resilience. They were built for a different time and a different level of complexity. Today's leaders need metrics that reflect adaptability, trust, and recovery in real time. Resilience is proven not by the absence of incidents but by the ability to sustain critical functions, pivot quickly, and preserve confidence under pressure. Organizations that continue to rely on outdated measures will remain blind to their fragility. Those that adopt new models will see resilience not as an illusion but as a measurable, living capability.

3.2 MEASURING TRUST, ADAPTABILITY, AND RECOVERY

Resilience is often mistaken for a purely technical function. Too many organizations define it by uptime percentages, infrastructure robustness, or how quickly a system can be restored.

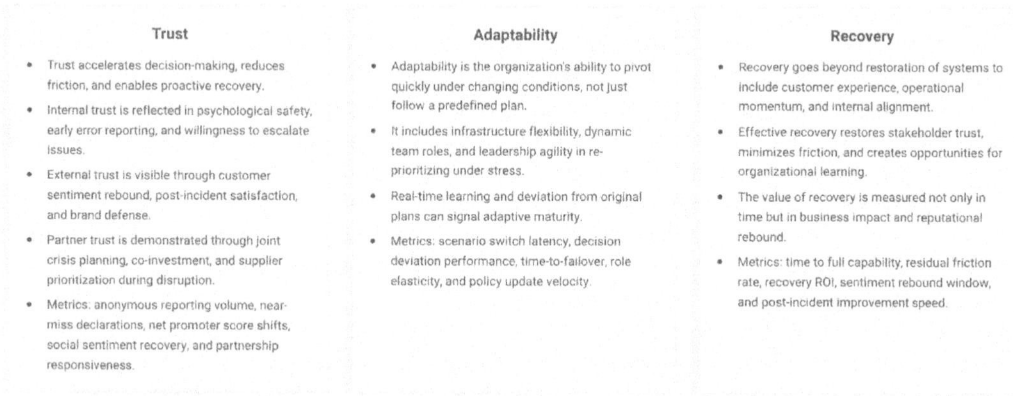

Figure 3.1 Measuring Trust, Adaptability, and Recovery.
Image created by the author using Gamma.

Those elements matter, but they are not resilient. Real enterprise resilience is a strategic capability. It is embedded in systems, processes, and people, and it rests on the pillars of trust, adaptability, and recovery.

Traditional metrics rarely capture this. They track continuity of services or compliance against a checklist. These metrics look good on paper, but they do not reveal how an organization behaves when real disruption arrives. Resilience is tested in chaos, not routine. The difference between success and failure is found in the trust teams have in one another, the adaptability of leadership and systems, and the speed and impact of recovery. To measure resilience meaningfully, leaders must ask if the organization can build trust, pivot with clarity, and recover in ways that create lasting strength. See Figure 3.1: Measuring Trust, Adaptability, and Recovery.

Trust is often dismissed as a soft measure, but it drives hard outcomes. It is the hidden currency that reduces friction, accelerates coordination, and enables confident decision-making. Where trust is strong, teams escalate issues early, leaders take decisive action, and stakeholders remain steady in uncertainty. Where trust is weak, hesitation and doubt can turn small problems into major failures.

Trust shifts over time. It depends on leadership behavior, communication consistency, transparency, and competence. Measuring it requires more than an annual survey. It requires a continuous, multisignal approach. Internally, trust shows up in how employees behave. *Do they raise concerns without fear? Are errors reported early or buried until it's too late? Are post-incident reviews honest or guarded?* Anonymous reporting, escalation timing, and near-miss declarations all reveal how much faith employees place in their system and leadership.

Externally, customer behavior reflects trust. Net promoter scores, post-incident surveys, and complaint patterns provide signals, but the most telling indicators come from how quickly customers return and whether they advocate for the organization after disruption. Social sentiment, recovery windows, and transparency in communication matter more than polished talking points.

Trust also extends into partnerships. Resilient ecosystems are built on vendor reliability and aligned priorities. When disruption hits, does your supplier stand with you or protect themselves first? Shared contingency plans, co-investment in controls, and joint communication exercises show whether operational trust exists. Trust is not blind faith. It is confidence earned. Build it in calm periods, and it becomes a reserve you can draw on in crisis. Neglect it, and disruption will leave you isolated.

Adaptability is more than planning. Continuity plans outline what to do, but adaptability reveals how quickly and effectively the organization can pivot when the unexpected happens. It is the ability to change course without losing direction.

Measuring adaptability means looking at indicators of speed and alignment. Scenario switch latency measures how quickly teams abandon a failing strategy and activate an alternative. Decision deviation tracking shows when leaders move beyond existing playbooks and whether those deviations improve results. Organizations that learn in real time outperform those bound by outdated procedures.

System design also matters. Flexible, loosely coupled application programming interface (API)-driven architectures allow workloads to shift quickly without major disruption. Metrics such as time-to-failover, container redeployment speed, and rollback efficiency reveal this flexibility.

People are equally important. Role elasticity, such as how often individuals can take on new responsibilities in crisis, signals human adaptability. Participation in cross-functional exercises and ownership of backup duties demonstrate whether teams can move fluidly when pressure mounts.

Leadership adaptability is a separate measure. *Do executives shift priorities quickly when conditions change? Do they centralize decisions unnecessarily, or empower distributed action?* Metrics such as time-to-shift in decision-making, intervention rates, and strategy reallocation cycles provide answers.

Finally, adaptability includes structural learning. Organizations that implement post-incident recommendations quickly and adjust policies in real time show maturity. Adaptability is not only about moving fast, but also about learning and growing stronger with each cycle.

Recovery is too often reduced to technical timelines. Recovery time objectives and service availability dominate reports, but these overlook the bigger picture. The real test is whether confidence was restored, whether critical business capacity returned, and whether the recovery created strategic value.

Metrics must extend beyond system uptime. Time to full business capability is critical. How long does it take for processes to operate at expected throughput? How quickly do revenues normalize? How fast do regulators, partners, and customers regain alignment?

Residual friction must also be tracked. Systems may be back online, but if teams are weighed down by workarounds, exceptions, or poor communication, recovery is incomplete. Hours of manual effort, unresolved incident threads, and temporary exceptions reveal hidden costs.

Recovery ROI ties actions to outcomes. Did the response protect customer loyalty, revenue, and brand reputation? Metrics like churn deflection, revenue rebound rate, and sentiment recovery curve matter far beyond IT. They shape board decisions and investor confidence and reflect the very nature of why this approach is strategic.

Recovery is also an opportunity for uplift. Post-event retrospectives, recommendation adoption rates, and measurable capability improvements show whether disruption produces real learning. A quick technical recovery without organizational learning wastes the crisis.

Finally, trust recovery completes the cycle. Analyst ratings, stakeholder reassurance timelines, and sentiment rebound provide the full picture. Recovery is not finished when systems are restored. It is finished when belief in the organization returns. See Figure 3.2: Case in Point.

Measuring resilience requires more than status checks. It requires insight into how people act, how systems shift, and how the organization restores confidence. Trust, adaptability, and recovery together form the true lens of resilience.

Each pillar demands its own metrics and ownership, but numbers only matter if they drive behavior and decisions. A trust score should inform leadership practice. An adaptability measure should shape strategy. A recovery ROI figure should influence investment.

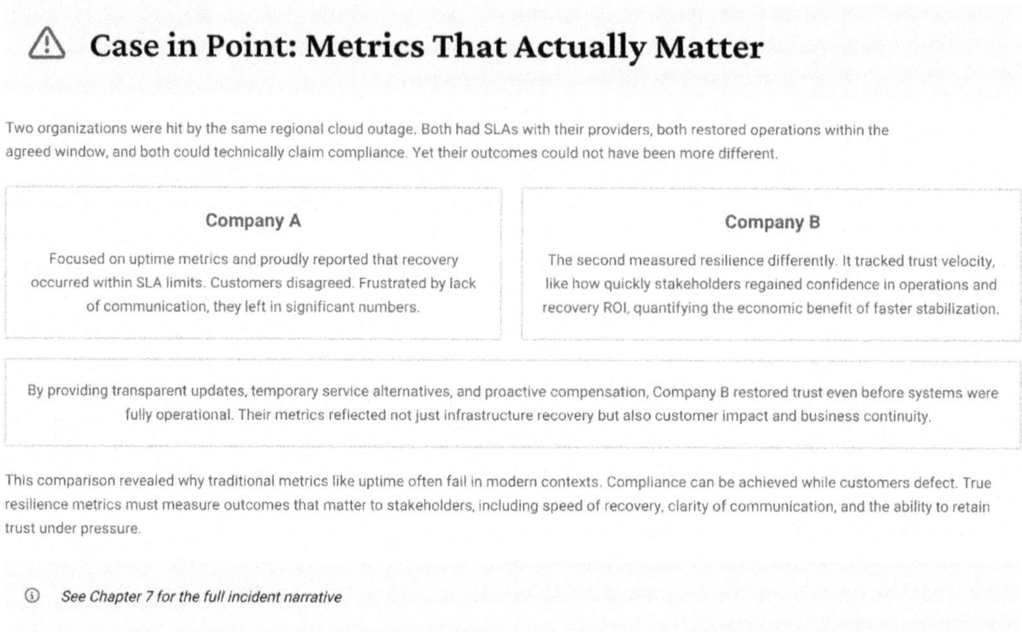

Figure 3.2 Case in Point.

Image created by the author using Gamma.

Resilience often comes in the wake of disruption. It is built in the ways organizations prepare, the ways they earn trust, and the ways they design flexibility into systems and teams. Measuring what matters reveals truth. Acting on that truth builds resilience. And making resilience visible turns it into a strategic advantage.

3.3 CONTROL INTEGRITY UNDER STRESS CONDITIONS

Resilience is never proven in calm waters. It shows itself when strain is applied. Cyberattacks, supply chain failures, or unexpected outages expose whether organizational controls hold firm or collapse. Too often, organizations measure the existence of controls rather than their endurance. They validate paperwork instead of behavior. Real resilience depends on whether a control functions when the system is stretched to its limits. See Figure 3.3: Control Integrity under Stress Conditions.

Controls erode quietly. Drift creeps in as systems evolve, roles shift, or infrastructure changes. An access control that once worked may be undermined by an unmonitored exception. A change control designed for monolithic releases can become irrelevant in a continuous deployment pipeline. Unless controls are tested under stress, resilience remains a concept, not a capability.

One key metric is the control degradation rate, which shows how quickly effectiveness drops under increased load or complexity. Does multifactor authentication (MFA) still perform during a sudden surge in remote work? Can fraud detection logic keep pace when transaction volumes spike? This is why simulated stress testing is critical. Audits validate existence, but resilience requires proof of behavior during disruption. High-risk controls should be tested under simulated loads, adversarial conditions, and cross-system failures.

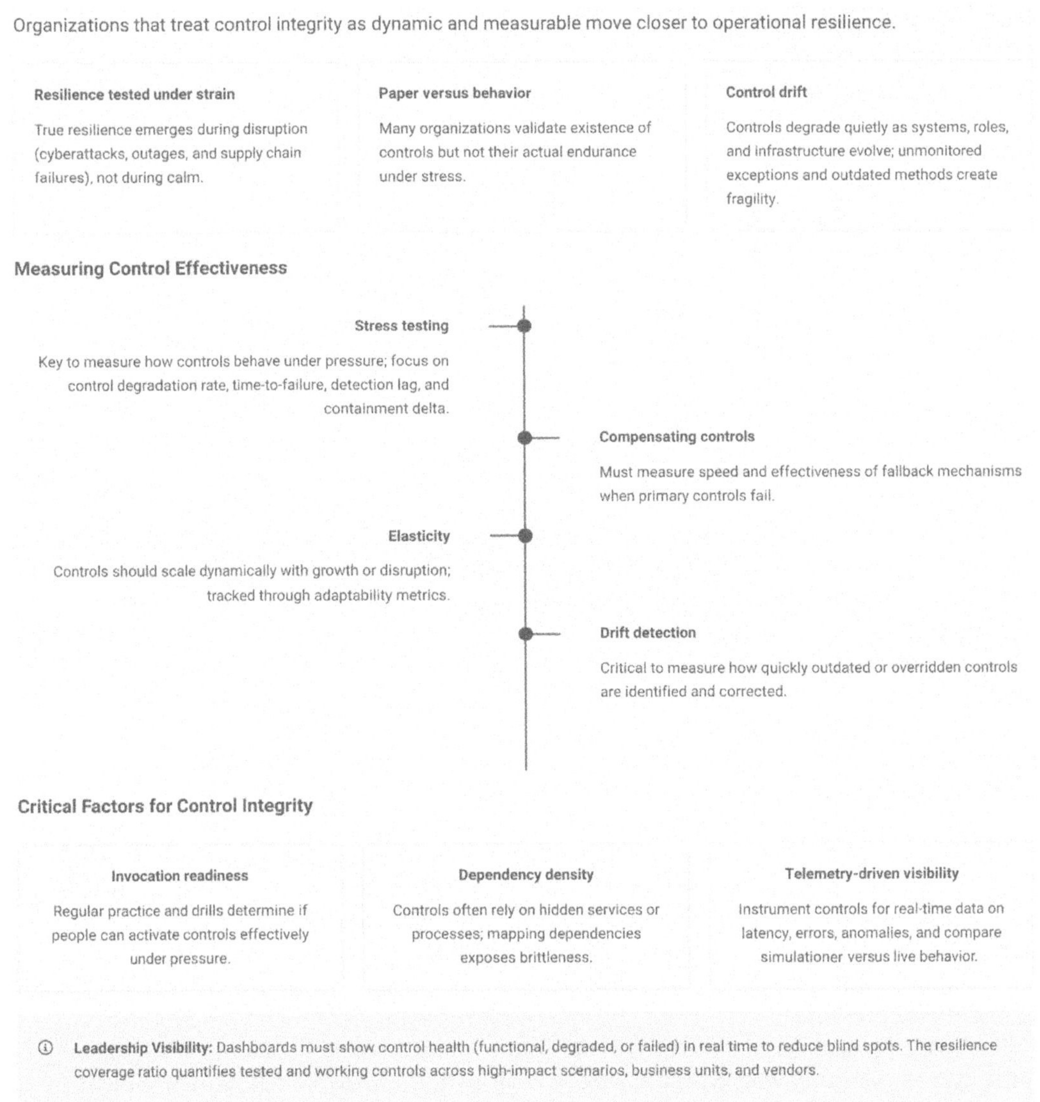

Figure 3.3 Control Integrity under Stress Conditions.

Image created by the author using Gamma.

Metrics such as time-to-failure, containment delta, and detection lag reveal whether resilience is real or assumed.

Compensating control responsiveness is just as important. Primary controls will fail at some point. The question is how quickly compensating mechanisms engage. Organizations should measure response speed, decision latency, and impact containment. How fast do alternate pathways activate when a primary control fails? What damage is avoided by fallback actions?

Elasticity should also be tracked. Controls must adapt dynamically when growth or disruption changes demand. For example, can provisioning controls expand automatically if a environment scales during a crisis? Elasticity metrics quantify adaptability on demand.

Drift detection is another signal. It shows how long misaligned, outdated, or overridden controls persist before discovery and correction. A high drift velocity means systems are evolving faster than governance can keep pace, which signals fragility.

Control invocation readiness matters as well. It measures how often people practice activating controls, how quickly those controls can be executed, and whether there is confidence in the outcome. The best runbooks are useless if no one drills them.

Another layer is control dependency density. Most controls rely on services, identities, pipelines, or processes beneath them. Mapping and scoring these dependencies reveal brittleness. A control with ten hidden dependencies is fragile if one of them fails.

Telemetry changes the game. Controls can now be instrumented for live data on latency, error rates, and anomalies. A control that works in testing may falter under real-world pressure. Tracking the gap between simulation and live events closes blind spots and corrects untested assumptions. The resilience coverage ratio adds perspective. It measures the percentage of high-impact scenarios that have tested, visible, working controls. It prevents false confidence from blanket policies and validates preparedness across threat types, business units, and vendors.

Finally, visibility is the cornerstone. Leaders must see the health of critical controls in real time. Dashboards should reflect whether controls are functional, degraded, or failed. Most blind spots during incidents result from lack of visibility, not lack of intention. Resilience depends on measuring how controls perform under stress, not how they look in policy. Organizations that treat control integrity as a living, active capability move closer to operational resilience.

3.4 RECOVERY RETURN ON INVESTMENT

Recovery has long been misunderstood. It is often reduced to a single milestone, a signal that systems are back online and that the crisis has ended. That framing is not only outdated but also dangerous. Recovery is not the final scene in a disruption story. It is a stress test of every claim an organization has ever made about its resilience. In recovery, the truth emerges. It is where teams, processes, systems, and investments prove whether they are capable of performing under real pressure.

When we treat recovery as the proving ground, we stop seeing it as a burden and start recognizing it as the stage where organizational maturity is on display. It is the moment where assumptions are validated or exposed. It shows whether the governance models we designed, the tools we procured, and the exercises we rehearsed were built for reality rather than for presentations. Recovery is where investment choices either justify themselves or reveal costly gaps.

Too many organizations still view recovery as a tactical clean-up operation. They focus on how quickly IT restores servers or how soon the network comes back online. That view misses the larger opportunity. Recovery should be treated as a value-generating capability, one that strengthens trust, preserves brand equity, and accelerates the return to value.

Recovery is not only about restoration. It is also about confidence. Customers, regulators, employees, and shareholders all watch closely to see how an organization behaves under strain. The real outcome of recovery is not just operational uptime but preserved trust and accelerated momentum. That is why measuring recovery ROI is essential. It allows leaders to evaluate recovery not as a sunk cost but as a driver of business performance.

Traditional recovery metrics, such as recovery time objective and recovery point objective, still have their place. They tell you how long it took to bring a system back or how much data was lost. But they fail to tell the full story. They do not reveal whether customers stayed,

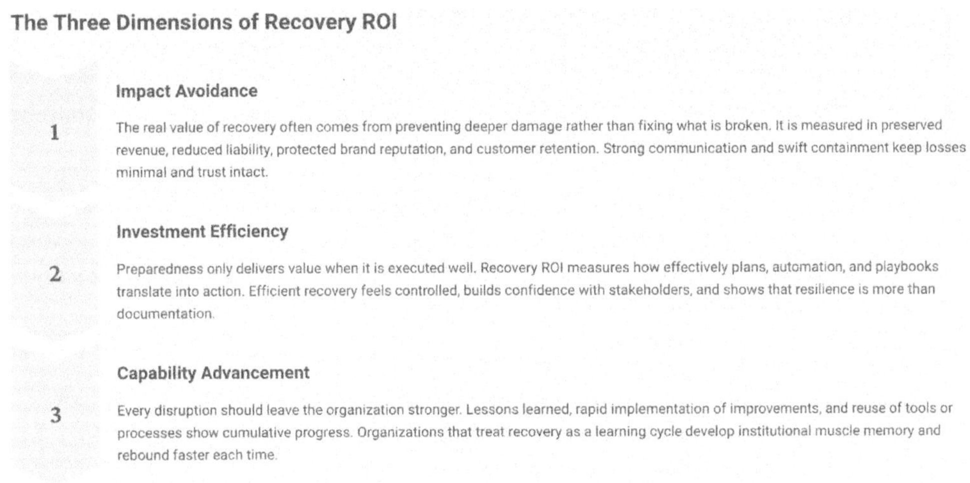

Figure 3.4 The Three Dimensions of Recovery ROI.
Image created by the author using Gamma.

whether revenue rebounded, or whether decision-makers had the clarity they needed during uncertainty.

A database that comes online in 15 minutes is irrelevant if customers have already lost faith because communication was absent or confusing. A business can restore technology while still losing trust. That disconnect is why recovery ROI must extend beyond technical measures to include outcomes that matter to the business.

To measure recovery ROI properly, we first need to redefine recovery itself. Recovery is not the restoration of infrastructure. It is the return to full business capability. What full capability means depends on the context.

For a logistics company, recovery might mean supply chain visibility is restored, allowing goods to flow again. For a hospital system, it means patient care resumes without dangerous delays. For a fintech platform, it might mean restoring user confidence more quickly than a competitor, ensuring customers do not move their accounts elsewhere. Recovery is always situational, which means recovery metrics must be aligned to the outcomes that matter most in that organization's world. See Figure 3.4—The Three Dimensions of Recovery ROI.

3.4.1 The dimensions of recovery ROI

1. Impact Avoidance
   The first dimension concerns what was prevented. Much of the value of recovery does not come from fixing what broke but from avoiding more serious damage. This is measured in revenue retention, reduced liability, preserved brand strength, and customer loyalty.

An outage that is contained within an hour, with clear and transparent communication, may result in minimal customer loss. The same outage, if mismanaged, can create years of reputational damage. That difference is measurable.

Key indicators include:

- Revenue preserved during the disruption window
- Avoidance of legal or regulatory penalties through timely disclosure
- Retention of strategic accounts and partners

- Reduction in compensation payouts or SLA breaches
- Speed of brand sentiment recovery

These indicators elevate resilience from a technical matter to a driver of shareholder value.

2. Investment Efficiency
The second dimension is efficiency. How effectively did the organization translate investments into action? Enterprises pour resources into continuity plans, automation tools, playbooks, and templates. Yet unless those assets are activated and executed during a crisis, they remain theoretical.

High-efficiency recovery shows up in:

- Playbook activation rate during live incidents
- Proportion of actions executed through automation rather than manual labor
- Speed and precision of resource reallocation during the event
- Consistency and cadence of stakeholder communication

When efficiency and communication are high, the crisis feels controlled. Stakeholders sense competence. Teams execute with confidence instead of improvisation. That perception is as important as the technical response, because it shapes trust.

3. Capability Advancement
Recovery should not end with containment. Each disruption exposes gaps but also surfaces hidden strengths. Mature organizations treat recovery as a learning opportunity. They embed lessons, uplift capabilities, and reduce the chance of repeating mistakes.

Metrics include:

- Time to conduct structured after-action reviews
- Speed of implementing recommendations into processes and policies
- Uplift in measurable detection, containment, or communication capability
- Reuse rate of tools or templates in future incidents

Capability advancement demonstrates that resilience is cumulative. Each incident becomes part of the organization's institutional muscle memory. The organization grows stronger with every challenge.

Recovery can be quick but still costly in ways that accounting does not capture. When teams work overtime, when decision fatigue sets in, and when workarounds pile up, the hidden cost is real. This friction shows up in employee burnout, drops in morale, and shortcuts that create new risks. Low-friction recovery is efficient and humane. It reduces burnout, preserves performance quality, and strengthens a culture of readiness. Indicators include overtime spikes, surges in customer service tickets, deviation from standard procedures, and post-incident declines in employee sentiment.

Recovery ROI is most powerful when compared over time. Trends reveal whether resilience is truly improving. Comparisons can also extend outside the organization. Benchmarking recovery against industry peers highlights competitive positioning. Stock price behavior after major incidents, for example, becomes a real-time signal of market trust.

While recovery is judged internally, regulators, auditors, and legal authorities also watch it closely. Their evaluation often hinges on disclosure speed, regulatory compliance, and corrective actions. Recovery metrics can demonstrate that the organization acted responsibly and transparently. Timely notification, swift closure of audit findings, and reduction of legal costs through early resolution are all tangible benefits of mature recovery practices. These indicators influence not only compliance outcomes but also the degree of trust regulators extend to the enterprise.

Metrics have no value if they do not reach decision-makers. Recovery ROI must be embedded into executive dashboards, board reports, and planning processes. When recovery metrics sit alongside financial indicators, they inform technology investments, budget allocations, and risk posture decisions. This integration ensures resilience is treated as a living capability that evolves with the business. Executives gain visibility into strengths and weaknesses. Boards see evidence of progress. Investors and employees see that resilience is measurable and actively managed.

Recovery is an opportunity to prove maturity, demonstrate trustworthiness, and strengthen strategic alignment. Measuring recovery ROI transforms recovery from a technical function into a source of enterprise value. Recovery ROI demonstrates that resilience is measured not only in technical terms but also in the preservation of value and confidence. Yet value cannot be preserved without trust. Trust is the accelerant that turns recovery into renewed momentum. It determines how quickly stakeholders forgive, how rapidly customers return, and how confidently employees reengage. To move beyond restoration into advantage, organizations must measure trust velocity with the same rigor they apply to systems and controls.

3.5 TRUST VELOCITY AS A BUSINESS ENABLER

Many organizations must think of trust not as a static perception but as a dynamic resource. Trust moves through systems, processes, and relationships, shaping the speed and quality of decisions. It fuels customer loyalty, accelerates partnerships, and determines how quickly an organization can act when conditions change. When trust builds, recovers, or expands with speed, it becomes a catalyst for resilience. Companies that demonstrate high trust velocity consistently respond to disruptions with greater agility and adapt to shifting conditions more effectively than those that lag.

Traditional approaches to measuring trust have fallen short. Surveys, satisfaction scores, and employee engagement snapshots are useful, but they capture a moment in time rather than the movement of trust. Trust velocity tracks momentum. It asks how fast trust builds, how quickly it erodes, and how effectively it rebounds after stress. This dynamic perspective explains why some organizations surge ahead while others stall or collapse when confronted with a crisis or uncertainty.

Measuring trust velocity begins by identifying the key moments where trust peaks or collapses. These moments often appear in disclosures after an incident, leadership updates during disruption, customer communications, employee feedback, or regulator interactions. Time-based measures create clarity, such as the time it takes to acknowledge an issue once discovered, the time required to engage stakeholders with meaningful updates, the time gap between recognition and remediation, and finally, the curve that shows how long it takes for sentiment to recover. Each interval reveals how seriously the organization treats accountability and how well it translates words into action.

Time-to-acknowledge is often the most visible indicator. Stakeholders form their impressions quickly based on how fast an issue is confirmed. Delayed acknowledgment creates suspicion, while early confirmation signals transparency. Time-to-engagement matters just as much. Customers want accurate updates, investors seek confidence, regulators require disclosure, and partners need assurance. The faster the engagement and the more substantive the information, the stronger the confidence that develops. Time-to-remediation measures whether the organization connects acknowledgment to decisive action. Admitting a problem without deploying remedies undermines confidence, but swift corrective steps preserve it. Finally, time-to-sentiment recovery shows how long it takes for trust to return to baseline—or climb above it—measured through customer feedback, media tone, or social signals. A short recovery curve often points to operational maturity and a culture that prioritizes credibility.

Trust velocity is just as important inside the organization as it is outside. Internally, it determines how quickly decisions move and how easily teams collaborate. When employees trust leadership and colleagues, escalation happens without hesitation, approvals require fewer layers, and decisions move faster. Leaders themselves set the tone. Executives who act quickly and communicate promptly establish a rhythm that cascades through the organization. Their response time to emerging risks and their willingness to provide visible direction are signals of the trust resources they command.

Externally, customer trust velocity can be measured through conversion rates, onboarding friction, and referral activity. Customers who trust the platform or service move faster to adopt and to recommend. After a disruption, the speed with which referrals recover is a clear indicator of trust regained. Supply chains provide another view. Partners who respond quickly to changes and disruptions show alignment rooted in shared confidence, while delays often expose gaps in collaboration and reliability.

Trust does not move at the same speed for every audience. Customers may forgive faster than employees. Regulators may take longer to acknowledge recovery than investors. Recognizing this asymmetry is critical. Organizations that measure these differences can design targeted interventions, focusing resources where trust is slow to recover rather than treating all groups the same.

Visualizing trust velocity requires tools that make movement visible. Dashboards that track time since the last trust-impacting event, current direction of trust flow, and estimated time to recovery allow leaders to see beyond static scores. These systems provide early warning in normal operations and become indispensable during a crisis. Training and preparedness amplify this further. Teams that rehearse responses, practice customer engagement, and build habits of transparency develop faster, more reliable trust acceleration.

A single trust velocity score will always be misleading. Employees, customers, partners, and regulators each require their own measures. Precision at the audience level enables organizations to shape their communications, refine their investments, and drive cultural improvements that matter where trust gaps exist.

Enterprises that achieve high trust velocity gain more than resilience. They gain speed, confidence, and credibility in their operations. They are able to innovate more quickly, take bolder positions, and execute more effectively. High trust velocity also provides breathing room during emergencies, reducing the need for excessive controls and creating an environment where experimentation is safe. Organizations that protect and grow this asset consistently outperform those that see trust only as a static perception. In practice, trust velocity is not just a measure of resilience. It is a measure of competitive advantage, the difference between merely surviving and leading with confidence in uncertain times.

Trust velocity shows that resilience has direction and speed, not just status. But trust, control, integrity, and recovery ROI only create advantages if they are made visible at the executive level. Metrics must inform decision-making, not sit buried in technical reports. This is where the design of executive dashboards becomes decisive, turning abstract measures into actionable guidance.

3.6 DESIGNING METRICS FOR EXECUTIVE DECISION-MAKING

Resilience metrics only matter when they influence decisions. Too often, executive dashboards are still anchored in compliance reporting. They display uptime percentages, incident counts, audit completions, and control checklists. While these numbers may satisfy regulatory requirements, they rarely give leaders what they need to steer through disruption and uncertainty. Executives need more than static health reports. They need signals that show what is shifting, where attention must go, and how quickly they must act. The true value of resilience metrics lies not in their collection but in their ability to shape timely and informed decisions.

The starting point is alignment with business priorities. That sounds obvious, but in practice, most organizations measure what is easy rather than what is essential. If customer loyalty and brand trust are central to growth, then trust velocity should be a primary indicator. If operations are scaling at speed, then adaptability, elasticity of controls, and recovery efficiency become vital. Every metric must serve a strategic purpose. It should not simply exist for reporting's sake but should answer questions the business is already asking.

For this alignment to be meaningful, metrics must translate across layers of the enterprise. Executives need composite signals, directional trends, and comparative views. They need to know whether trust is rising or falling, whether controls are holding under stress, and whether recovery speeds are improving over time. These signals must be simple enough to guide decisions, but not simplistic to the point of distortion. Functional leaders, on the other hand, require the ability to drill into causes. They need to see the logs, the incident histories, and the capacity indicators that explain why a number is moving. A well-designed dashboard functions as a conversation across different levels of responsibility, balancing summary signals with depth where it is needed.

A metric that does not lead to action is noise. Actionable metrics tell a story. They highlight what is changing, why it matters, who is accountable, and what must happen next. That requires both quantitative signals and qualitative context. For example, a dashboard might show a decline in trust velocity after a customer-facing outage. By itself, that number only hints at trouble. When paired with a short narrative about the cause of the outage, its duration, and the measures being taken, it becomes a catalyst for action and support.

Visualization plays a critical role. Executives are already overloaded with information. A useful dashboard should cut through that noise with clarity. The use of color gradients, directional arrows, confidence ranges, and impact tags can highlight where focus is required, but restraint is essential. Many dashboards attempt to impress rather than inform. A simple downward green trend line is more valuable than an ornate chart that lacks context. Every visual element should reinforce the story behind the data, not distract from it.

Metrics also live on different timelines. Some are real-time, designed to capture deviations the moment they occur. Others are retrospective, useful for evaluating performance after the fact. The dashboard must clearly distinguish between the two. A lagging trust score is only useful when paired with leading indicators such as early sentiment dips, changes in social media tone, or signs of internal confidence slipping. Recovery ROI has little value unless tied to a defined window of time and scope of impact. Precision about time prevents misinterpretation and strengthens the quality of decisions.

Executives need predictive signals, not only status updates. That means resilience dashboards must look forward as well as backward. Metrics such as scenario deviation velocity, decision latency, and early warning amplification help identify disruption before it becomes a crisis. These are not predictions of certainty. They are patterns that indicate where intervention will be needed if current conditions continue. Anticipation is what allows leaders to act with foresight rather than hindsight.

No metric should exist without ownership. A consistent failure in metric programs is the absence of accountability. Each resilience metric must have a designated owner responsible for accuracy, interpretation, and follow-through. When trust indicators dip below target, it should be immediately clear who investigates and who acts. Clear ownership transforms dashboards from observational tools into instruments of execution.

Metrics should also create opportunities for comparison. A single score can reveal status, but comparison over time or across teams unlocks real learning. *Are we recovering faster than last quarter? Do some regions regain customer trust more quickly than others? Are certain business units adapting more effectively to disruption?* Comparative framing moves metrics from passive reporting to active guidance.

Leadership engagement is what cements the role of metrics. When board members and executives begin asking about trust velocity or control readiness instead of focusing only on SLA percentages, it shifts the culture. Metrics gain power when they are referenced in leadership meetings, strategy reviews, and budget discussions. When resilience indicators inform resource allocation and leadership assessments, they become embedded in the operational rhythm of the organization.

The integrity of the data is paramount. A dashboard built on outdated, inconsistent, or unverifiable information will quickly lose credibility. Data sources must be validated, definitions standardized, and update cycles consistent. Trust in the dashboard reflects trust in the organization's ability to see itself accurately. The concept of trust resilience applies equally in this kind of situation as it does with customers. A metric that cannot be explained or audited will be dismissed. Governance must ensure every signal is defensible, timely, and relevant.

Resilience dashboards must evolve. Threats change, technologies advance, and customer expectations shift. A static dashboard in a dynamic environment becomes irrelevant. Metrics should be reviewed regularly, with new indicators added, outdated ones retired, and alignment checked against the current strategy. A dashboard is not a finished product. It is a living, adaptive framework that must grow with the business.

In organizations that lead, resilience dashboards are not saved for crises. They are embedded into everyday operations, planning cycles, and transformation efforts. They highlight weak signals before they turn into losses. They reveal strengths that deserve investment. They create a shared language across IT, operations, risk, compliance, and leadership, giving everyone the same picture of readiness.

When built and used effectively, these dashboards become sources of confidence. Not because they suggest perfection, but because they reveal or at least resemble reality. They show what is stable, what is fragile, and where momentum is shifting. They allow executives to lead from a place of informed visibility rather than assumption. The most critical resilience metric in the coming decade may not be whether systems remain online. It may be the speed at which trust is lost and the speed at which it can be restored. That velocity will define competitive advantage. Dashboards that can measure it, explain it, and help shape action around it will be central to leadership itself.

Dashboards that capture trust velocity, control performance under stress, and recovery ROI transform resilience into a living capability. They give leaders the same clarity about resilience that they expect about revenue or risk. This sets the stage for a broader realization that resilience is not a fixed state but an operational discipline that must be measured, managed, and lived across the enterprise.

3.7 IAMM AND METRICS EVOLUTION

Metrics define how leaders perceive and manage resilience. The Metrics and Reporting domain within IAMM gives structure to that understanding. It moves organizations from tracking activity to measuring outcomes, a shift that changes how resilience is seen and managed.

At Level 1, measurement is scattered or missing. Teams record what they can, often through manual spreadsheets. One team counts vulnerabilities, another tallies incident tickets, while another measures uptime. The data remains fragmented, offering executives only partial visibility. No one can say with confidence whether resilience is improving or fading.

Level 2 brings standardization but not depth. Metrics focus on activity. Organizations count implemented controls, completed audits, or training sessions delivered. Dashboards show green indicators that reflect effort rather than effect. Leaders see activity but not improvement. The numbers offer comfort, not clarity. Often, sourcing data out of convenience, rather than planned data, with the express purpose and design of making decisions.

By Level 3, coordination improves, and reporting begins to align with business outcomes. Metrics such as recovery time objectives and incident containment times appear. Dashboards start to connect control performance with operational outcomes. Measures like average detection time and average response time begin to matter. Yet these remain static snapshots. They do not show whether resilience holds over time or whether stakeholders continue to trust the enterprise.

Level 4 transforms measurement into a forward-looking practice. Metrics now capture business impact. Trust velocity becomes central, showing how fast confidence is restored after disruption. Recovery ROI reveals whether investments in resilience yield measurable value. Leaders gain real-time insight into performance under stress. These measures support informed decisions about priorities, trade-offs, and investments.

At Level 5, measurement becomes part of the enterprise's fabric. Metrics are verified through continuous telemetry rather than periodic sampling. Reporting becomes tailored for each stakeholder group. Boards see assurance performance besides financial results. Customers receive transparent visibility into resilience measures. Regulators see verified evidence of continuous improvement. Metrics evolve into expressions of organizational identity. Resilience is proven through data.

Consider a global retailer facing a cyber outage. At Level 2, executives might see a report showing that 90 percent of controls were implemented and 100 percent of staff were trained. The data would say nothing about recovery effectiveness. At Level 3, reports might show that recovery time objectives were met but omit customer sentiment. At Level 4, the organization would track trust velocity, showing how quickly satisfaction levels returned. At Level 5, it would measure recovery ROI, proving that resilience investments returned value through loyalty and reputation gains.

Enterprises that remain at Level 2 often deceive themselves. Dashboards full of green indicators create an illusion of safety while saying little about how the organization performs under stress. Level 4 and 5 organizations, by contrast, can demonstrate that their controls preserve trust even when challenged. They measure resilience in ways that boards, regulators, and customers can recognize as credible.

Barriers to maturity usually come from habit. Teams measure what is simple instead of what is significant. Some avoid outcome metrics because the results may expose weaknesses. IAMM provides structure for overcoming these habits. It maps a clear progression from activity-based reporting to outcome-based measurement, from compliance indicators to trust indicators.

Reflection and recalibration drive the journey. Dashboards must evolve from showing what has been done to showing what has been achieved. Metrics must align with business priorities and reflect the experience of stakeholders. Recovery ROI must be tracked and communicated. These steps turn metrics into decision instruments rather than static reassurance.

IAMM affirms that resilience is not proven through counts of completed activities. It is shown through outcomes that can be seen, tested, and trusted. The maturity of an enterprise's metrics defines whether it operates for compliance or for confidence.

3.8 CONCLUSION

Resilience has long been framed as a static condition. Leaders ask whether the enterprise is "resilient," as if it were a permanent state that can be declared once and checked off a list. That framing is both misleading and dangerous. Resilience is a living capability. It changes as threats evolve, as people adapt, and as systems face pressures they were not designed to handle. Organizations that view resilience as a destination will remain vulnerable. Those who view it as a discipline to be measured, refined, and lived will thrive in environments defined by disruption.

This chapter began by dismantling the illusions of traditional metrics. Uptime percentages, SLA compliance, and audit completions have dominated executive dashboards for decades. They were simple, familiar, and easy to benchmark. But as we explored, they are backward-looking, fragmented, and hollow. They provide reassurance without truth. They describe surface stability without revealing underlying fragility. They create false confidence that encourages leaders to make bold decisions on the basis of distorted views. The green dashboards and polished compliance reports that once symbolized readiness are, in fact, warning signs of brittleness.

That critique matters because measurement shapes behavior. What leaders choose to measure signals to teams what is valued and what will be rewarded. If uptime is the ultimate measure, then staff will chase availability, even if it means masking fragility. If compliance checklists define resilience, then teams will rehearse paperwork rather than rehearse a crisis. When activity counts more than outcome, the culture adapts accordingly, optimizing for shallow success while real risks multiply in the shadows. Metrics are never neutral. They direct attention, influence investment, and decide what gets ignored. Measuring the wrong things does not merely fail to capture resilience. It actively undermines it.

To break this cycle, resilience must be redefined. It is not the absence of failure but the presence of adaptability. It is not measured by how rarely things go wrong but by how quickly and effectively the organization pivots when they inevitably do. Real resilience lives in the confidence stakeholders maintain, the speed with which trust is restored, and the clarity of action when pressure mounts. It is a system's ability to bend without breaking and a culture's ability to move with purpose in the midst of uncertainty. For leaders, that means moving beyond legacy indicators and embracing a new set of measures that reflect how resilience actually works.

The first of these is trust velocity. Trust has often been treated as an intangible quality, spoken of in vague terms but rarely measured with rigor. In practice, it is one of the most powerful accelerants of resilience. When trust is high, issues are escalated early, decisions are made quickly, and stakeholders remain steady even when disruptions occur. When trust is low, hesitation spreads, leaders second-guess, and customers abandon. Trust velocity captures not just whether trust exists but how it moves. How quickly is it built? How rapidly does it erode? How effectively does it rebound? By tracking acknowledgment times, engagement lags, remediation speed, and sentiment recovery, leaders gain visibility into the true tempo of confidence. Trust velocity becomes a leading indicator of how resilient the enterprise feels to those who matter most.

The second is control integrity under stress. Controls look effective in policy documents, in staged audits, or in routine operations. But resilience is not proven in calm waters. It is revealed when strain is applied. A control that works in a test may collapse when transaction volumes spike, when remote access surges, or when attackers adapt in real time. That is why organizations must measure degradation rates, containment deltas, and drift detection cycles. They must treat controls not as static safeguards but as living defenses whose endurance must be tested and validated. Controls that cannot hold under stress are illusions, and resilience built on illusions is no resilience at all.

The third is recovery ROI. Too many organizations still view recovery as a cleanup task to be finished as quickly as possible. That mindset reduces recovery to timelines and technical milestones. In reality, recovery is where every investment in resilience is tested. It is where leadership demonstrates credibility, where customers decide whether to remain loyal, and where regulators judge competence. Recovery ROI reframes the question from "how quickly were we back online?" to "what did we preserve, what losses did we prevent, and what capabilities did we improve?" By evaluating impact avoidance, efficiency of response, and capability advancement, recovery ROI converts a crisis from a cost center to a proving ground. Leaders who treat recovery as a strategy gain trust, strengthen brand equity, and accelerate momentum even in disruption.

Together, trust velocity, control integrity, and recovery ROI form a model of resilience that is dynamic, measurable, and actionable. They answer the questions executives actually face: Do our stakeholders still believe in us? Do our defenses hold when it counts? Do we emerge from disruption stronger than before? These are not IT questions or operational side notes. They are boardroom issues, directly tied to enterprise value, market confidence, and competitive advantage.

Yet even the right metrics mean little if they are not made visible at the leadership level. That is why executive dashboards play such a critical role. Too many dashboards still display static uptime percentages and audit completions, mistaking health for resilience. What leaders need are dashboards that integrate trust velocity scores, real-time control performance, and recovery ROI trends. They need directional signals that show what is stable, what is degrading, and where attention must shift. They need predictive indicators that highlight emerging stress before it leads to loss. When metrics are integrated into executive decision-making, they cease being numbers on a page and become catalysts for action.

A dashboard that reveals where trust is slipping can trigger communication strategies before churn accelerates. A dashboard that shows control degradation under load can redirect investment to shore up defenses before adversaries exploit weaknesses. A dashboard that tracks recovery ROI across incidents can demonstrate to investors and regulators that resilience is not just claimed but proven. When resilience metrics stand beside financial and risk indicators, they anchor resilience as a strategic function of the enterprise rather than a technical afterthought.

The lesson of this chapter is clear. Resilience cannot be measured by the comfort of familiar numbers. Legacy metrics mislead because they are simple when reality is complex, backward-looking when the future is uncertain, and polished when truth is messy. They tell leaders what they want to hear instead of what they need to know. The alternative is not to abandon measurement but to measure differently. By adopting metrics that reflect trust, adaptability, and recovery, leaders gain a truer picture of readiness. By embedding those metrics into executive dashboards, they turn resilience from rhetoric into reality.

For boards and executives, the implications are profound. The enterprise will be judged not by how often it avoids disruption but by how it behaves when disruption comes. Customers will ask whether trust is restored quickly. Regulators will ask whether controls are held under stress. Investors will ask whether recoveries preserve value. The answers will not be found in uptime charts. They will be found in resilience metrics that capture the lived reality of performance under pressure.

Resilience is not survival. It is leadership in uncertainty. Organizations that measure what matters most will move faster, decide with confidence, and recover with strength. They will stop being defined by the disruptions they endure and start being defined by the trust they

This checklist turns resilience metrics into guiding questions for leaders. It shifts focus from technical uptime to business critical capabilities like trust, adaptability, and recovery. Use these questions to validate whether your organization is truly ready to perform under stress and to align resilience measurement with strategic outcomes.

1

Shifting Beyond Legacy Metrics

- ☐ Are uptime and SLA compliance being treated as supporting signals rather than the main measure of resilience?
- ☐ Do our metrics reflect readiness under stress, or only availability under normal conditions?
- ☐ Have we built impact severity and interdependencies into how we evaluate performance?

2

Measuring Trust Velocity

- ☐ How quickly do we acknowledge issues to employees, customers, and regulators once they are detected?
- ☐ Are we engaging stakeholders with meaningful updates at the right speed?
- ☐ Do we move from acknowledgment to concrete remediation actions quickly?
- ☐ What does our sentiment rebound curve look like after disruptions and do trust levels return quickly?
- ☐ Do we make internal decisions quickly, for escalations to occur, or approvals to move forward?
- ☐ Are our ecosystem partners aligned and responsive when a disruption occurs?

3

Testing Control Integrity Under Stress

- ☐ Have we stress-tested our most critical controls under high load or adversarial scenarios?
- ☐ Do we have an acceptable rate of degradation when controls are pushed to their limits?
- ☐ Do compensating controls activate quickly when a primary control fails?
- ☐ Are we tracking drift and how long do outdated or misaligned controls remain undetected?
- ☐ Can our controls scale dynamically as systems expand or during a crisis?
- ☐ Do we have live telemetry showing how controls actually behave under real-world stress?

4

Quantifying Recovery ROI

- ☐ Do we define recovery as a return to full business capability, not just system restoration?
- ☐ Do we track measurable damage avoided (revenue loss, penalties, or churn) through effective recovery?
- ☐ Do our playbooks activate, does automation cover critical actions, and do communications maintain confidence?
- ☐ Do we implement lessons learned and achieve measurable improvements in capability after events?
- ☐ How do regulators, auditors, and legal bodies perceive the effectiveness of our recovery performance?

5

Designing Executive Dashboards That Matter

- ☐ Are our resilience metrics directly aligned to business priorities like growth, trust, and adaptability?
- ☐ Do our dashboards provide tiered views, including high-level signals for executives and drill-down detail for operators?
- ☐ Is every resilience metric clearly owned by a leader who ensures accuracy and follow-up?
- ☐ Are we monitoring leading indicators such as decision latency, early warnings, and scenario deviations?
- ☐ Does our dashboard tell a clear story that informs decisions instead of just reporting data?
- ☐ Do we regularly review and update our dashboards to reflect evolving risks and business realities?

☐ **Executive Action:** Move resilience metrics out of compliance dashboards and into strategic decision-making. Measure trust, adaptability, and recovery as living indicators of capability. Ensure metrics drive ownership, clarity, and investment that strengthens resilience as a competitive advantage.

Figure 3.5 Practical Checklist: Resilience Metrics.

Image created by the author using Gamma.

earn, the adaptability they show, and the value they protect. In a world where volatility is constant, that shift is not optional. It is the difference between fragility and advantage, between enduring loss and creating momentum.

The call to leaders is straightforward. Stop counting the wrong things. Start measuring the reality of resilience. Demand metrics that reveal trust velocity, test control integrity, and prove recovery ROI. Place those measures on the same dashboards that guide revenue and risk. Let them shape strategy, investment, and culture. Because what you measure is what you build. And if you build on measures that matter, you will not only endure disruption but also convert it into strength. See Figure 3.5: Practical Checklist: Resilience Metrics.

Part II

Organizational Change in Motion

Chapter 4

Breaking the Culture of Siloed Defense

4.1 SHIFTING FROM SILOED DEFENSE TO SHARED OWNERSHIP

For decades, cybersecurity and operational risk functions have developed in parallel but separate tracks. That separation was not malicious or careless. It emerged from a mix of scale, specialization, and mounting regulatory pressure. As technology grew more capable, organizations answered by forming dedicated teams to manage distinct areas of responsibility. Infrastructure groups focused on core systems, application teams built and supported software, and compliance groups interpreted evolving rules. Security, governance, and operations units followed, each developing its own tools, methods, and accountability practices. But over time, this specialization hardened into isolation. What began as a logical division of labor gradually became a systemic vulnerability.

This fragmentation shows up as siloed defense in most organizations. Security teams operate as external validators rather than embedded partners. IT operations prioritize uptime, performance, and delivery metrics. Business units push for speed and innovation. These functions are rarely aligned on how to evaluate, prioritize, or own risk. They speak different languages, operate on different cadences, and respond to different incentives. The result is friction that compounds risk rather than containing it.

That friction is not theoretical. It materializes in missed deadlines when security is brought in too late. It shows up in tense meetings where operational teams feel caught off-guard by new controls. Blame surfaces fast when something breaks, and no one can point to the moment a decision created the opening. It wears people out, and it also leaves quiet gaps that determined attackers know how to exploit. Adversaries move easily through the space that forms between teams. They succeed where handoffs are messy, where ownership is vague, and where risk signals are overlooked or ignored because they fall outside someone's domain.

The boundaries that were once intended to protect responsibilities now constrain collaboration. They prevent organizations from seeing risk holistically. They make it difficult to detect compound risks that span technology, operations, and business processes. And they slow down the very decision-making required to respond to dynamic threats. In a world where attackers move fast and exploit complexity, silos are not just inefficient. They are dangerous.

Integrated Assurance is the antidote to siloed defense. It reframes risk not as a departmental issue, but as a shared operational concern. It asks every function to participate in protecting the enterprise. That participation begins with visibility. Each team must understand the risk landscape relevant to its domain. Product teams must see how design choices affect data privacy. Operations teams must grasp how system changes could impact control effectiveness. Procurement must recognize the risk implications of third-party decisions. Risk ownership is no longer the domain of a few; it is the responsibility of all.

DOI: 10.1201/9781003685982-6

This does not mean everyone must become a cybersecurity expert. It means that every team must develop basic fluency in how risk appears within its sphere of influence. The real lever is contextual accountability. Risk literacy only has real value when it connects to the choices a team makes, the systems it relies on, and the outcomes it is working toward. When people understand risk in that setting, the organization starts to notice issues sooner, bring them forward without hesitation, and act before a central check or security gate is needed.

The hard part is weaving this mindset into daily work. Adjusting a process will not be enough. New tools and dashboards can provide clarity, but they cannot carry the weight on their own. Moving away from isolated lines of defense toward shared responsibility is a cultural shift. It calls for new thinking about risk, clearer incentives, and a more direct approach to accountability.

In many organizations, the first sign of this cultural gap is how leaders ask questions. When decision-makers ask, "Did security sign off on this?," they reinforce the idea that risk is someone else's concern. That question isolates accountability. It turns security into a permission gate rather than a strategic partner. The better question is, "How are we managing the risk of this initiative together?" That shift in language signals shared ownership. It invites cross-functional thinking. It opens the door to better decisions, made earlier, with broader input and clearer trade-offs.

Language will not close the gap on its own. Teams need to learn how to evaluate risk within the full context of the business and the systems they support. Incentive models that favor speed over resilience need a hard look, and many will need to be rebuilt. Governance must also evolve so that security, risk, and operations no longer move on separate tracks but operate as one connected function with shared outcomes.

This is where many transformation efforts stall. Culture change is slow. It requires visible leadership commitment and structural reinforcement. It demands that we embed security advisors and risk champions into operational teams. It calls for updated metrics that measure not only how fast we ship but how well we protect. It requires performance reviews and promotion criteria that reward collaboration, transparency, and proactive risk management.

Shared ownership does not mean consensus. Every decision does not need to pass through a committee. What it does require is clarity. Clarity on who owns what risk. Teams need to understand how to evaluate risk in the context of the business they serve and the systems they rely on. Incentive structures that reward speed at the expense of resilience deserve serious scrutiny, and many will need to be redesigned from the ground up.

This level of integration is not a theoretical goal. It is already happening in high-performing organizations. We see it in organizations that embed security into agile delivery teams, where vulnerability scanning and control validation happen during development, not after release. We see it in joint procurement and security committees that evaluate vendors based on both cost and risk exposure. We see it in business units that own the consequences of system misconfigurations or data mishandling. This is not because security says so, but because they understand the downstream impact on customers and reputation.

What separates these organizations is not a spotless record. They make mistakes like everyone else. The difference is in how quickly they recover, how deeply they learn, and how rarely they repeat the same problems. That is what shared ownership creates. It spreads accountability in a way that sharpens response, strengthens resilience, and builds real trust.

Resilience does not come from one team trying to carry the full weight. It grows when many teams work together, spot risks early, and act as a coordinated system. In that environment, security stops being a standalone function. It becomes an organizational skill. That skill grows out of the daily habits, choices, and expectations that guide people far more than any chart or reporting line ever will.

The shift from isolated defense to real shared ownership is challenging, and it rarely happens overnight. It has to be built into the work. It has to be understood, practiced, and carried out. That shift takes time. Each conversation that widens perspective, each choice that reaches beyond familiar lines, and each structural change that brings people together pushes the enterprise in the right direction. It shapes an organization that becomes safer, more adaptable, more trusted, and ready for whatever comes next.

4.2 THE CULTURAL BARRIERS TO INTEGRATION

Many of the forces that block real integration across cybersecurity, risk, and operational functions do not come from technology gaps. The tools are strong, and the capabilities continue to advance. The deeper challenge sits in the culture that surrounds those tools. Even as organizations mature digitally, many of their habits remain rooted in old patterns and long-standing assumptions. These patterns create a sense of stability, yet they also reinforce silos that quietly weaken resilience. What looks like discipline on the surface often conceals structural friction that drains the organization's ability to adapt.

A major source of this friction comes from how people understand risk ownership. In many companies, cybersecurity grew out of regulatory demands or public pressure after major incidents. These teams were asked to protect the business, yet were positioned outside of the daily flow of operations. They were seen as guardians who stood apart from the work, rather than as partners woven into it. Meanwhile, operations, engineering, and product teams were chartered to build, release, and support. Their mandate centered on performance and speed. Their metrics reflected that focus.

At first glance, this separation seems rational. It offers checks and balances. In practice, it creates a quiet misalignment. Security is framed as a barrier to progress, stepping in to block or slow work. Operations are framed as risk takers who push ahead without caution. With every missed signal or last-minute conflict, the space between teams stretches further. Blame takes root. Respect thins out. Over time, resilience erodes.

These tensions are reinforced by how teams are evaluated. Security is judged by incident prevention, compliance adherence, and control strength. Operations are judged by uptime, delivery speed, and cost efficiency. Each group behaves in line with its incentives. When a risk decision arises, these incentives collide. A single vulnerability discovered just before a planned release becomes a battleground. Security urges immediate action. Operations pushes to stay on track. Neither group is wrong. Both operate from a reasonable view of success. Yet the organization is forced into a lose–lose decision. Over time, these moments create frustration that sits below the surface and quietly shapes how teams perceive one another.

Language becomes another barrier. Words that appear straightforward carry different meanings across functions. Threat, vulnerability, exposure, readiness, tolerance: Each of these terms can shift depending on who is speaking. Security tends to think in terms of adversaries and attack paths. Business leaders think about customers, revenue, and market risk. Operations focuses on system stability, service reliability, and delivery cadence. Each group speaks fluently within its own frame but struggles to translate that fluency across the organization. Even when everyone agrees on the need to manage risk, the conversation breaks down when shared language is missing.

These language gaps slow decisions and distort intent. Teams talk past each other without realizing it. They misread urgency or underestimate impact because information was presented in an unfamiliar frame. People grow hesitant to elevate concerns if they expect misunderstanding or conflict. Risk signals then arrive late or not at all. This is not a communication flaw in individuals. It is a structural design flaw in how cross-functional work is organized.

The most difficult barrier to confront is trust. Trust is not abstract. It shapes every decision, escalation, and interaction. When trust is low, teams protect themselves. Security teams feel the weight of responsibility without the authority to influence core decisions. They work in constant reaction, often under-resourced and excluded from early planning. Operations teams feel pressure to deliver at speed while staying within narrow guardrails. They grow weary of being held responsible for risks that were never discussed openly. In this environment, people default to caution. They share less. They reveal less. They wait to be asked rather than volunteer insight. None of this is done with harmful intent. It is a survival response.

Without psychological safety, organizations cannot integrate. Integration requires people to raise uncomfortable issues, acknowledge uncertainty, and collaborate through trade-offs. If the environment punishes transparency, these behaviors never emerge. Integration remains a slogan rather than a lived practice.

For organizations that want to adopt Integrated Assurance, the starting point cannot be new tooling or procedural updates. The starting point is culture. Trust must be shaped with intent. It has to be visible in how leaders make decisions, how teams communicate, and how outcomes are measured. Cross-functional meetings alone are not enough. Leaders must demonstrate shared accountability, invite input from diverse functions, and show that resilience is a collective aim, not an isolated responsibility.

Incentives must also shift. As long as security and operations are measured against opposing goals, friction will continue. Shared outcomes matter. Time-to-risk-mitigation, control integrity across workflows, resilience indicators that combine availability and protection: These kinds of measures help reframe success as a joint accomplishment. When teams are aligned on what "good" looks like, cooperation becomes natural rather than forced.

Communication must mature as well. This involves more than swapping vocabulary. It involves understanding what each group values. Security leaders benefit from understanding what drives product growth. Business leaders benefit from understanding the operational impact of risk decisions. Operations teams benefit from a space where concerns can be raised without being labeled an obstacle. These skills influence survival in a complex enterprise environment. They determine how well an organization turns risk into informed action.

Visibility also plays a key role. When teams share the same view of telemetry, dashboards, and indicators, they operate with the same understanding of reality. This reduces suspicion and brings clarity. Decisions are made faster and with more confidence. Risk becomes part of the operational rhythm rather than an external judgment that arrives after work is already planned.

Risk conversations must also move into earlier stages of planning. Too often, organizations treat risk as a final checkpoint or a compliance requirement. When risk is brought in only after decisions have been made, it has little influence beyond slowing the process. When risk is part of design reviews, budgeting, and strategy sessions, it becomes a tool for shaping clearer and stronger decisions.

Culture might seem intangible, yet it can be shaped deliberately. It is influenced by the structures leaders create, the signals they reinforce, and the behaviors they recognize. To break the cultural barriers that slow integration, organizations must treat trust as a foundation, not a byproduct. They must refine shared language, align incentives, and make collaboration a practiced habit rather than a periodic effort.

This work takes time. It requires persistence and an honest look at how teams actually interact. But the payoff is real. As barriers dissolve, ownership becomes shared. Integration becomes routine. Risk management shifts from reactive control toward anticipatory guidance. Resilience becomes a daily capability.

Organizations that choose this path gain an advantage that technology alone cannot deliver. In a world filled with complexity and speed, cultures built on trust and shared purpose hold

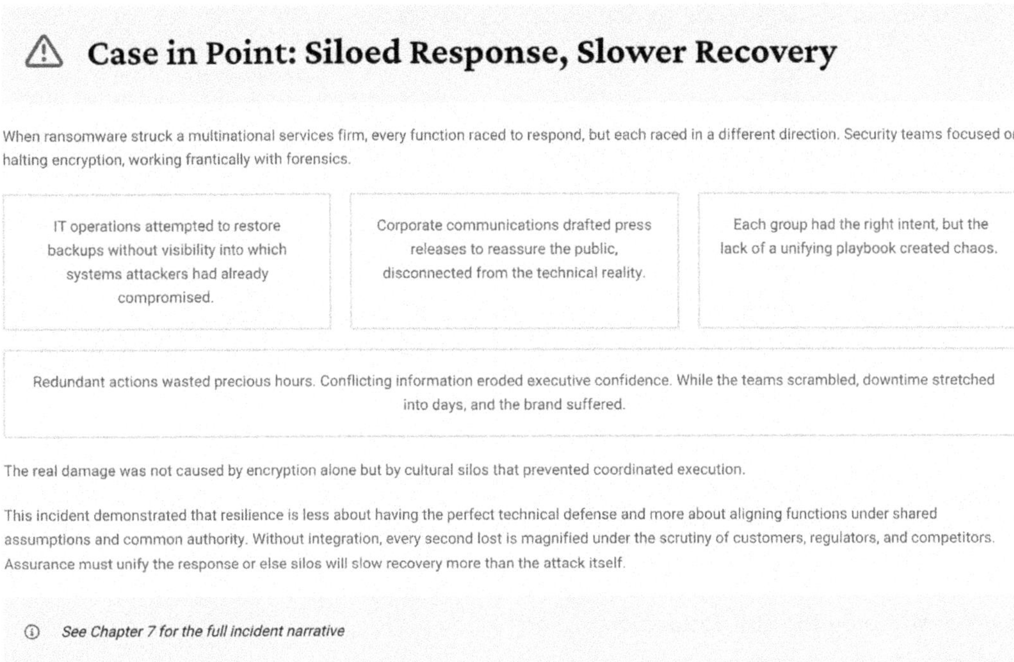

Figure 4.1 Case in Point.

Image created by the author using Gamma.

the greatest resilience. Integrated Assurance becomes not only attainable but also essential for organizations that want to navigate uncertainty with clarity and confidence. See Figure 4.1: Case in Point.

4.3 THE PSYCHOLOGY OF RISK

Breaking the culture of siloed defense requires more than new workflows or shared dashboards. It begins with an honest look at how people experience and interpret risk. Enterprise risk is not only a technical issue or a governance problem. It is a human behavior challenge. The decisions people make, the signals they react to or dismiss, and the urgency they assign to an issue are all shaped by habits, bias, and emotion. When these dynamics remain unaddressed, even the most mature frameworks struggle to gain traction. See Figure 4.2: Designing for Risk Rationality.

Most people do not assess risk through a purely objective lens. They make judgments under time pressure, with incomplete information, and in environments where reputation and authority influence every interaction. In those situations, individuals rely on mental shortcuts that operate beneath conscious awareness. These shortcuts shape a familiar pattern of distortions that affect coordination, reporting, and response.

Loss aversion offers a clear example. People feel the weight of loss more intensely than the satisfaction of an equivalent gain. In practice, this is evident when teams resist security measures that introduce short-term inconvenience. Even when the long-term value is obvious, the immediate sense of reduced speed creates a stronger emotional pull. The trade-off that strengthens resilience is eclipsed by the discomfort of slowed delivery. This bias makes it harder to adopt controls that serve the larger mission.

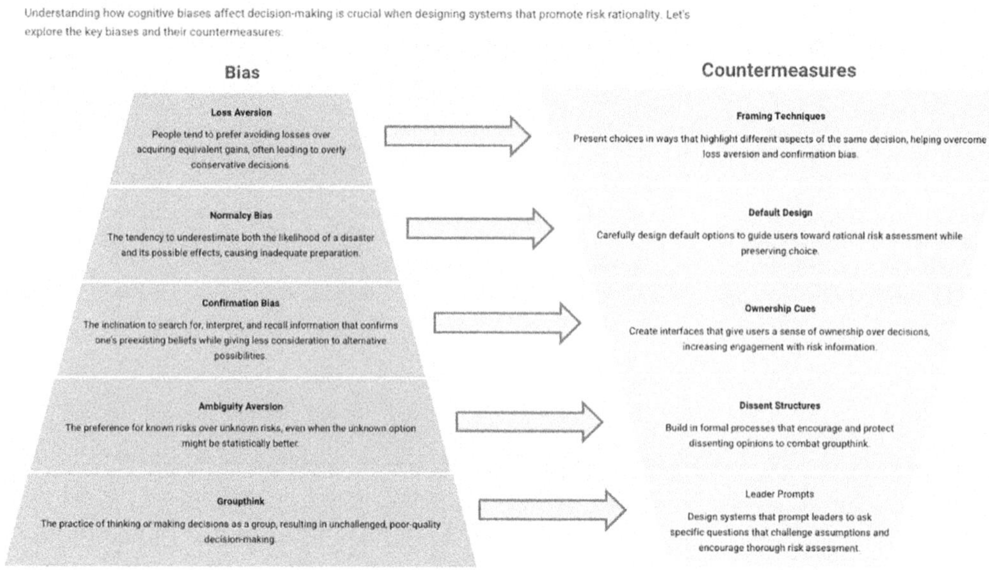

Figure 4.2 Designing for Risk Rationality.
Image created by the author using Gamma.

Confirmation bias creates its own challenges. Individuals tend to favor information that supports their current beliefs and discount what contradicts them. A product team eager to ship may overlook early signs of instability or security risk. A compliance group may focus on checklists that validate its existing approach while ignoring operational concerns about usability. When each function operates inside its own validation loop, shared understanding becomes fragmented.

Normalcy bias also affects how organizations interpret unusual signals. When teams assume the future will resemble the past, they underestimate the potential for rare but damaging events. Stability becomes a substitute for safety. The absence of recent incidents comforts people into thinking risk is low. Early indicators of trouble are dismissed as noise until disruption forces a response that could have come much earlier.

These patterns are not failings of character. They are common features of human reasoning. Their impact, however, is significant. They influence which issues get raised, which warnings get ignored, and how teams coordinate in moments of uncertainty. If these tendencies are not addressed, they compound across the enterprise and turn cultural friction into structural exposure. Improving risk management requires a shift in how risk is framed and acted upon in everyday work.

Framing is one of the most effective tools. Research consistently shows that the way information is presented can influence decisions as strongly as the information itself. A vulnerability described as having a 20 percent chance of exploitation in the next month is more likely to create urgency than one described as having an 80 percent chance of no incident. When security teams frame risk through customer impact, financial cost, or operational consequence, stakeholders see the relevance more clearly. Translating technical concerns into outcome-based language narrows the distance between intent and action.

Defaults also guide behavior. People usually follow the path that requires the least effort. In many organizations, secure choices require extra steps, while unsafe choices are easier. To counter this, security should be built into the default experience. Contract templates should already contain essential security provisions. Repository settings should enforce sensible restrictions without relying on developer initiative. Procurement platforms should identify vendors with elevated risk and trigger early review. These defaults tilt daily decisions toward safer outcomes without overwhelming teams.

Ambiguity aversion introduces another barrier. When ownership of a risk signal is unclear, or when escalation criteria are not explicit, people naturally avoid taking action. Issues linger because no one knows who must respond or when. To resolve this, risk processes should offer immediate clarity. Each signal should answer three questions: Who is responsible, what action is needed, and when escalation is required. This reduces hesitation and allows teams to move with confidence.

Groupthink brings its own hazards. When teams value harmony over challenge, they suppress dissent and overlook evidence that would sharpen judgment. Risk signals are softened to avoid conflict. Decisions follow perceived alignment rather than genuine analysis. Organizations can counter this by formalizing a role for challenge. A designated questioner in planning sessions, a premortem exercise before major initiatives, or a retrospective that focuses on overlooked signals can help teams surface alternative views. This creates space for constructive disagreement that strengthens decision quality.

Leadership plays an essential role in shaping these habits. Leaders influence how teams think as much as how they act. When leaders name potential blind spots, question easy assumptions, and invite alternate viewpoints, they signal that reflection is part of the work. They guide conversations toward the risks that are easy to ignore. They encourage people to examine which signals they may have filtered out without realizing it. This sets a tone where transparency is valued, and accountability becomes a shared responsibility.

When organizations build awareness of these behavioral forces into daily operations, risk conversations begin to shift. Teams respond with curiosity rather than defensiveness. Decisions feel more grounded and less reactive. People recognize how bias shapes their instincts and compensate with deliberate checks. The goal is not perfect rationality. The goal is a more intentional approach to uncertainty.

Organizations that understand the psychology of risk do not rely on awareness alone. They design better defaults, use clear narratives to align understanding, and create systems that lift signals before they become incidents. They recognize that most failures emerge from gaps in perspective rather than gaps in logic. Integrated Assurance becomes the mechanism that closes these gaps. It creates alignment across behavior, language, and structure so that bias loses its influence and decisions improve.

Seen in this way, Integrated Assurance becomes a behavioral design system as much as a governance model. It accounts for how people actually behave rather than how they are expected to behave. It treats trust, clarity, and responsibility as foundational elements. Resilience grows from the alignment of these elements with the enterprise strategy. Understanding the psychology of risk does not sit at the edge of integration. It sits at the center. It turns culture into a source of strength and helps the enterprise manage risk with clarity, consistency, and collective purpose.

4.4 BUILDING A CULTURE OF COLLECTIVE RESPONSIBILITY

In today's operating environment, risk no longer lives inside cybersecurity teams or within compliance checklists. It moves through every part of the business and touches every function. That reality makes resilience a responsibility shared across the entire organization. While technologies help and policies provide structure, neither can create resilience on their own. The real work begins with people who understand that risk belongs to all of them.

Moving from narrow accountability to collective responsibility becomes the foundation of a resilient enterprise.

Many companies still operate with habits formed long before the current threat landscape emerged. Risk is treated as something that can be delegated. It is assigned to legal teams, internal auditors, cybersecurity specialists, or enterprise risk managers. Although these groups often carry deep expertise, they remain limited by the organizational boundaries around them. The rest of the company keeps moving at full speed and assumes that someone else is handling the problem. That sense of distance creates genuine vulnerability. When responsibility feels remote, accountability fades into the background. No one steps forward because everyone believes someone else already has.

Shifting this mindset requires more than new documentation or a broad awareness campaign. It calls for a fundamental rethinking of how the organization sees risk and who owns it. In a resilient enterprise, risk becomes an operational factor that shapes every level of activity. People view it as part of planning, decision-making, and routine execution. This begins by positioning risk as a business concern that influences outcomes rather than a technical concern reserved for specialists. Every individual should understand how their work affects the organization's exposure. The goal is not to turn the workforce into cybersecurity experts. The goal is to help people see how their decisions create consequences that travel far beyond their immediate tasks.

A product manager planning a release should recognize the privacy, trust, and misuse implications of their decisions. A procurement leader reviewing a contract should consider the security posture of the vendor and what it brings into the environment. A marketing director preparing a campaign should understand the reputational and regulatory considerations that accompany their strategy. When people see risk in these daily choices, it becomes tangible. Once it is tangible, they begin to make different choices. Curiosity grows. Transparency improves. Alignment with the organization's resilience goals becomes natural rather than forced.

This kind of culture only grows when leadership shows what it looks like in practice. An executive team cannot rely on endorsements of security programs to set the tone. They must demonstrate risk-informed behavior in visible ways. This includes incorporating risk discussions into strategy sessions, framing decisions with a clear awareness of their full impact, and acknowledging trade-offs with honesty. When leaders treat risk as an operating reality rather than a side conversation, the message resonates across the organization.

Leadership must also model healthy responses to failure. Too many organizations treat incidents as moments that require blame instead of understanding. That pattern discourages openness. To break this, leaders need to show that raising concerns is preferable to silence. Transparency should be rewarded, especially when mistakes occur under pressure. Culture is shaped by what leaders accept and what they recognize. If leaders want widespread ownership of risk, they must call attention to those who demonstrate it.

Shared retrospectives are a powerful tool for reinforcing these values. These sessions should be routine ways of examining incidents or major projects. The purpose is to understand what happened and why, not to determine who erred. When people from across the organization participate, the conversation becomes richer. Teams see how signals were missed or where processes fell short. This widens their perspective beyond the limits of their functional roles. Retrospectives help normalize the idea that learning sits at the center of effective operations.

Healthy feedback loops support this cultural foundation. Psychological safety becomes essential. If people worry about repercussions when raising concerns, those concerns will remain hidden. The veneer of smooth operations masks a fragile reality. By encouraging questions and rewarding the early surfacing of issues, leaders help create an environment where risk signals move quickly through the organization. A simple test often applies. If no one is raising low-level concerns, the culture is likely suppressing them.

Structures must reinforce these cultural expectations. Performance metrics and incentives should reflect the organization's commitment to resilience. Success cannot be measured only by delivery speed, uptime, or efficiency. Evaluations must consider how well individuals anticipate risk, communicate during uncertainty, and collaborate when challenges appear. When these expectations are built into the definition of strong performance, people understand that responsible behavior is not optional. It is part of the job.

Recognition matters as well. Employees who surface difficult truths or challenge assumptions often show the highest form of leadership. Too often, these actions go unnoticed. Highlighting them in leadership communications, internal awards, or peer-recognition programs makes the behavior visible. Over time, others begin to follow that example. The message becomes clear. Owning risk is not a burden. It is a contribution to the health of the enterprise.

When this cultural shift takes hold, an organization begins to work differently. Individuals step forward rather than wait for instruction. Teams respond with speed because they understand the context. Risk becomes something that is shared rather than delegated. The organization starts to behave like a living system with the capacity to detect weakness, respond to pressure, and adapt to change. Resilience stops being a program. It becomes a property of how the enterprise functions.

Building such a culture requires patience and persistence. It requires repeated reinforcement and consistent leadership support. Yet the benefits are considerable. Organizations that succeed in this shift reduce blind spots and improve their response to uncertainty. They make decisions faster because they trust their people to act with judgment. They create confidence among customers, partners, and regulators by demonstrating that risk is truly owned. They become more capable of navigating complexity and recovering from disruption.

A culture built on collective responsibility does not avoid risk. It understands it. That understanding strengthens the organization and supports resilience that lasts.

4.5 IAMM AND CULTURE MATURITY

Culture is the foundation on which all assurance stands. Policies, tools, and frameworks cannot compensate for a culture that views assurance as someone else's responsibility. IAMM's Culture and Collaboration domain makes that truth visible by showing how maturity in culture determines whether resilience is fragmented or shared.

At Level 1, culture is reactive and disconnected. Teams protect their own priorities and rarely collaborate outside their function. Security is seen as an obstacle to delivery, and risk management is regarded as paperwork. Communication between departments is limited to escalation during incidents. When a breach or failure occurs, blame follows instead of analysis. This environment creates fatigue and mistrust. People work around controls rather than within them. Assurance efforts fail because the culture resists alignment.

Level 2 introduces awareness but not integration. Awareness campaigns and compliance training become common, yet the impact remains surface-level. Employees can recite policy slogans but do not see how assurance relates to their day-to-day work. Risk and compliance are still perceived as external authorities rather than embedded disciplines. Teams comply when required but disengage otherwise. The culture values avoidance more than improvement.

At Level 3, collaboration begins. Leaders establish cross-functional working groups and begin to recognize the importance of shared responsibility. Information flows between business units and security teams. Joint exercises, such as tabletop simulations or resilience drills, become part of the routine. Trust starts to form between groups, and individuals begin to understand that assurance benefits everyone. However, these behaviors are often dependent on personalities. When key advocates leave, progress can stall. The culture is maturing, but it has not yet become self-sustaining.

Level 4 marks the transition from coordinated effort to embedded accountability. Assurance becomes part of how people define success. Objectives in performance reviews reflect shared outcomes. Collaboration is formalized through governance structures, and teams act from a shared understanding of resilience goals. A developer no longer waits for a security review at the end of a project but includes security checks in their build process because the behavior is expected. Cultural maturity at this level ensures that assurance is not dependent on management oversight. It becomes instinctive.

Level 5 institutionalizes assurance culture. Leadership models behavior not only through communication but also through visible engagement in assurance activities. Recognition programs reward teams that strengthen resilience, and lessons from incidents are shared transparently. Collaboration is continuous, not event-driven. Employees understand that assurance protects the enterprise and its reputation. When disruption occurs, teams act collectively without waiting for directives. This level of maturity transforms assurance from an organizational function into a cultural identity.

Consider an example from a healthcare provider. At Level 2, compliance training is completed annually, and staff acknowledge policies. Yet when a phishing campaign occurs, many still click on malicious links. At Level 3, departments begin joint response exercises, and awareness improves. At Level 4, employees report suspicious emails proactively and share insights. At Level 5, they collaborate across departments to improve detection and strengthen policies. The difference lies in ownership. Assurance becomes part of how people work, not an afterthought.

Organizations that fail to invest in culture often experience cycles of improvement and regression. Controls may strengthen temporarily, but behaviors revert under pressure. IAMM shows that sustainable assurance requires a culture that values accountability, transparency, and shared purpose.

To build this maturity, enterprises can begin with simple reflection. Are teams working together toward shared resilience goals? Are assurance responsibilities embedded in job descriptions? Do leaders model desired behaviors? Are failures discussed openly to learn from them? The answers reveal where culture stands on the maturity path.

IAMM's Culture and Collaboration domain provides a roadmap for creating a workforce that responds to risk not with fear but with confidence. Culture determines whether assurance survives change or disintegrates when challenged.

4.6 EMBEDDING CROSS-FUNCTIONAL RISK LITERACY

Embedding cross-functional risk literacy is not a compliance task. It is a business requirement. In most organizations, resilience depends on more than the strength of technical controls. It depends on how well every function understands the risks around its daily work. Risk literacy is the ability to notice, interpret, and respond to signals that influence the health of the business. It is not an attempt to turn the entire workforce into cybersecurity specialists. It is an attempt to help every team make choices that respect the realities of risk while supporting operational speed, strategic goals, and long-term trust.

Many organizations still treat risk literacy as a fixed obligation. They introduce required training, publish policy packets, or rely on onboarding videos. These measures allow leaders to assure auditors that the box has been checked. They rarely influence how people behave.

They do not develop real capability. They do not help employees recognize new forms of exposure, collaborate across functions, or weigh trade-offs when pressure rises. The outcome is a workforce that knows the rulebook but does not know how risk shapes its decisions. This produces confidence that is thin and fragile, and it collapses when the organization faces real adversity.

A shift from this passive stance to a more resilient posture requires literacy that is embedded in daily work. It must be relevant, grounded, and supported by the tools and conversations that shape decisions. This begins with learning that fits the realities of each function. The risk landscape for software developers differs from the one faced by procurement or human resources. Developers need insight into secure coding practices, cloud configuration concerns, and risks connected to the software supply chain. Procurement must understand contract language, assessment frameworks for vendors, and the security obligations within service agreements. Human resources teams must be equipped to understand insider threats, sensitive personnel transitions, and privacy obligations.

Generic training ignores these distinctions. When literacy reflects the context of each role, it becomes practical. Employees start to see clear connections between their responsibilities and the exposures that come with them. They understand their part in the broader resilience of the enterprise. This creates a more connected system where information travels freely, risk signals are noticed earlier, and responses are coordinated rather than scattered.

Embedding literacy extends far beyond training. It must be present in operational rhythms. Risk discussions should occur at the point where decisions are made, not only in annual reviews or formal risk councils. If risk is discussed only in security meetings or governance boards, it becomes detached from the pace of real work. It must appear in sprint planning, vendor negotiations, marketing reviews, and business planning cycles. This is where Integrated Assurance brings value. When risk and security advisors work directly with cross-functional teams, risk considerations surface naturally at the beginning of the process rather than at the end.

This change also calls for clearer language. The vocabulary of security can feel remote to people who do not work in the field. Terms that carry weight among analysts or engineers often feel abstract to business leaders. To strengthen risk literacy across functions, we must translate these ideas into business outcomes. Leaders are more likely to engage when conversations connect to revenue, trust, operational continuity, or regulatory exposure. A marketing leader will participate more fully when risk is linked to customer confidence. A product manager will make better judgments when the relationship between rapid feature delivery and platform stability is clear.

Organizations that advance in this area often rely on narrative to reinforce understanding. People remember stories, particularly when the narrative mirrors their world. Tabletop exercises, breach simulations, and case studies bring risk to life. A story about a phishing attack that disrupted a payroll cycle becomes far more memorable than a list of technical concepts. These experiences build readiness and reduce resistance. Over time, employees begin to view risk as a regular element of their work rather than an external disruption.

Leadership has a significant influence in shaping this culture. Executives must do more than sponsor training or approve policy documents. They must engage in risk discussions, ask thoughtful questions, and show how trade-offs can be managed without fear. When leaders use risk analysis in strategic planning and recognize transparency about exposure, they set a powerful example. Mid-level managers then adopt the same approach, and the mindset cascades through the organization.

Technology must reinforce this environment. Risk awareness cannot rely on occasional reminders. It must be visible in the daily workflow. Dashboards and operational platforms should surface relevant indicators in real time. Procurement systems can present vendor risk scores before a contract moves forward. Engineering tools can highlight known vulnerabilities during backlog refinement. When these signals appear naturally in the work environment, they help teams make decisions with greater clarity and consistency.

Organizational structure also matters. Cross-functional steering groups, embedded risk liaisons, and communities of practice help sustain literacy by encouraging communication across teams. These structures prevent blind spots, support rapid escalation, and promote shared learning. When functions compare how they interpret similar risks, they often uncover patterns that improve alignment and maturity.

Measurement is necessary for improvement. Participation rates or training completions offer little insight. The real signal comes from behavior. Are teams raising risks earlier? Are they engaging more consistently with risk and security partners? Surveys can reveal changes in confidence. Incident data can show which patterns are improving and which ones still require attention. These measures give leaders a more accurate sense of progress.

Risk literacy must continue to evolve. The threat landscape shifts. Regulatory expectations change. Business models introduce new forms of exposure. Literacy programs must adapt at the same pace. This requires champions who take responsibility for content, delivery, and refinement. Without ongoing stewardship, literacy loses relevance and credibility.

There is also potential to incorporate risk literacy into performance expectations. When it becomes a recognized competency, it influences career growth. Performance reviews can include assessments of how well individuals consider risk when making decisions. Teams that demonstrate strong risk awareness can be recognized through advancement or peer programs. This reinforces the reality that good risk management is a mark of leadership rather than a constraint.

At its core, cross-functional risk literacy gives the organization a common way to see the world. It supports collective understanding even when responsibilities differ. In complex environments that change quickly, this shared lens enables coordinated movement. It strengthens agility and trust. It shifts the organization from reacting after the fact to anticipating what may come.

This kind of change requires focus, iteration, and sustained commitment. Yet the benefits are profound. When every team understands how risk connects to its work, the organization becomes more adaptive. It responds faster. It learns faster. It grows more confident in uncertain conditions. As this foundation takes hold, the next step is to shape the organizational structures that reinforce this maturity. The following section will explore how design principles can place assurance at the center of how the enterprise operates and remove the friction that weakens resilience.

4.7 ORGANIZATIONAL DESIGN PRINCIPLES FOR ASSURANCE

Organizational design is one of the most powerful yet frequently overlooked levers for building real resilience. Within an Integrated Assurance model, it becomes an essential driver. No amount of training or new technology can offset the limits created by structures that encourage siloed behavior, scattered accountability, or reactive patterns. The way an organization is built shapes how people reason, collaborate, and respond. That structure, more than any directive or announcement, determines whether assurance functions work in alignment or fall into conflict.

Many organizations pour resources into culture, leadership training, and digital transformation while giving far less thought to the design of their operating model. This is a costly oversight. Since structure shapes culture, any effort to bring security, risk, compliance, and operations together must start with the architecture of the organization itself.

When the organizational chart reinforces divisions and misaligned incentives, cross-functional work becomes a hollow attempt at cooperation or empty performance. The real task is to shape the organization so that it supports shared outcomes instead of protecting isolated specialties.

One of the most effective design principles in advancing assurance is proximity. People do not build trust through long email threads or periodic reviews. Trust grows when teams sit together, plan together, and solve problems together. This requires security and risk professionals to be embedded in the functions they support. It is not a matrix model or a dotted-line arrangement. It is operational adjacency. Developers need security partners inside sprint planning sessions, not reviewing pull requests at the end. Procurement teams need risk advisors involved during vendor evaluation, not after the contract moves to legal review. Finance teams need visibility into exposure levels while shaping budgets, not after incident response costs arrive.

Proximity creates a learning loop. Security professionals gain fluency in the pressures and constraints of their host teams. Product and operational teams begin to view risk as a lens that strengthens outcomes rather than an audit hurdle. This exchange builds empathy, shared language, and joint ownership. It also lowers the cost of friction. Handoffs shrink. Escalation ladders shorten. Late-stage rework driven by misalignment becomes less frequent.

Another foundational design principle is aligned incentives. Incentive structures shape behavior with more influence than formal authority. Yet many organizations unintentionally reward silos. Security teams are measured by how well they block threats. Operations teams are measured by uptime and throughput. Finance is measured by cost control. Each group acts rationally within its domain, yet these isolated metrics often create tension across the enterprise.

To support Integrated Assurance, organizations need shared metrics that reflect cross-functional outcomes. Resilience scores, control effectiveness ratings, and recovery indicators can serve as unifying KPIs. These indicators should reflect how teams collectively manage uncertainty and perform under pressure. A successful product launch should be judged not only by adoption and speed, but also by security posture, privacy readiness, and its capacity to withstand failure.

Aligned incentives do not diminish specialized expertise. Instead, they bring risk-informed goals into the systems that shape performance. Bonus models, compensation plans, and reviews should account for how well teams integrate assurance into their work. A marketing group that protects brand trust during a campaign deserves recognition. An engineering team that reduces security debt while maintaining delivery pace should be rewarded. These models reinforce the idea that managing risk is part of delivering value.

Clarity in governance and escalation pathways is equally important. One of the most common sources of friction in risk decisions is ambiguity. Who holds the final authority? When must an issue be escalated? What thresholds require executive involvement? Without clarity, decisions stall. Risk gets pushed down until it becomes unmanageable or pushed up until urgency is lost.

A strong assurance model creates visible roles that operate across functions. Risk champions within business units, assurance stewards inside delivery teams, and executive sponsors who navigate trade-offs at the portfolio level create a distributed governance layer. This structure enhances accountability and accelerates action. Teams know what to raise, where to raise it, and how decisions will move forward. Leadership understands where assurance responsibilities sit and whether the organization remains within its defined appetite.

Agility is another essential element of modern organizational design. Traditional hierarchical models were built for stability. Today's risk environment demands flexibility and speed. Static reporting lines and rigid approvals cannot keep pace with evolving threats.

Organizations need fluid, networked structures that allow teams to self-organize in response to new challenges.

One effective mechanism is the use of cross-functional fusion cells. These groups can be quickly assembled to address emerging risks, analyze incidents, or develop integrated solutions. They bring together expertise from legal, IT, security, compliance, operations, and business units. They operate with clarity and speed. They bypass delays and create responses that line functions can scale.

To activate these principles, organizations should conduct a structural risk alignment review. This review is not an exercise in redrawing boxes. It is a diagnostic effort that examines where assurance responsibilities sit, where teams operate in isolation, and where governance forums lack necessary voices. It maps how decisions move, who has visibility into risk, and whether current structures enable real-time coordination or reinforce fragmentation.

Technology and data systems must mirror this integration. Assurance information must flow across boundaries. Shared platforms, unified dashboards, and real-time telemetry are vital. A product owner should see how backlog items relate to security risk. A supply chain leader should view vendor exposure through the same system used to manage sourcing. A CISO should track risk decisions by business impact, not only by control status.

The external interface of the organization must also reflect Integrated Assurance. Many organizations manage internal risk and third-party risk in separate domains. This creates gaps and inconsistencies. An integrated model brings vendor, partner, and supply chain risk into the same decision-making structure as internal operations. Shared onboarding processes, joint scorecards, and cross-functional steering groups ensure that external exposures are managed with the same rigor as internal ones. This also supports bidirectional learning from the broader ecosystem.

Resilient design requires leadership that is distributed yet coordinated. Centralized models slow decision-making. Leaders at all levels must be equipped to act within defined boundaries. This requires clear communication of risk appetite, structured delegation, and predictable mechanisms for upward reporting.

Empowered teams can take calculated risks, innovate with confidence, and escalate appropriately when limits are reached. This balance between autonomy and oversight creates operational speed without weakening control. When leaders trust their mandate and have real-time data and clear guidance, the organization becomes more responsive.

Assurance must also be woven into everyday business rhythms. Risk cannot operate on a separate track. It must be present during quarterly reviews, strategy discussions, product launches, vendor negotiations, and major transformation efforts. These moments shape the direction of the organization. Without assurance at the table, misalignment and exposure become more likely.

When risk appears on executive dashboards, when board meetings track it with the same rigor as growth metrics, and when portfolio decisions reflect it, the organization sends a clear signal. Assurance becomes a source of value. It becomes part of the conversation that guides the future. This visibility elevates its relevance and keeps it aligned with business priorities.

Organizational design for assurance is not about adding layers. It is about removing barriers that keep risk isolated. It aligns structure with strategy. It ensures that the way teams are grouped and governed reinforces the behaviors needed for resilience. When structural form supports functional intent, when incentives encourage integrated thinking, and when collaboration is strengthened by design, assurance becomes a natural part of how work gets done.

Integrated Assurance does not demand a wholesale reorganization. It demands intentional design. It requires examining where roles, incentives, and reporting lines promote integration or reinforce division. It also requires continuous attention. As threats evolve and business models shift, the structure of the enterprise must adapt.

Organizations that commit to these principles begin to limit the kind of fragmentation that slows decisions and weakens trust. Their teams move with greater clarity because functions that once operated on separate paths now coordinate their efforts with a shared sense of direction. This shift creates the early structure for resilience that is not easily disrupted. Over time, it becomes part of how the enterprise thinks and behaves.

4.8 EXAMPLES OF BREAKING SILOED HABITS

In every organization, silos are easier to form than to dismantle. They are the product of legacy structures, functional specialization, and well-intentioned efforts to bring focus and accountability to discrete domains. Over time, however, those same silos become friction points that impede collaboration, slow down decision-making, and weaken the organization's ability to respond to risk. What follows are real-world examples of organizations that made the shift toward Integrated Assurance by intentionally dismantling siloed habits. While every context is different, the principles of visible leadership, structural alignment, incentive redesign, and a deliberate investment in shared language and trust remain remarkably consistent. See the examples provided in Figures 4.3–4.6.

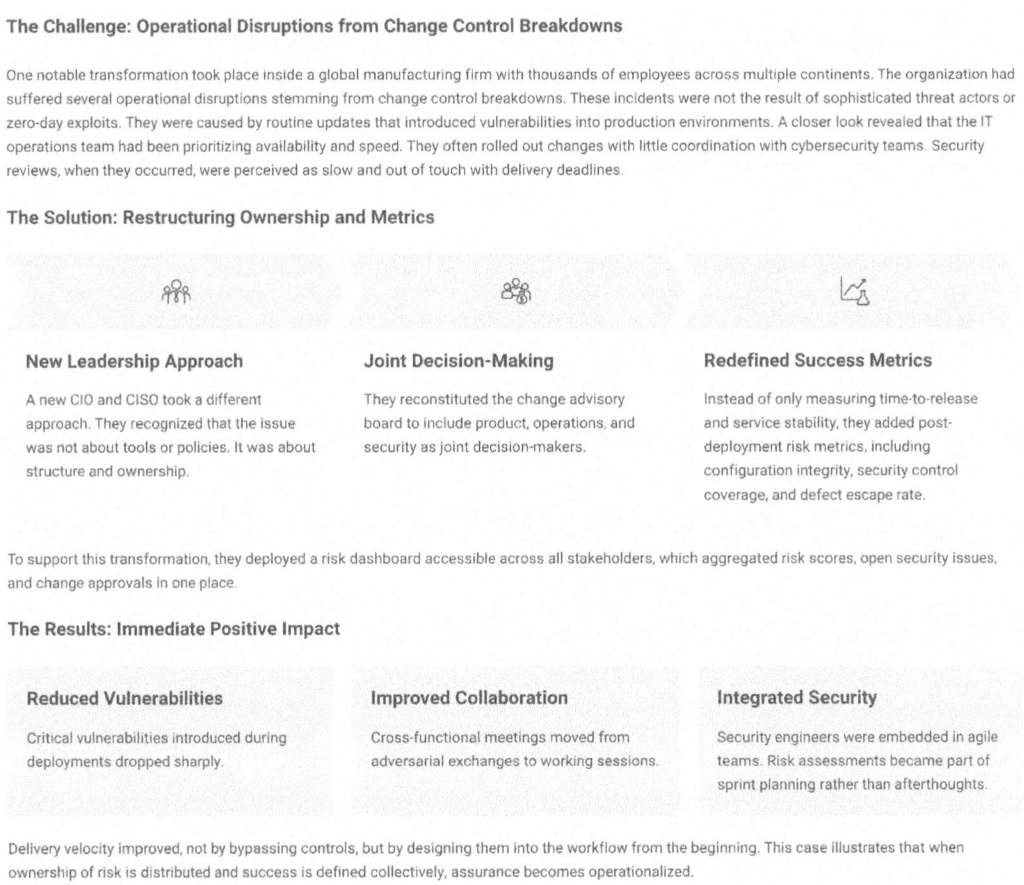

Figure 4.3 Example: Global Manufacturing Firm.

Image created by the author using Gamma.

A second example comes from a regional healthcare provider under increasing pressure to strengthen its third-party risk oversight. The procurement team traditionally operated in isolation from IT and security. Vendors were chosen based on price, availability, and service fit. Security reviews, if conducted at all, occurred after contracts were signed. The result was predictable. High-risk vendors entered production environments with little scrutiny. Go-live dates were delayed by last-minute risk findings. In some cases, retroactive remediation drove up costs and created friction with legal and compliance teams.

The Transformation

Problem Identification

Recognizing the pattern, the organization created a joint working group between procurement and cybersecurity. They met weekly to review vendor requests, assess risk levels, and align on assurance requirements.

Solution Development

The team developed a vendor risk tiering framework, which categorized suppliers based on data sensitivity, operational criticality, and regulatory exposure. Each tier came with predefined security requirements, contract clauses, and review timelines. Procurement staff were trained to interpret security assessments and factor them into RFP scoring models.

Measurable Results

Within a year, the organization dramatically reduced the number of high-risk vendors in its ecosystem. They renegotiated contracts to include clearer security obligations and implemented a third-party risk platform that provided end-to-end visibility across the vendor lifecycle.

Cultural Shift

Procurement and security developed a collaborative rhythm. Rather than operating in sequence or conflict, they co-owned the objective of enabling the business with confidence. The shift was not just procedural. It was cultural. They no longer viewed security as an obstacle. Security no longer saw procurement as reckless. They began speaking a shared language of business-enabling risk management.

Figure 4.4 Example: Regional Healthcare Provider.
Image created by the author using Gamma.

In financial services, the stakes are even higher. A multinational bank experienced a high-profile data breach traced to weak identity governance. The issue was not the absence of technology. Tools were in place. The problem was structural. Responsibility for identity management was fragmented across HR, IT, and security. There were no clear lines of accountability for provisioning, role design, or access revocation. Orphaned accounts accumulated. Privileged access was granted without proper oversight. When the breach occurred, no one could agree on where responsibility began or ended.

The Problem

Fragmented responsibility across departments with no clear accountability for identity management, leading to a high-profile data breach.

The Solution

Creation of an identity governance council with authority to make policy decisions, allocate resources, and set access governance strategy.

The Result

Identity governance transformed from a compliance burden to a business capability, with improved processes and shared accountability.

Governance Transformation

In response, the organization launched an identity governance council made up of HR, security, compliance, and IT leaders. The council was given authority to make policy decisions, allocate resources, and set access governance strategy. They redesigned the joiner–mover–leaver process to reflect real-time triggers from the HRIS. They embedded risk scoring into access provisioning tools. They also created a quarterly report for the audit committee that showed improvements in policy compliance, access exceptions, and audit findings.

Over time, identity governance moved from a compliance burden to a business conversation. New-hire onboarding included role-based access by design. Organizational restructuring included identity risk reviews. When new applications were introduced, access provisioning was part of the design, not a post-implementation fix. The breach had catalyzed a governance structure that turned fragmented ownership into shared accountability. What was once a liability became a capability.

Figure 4.5 Example: Financial Services.
Image created by the author using Gamma.

The Challenge: Siloed Security Operations

Public sector organizations face different constraints but the same core problem. In one large city government, cybersecurity and emergency management operated on completely separate planes. IT managed digital infrastructure. Emergency management handled physical crises, severe weather, and public safety. When a ransomware attack struck, both teams responded, but without coordination. Systems went offline. Communication channels failed. Responsibility was disputed. Recovery took far longer than necessary.

The Solution: Unified Incident Response

Collaborative Framework

To address the gap, the CIO and CISO worked with the director of emergency services to create a unified incident response framework.

Shared Protocols

They wrote shared playbooks that included cyber-physical response protocols. They ran tabletop exercises that included legal, communications, and public safety.

Integrated Dashboard

They implemented a shared operations dashboard that allowed all stakeholders to see incident data, mitigation progress, and escalation paths in real time.

The Results: Improved Resilience

The transformation showed its value during a subsequent cyber incident. The response was cohesive. Roles were clear. Communications were unified. Containment occurred before public disruption. The city received commendation from state auditors for its improved posture. More importantly, the experience changed how teams saw each other. Cybersecurity was no longer viewed as a narrow IT concern. It became part of the city's overall resilience strategy.

Figure 4.6 Example: Public Sector.

Image created by the author using Gamma.

These examples offer several lessons for organizations pursuing Integrated Assurance. First, structural integration must come before cultural change. Embedding shared roles, redesigning governance, and aligning incentives are necessary precursors to trust. When structures reinforce isolation, no amount of workshops or leadership messaging will build the behaviors required for integration.

Second, shared metrics are nonnegotiable. Each of these examples succeeded in part because they introduced measures that crossed functional lines. Whether it was deployment risk integrity, vendor exposure, access governance maturity, or incident containment speed, the organizations tracked what mattered across teams. Dashboards were not just tools for visibility. They were mechanisms for alignment.

Third, the best transformations begin with an acknowledgment of fragmentation. They do not pretend that collaboration can be improvised. They start by naming the silos, surfacing the friction points, and designing pathways toward collective ownership. They treat integration as an ongoing capability, not a one-time program.

Perhaps just as important is what these cases did not do. None of them assumed that more technology alone would solve the problem. All involved some tooling, but the real gains came from redesigning how people made decisions together. None relied solely on new hires or rebranding initiatives. They built durable mechanisms such as councils, embedded roles, recurring forums, and integrated platforms. And none treated risk as the exclusive domain of one function. Each invested in distributing responsibility where it could be best exercised.

Breaking siloed habits requires more than intent. It requires operational design that aligns authority, accountability, and action. Organizations that make this shift begin to experience a different rhythm. Risk signals are identified earlier. Responses become coordinated rather than fragmented. Decisions reflect cross-functional insight. Over time, the organization begins to learn as a system.

Integrated Assurance is not theoretical. It is already being practiced in leading organizations across sectors. What distinguishes these organizations is not the absence of risk, but their ability to manage it collectively. They have replaced internal conflict with shared understanding. They have turned control into capability. And most importantly, they have built a foundation for resilience that scales.

The path forward is not mysterious. The principles are clear. The examples are instructive. What remains is the choice to act. For organizations willing to confront fragmentation head-on, the payoff is not only reduced exposure. It is increased confidence, faster execution, and stronger alignment with the mission. That is what Integrated Assurance delivers when siloed defense is left behind.

4.9 CONCLUSION

The journey through this chapter has revealed a truth that many leaders know intuitively but struggle to act on, which is that siloed defense is no longer sustainable. In today's environment of persistent disruption, accelerated digital transformation, and adversaries who exploit every gap in coordination, functional isolation is not just inefficient. It is dangerous. Siloed defense slows down the enterprise, hides risk signals, fragments accountability, and impairs resilience at the moments when cohesion matters most.

What has made silos so difficult to dismantle is that they are not just structural. They are cultural. They are built into language, incentives, governance models, and the daily behaviors of teams that were designed to optimize for speed, efficiency, or compliance in isolation. But those optimizations now come at a cost. A delay in a product release because of last-minute security checks. A procurement decision that introduces third-party exposure. An operational push that bypasses controls to meet a deadline. These are not isolated events. They are symptoms of a deeper misalignment.

Integrated Assurance offers a different model. One that recognizes the interdependence of cybersecurity, operations, compliance, risk, and business performance. It is a shift from reactive control to proactive capability. From isolated expertise to shared understanding. From functional protectionism to enterprise-wide resilience. And it begins with breaking the cultural habits that keep teams apart.

This chapter has explored what that shift looks like in practice. It begins with a reframing of ownership. Security is not just the job of the security team. Risk is not just a line on a compliance report. Every function has a role to play. Every team makes decisions that influence the organization's exposure. And every employee needs to understand how their work connects to the resilience of the organization. That is what it means to move from siloed defense to collective responsibility.

We have seen that structural integration is essential to making this real. When risk professionals are embedded in delivery teams, when procurement and cybersecurity co-own vendor assessments, when identity governance is treated as a joint responsibility across HR, IT, and security, organizations move faster and with greater confidence. These changes are not theoretical. They are happening today in companies that have chosen to replace defensive posture with operational clarity.

Structure alone is not enough. Culture must shift, too. That means rethinking how success is defined. Uptime and velocity matter, but not at the expense of integrity. Control coverage matters, but not if it blocks delivery without context. Integrated Assurance brings the ability to act quickly while managing risk transparently, to align on outcomes even when trade-offs are required, and to surface and resolve tensions before they turn into vulnerabilities.

Use the following questions to test whether your organization is dismantling silos and moving toward Integrated Assurance.

1 Diagnosing Silos

- ☐ Do our teams (security, IT, operations, compliance, business units) still work in isolation when it comes to risk decisions?
- ☐ Are there recurring moments when projects stall or fail because of late-stage security involvement?
- ☐ Is accountability for risk decisions clear, or do we often defer or assign blame after the fact?

2 Shifting to Shared Ownership

- ☐ Do leaders ask, "How are we managing this risk together?" rather than "Has security signed off?"
- ☐ Are risk professionals embedded in delivery teams, procurement, HR, and other business functions?
- ☐ Do all teams have a baseline understanding of the risks in their domain, even if they are not experts?

3 Cultural Signals

- ☐ Are incentives aligned across functions, rewarding resilience and collaboration rather than just speed or uptime?
- ☐ Do leaders model transparency by surfacing trade-offs and owning outcomes with their peers?
- ☐ Is trust being deliberately built through psychological safety, open dialogue, and visible reinforcement of collaborative behavior?

4 Overcoming Biases

- ☐ Do we account for loss aversion, confirmation bias, and normalcy bias in risk decisions?
- ☐ Are risk signals framed in business-relevant language (customer impact, cost, trust) instead of purely technical terms?
- ☐ Do we use defaults, prompts, and storytelling to make risk literacy real and memorable?

5 Building Collective Responsibility

- ☐ Do retrospectives focus on shared learning instead of blame?
- ☐ Are people recognized and rewarded for surfacing difficult risks or challenging groupthink?
- ☐ Are cross-functional risk discussions part of planning, budget, and strategy—not just crisis management?

6 Organizational Design

- ☐ Are risk and security professionals operationally adjacent to the teams they support?
- ☐ Do we have clear escalation pathways and distributed governance roles (risk champions, assurance stewards, and executive sponsors)?
- ☐ Are shared metrics like resilience scores, recovery performance, and control integrity part of executive dashboards?

Executive Action: If your answers reveal persistent silos, unclear ownership, or a lack of shared incentives, the immediate step is to embed risk ownership into business functions and align incentives around resilience. Integration must be designed, not assumed.

Figure 4.7 Practical Checklist: Breaking the Culture of Siloed Defense.
Image created by the author using Gamma.

Language plays a pivotal role here. Teams must be able to talk about risk in a way that resonates across disciplines. Security terms must be translated into business impacts. Business metrics must reflect resilience indicators. And everyone must operate from a shared understanding of what is at stake. Without this common vocabulary, even the best-intentioned collaboration falters.

Trust is another critical enabler. It cannot be mandated, but it can be designed. When teams feel psychologically safe, when they see leaders modeling transparency, when risk surfacing is rewarded rather than penalized, trust takes root. That trust becomes the fuel for faster decisions, better alignment, and fewer surprises. It is the foundation of a culture where risk is not something to avoid, but something to manage together.

The case studies in this chapter show how organizations across industries have taken practical steps to move in this direction. From manufacturing to healthcare, finance to public sector, the pattern is clear. Leaders made integration a priority. They aligned incentives. They embedded roles. They created forums for cross-functional decision-making. And they committed to measurement, feedback, and continuous learning. The results were measurable reductions in exposure, improved delivery velocity, and stronger stakeholder trust.

What these organizations share is not perfection. It is persistence. They did not wait for an ideal moment or a perfect toolset. They started by naming the fragmentation, inviting shared accountability, and redesigning how risk is managed at every level. They treated Integrated Assurance not as a compliance obligation, but as a business capability. And that capability has paid dividends in resilience, agility, and performance.

For organizations looking to make this shift, the roadmap is straightforward but demanding. Start by embedding security into the places where business decisions are made. Treat procurement, HR, engineering, marketing, and operations as partners in resilience. Build a shared language around risk. Align metrics and incentives to reward cross-functional outcomes. Create structures that enable collaboration, not just talk about it. And above all, we must lead by example. Show that risk ownership is a leadership behavior, not a delegated task.

This is not a transformation that happens overnight. But it is a transformation that must happen. The complexity of modern organizations, the velocity of change, and the sophistication of today's threats leave no room for fragmented defense. Organizations that succeed in breaking these habits will not only reduce their risk. They will unlock new levels of speed, innovation, and trust.

The future of security is not isolation. It is integration. The future of risk management is not control for its own sake. It is the ability to operate with confidence in the face of uncertainty. Integrated Assurance is how we get there. It is not a new team. It is a new way of thinking. A way that makes resilience everyone's business. See Figure 4.7: Practical Checklist: Breaking the Culture of Siloed Defense.

Chapter 5

Operating at the Speed of Trust

5.1 REAL-TIME OPERATIONS ENABLED BY TRUST

Speed has long been celebrated as a marker of business strength. Yet speed alone tells only part of the story. The fastest servers, the most efficient sprints, or the most aggressive delivery timelines do not guarantee an advantage if each step forward is slowed by hesitation or blocked by uncertainty. What truly defines modern performance is not how rapidly machines process tasks, but how quickly an organization can move forward with confidence. That confidence rests on trust. The enterprise that embeds trust into its architecture, workflows, and governance is able to make decisions without delay, to act on evidence rather than assumption, and to adapt to external pressures without constant reinvention. In this way, trust becomes the true accelerator of real-time operations.

In the past, trust was established through layers of review and human validation. A new product feature might sit in a queue waiting for approval from a compliance officer. A procurement decision might require signatures from multiple committees before moving forward. These controls created checkpoints that were intended to manage risk, yet they also created significant drag. When markets moved slowly, such delays were tolerable. When infrastructure was centralized and predictable, oversight could be handled in cycles measured in weeks or months.

That environment no longer exists. Today's enterprise moves across shifting boundaries of cloud infrastructure, dynamic partner ecosystems, and distributed workforces. Code is deployed within hours. Business services expand into new jurisdictions in days. Customer expectations change with every interaction. In this setting, static checkpoints designed for a slower era collapse under the weight of demand. Trust must evolve from a manual process into a built-in capability. It must operate continuously, without waiting for signatures or meetings.

This is not about eliminating oversight, but it is about repositioning it. Oversight must become real-time and embedded, operating through systems rather than standing apart from them. In doing so, trust becomes part of the operational fabric instead of a bureaucratic hurdle.

Traditional control models treated trust as something fragile, to be verified cautiously and only after deliberate analysis. A project could not proceed until an approval was granted. A system could not change until a review board signed off. Risk was considered manageable only by slowing down. This perspective fails in an environment defined by constant motion. Businesses cannot afford to treat trust as a brittle asset. Trust must be resilient enough to keep pace with rapid change.

When trust is embedded in architecture and reinforced by evidence, it does not weaken with speed. It grows stronger. Real-time telemetry validates the current state of systems. Automated policies enforce requirements at runtime. Identity verification adapts as conditions change. These mechanisms ensure that trust is not episodic. It is continuous. The

DOI: 10.1201/9781003685982-7

organization no longer rebuilds confidence from scratch with every decision. Confidence flows naturally because it has been engineered into the system itself.

The concept at the core of Integrated Assurance is that trust is no longer merely a human judgment. It is a property of the system. When designed as such, it can be monitored, adjusted, and scaled with the same rigor as any technical function. Architecture becomes the place where trust is expressed, not just where operations occur.

Consider the response to a regulatory change around data residency. Under legacy models, the enterprise might launch an extended compliance assessment, followed by redesigns, legal reviews, and organizational approvals. The process could take months, during which the enterprise would remain exposed and slow to adapt. In a trust-enabled system, however, the organization responds in days. Policies are written as code. Compliance engines validate data placement continuously. Telemetry provides evidence of adherence in real time. Decisions occur with confidence because trust is already woven into the system, not reconstructed after the fact.

This example illustrates the difference between reactive oversight and proactive design. By embedding trust directly into architecture, the enterprise ensures that regulatory obligations, operational risks, and business demands can be balanced at the speed at which they arise.

Real-time trust requires systems that are transparent by design. Every action must be observable. Every identity must be verifiable. Every policy must be enforceable at the moment of execution. Transparency eliminates assumptions. It ensures that trust is not derived from expectations but from actual state and context.

Transparency also changes organizational behavior. When systems provide clarity, teams do not hide work in shadow processes. When controls operate automatically, employees do not view governance as an obstacle. When oversight is visible but unobtrusive, compliance becomes part of normal operations rather than an interruption.

This level of transparency is not achieved through more reporting or larger compliance teams. It is achieved through intentional architectural choices that favor observability, context-rich telemetry, and automated enforcement.

Real-time trust is not a purely technical shift. It requires a cultural transformation in how security, compliance, and risk functions are positioned within the enterprise. Too often, these groups have been seen as inhibitors of speed, creating barriers rather than enabling flow. This adversarial positioning breeds resentment, drives work into informal channels, and erodes confidence between teams.

Integrated Assurance reframes these functions as accelerators. When governance is embedded into workflows and toolchains, security and compliance no longer appear as late-stage gatekeepers. They become contributors to speed. Controls operate invisibly in the background, protecting activity without obstructing it. Instead of asking how to slow things down in order to verify, professionals ask how to verify without slowing things down. That single shift in perspective transforms both design philosophy and organizational culture.

Legacy security models relied on controls at rest. They assumed known environments and stable conditions. Yet today's digital enterprise is fluid, with workloads moving across regions, identities shifting across devices, and partners interacting with sensitive systems in unpredictable ways. Trust cannot remain static in this setting. It must adapt dynamically.

An employee pushing code from a new location should trigger validation that considers behavioral history, current context, and risk posture. A partner requesting system access must be evaluated not only by role but by observed activity and system integrity. These adjustments are not complications. They are requirements for relevance. Adaptive trust ensures that operations continue securely even as conditions evolve in unpredictable ways.

Architecture is the medium through which trust is scaled. A well-structured architecture allows controls to be modular, reusable, and transparent. Policies expressed as code can be tested, versioned, and enforced consistently across cloud platforms, development pipelines, and business workflows. When policy is treated as infrastructure, trust becomes portable. It follows workloads and identities wherever they move, enabling real-time validation without reimplementation.

This architectural shift transforms trust from a localized decision into an enterprise-wide capability. Instead of a single compliance officer providing approval, the system itself enforces policy at every layer. Instead of trust being built manually for each change, it is provisioned continuously. Scale is achieved not by expanding oversight teams but by designing systems that carry assurance with them.

None of this is possible without observability. Organizations cannot claim to trust what they cannot see. Logs and metrics are insufficient unless enriched with identity, policy, and behavioral context. The question that must always be answered in real time is "Does the system behave as intended?"

Shared telemetry provides this answer. It ensures that every function views the same reality. Siloed systems give way to coordinated understanding. Decisions made in one part of the enterprise become visible and meaningful to others. With shared telemetry, trust decisions are no longer isolated. They are distributed and transparent, creating confidence across boundaries that might otherwise fragment.

The advantages of real-time trust ripple across the enterprise. Finance departments gain faster audits through continuously validated controls. Legal teams rely on live evidence to support contractual obligations. Customer service operations access sensitive information quickly and securely without depending on manual approvals. Procurement evaluates vendor risk dynamically rather than annually. In each case, trust embedded into systems reduces delay, improves confidence, and strengthens alignment.

Perhaps most importantly, innovation accelerates. Developers move faster because policy violations are flagged automatically rather than discovered later. Product managers design boldly because privacy and compliance risks are surfaced early in the process. Teams collaborate more openly because governance is perceived as a partner, not an adversary. Trust becomes the connective tissue linking assurance to creativity.

For real-time trust to be sustainable, it must be measurable. Vague confidence is not enough. Organizations must track the integrity of controls, the adoption of policies, and the quality of assurance signals. Dashboards must provide real-time trust indicators that guide both strategic and operational decisions.

Measurement also ensures resilience. Systems must be designed to withstand failure, to degrade gracefully when telemetry is unavailable, and to provide auditable manual overrides when automation cannot function. In this sense, real-time trust is not only about moving quickly when all goes well. It is also about responding confidently when disruption occurs.

The absence of trust shows itself in hesitation. Projects stall. Work is duplicated. Manual handoffs multiply. Regulatory risk grows. Teams lose confidence in one another. Customers sense uncertainty. These costs are difficult to measure directly but manifest clearly in performance, morale, and market reputation. The modern market rewards those who move with clarity and punishes those who pause. To operate without embedded trust is to operate at a disadvantage. Speed without trust leads to chaos. Speed with trust leads to excellence.

Enterprises that succeed in embedding trust into their systems and cultures will not only move faster but will also move further. They will treat trust as an architectural property, as a cultural enabler, and as an operational discipline. By doing so, they will transform hesitation into momentum and oversight into confidence.

Operating at the speed of trust is not a slogan. It is a measurable capability, a design requirement, and a competitive advantage. It allows organizations to act without seeking permission because permission has already been codified into policy, validated through telemetry, and reinforced by context. It ensures recovery is swift because recovery paths are embedded into systems. It promotes collaboration because trust is shared across functions rather than hoarded in silos.

Speed is essential. But speed alone is insufficient. The true differentiator is trust that moves faster than uncertainty. Trust that enables execution without delay. Trust that sustains resilience even in disruption. This is what makes real-time operations possible. It is not performance without risk, but performance with confidence. That is the transformation enterprises must embrace to lead in the digital era.

5.2 UNDERSTANDING TRUST VELOCITY

Most organizations measure speed with technical indicators. Metrics like uptime, latency, transaction throughput, and response time create the illusion of a high-functioning digital environment. But when business processes stall without a clear root cause, infrastructure alone is rarely to blame. The real limiter is trust—more specifically, the speed at which trust can be established, validated, and acted upon. That is trust velocity.

Trust velocity reflects how quickly an organization can make confident, informed decisions based on assurance in its identities, behaviors, data flows, and systems. In the past, trust was earned over time and validated through manual oversight. That model collapses under the pressure of real-time digital operations. The current pace of change demands a trust model that moves as fast as the business it supports.

Across most organizations, critical decisions are not delayed due to insufficient resources. They are delayed due to ambiguity. Unanswered questions create drag. Who owns this dataset? Has this vendor been risk-scored? Is the user requesting access approved for this level of privilege? Did this control pass its last test? Without answers, confidence stalls. Trust velocity addresses these gaps by removing blind spots that interrupt execution.

A useful comparison comes from early internet performance. When websites took minutes to load, user patience adapted. Today, milliseconds of delay cause abandonment. Trust operates the same way. If your organization takes days to approve access or weeks to onboard a third-party partner, you are working with unacceptable latency. Your competitors are not waiting. Neither are your customers. And your regulators are watching in real time.

Trust velocity goes beyond measuring elapsed time. It requires understanding the three domains that underpin trust decisions including identity, activity, and integrity. See Figure 5.1: Trust Velocity.

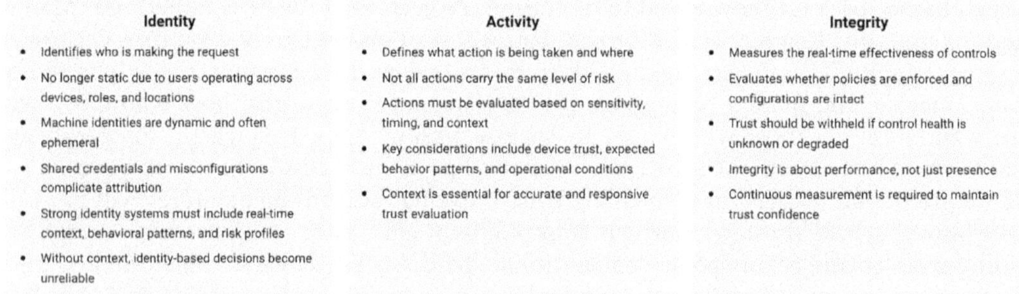

Figure 5.1 Trust Velocity.

Image created by the author using Gamma.

5.2.1 Identity

Identity answers the question: Who is making the request. That used to be a static value, but today's digital identities are fluid. Users move across devices, locations, and roles. Machine identities spin up and down dynamically. Shared credentials and misconfigured accounts complicate attribution. A strong identity system must tie into real-time context and be enriched by behavioral patterns, risk profiles, and environmental data. Without this context, identity becomes guesswork.

5.2.2 Activity

What action is being taken, and where is it occurring? Not all operations carry the same risk. Downloading a public report does not require the same scrutiny as modifying access privileges. Reading a record is not the same as deleting one. Decisions must account for the sensitivity of the action, the timing, and the conditions in which it takes place. Was the action initiated from a sanctioned device? During normal hours? Within an expected usage pattern? Context is not a luxury. It is foundational to reliable trust assessment.

5.2.3 Integrity

This domain speaks to the current state of your controls. Are they functioning as expected? Has configuration drift occurred? Are baseline policies still enforced? Even if identity and activity appear legitimate, trust should not be granted if control health is unknown or degraded. Integrity is not defined by the presence of controls alone. It is demonstrated through their effectiveness, which is measured continuously.

5.2.4 Combined

When these three domains are evaluated together, trust decisions can be made at pace and with confidence. This is the prerequisite for adaptive, risk-aware operations.

But trust velocity is fragile. Silos are the primary threat. When systems and teams operate in isolation, manual handoffs are required. Security waits for IT logs. Legal waits for procurement clauses. Compliance waits for security attestations. Each delay compounds risk. The friction is rarely intentional. It is structural. Disconnected trust systems slow everything down.

Fixing this requires shared telemetry and a common language for risk signals. Trust velocity improves when policy engines integrate with access controls, when risk scoring connects to workflow automation, and when identity signals shape authorization logic. This does not mean centralizing every decision. It means designing a federated trust architecture where data flows across systems without obstruction, and controls are enforced without coordination bottlenecks.

Consumer finance offers a compelling analogy. In the past, loan approvals required paperwork and in-person meetings. Today, creditworthiness is scored in real time using behavioral data, identity verification, and fraud analytics. The trust model was not eliminated. It was automated. Financial institutions improved velocity by enriching the data, removing guesswork, and embedding decision logic into workflows. That same shift must happen inside the enterprise.

Quarterly access reviews should be replaced with continuous authorization. Static attestations must give way to real-time control health checks. Policy exceptions should be handled by automated guardrails, not approval committees. These adjustments make governance more responsive and aligned with the velocity of modern operations.

Clarity in policy is essential. Vague, subjective, or inconsistently applied policies bring trust systems to a halt. Unclear rules generate hesitation. Teams delay deployments. Exceptions multiply. Policies must be understandable by both people and machines. They should be version-controlled, testable, and traceable. They must evolve alongside the business.

Policy-as-code delivers on this need. It lets organizations codify requirements in formats that integrate directly into pipelines and runtime environments. Developers receive immediate feedback. Systems enforce policies automatically. Trust becomes measurable, actionable, and predictable.

Signal quality is equally important. In noisy environments, weak or misleading signals can cause just as much damage as no signal at all. False positives exhaust teams. False negatives leave the door open to threat actors. To sustain high trust velocity, organizations must invest in data governance, enrichment, and telemetry quality. Signal sources must be validated for authenticity and timeliness. If the signals cannot be trusted, neither can the decisions that rely on them.

This is why trust velocity must be treated as an enterprise capability. Security must ensure access controls are auditable. Operations must prioritize observability and telemetry. Risk and compliance must define acceptable thresholds. Business leadership must align expectations and drive decisions based on current trust posture. When these functions operate in sync, trust velocity becomes scalable.

It is tempting to equate trust velocity with speed alone. But that misses the point. Fast decisions made without sufficient data create exposure. That is not trust. That is recklessness. Trust velocity is about confident execution. It represents the ability to act at pace without compromising safety or integrity.

Here are tangible ways to measure capability:

- Time to approve access based on risk context
- Frequency of manual exceptions to policy
- Enforcement consistency across business units
- Time to detect and respond to control failures
- Volume of real-time trust decisions made by systems

These metrics reveal bottlenecks, signal the need for automation, and guide investment in systems that accelerate decision-making without losing control.

It is important to assess trust velocity under pressure, not just during optimal conditions. How fast can access be revoked in response to an incident? How quickly can unauthorized changes be detected? What is the time required to restore baseline trust after disruption? These are the moments that reveal whether trust systems are robust or brittle.

Trust velocity also impacts the user experience. Delays caused by opaque models erode confidence. Users seek workarounds. Engagement drops. Systems with high trust velocity eliminate unnecessary obstacles while preserving oversight. They allow users to operate confidently within defined and observable parameters.

Over time, trust velocity becomes a strategic asset. It accelerates onboarding, reduces friction in product delivery, and enhances responsiveness to market shifts. It strengthens the alignment between risk posture and business agility. Organizations that invest in trust velocity gain an advantage not because they are taking more risks, but because they are managing risk more deliberately and more efficiently than their peers. See Table 5.1: Mean time to respond (MTTR) versus trust velocity.

Table 5.1 Mean time to respond (MTTR) versus trust velocity

Dimension	*Traditional MTTR metrics*	*Trust velocity indicators*	*Why it matters*
Primary Focus	Technical recovery speed (infrastructure uptime, service restoration)	Speed of decision-making, stakeholder confidence, and trust restoration	Moves from systems-only to a holistic enterprise lens
Unit of Measure	Minutes or hours to detect, contain, and restore systems	Time to restore confidence (customer reassurance, employee clarity, and investor confidence)	Captures impact beyond IT dashboards
Key Questions	How quickly was the system restored? Was downtime within RTO/RPO targets?	• How quickly did leadership communicate with clarity? • How fast did customers/users return? • How long until teams acted with full confidence?	Trust questions are closer to what executives/boards care about
Data Sources	Incident logs, monitoring tools, ticketing systems, and uptime dashboards	Customer sentiment (surveys, net promoter score (NPS), and churn), employee engagement, social media trust signals, time to effective cross-functional alignment	Expands metrics beyond IT systems
Examples	MTTR = 90 minutes to restore system after outage Mean time to contain (MTTC) (Containment) = 60 minutes to stop attack spread	• Trust restoration in 6 hours (customer communications stabilized churn) • Employee decision lag dropped from 2 days to 4 hours	Trust velocity provides a "so what" layer
Limitations	Focuses on infrastructure only Doesn't account for reputational or trust loss Often backward-looking and compliance driven	• Harder to quantify consistently • Requires behavioral and perception data • Needs cross-functional integration	Trust velocity is newer but gives strategic insight
Executive-Level Metric	"We restored service in under 2 hours."	"We restored customer confidence and employee alignment within the same day."	Translates resilience into language boards and market value

5.2.5 How to implement trust velocity measurement

- Define trust checkpoints: Communication clarity, employee alignment, and customer reassurance.
- Instrument real-time signals: Sentiment tracking, employee decision latency, time-to-re-engagement after disruption.
- Link to outcomes: Correlate trust recovery with revenue stabilization, reduced churn, or faster crisis resolution.
- Benchmark over time: Track whether the organization is reducing lag between system restoration and stakeholder trust restoration.

5.3 ARCHITECTING FOR SPEED AND AGILITY

Enterprises often confuse speed with momentum. Delivering something faster is not the same as sustaining performance at scale. The organizations that fail are usually those that equate rapid delivery with resilience, only to discover that fragility multiplies with every rushed decision. Agility collapses when it is not supported by structural integrity. In order to make speed sustainable, assurance must be treated as part of the architecture rather than as a review step or a compliance gate. Assurance is not simply about controls. It is about the ability to demonstrate, at any given moment, that systems, teams, and decisions remain within tolerable risk boundaries. Without this capability, velocity creates exposure instead of confidence.

In older models, assurance was often introduced after the fact. Development teams built systems, and risk functions verified them once complete. This approach introduced deliberate pauses, often seen as necessary. Delays were tolerated because they gave decision-makers time to interpret evidence and confirm whether the system could be trusted. That world has disappeared. Today's enterprise operates across multiple clouds, relies on vendors that can be onboarded in hours, and deploys code continuously. Business leaders expect responsiveness in days, not quarters. In this environment, assurance cannot be a checkpoint. It has to move with the system, keeping pace with every change.

The challenge is architectural in nature. To maintain trust velocity, assurance must be embedded in the design of infrastructure, software, and workflows. It is not enough to have scattered controls or occasional reviews. The architecture itself must carry the properties of trust. This means that assurance is portable, observable, enforceable, and measurable at every point where decisions are made. If the design does not support these attributes, then no amount of process will compensate.

This section explores five principles that can shape such an architecture, including composability, observability, policy orchestration, federated execution, and trust-centric data models. These principles are not independent. They reinforce one another. When applied together, they transform governance and assurance from inhibitors of speed into the very mechanisms that make velocity reliable.

In modern enterprise environments, systems are assembled from many moving parts. Microservices, containers, cloud-native functions, and infrastructure templates define the operating model. The modularity of these components is often praised for enabling innovation and scale. Yet modularity without assurance creates blind spots. A component may be efficient but still fail to meet compliance or security requirements. The result is rework, stalled projects, and regulatory exposure.

Composability addresses this by ensuring that every component carries its own assurance attributes. A microservice is defined not only by its code but also by its runtime checks, logging defaults, and risk classification. An infrastructure template is not only a design blueprint but also a unit that comes with enforced identity controls and performance baselines. These assurances travel with the component wherever it is deployed. They do not have to be reapplied manually or rediscovered in each environment.

This design philosophy means that developers can focus on building and innovating without constantly seeking approvals for previously validated elements. Security and risk teams gain confidence that the foundations already meet the required standards. Business leaders benefit from reduced delays because every deployment leverages components that are trusted from the start. In practice, composability creates a library of trusted building blocks, each with embedded evidence of integrity. The enterprise then scales not by repeating manual reviews but by assembling proven units.

No system can be trusted if its behavior cannot be observed. Observability ensures that every component and interaction can be evaluated against intended outcomes. This is not the same as monitoring. Monitoring collects metrics, but often in isolation. Observability creates context by enriching those metrics with information about identity, activity, and policy compliance. It allows leaders to answer not only whether the system is working, but whether it is working within defined trust boundaries.

In a highly distributed enterprise, observability must cover diverse environments. Logs from cloud workloads must connect with access records from identity platforms. Application performance must align with risk thresholds defined by compliance teams. Telemetry has to be shared across roles rather than locked into silos. Developers require feedback on whether their code introduces vulnerabilities. Security teams need baselines of expected behavior. Executives need dashboards that correlate control integrity with business performance.

The value of observability is not limited to detection. It is also about prevention. Real-time visibility allows systems to correct themselves before failures become incidents. A policy violation can trigger an automated control adjustment rather than waiting for a quarterly audit. A deviation in access behavior can initiate risk scoring without interrupting the workflow. With this approach, assurance is not retrospective. It becomes an active capability that supports decision-making as it happens.

In many enterprises, policies exist in documents rather than in systems. They are described in language that humans can interpret but machines cannot. This leads to inconsistency, because policies must be interpreted by individuals across teams and technologies. The result is fragmented enforcement, with some controls applied rigorously in one environment and ignored in another.

Policy orchestration addresses this challenge by translating governance into executable logic. Instead of a policy that states "data must be encrypted at rest," the orchestration layer enforces encryption as part of every storage configuration. Instead of requiring developers to interpret privacy standards, the orchestration system integrates those standards directly into pipelines. In this model, the policy is not a reference point. It is an operational fact.

The advantage of orchestration is that it eliminates the need for constant interpretation. Teams across infrastructure, applications, and procurement operate within the same framework of executable rules. Policy becomes testable and version-controlled, like software. Updates can be applied rapidly across all environments. Compliance is no longer a static event but a continuous state.

By embedding governance into the architecture, enterprises reduce ambiguity. Workflows no longer stall while teams seek clarification. Disputes over interpretation diminish. Assurance moves from being a matter of persuasion to a matter of fact, visible in system behavior and enforceable in real time.

Centralized decision-making cannot keep up with the speed of modern business. If every risk decision requires escalation to a central authority, the result will be bottlenecks and resentment. Teams will work around the system, creating shadow processes that undermine both security and compliance.

Federated execution provides an alternative. Instead of a single gatekeeper, authority is distributed to the teams that operate closest to the decision. Developers, operations staff, and business units are empowered to act within defined boundaries. These boundaries are enforced by automated controls, continuous telemetry, and shared governance. If activity exceeds the acceptable profile, escalation occurs automatically.

The benefit of this model is that speed does not rely on a single point of approval. Decisions happen where they are needed, but always within guardrails that preserve assurance. Local teams gain autonomy without sacrificing accountability. Central teams shift their focus from controlling every action to designing the systems that make safe autonomy possible.

This approach changes organizational culture. Teams no longer see governance as a blocker. They experience it as a framework that allows them to operate confidently. Central oversight shifts from gatekeeping to stewardship. Trust flows throughout the enterprise because the boundaries are clear, the signals are transparent, and the evidence is always available.

Trust is often described in abstract terms, but in a real-time enterprise, it must be structured as data. Every transaction, identity, and workload should carry attributes that describe its trust posture. These attributes might include the current state of controls, recent behavioral patterns, policy compliance status, or contextual risk scores.

When trust is modeled as data, it can be queried, audited, and integrated into decision flows. A deployment pipeline can halt automatically if a component's trust score falls below a threshold. A partner system can be restricted if its assurances are outdated. An access request can prompt additional verification if contextual risk increases. Trust becomes more than a judgment. It becomes an operational fact, expressed and acted upon in real time.

This transformation has significant implications. It enables organizations to deliver assurance as a service. Any system can request validation of trust attributes before proceeding. Controls become composable and portable because trust is not tied to a single environment. The enterprise gains agility without sacrificing clarity, because trust decisions are grounded in evidence rather than assumptions.

Each of these principles has value on its own. Composability makes assurance portable. Observability creates visibility. Policy orchestration enforces consistency. Federated execution distributes authority safely. Trust-centric data models make assurance measurable. When combined, they create an architecture that transforms velocity into resilience.

The outcome is not theoretical. Enterprises that adopt these principles find that audits become faster because evidence is always available. Incident response improves because trust signals guide containment. Partner onboarding accelerates because requirements are enforced through policy rather than contracts alone. Developers innovate more confidently because they know compliance is embedded in pipelines. Customers gain confidence because assurance is visible in outcomes rather than promised in statements.

This is not simply a technical exercise. It is a shift in how organizations think about control, risk, and speed. The old model treated assurance as a weight that slowed the system. The new model treats assurance as part of the system's design. Velocity becomes sustainable because it rests on a foundation of trust.

5.4 DESIGNING SHARED TELEMETRY SYSTEMS

Telemetry has moved from being a useful technical feature to being the lifeblood of enterprise assurance. In the past, organizations could afford to make decisions based on lagging reports, occasional audits, and manually gathered evidence. That world has ended. The pace of modern operations means that waiting for confirmation equates to operating on guesswork. Executives are asked to make decisions in hours, not quarters. Developers are expected to release code daily. Regulators and customers demand proof of compliance in real time. In this environment, telemetry becomes the foundation of trust. Without it, the organization stumbles forward in partial darkness. With it, assurance becomes a continuous capability that supports every decision and every action.

Yet simply collecting more data does not guarantee better outcomes. Many organizations drown in telemetry while struggling to extract clarity. Signals are scattered across monitoring platforms, log aggregators, identity tools, and security systems. Each produces output in its own language, using its own formats, and reporting to its own audience. The result is fragmentation. Instead of insight, leaders get noise. Instead of confidence, teams experience hesitation. The challenge is not about volume. It is about quality, consistency, and relevance. Shared telemetry is the architectural response to this challenge. It is the discipline of designing

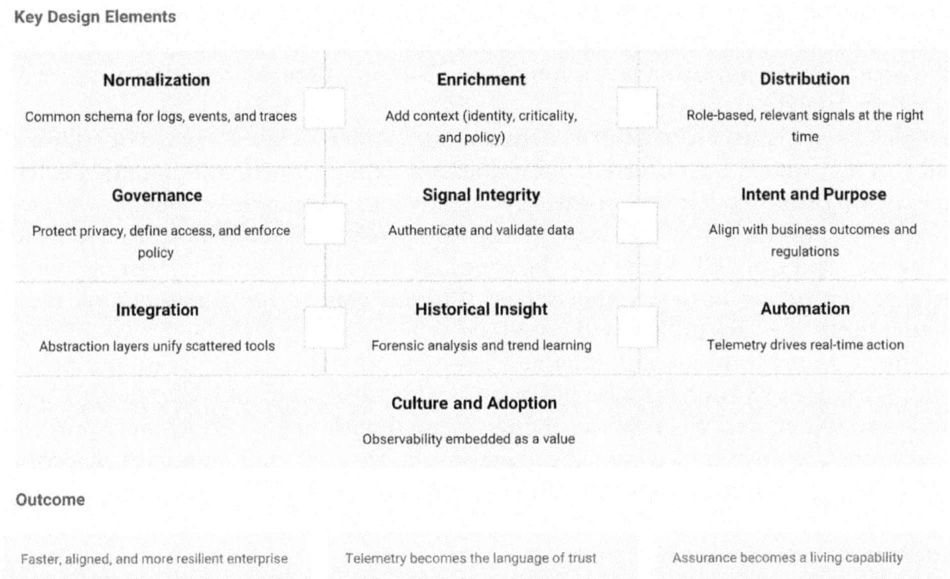

Figure 5.2 Designing Shared Telemetry Systems.

Image created by the author using Gamma.

a unified, contextual, and trustworthy information fabric that allows risk, performance, and compliance decisions to be made in real time. See Figure 5.2: Designing Shared Telemetry Systems.

The core value of shared telemetry lies in its ability to create a single version of truth across the enterprise. When different teams rely on different data streams, their interpretations of events diverge. Security may interpret a spike in traffic as suspicious. Operations may see it as normal growth. Finance may ignore it altogether. The lack of alignment creates delay, disputes, and errors. Shared telemetry prevents these breakdowns by ensuring that every function speaks from the same evidence base. This is not about centralizing control. It is about consistency. A shared data language allows leaders to coordinate faster, reduces misunderstandings, and removes the excuses that stem from siloed interpretation.

To achieve this, telemetry must be designed as a system capability rather than a collection of tool outputs. That means thinking in terms of normalization, enrichment, distribution, governance, and integrity. Each of these functions turns raw data into reliable assurance. Each must be considered carefully, because any weakness undermines trust across the enterprise.

The first discipline is normalization. Raw telemetry comes in many shapes. Without a common schema, these signals cannot be correlated or compared. A failed login may be recorded in three different systems with three different field names. One system calls it "auth_fail." Another calls it "invalid_login." A third uses a numerical code. If these records cannot be aligned, an analyst cannot see that the same user failed across multiple domains within a short period. The signal loses meaning, and the organization loses the opportunity to detect risk.

Normalization imposes a consistent structure by requiring schemas that define the essential attributes every signal must carry. Each telemetry item must specify what occurred, the time of occurrence, the location, the entities involved, and the conditions under which the event took place. While the specific details can vary across systems or domains, this core structure ensures that signals can be correlated and interpreted in a unified way. Industry standards such as OpenTelemetry offer valuable guidance, yet the greatest benefit emerges when an enterprise establishes and enforces its own internal baseline. When all signals conform to a shared schema, the organization lays a foundation for automation, cross-domain correlation, and confident analytical insight.

Normalized data is structured, but structure alone is not enough. A record of a file transfer may tell you that something occurred, but it does not explain whether it matters. Enrichment adds the missing context that transforms raw signals into meaningful evidence. This involves attaching metadata that allows the signal to be interpreted within the business environment. For example, a spike in CPU usage may be expected if a payroll batch is running, but it may be alarming if it occurs on a dormant server. Without context, both events look the same. With enrichment, they are understood correctly.

Enrichment draws from identity attributes, system criticality, policy tags, and behavioral baselines. A change in a configuration file means little unless you know who made it, whether they had permission, and whether the change aligned with policy. Enrichment ensures that these questions are answered within the signal itself. This not only improves detection and analysis but also supports traceability. When signals carry context, they can be linked to specific users, workflows, or business outcomes. That makes audits easier, investigations faster, and automated responses more reliable.

A common failure in telemetry design is assuming that every stakeholder should see the same data. In reality, different roles require different levels of visibility. Developers need performance metrics. Security teams need behavioral anomalies. Compliance officers need to control the evidence. Executives need high-level indicators of risk and trust posture. If all parties are given the same stream of raw data, none of them gets what they truly need. Developers drown in regulatory language. Executives get lost in log entries. Security analysts chase irrelevant alerts.

Distribution solves this by tailoring telemetry delivery to the needs of each role. This involves designing dashboards, reports, and alerting mechanisms that align with the decisions users are expected to make. Role-based observability ensures that every person sees signals in a form that supports their responsibilities. Routing logic must also filter noise, prioritize relevance, and ensure that the most important signals reach decision-makers without delay. Effective distribution does not mean giving everyone more data. It means giving everyone the right data, in the right form, and at the right time.

Shared telemetry creates enormous visibility, but visibility without governance introduces new risks. Sensitive data may appear in logs. Signals may be misused for purposes beyond their intent. Retention practices may conflict with privacy or regulatory obligations. Without clear guardrails, telemetry can become a liability rather than an asset.

Governance addresses this by defining who can access what signals, under what conditions, and for what purposes. It requires classification of telemetry streams, access control policies, and audit logs that record who accessed which signals. Governance must also account for regional regulations. What is observable in one jurisdiction may be restricted in another. The goal is to achieve transparency without overexposure. Properly governed telemetry supports accountability, protects privacy, and ensures that observability remains defensible.

Even the most well-designed telemetry system fails if the data cannot be trusted. Attackers may attempt to spoof logs, tamper with traces, or inject false signals to mislead defenders. Internal errors may corrupt data. If decision-makers cannot trust the authenticity of telemetry, every assurance system collapses. Signal integrity is therefore a foundational requirement.

To safeguard integrity, telemetry pipelines must include cryptographic validation, provenance tracking, and transformation auditing. Every signal should be verifiable back to its source. Any manipulation should be logged. Systems producing telemetry must be hardened against compromise. These measures ensure that telemetry is not only visible but also reliable.

Leaders can base decisions on the signals with confidence, knowing that they reflect reality rather than distortion.

Not every telemetry stream serves the same purpose. Some are collected to tune performance. Others are used for threat detection. Still others support compliance reporting. Designing shared telemetry requires clarifying the intent of each stream. This prevents misalignment where signals are collected without a clear value or used inappropriately. It also ensures that telemetry design supports business priorities directly.

For global organizations, intent must also consider regional and regulatory constraints. Telemetry that is useful in one region may be restricted in another due to privacy laws or data sovereignty rules. Aligning signals with purpose prevents accidental violations and keeps telemetry relevant to the mission of the business.

One of the greatest challenges in telemetry design is fragmentation across tools. Each vendor produces its own format and interface. Forcing all systems to conform to a single standard often proves costly and disruptive. Instead, advanced organizations deploy abstraction layers that map diverse signals into a normalized schema. This allows for correlation and analysis without requiring wholesale replacement of existing systems. It also enables integration with automation platforms, analytics tools, and assurance workflows.

By embedding telemetry integration into the architecture itself, the organization builds connective tissue across infrastructure, security, compliance, and operations. This transforms telemetry from a set of isolated tool outputs into a coherent enterprise capability.

Real-time telemetry is essential, but historical telemetry is equally valuable. Looking back at signal histories allows organizations to trace the slow decay of trust, identify when controls weakened, and reconstruct the chain of events leading to an incident. Historical analysis informs adaptive learning. It strengthens forensic investigations. It allows leaders to see not only what is happening now but also why patterns emerged and how they can be prevented in the future.

Combining real-time observability with historical insight creates a dual lens. Organizations can respond immediately to current conditions while learning continuously from past performance. This combination is critical to building resilience that grows stronger over time.

Telemetry achieves its greatest impact when it drives action. Shared telemetry should not only inform dashboards and reports. It should feed automation engines that enforce policy, adjust access, and remediate controls. When a trust score drops below the threshold, the deployment pipeline can pause. When suspicious behavior is detected, access can be restricted instantly. When control degradation is identified, remediation can be triggered without waiting for manual intervention.

Automation is not about removing humans. It is about ensuring that humans are focused on higher-level decisions while routine enforcement occurs at machine speed. Telemetry provides the evidence. Automation translates that evidence into a response.

Even the best technical design fails if the culture does not support it. Teams must value observability. They must understand how telemetry enables trust, reduces risk, and accelerates recovery. Without cultural alignment, telemetry becomes another compliance requirement rather than a strategic capability.

Cultural adoption requires training, champions, and reinforcement. Teams need to see how telemetry helps them achieve their goals faster and with more confidence. Recognition systems should reward contributions to observability. Dashboards should highlight not only problems but also improvements. When people see the benefits of shared telemetry in their own workflows, adoption grows organically. Over time, observability becomes part of the organizational identity, not just an IT function.

When designed properly, shared telemetry transforms enterprise performance. Audits become faster because evidence is continuously available. Investigations become sharper because signals carry context. Decision-making accelerates because leaders operate from the same evidence base. Risk management becomes proactive rather than reactive. Compliance shifts from episodic to continuous. Most importantly, the enterprise gains confidence. It no longer operates on assumptions. It acts on evidence.

The payoff extends to customers and partners as well. Customers gain confidence that their data is protected. Partners see assurance as part of every transaction. Regulators view the organization as credible and trustworthy. Telemetry, when shared and governed, becomes a competitive differentiator. It strengthens relationships, accelerates transactions, and builds resilience into the core of the business.

5.5 IAMM AND OPERATIONS INTEGRATION

The IT and Operations domain within IAMM represents the point where design becomes reality. Governance defines direction and culture builds intent, but it is operations that prove whether assurance has taken root. This domain traces how organizations progress from scattered reactions to a disciplined, automated form of resilience.

At Level 1, operations are reactive. Incidents are handled by improvisation, and recovery plans are fragmented across shared drives or personal notes. Teams rely on individual experience instead of dependable processes. When a disruption occurs, decisions rest on instinct rather than evidence. Post-incident reviews may capture lessons, but few are applied. The organization endures each event yet repeats the same mistakes, learning in fragments instead of systems.

Level 2 introduces structure. Procedures are documented, and continuity plans exist in formal templates. Teams use checklists, maintain inventories, and follow defined playbooks. The progress feels substantial but remains shallow. Many enterprises stall here, mistaking documentation for preparedness. Plans are rarely tested, and functional silos persist. Drills occur on occasion but lack full participation. Control has improved, but agility has not.

Level 3 begins the shift toward coordination. Operations, IT, and security teams start aligning objectives and sharing telemetry. Response plans are validated through scheduled exercises. Service dependencies are mapped, and recovery targets are tested against actual performance. Automation appears in fragments through scripts or workflow tools. Predictability increases, though manual effort still dominates.

At Level 4, operations turn proactive. Assurance integrates into daily workflows rather than after-action reports. Infrastructure-as-code applies recovery standards automatically, while policy-as-code checks configurations against approved baselines. Telemetry moves across environments in real time, creating a unified operational picture. Regular recovery drills feed automation routines that correct deviations instantly. Collaboration among teams ensures that continuity, security, and performance remain synchronized. Confidence grows because assurance is designed into the system itself.

Level 5 institutionalizes operational excellence. Continuous monitoring validates every control, and anomalies trigger correction without delay. Shared dashboards connect operations and security, allowing visibility across the enterprise. Metrics such as mean time to detect and mean time to recover are integrated into performance reviews. Routine remediation is automated, allowing staff to focus on long-range improvement and strategy. At this level, the enterprise no longer reacts to failure; instead, it anticipates and adapts before disruptions escalate.

A manufacturing enterprise illustrates the path. At Level 2, it kept recovery documents and offsite backups but faltered during outages. By Level 3, cross-site failover tests confirmed dependencies and bottlenecks. At Level 4, automated deployment pipelines enforced configuration integrity across facilities. Reaching Level 5, continuous monitoring and self-healing systems minimized human intervention. Each step reduced downtime, improved recovery speed, and strengthened customer confidence.

IAMM defines operational maturity not by the number of documents written but by the performance of the systems those documents describe. Many organizations uncover this truth during an actual disruption, when static plans fail to match real-time demands. True assurance depends on continuous validation and adaptation.

The maturity of an enterprise is visible in its habits. Recovery standards that enforce themselves, response times that improve with every incident, telemetry shared across domains, and lessons from drills that reshape future operations all reflect assurance as a living function. IAMM's IT and Operations domain converts resilience from a concept into a capability. It ensures that trust is built through consistent, verifiable execution rather than intention or policy.

5.6 GOVERNANCE STRUCTURES THAT SUPPORT TRUST-DRIVEN OPS

Governance is widely misunderstood. In many organizations, it is synonymous with bureaucracy. Reviews, approvals, documentation, and oversight are all necessary components, yet they are often implemented in ways that obstruct decision-making, slow innovation, and distance risk ownership from operational reality. This has led many teams to view governance as a barrier, something to navigate around rather than a system that enables enterprise value. However, governance does not have to be slow. When designed with intent, it becomes a mechanism that accelerates trusted decision-making without sacrificing safety. Proper governance is not a drag on speed. It is the structure that makes speed sustainable. It provides the scaffolding that enables fast, accountable action while keeping the organization aligned with its policies, values, and external obligations.

In a trust-driven organization, governance is not a static series of approvals. It is a dynamic capability. It adjusts oversight based on risk, automates control through policy, and distributes authority closer to the point of action. This model of governance is built to support operations, not hinder them. It facilitates velocity by providing clear guardrails, real-time feedback, and shared accountability. Achieving this shift requires a rethinking of how governance is constructed, how policies are expressed, and how decisions are made. Traditional governance models were built for slower environments where change was infrequent and infrastructure was fixed. That world no longer exists. Infrastructure now evolves daily. Code ships multiple times a day. Third-party access is provisioned and revoked constantly. Regulatory expectations shift in near-real time. Governance must evolve to match this pace.

The first step is treating governance as code. Policies should be expressed in formats that can be executed automatically, versioned with confidence, and integrated directly into digital workflows. This model, often referred to as policy-as-code, eliminates ambiguity. A system can evaluate policy consistently and immediately, avoiding delays and minimizing subjective interpretation. Enforcement happens when and where the decision is made, not after an audit. When governance is codified, it becomes testable, repeatable, and responsive. It supports agility. A policy change can be implemented across environments without waiting for manual updates or human interpretation. The speed of deployment matches the speed of control. Risk is not deferred. It is addressed in real time.

Codification also requires visibility. Instead of relying on quarterly audits and spreadsheets, modern governance uses assurance APIs to expose control state continuously. These APIs provide on-demand evidence of compliance and risk posture. They enable security teams to verify that a policy is working and empower operational teams to course-correct without external intervention. This transforms governance from oversight into collaboration.

Another core principle is federated authority. Centralized governance models require every risk decision to be escalated, every exception to be reviewed. This creates bottlenecks and disconnects decision-makers from the operational context. In contrast, federated authority gives teams the autonomy to act within defined risk boundaries. Those boundaries are enforced through telemetry, automation, and shared policy. In this model, developers can deploy services within predefined risk profiles. If their activity exceeds those profiles, automatic escalation occurs. Business units can engage vendors, provided those vendors meet specific assurance criteria. These trust requirements are enforced at the system level through integrations across security, legal, and procurement workflows.

Federated governance scales. It allows the organization to move without losing control. It defines when local action is allowed and when oversight is required. It ensures that all activity is logged, exceptions are tracked, and risk signals are monitored in real time. Governance becomes distributed but not diluted. To make federated governance effective, organizations must invest in shared dashboards and collaboration platforms that surface assurance data to the right people at the right time. Governance boards must shift from periodic oversight to continuous visibility. Teams must align on thresholds, definitions, and accountability mechanisms.

Many organizations form digital trust councils or assurance boards to support this evolution. These groups bring together leaders from risk, compliance, legal, IT, security, and the business. Their role is not to manage every exception but to design and monitor the architecture of trust. They align on tolerances, detect where controls are too tight or too weak, and track assurance health across systems. They ensure governance keeps pace with change.

These governance bodies replace gatekeeping with stewardship. They focus on making sure guardrails are effective and well-calibrated. They do not block change. They make change safer. They use dashboards and performance indicators to understand where governance is enabling flow and where it is causing drag.

Friction is treated as a signal. A policy that is repeatedly bypassed is not a failure. It is a data point. It prompts inquiry. *Is the policy unclear? Is it out of sync with operational reality?* Feedback loops like these allow governance to evolve continuously. The system improves through observation, not disruption.

Adaptability is another defining trait of trust-driven governance. Not every situation requires the same level of scrutiny. Governance should respond to context. If a user is operating within expected patterns, controls can remain quiet. If risk signals emerge, governance can respond with additional checks. This approach, known as contextual governance, ensures that oversight is applied proportionally to the level of risk.

To support contextual governance, systems must integrate with real-time identity, behavior, and telemetry platforms. Policies must adapt dynamically. Oversight must be precise. Controls must be informed by data, not static rules. This shift also requires a cultural transformation. Governance professionals must transition from enforcing rules to designing systems. Their work is no longer limited to writing policy documents. They must collaborate across disciplines to embed policy into the design of software, the structure of pipelines, and the planning of digital initiatives.

This requires new capabilities. Governance teams must understand development workflows, continuous integration/continuous deployment pipelines, automation frameworks, and telemetry systems. They must be fluent in how policy-as-code works and how assurance signals are generated. This is not just about learning new tools. It is about participating in new ways of working.

Metrics must evolve as well. The success of governance is no longer measured by the number of approvals processed or the amount of documentation produced. It is measured by policy adherence, incident reduction, trust velocity, and alignment with business outcomes. These metrics reveal whether governance is helping the enterprise move with confidence or simply adding weight.

Technology plays a foundational role in this model. Governance must be embedded into the systems that power development, infrastructure, and procurement. Policies must be enforceable at runtime, not just reviewable after the fact. Risk scoring must be real-time. Control telemetry must be available on demand. Evidence generation must be automated. At the same time, governance tooling must be protected. With automation comes the potential for unintended consequences. Policy changes must be versioned, peer-reviewed, and staged before deployment. Governance activity must be logged and auditable. Access to governance systems must follow least privilege principles. The control plane must never become a vulnerability.

None of this implies loosening standards. Trust-driven governance is not about relaxing oversight. It is about applying oversight in smarter, faster, and more adaptive ways. It ensures that resources are focused on the risks that matter most. It enables the organization to move without losing sight of its obligations or exposing itself to unmanaged risk.

Organizations that embrace this model experience a powerful shift. Governance no longer works against the speed of innovation. It becomes the reason innovation is sustainable. It reduces uncertainty. It sharpens decision-making. It strengthens alignment across business and technical functions. It shifts governance from being reactive to being operational. This is not theoretical. It is a practical model that has already been adopted by leading organizations seeking to scale with confidence. The choice is not between speed and control. The goal is speed with control. Trust-driven governance delivers both. This is the model that enables real-time, high-trust enterprise operations. It does not resist change. It enables it with precision, visibility, and confidence.

5.7 CONCLUSION

Organizations no longer have the luxury of choosing between speed and control. In today's enterprise landscape, the ability to move quickly while remaining secure, compliant, and coordinated is no longer aspirational. It is mandatory. This chapter has shown that trust, once considered a philosophical or interpersonal concept, has become an architectural requirement. It is the infrastructure that enables real-time action. It is the signal that validates decisions. It is the control layer that moves with the system rather than lagging behind it.

Organizations should be built on dynamic infrastructure, composable services, distributed workforces, and partner ecosystems that evolve rapidly. That complexity cannot be managed through legacy control models that depend on manual review, committee sign-off, or quarterly attestation. Those approaches were designed for a different era. Today, they introduce latency, create uncertainty, and erode business confidence. By contrast, organizations that embed trust into systems, telemetry, and governance gain a measurable advantage. They are not simply moving fast. They are moving with clarity, confidence, and control.

Trust velocity captures this dynamic. It shifts the focus from how many controls are deployed to how quickly those controls support informed, accountable decisions. Organizations with high trust velocity do not delay execution while waiting for assurance. They already have assurance built into their architecture. They operate with continuous feedback. They know who is doing what, under what conditions, and with what level of risk. And they act accordingly, not by exception but by design. Embedding trust into architecture begins with design principles, not tools. Composability ensures that systems are modular and include their own embedded assurances. Observability provides real-time insight into whether controls are operating as intended. Policy orchestration translates governance into code that can be enforced consistently across environments. Federated execution allows teams to make decisions close to the point of action, within clearly defined trust boundaries. Trust-centric data models enable systems to reason about trust as a structured, measurable property rather than a static approval.

Telemetry brings these elements to life. It provides the raw signals and enriched context that allow trust decisions to be made in real time. When telemetry is normalized, enriched, and distributed to the right roles, it becomes a shared language across security, operations, compliance, and business leadership. When signal integrity is protected and aligned with clear governance, telemetry becomes a strategic asset. It not only tells the story of system behavior. It drives adaptive response.

Governance ties it all together. When governance is codified, contextual, and continuous, it scales with the pace of change. It enables agility by making oversight automatic, not bureaucratic. Policy-as-code replaces ambiguity with clarity. Assurance APIs replace static audits with live evidence. Federated authority replaces gatekeeping with alignment. And governance boards focused on stewardship ensure that trust systems are evolving in step with business priorities.

The cultural transformation cannot be overstated. Trust-driven operations require a mindset shift across the organization. Security professionals must design for verification without friction. Compliance leaders must focus on outcomes, not artifacts. Developers must treat assurance as a design constraint, not a blocker. Product teams must build with privacy and control integrity from the first sprint. And executives must lead with data that reflects trust posture as much as financial performance.

Metrics will reinforce this transformation: time to trust decisions, frequency of manual policy exceptions, integrity of control telemetry, and recovery speed after drift or failure. These are the signals that tell leaders whether their trust infrastructure is working. These are the numbers that correlate with reduced rework, faster delivery, and stronger customer confidence.

There are tangible business outcomes that come from this transformation—faster partner onboarding; reduced audit cost and effort; and quicker time to market for regulated services. More resilient incident response. Greater confidence in data integrity and system behavior. These are not theoretical benefits. They are already being realized by organizations that have treated trust not as a byproduct of policy but as a core operating capability.

Trust as infrastructure changes how organizations design, deliver, and govern digital systems. It moves assurance from the periphery to the core. It makes compliance continuous. It turns architecture into a control system. And it enables speed that is both sustainable and safe. This is what it means to operate at the speed of trust.

As business leaders and security architects, we must stop treating trust as something to be retrofitted. We must design for it from the beginning. We must ensure that every system, every workflow, and every interaction reflects a current, accurate, and contextual understanding of risk. That is not a future state. It is an architectural requirement right now.

To lead in this environment, organizations must invest in the capabilities that support trust velocity. That means more than automation. It means deliberate design, shared language, collaborative governance, and measurable outcomes. It means putting telemetry at the center of assurance. It means enabling policy decisions through evidence, not instinct. It means building trust that is observable, portable, and resilient.

The speed of business will only increase. Regulatory pressure will not slow down. Customer expectations will continue to rise. Resilience will be tested more frequently and more

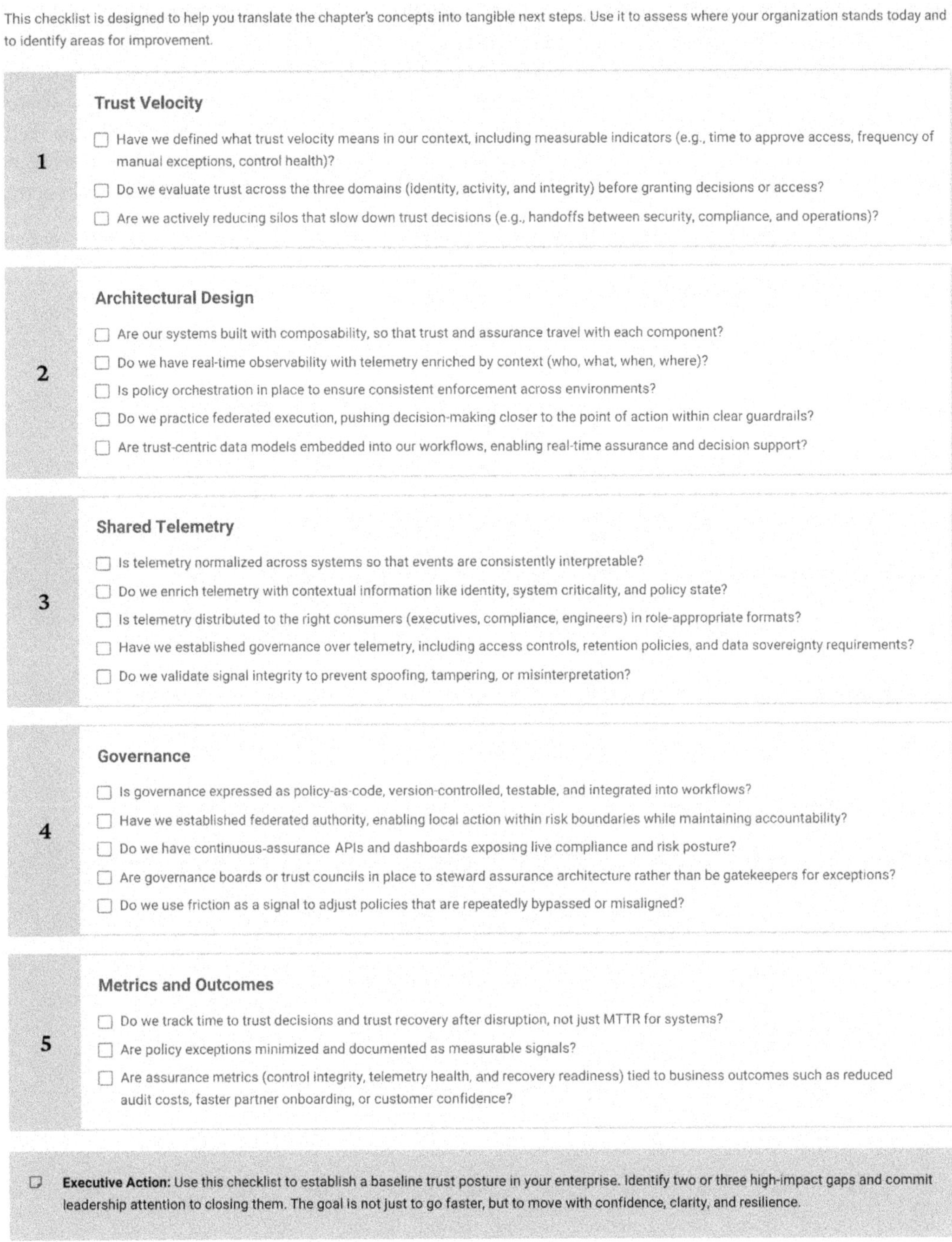

Figure 5.3 Practical Checklist: Operating at the Speed of Trust.
Image created by the author using Gamma.

publicly. The organizations that thrive in this environment will not be those with the most controls. They will be the ones with the most clarity, the most coordination, and the most confidence. Trust is not a feeling. It is not a slogan. It is a system. It is the ability to know that you are operating within acceptable risk, to act accordingly, and to adapt when that context changes. Trust is now operational. It is measurable. It is enforceable. And when built correctly, it becomes the engine of enterprise velocity.

In the end, speed without trust is unsustainable. It leads to failures, workarounds, and rework. But speed with trust creates advantage. It enables scale. It builds resilience. It fosters innovation. And it aligns every part of the organization around shared accountability. Trust does not slow you down. It is how you move forward with confidence. That is the real transformation. That is the future of operations. That is how we lead. See Figure 5.3: Practical Checklist: Operating at the Speed of Trust.

Chapter 6

Boardroom to Break Room

6.1 FROM BOARDROOM TO BREAK ROOM

In many organizations, assurance strategies are crafted with care in the executive suite, yet they lose momentum once they meet the realities of day-to-day operations. A clear intent to weave risk awareness and resilience into how the business runs can gradually fade as it moves closer to the frontline. By the time it reaches teams responsible for execution, the message is often softened, misinterpreted, or set aside altogether. This is rarely the result of indifference or weak technical capability. More often, it reflects a gap between how assurance is designed at the strategic level and how it is expected to function in practice. Making assurance real requires more than policies and dashboards. It demands that assurance becomes an intuitive part of how people work, decide, and respond throughout the organization.

The core challenge is when assurance programs that only live in the boardroom do not survive the complexity and pace of the business unless they are intentionally embedded into every layer of operations. Frameworks and governance models matter, but they cannot replace daily reinforcement and practical support. A data center technician, a call center representative, a warehouse supervisor, and a marketing analyst all shape enterprise trust through routine decisions. When that connection is unclear, assurance becomes theoretical and loses its value.

Assurance becomes real only when people can see it and relate to it. Employees need a clear line of sight between their role and the organization's ability to withstand disruption. Generic training and annual checklists do not create that connection. What does work is role-aware, timely feedback that fits naturally into how work is done. When a logistics coordinator adjusts routing schedules, for example, they should see how that choice affects regional supply chain resilience. Visibility at that level turns risk from an abstract idea into something concrete and manageable.

Transparency is the first step in closing the gap between strategy and execution. This includes upward, downward, and lateral flows of assurance information. Executives need summary dashboards, but frontline teams need operational views that help them take action. Middle managers need contextual KPIs to align performance objectives with assurance goals. In practice, this means designing telemetry systems that are comprehensive yet support different roles. A one-size-fits-all approach to reporting will fail. Instead, each layer of the organization must receive the information it needs to make better decisions in its context.

Storytelling is another powerful tool in this transition. Abstract metrics and frameworks rarely inspire behavioral change, but stories do. Stories provide emotional resonance and operational clarity. When a team hears how early threat detection prevented a major outage, or how a procurement analyst's risk identification avoided a reputational crisis, they begin to see assurance as something real and valuable. Stories also humanize assurance. They make it clear that everyday work has meaning beyond task completion. Leadership should use real

DOI: 10.1201/9781003685982-8

stories to reinforce assurance values, pass along hard-earned lessons, and recognize people whose decisions reflect the model in practice.

Making assurance tangible requires a different view of how work is defined and how performance is measured. In many organizations, employee evaluations still revolve around speed, throughput, or customer satisfaction, while resilience is treated as someone else's responsibility. That leaves important signals unnoticed. A customer service representative might be the first to spot a phishing attempt simply by recognizing an unusual calling pattern. If their role is not designed to value that kind of judgment, the warning is easy to dismiss. Assurance has to be built into the fabric of the job itself. It belongs in role definitions, evaluation criteria, and incentive models so employees understand that noticing and acting on risk is part of doing the job well.

The design of tools and systems also plays a pivotal role. Assurance must be intuitive and frictionless. When risk decisions are the easiest choices available, adoption becomes natural. For example, a cloud engineer should not have to consult three different dashboards to verify control status. Their development environment should automatically flag risk exposures and offer approved remediations in real time. When systems are designed with user experience in mind, assurance becomes embedded in behavior rather than being a task added on top.

Cultural reinforcement matters just as much as formal structure. What happens in the break room or after a meeting often shapes behavior more than any written policy. When people talk through a recent incident over coffee, when a manager frames a team meeting around shared responsibility, or when a post-incident discussion focuses on learning instead of fault, assurance starts to feel normal rather than imposed. These moments cannot be ordered into existence, but they can be encouraged. Organizations that invest in peer learning, informal recognition, and communities of practice give assurance room to take root in ways that feel natural and credible.

Leadership must also redefine its engagement model. Too often, executive teams receive polished assurance reports that obscure frontline realities. This disconnect leads to false confidence and slow reaction. Leaders must require operational indicators that reflect lived conditions. These efforts rely on measures such as time to trust recovery, rates of control erosion, and the lag between a warning signal and a meaningful response. When these measures are brought to the boardroom, they stop being abstract concepts. They become expectations. Leadership attention signals that assurance is not optional and that priorities in this area will be reinforced through visible executive action.

Psychological safety underpins all of this work. When people do not feel safe raising concerns or challenging assumptions, early warning signs never surface. Cultures driven by fear quiet the very voices that enable timely detection and adjustment. Assurance takes hold in environments where speaking up carries no penalty, where missteps are examined rather than hidden, and where openness is valued. Leaders set that tone. They invite dissent, acknowledge what they do not yet know, and make it clear that honest dialogue is essential to resilient operations.

Another critical element is localized empowerment. Assurance cannot depend solely on central oversight. It must be distributed. Business units should have risk champions who contextualize enterprise priorities within local operations. These champions act as translators and advocates. They help their teams understand how to act on assurance signals, adapt processes, and align with enterprise standards. Their presence reinforces a simple but critical message. Assurance is not something imposed on the business. It is something the business actively owns and practices.

Training and enablement must change as well. Traditional compliance training falls short because it treats assurance as a periodic requirement instead of an everyday capability. Effective assurance learning is continuous, grounded in real context, and shaped by experience. Scenario exercises, simulations, and well-designed challenges help teams practice under conditions that resemble real operations. The goal is not memorization of policy. It is judgment. People need to learn how to spot emerging risks, weigh trade-offs, and know when to escalate. Tools that deliver guidance inside normal workflows support better decisions at the moment they matter.

Recognition plays an equally important role in reinforcing this shift. Assurance behaviors must be visible if they are going to spread. When a product team uncovers a control gap before release and chooses to delay delivery, that choice should be acknowledged rather than questioned. When an operations team creates a local contingency plan that strengthens supply chain resilience, that effort should be shared and learned from. Recognition does more than reward individuals. It clarifies what the organization truly values.

Technology supports this model, but only when it is built for openness and shared understanding. Assurance data should not live in isolated risk tools that few people ever see. It belongs inside collaboration platforms, delivery tools, and the systems leaders already use to run the business. Alerts should reflect business impact rather than raw volume. Signals should add clarity, not noise. The aim is a common operational view of trust that teams can see, understand, and act on together.

Over time, assurance must blend into the daily rhythm of work. Sprint reviews, sourcing decisions, planning cycles, and customer debriefs should all include deliberate assurance moments. When assurance becomes part of how work is done, it stops feeling like an interruption and starts functioning as a core business capability. Not as compliance items, but as strategic touchpoints. For example, during a product retrospective, teams should discuss not just what was delivered, but how well it held up under real conditions. During a vendor negotiation, procurement should review the vendor's latest telemetry and risk posture as part of the scoring model.

The shift from boardroom intent to everyday practice does not happen all at once. It unfolds over time through consistent choices about how decisions are made, how people are expected to act, and how resilience shows up when conditions change. It takes sustained leadership attention, patience, and a readiness to rethink structures that no longer support the outcome the organization claims to value. The return on that effort is meaningful. When assurance is embedded into how work actually gets done, organizations are more prepared to see disruption coming, withstand its impact, and regain momentum faster. Over time, this discipline builds credibility. That credibility earns trust from customers, confidence from investors, and an advantage that competitors struggle to replicate.

Assurance cannot remain a domain of risk officers and compliance auditors. It must become a shared competency across the organization. Every employee should understand how their actions contribute to enterprise trust. Every team should have the tools and knowledge to respond to disruptions with confidence. Every leader should model assurance behavior and reinforce its importance. When this becomes the norm, assurance ceases to be a checkbox. It becomes a muscle. And like any muscle, it grows stronger with use, feedback, and alignment. That is the true path to making assurance real.

To close this gap, assurance must be embedded not only in governance models but in the everyday actions of the business. That requires alignment across layers, integration into core functions, and reinforcement through culture.

6.2 ALIGNING LEADERSHIP, MANAGEMENT, AND FRONTLINE ACTIONS

For Integrated Assurance to move beyond theory and become a performance engine, the organization must operate as a coordinated system. Effective coordination depends on

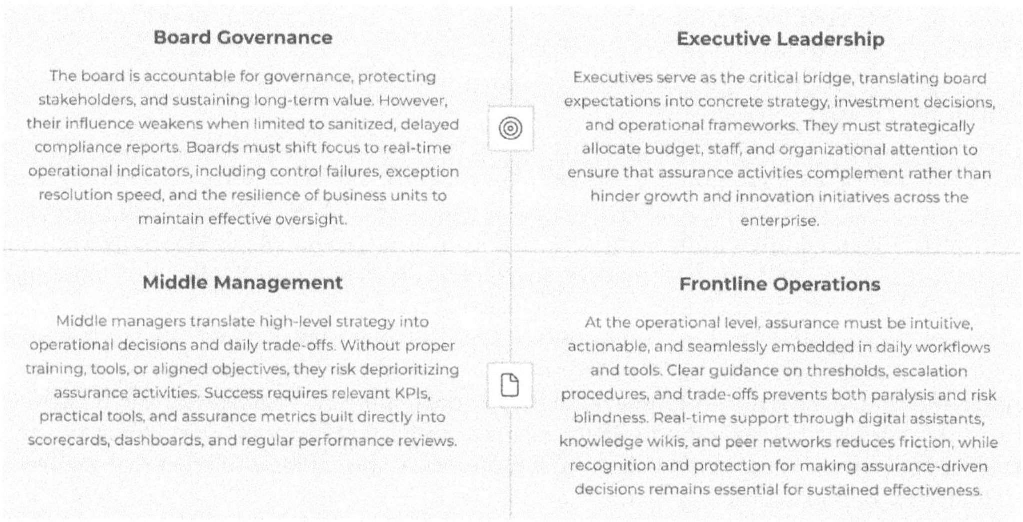

Figure 6.1 Aligning Leadership, Management, and Frontline Actions.

Image created by the author using Gamma.

alignment across three layers—leadership, management, and frontline operations. When these groups share a clear view of assurance priorities, reinforce those priorities through day-to-day decisions, and are given the authority and tools to act, resilience becomes part of how the organization functions. It is no longer something activated only during a crisis.

In practice, assurance efforts often break down. Boards and senior executives set risk principles and launch strategic programs, but that intent weakens as it moves through the organization. Middle management struggles to translate strategy into execution. Frontline teams receive mixed signals or little guidance at all. The gap shows up quickly. Strategies stall. Controls are worked around. When disruption hits, responses are uneven and slow, increasing exposure and extending recovery far beyond what leadership expected. See Figure 6.1: Aligning Leadership, Management, and Frontline Actions.

True alignment starts with leadership at the top. Boards of directors hold the responsibility for governance and remain accountable for protecting stakeholders and sustaining long-term value. Their influence weakens, however, when it is limited to reviewing audit results and compliance scorecards. Many assurance reports arrive late, stripped of nuance and disconnected from what is actually happening inside the business. They summarize conditions after the fact rather than illuminating them as they evolve. If boards want to play a more effective role, they need to move beyond static dashboards and compliance packages and engage directly with operational signals that reflect reality in motion. The ability to spot control breakdowns as they occur, understand how quickly exceptions are resolved, and see how different parts of the organization respond under stress becomes far more valuable than reviewing historical attestations. In this model, assurance becomes a living conversation about performance, not a retrospective exercise in documentation.

Once expectations are set at the board level, responsibility shifts to executive leadership to make those expectations real. This is where intent must translate into action. If assurance truly matters, it has to show up in how leaders allocate funding, staff critical roles, and prioritize attention. Security and resilience should not be framed as obstacles to growth. They need to be treated as enablers that sit alongside innovation and expansion. That requires embedding assurance into strategic planning, investment decisions, and execution models, not bolting it on afterward.

Consider the launch of a new digital product. Assurance should be part of the design from the outset, not a final checkpoint before release. Product and engineering teams need both the budget and the authority to build in observability, automated controls, and policy enforcement throughout the development lifecycle. Risk and compliance functions should be present during early design discussions, shaping decisions rather than reviewing them once they are already locked in. Customer experience leaders should have visibility into operational telemetry that influences service reliability and customer trust. When assurance is integrated this way, it supports speed and adaptability instead of slowing them down.

In many organizations, the greatest friction appears in the middle layers of management. These leaders convert strategy into daily decisions. They decide how teams spend their time, which trade-offs are acceptable, and what gets attention when priorities collide. When middle managers are not aligned with assurance objectives, progress stalls quickly. Telemetry initiatives get postponed to meet release deadlines. Control weaknesses are tolerated because they complicate delivery metrics. In some cases, managers simply lack the context or training to see how their choices affect enterprise-level assurance.

That is why engaging middle management is essential. Managers need practical guidance, clear accountability, and metrics that connect assurance to outcomes they already own. A procurement leader should understand how to escalate vendor risk events and why that escalation protects supply continuity. An operations manager should know how to interpret early signs of control degradation and adjust staffing or processes before service levels are affected. A marketing leader should recognize which datasets require heightened oversight and how data quality issues can translate into regulatory or reputational risk. When managers see assurance as part of their operational responsibility, it stops being abstract and starts driving better decisions across the organization.

Assurance must be integrated into the operating system of management. Scorecards, team dashboards, planning meetings, and performance reviews must include indicators that reflect control maturity, risk responsiveness, and trust performance. This ensures that assurance is not a side conversation, but a core dimension of how business performance is assessed.

One practical method is the introduction of assurance KPIs at the departmental level. These indicators should not be abstract or technical. They should reflect operational relevance. For example, a customer support department might track the number of escalations resolved within the approved trust window. An engineering department might track test coverage for business-critical features and mean time to validate fixes for control regressions. Procurement could measure the percentage of vendors with live telemetry integrations or completed joint incident exercises. These KPIs link behavior to outcome and create a foundation for meaningful accountability.

For frontline teams, assurance must be made intuitive and actionable. Policies and frameworks provide structure, but people on the ground need guidance at the moment. They need clarity about what decisions they are authorized to make, what thresholds require escalation, and what trade-offs are acceptable. In the absence of clarity, people default to speed or familiarity. This can result in risk blindness or decision paralysis. To address this, organizations must embed assurance into tools, workflows, and routines. User interfaces should offer embedded prompts when a decision could affect trust posture. Role-specific playbooks should define escalation paths and decision criteria. Contextual alerts should prioritize risk signals by impact, not frequency. And when employees make the right call, even if it slows down delivery or highlights an uncomfortable truth, their actions must be recognized and protected.

Real-time support systems also play a role. Employees should not have to interpret long policy documents to take appropriate action. They should be able to access digital assistants, internal wikis, or peer networks that help them resolve uncertainty quickly. These systems reduce friction, support confident decision-making, and ensure that assurance expectations are operational, not theoretical.

Leadership modeling reinforces alignment across all layers. When executives and managers ask about trust indicators in meetings, review risk dashboards during planning sessions, and surface assurance concerns alongside growth metrics, they normalize risk-informed behavior. When they participate in postmortems, support control remediation efforts, or delay a launch to address unresolved vulnerabilities, they send a clear message that assurance is a strategic priority.

Psychological safety underpins all of this. Teams must feel safe raising concerns, challenging assumptions, and admitting uncertainty. Assurance falters in organizations where people fear blame, dismissal, or reputational damage for surfacing risk. Leaders must model vulnerability by acknowledging unknowns, thanking employees for surfacing concerns, and prioritizing resolution over punishment. A culture that encourages curiosity and transparency will always outperform one that relies on fear and silence.

Another key element is cross-functional coordination. Risk rarely confines itself to one function. A delay in vendor payment due to compliance checks can lead to service outages, legal exposure, and customer dissatisfaction. Organizations must create governance structures that enable collaborative assurance. This includes integrated risk councils, incident response forums, assurance working groups, and shared planning cadences. These structures break down silos, surface blind spots, and allow teams to act in concert when threats emerge.

Alignment also requires bidirectional feedback. Frontline teams must have a voice in shaping assurance practices. They see where controls fail, where guidance is unclear, and where processes break under pressure. Their input should be actively solicited through surveys, retrospectives, and informal conversations. When that input leads to improvement, it reinforces the value of contribution. Conversely, executives must cascade strategic updates down to frontline teams in ways that are understandable and relevant. This feedback loop is what allows assurance practices to remain grounded, adaptable, and effective.

Recognition ties the system together. When alignment between leadership, management, and frontline actions results in successful disruption prevention, fast recovery, or strengthened stakeholder trust, those achievements must be visible. Celebrating the team that identified a latent vendor risk before contract renewal, the engineer who improved control telemetry without being asked, or the customer support rep who recognized and escalated a phishing pattern reinforces the behaviors that make assurance work.

In the end, alignment is not about everyone doing the same thing. It is about everyone doing different things with the same purpose. The board provides direction and oversight. Executives translate that direction into strategy and investment. Managers turn strategy into operations. Frontline teams execute with clarity and confidence. When these layers are synchronized, the organization becomes capable of navigating disruption without losing coherence. That coherence is what defines true operational resilience. Assurance ceases to be a program and becomes a way of operating. That is the ultimate goal of Integrated Assurance. See Figure 6.2: Case in Point.

Once alignment is established at the system level, the next challenge is to integrate assurance into the specific domains where risk materializes.

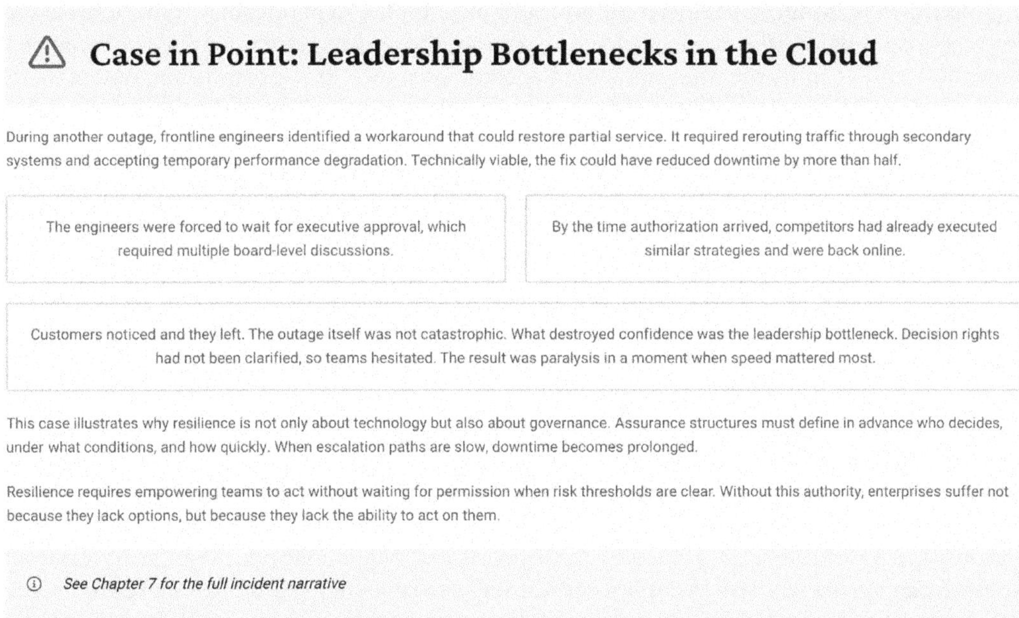

Figure 6.2 Case in Point.

Image created by the author using Gamma.

6.3 EMBEDDING ASSURANCE IN CORE BUSINESS FUNCTIONS

Integrated Assurance cannot remain a leadership talking point or a governance framework confined to a slide deck. Its true power lies in execution across the day-to-day operations of business functions. Risk lives where work is performed, not just where it is measured. Therefore, assurance must be designed to function within the language, incentives, workflows, and pressures of each business unit. Success comes not from pushing security objectives into functions but from embedding risk awareness and assurance outcomes into what those functions already value.

Every department within an organization manages its own ecosystem of responsibilities, decisions, and tools. Finance evaluates investments and manages cash flow. Legal interprets and enforces compliance obligations. Human Resources handles identity, culture, and behavioral norms. Engineering builds and ships the core infrastructure of the organization. Procurement expands and maintains the organization's external ecosystem. These departments are not appendages to enterprise risk management. They are the operational surface where risk either materializes or is mitigated. Assurance that fails to account for the distinct language and logic of these business functions becomes irrelevant, or worse, disruptive.

The starting point for effective integration is recognizing that each function already manages risk, just through a different lens. For example, finance departments conduct risk-adjusted return analysis as a matter of course. They evaluate trade-offs, model downside exposure, and hedge investments. The question is not whether they manage risk, but whether they are equipped to see risk through the lens of resilience, continuity, and assurance. To bridge this gap, organizations must provide assurance signals in the format each function can interpret and act on.

A practical illustration lies in the financial planning process. Consider a business unit seeking approval for a large investment in a cloud-based analytics platform. The financial analysis will likely focus on ROI, operational efficiency, and potential revenue growth. But what if the platform introduces telemetry blind spots or complex dependencies that increase incident response time? Without assurance integration, those downstream risks are invisible to finance leaders. With it, the analysis would include recovery ROI projections, potential risk offsets, and assurance capability uplift tied to the investment. This makes decision-making more complete.

Similarly, engineering teams often move at high velocity, delivering code and infrastructure in rapid iterations. Traditional security reviews are perceived as friction in this environment. However, embedding assurance in engineering means engineering teams are not being asked to slow down, but rather to build resilience into their own cadence. Security debt becomes part of the backlog, telemetry coverage becomes a sprint metric, and control thresholds become build gates. Rather than being outside stakeholders, security and assurance become embedded properties of the code itself. This shifts assurance from being a separate layer to being part of the fabric of development.

Legal teams are another area where integration unlocks significant value. Contractual language often mandates adherence to industry standards, such as ISO 27001 or National Institute of Science and Technology Cybersecurity Framework. Yet if those requirements do not align with actual operational controls, the result is legal exposure and strained vendor relationships. Embedding assurance in legal processes means mapping regulatory and contractual language to real-world capabilities. It means ensuring legal templates reflect telemetry-sharing expectations, define breach escalation procedures in operational terms, and align with how the organization actually measures control effectiveness. This alignment turns legal from a blocker into a builder of operational trust frameworks.

Human Resources plays a more strategic role than is often acknowledged in risk discussions. HR is the gatekeeper of who joins the organization, how they are trained, how their access is managed, and how departures are handled. These are all critical junctures in identity governance. Assurance integration here involves tiered access provisioning based on role risk, behavior-driven escalation policies, and embedded training programs that equip employees to spot and respond to emerging risks. HR also stewards culture. Signals such as whistleblower activity, engagement surveys, and attrition spikes are early indicators of risk pressure building inside the organization. An assurance-aware HR function becomes a vital sensor for detecting and mitigating cultural drift before it manifests in operational failure.

Procurement, though often viewed through a cost-efficiency lens, has become a pivotal actor in enterprise assurance. Every new vendor added to the ecosystem expands the potential attack surface, introduces new dependencies, and creates shared responsibility zones. Embedding assurance into procurement means evaluating vendors not just on price or delivery performance, but on their control maturity, transparency capabilities, and joint response readiness. Assurance-aware procurement teams negotiate for real-time telemetry feeds, contractually defined incident response obligations, and proof of control performance as part of ongoing business relationships. These expectations must be normalized across the vendor lifecycle, from due diligence to renewal.

Beyond the unique contributions of each function, the organization must align around common principles. The first is translation. Risk language must adapt to the functional context. It is unproductive to ask a procurement officer to assess third-party exposure using control IDs from a cybersecurity framework. Instead, they should evaluate vendor response times, audit participation, and data-sharing maturity. Translation is not dumbing down risk. It is making it actionable in the functional domain where decisions are made.

The second principle is resourcing. Too often, business units are asked to adopt assurance responsibilities without corresponding investment. Telling engineering to remediate telemetry gaps without allocating development capacity creates tension, not traction. Expecting procurement to vet cybersecurity controls without giving them access to a vendor intelligence platform is unrealistic. Integration requires capability alignment. If new expectations are placed on a function, they must be matched with resources, tools, and training.

The third principle is measurement. Assurance cannot remain an abstract good. It must be translated into metrics that matter within each function. In HR, this might mean tracking how many roles have context-aware onboarding tied to risk tiers. In finance, it may involve measuring capital allocations for resilience initiatives or quantifying avoided losses due to early detection. In legal, performance may be tied to the percentage of contracts that include enforceable control-sharing terms. These metrics turn assurance into operational currency.

The fourth and perhaps most transformative principle is distributed accountability. Assurance must move from being the sole domain of risk and compliance teams to a shared responsibility across the enterprise. Each function owns part of the organization's resilience. This means having risk champions within each business unit who act as both advocates and advisors. It means embedding assurance into the operational cadence, into standups, retrospectives, quarterly business reviews, and planning cycles. Assurance conversations should be as normal as financial performance updates or customer satisfaction scores.

Technology plays an enabling role, but not a leading one. Dashboards and tooling must support role-based visibility and relevance. Legal professionals need exposure summaries, not vulnerability scores. Finance leaders need risk-adjusted forecasting tools, not security incident reports. Engineering teams need embedded CI/CD feedback loops, not static compliance documents. Technology must meet people where they work and present information in a format they can understand and act upon.

At a system level, integrating assurance into business functions transforms fragmented risk ownership into a coordinated, cross-functional resilience model. When procurement evaluates a vendor, they consider not just cost and compliance but real-time operational trust. When HR designs a job role, they build in behavioral risk indicators and escalation pathways. When finance reviews a budget, they factor in risk offsets and capability readiness. When engineering builds a feature, they ensure it can be observed, defended, and recovered. This alignment changes how the organization moves, responds, and adapts.

Ultimately, integration of assurance across core business functions is not an overlay. It is a reanchoring of how value is created, protected, and sustained. Assurance becomes a performance multiplier, not a constraint. The end goal is not just better security or improved compliance. It is enterprise resilience that is intelligent, distributed, and continuously improving. That level of operational maturity is what enables businesses to move fast without fear, innovate without blind spots, and grow with confidence in an environment where uncertainty is the only constant.

6.4 HR, LEGAL, FINANCE, ENGINEERING, AND PROCUREMENT

Integrated Assurance cannot thrive as a standalone function. It must be expressed through the everyday actions, decisions, and systems of the business. This means assurance must be operationalized across all major business functions, each of which interacts with risk in unique and consequential ways. Human Resources, Legal, Finance, Engineering, and Procurement are not just internal service providers or support domains. They are active contributors to the organization's trust posture. Their role in risk sensing, mitigation, and response must be made explicit, not implied. Embedding assurance into these core functions creates a connected web of resilience that is far stronger than any centralized oversight model.

Each of these domains comes with its own language, objectives, and operational cadence. Integrated Assurance does not ask these functions to become security experts. Instead, it equips them to express assurance through their own workflows. The goal is not to introduce parallel processes, but to embed assurance as a natural part of decision-making and performance execution.

6.4.1 Stewards of trust and organizational behavior

Human Resources is often overlooked in security and risk programs, yet it sits at the center of many assurance activities. HR determines who joins the organization, how they are introduced, how their access is handled, how their performance is reviewed, and how they eventually depart. Each of these stages carries both risk and opportunity.

Assurance begins with hiring. Job descriptions should reflect the level of sensitivity tied to each role. Positions with access to financial systems, critical data, or infrastructure require greater scrutiny. This may involve deeper background checks, behavioral assessments, or additional interview steps to identify risk factors that relate to trust. The purpose is not exclusion but informed decision-making that aligns risk posture with role responsibilities.

When a new employee starts, onboarding becomes the first point where assurance must be reinforced. Instead of overwhelming people with dense policy manuals, training should be tied to the real decisions they will face. A marketing specialist can be shown how misuse of customer information creates compliance risk. A developer can review a case where a monitoring gap concealed a breach. These practical examples turn abstract policies into experiences that shape behavior.

Identity and access management is another joint responsibility of HR and IT. Assurance depends on precise access provisioning, continuous monitoring, and timely updates. Job changes, project reassignments, or extended leave can all open gaps if not tracked properly. HR must maintain accurate role data and coordinate with technical systems to ensure access aligns with current responsibilities. When an employee leaves, accounts must be deactivated immediately. Any delay increases exposure.

HR also provides insight into the cultural health of the organization. Engagement surveys, retention patterns, performance issues, and whistleblower reports all serve as signals of potential risk. An HR team that understands assurance treats these indicators as part of the enterprise risk picture. They bring forward concerns, coordinate with other functions, and help design responses that reduce exposure without eroding trust.

Finally, assurance must be built into job expectations and performance management. Employees who surface risks, improve processes, or guide peers in responsible decision-making should be recognized. When trust and resilience are factored into advancement and compensation, they become part of daily leadership and performance standards.

6.4.2 Translating policy into operational contracts

Legal departments act as both guardians of organizational integrity and partners in strategic risk management. Their central task is to ensure that commitments written into contracts can be met in practice. Too often, agreements include requirements that cannot be delivered or clauses that heighten operational risk. Integrated Assurance provides the structure to connect legal terms with the actual control environment.

This alignment begins with early involvement. Legal should not enter the process only when negotiations close or a launch nears completion. Their participation is critical in the planning and design phases, particularly where third-party data handling, privacy concerns, or regulatory exposure is at stake. When present at this stage, legal teams can shape agreements for shared control ownership, telemetry exchange, and escalation procedures that fit the organization's assurance model.

Contract templates also need to evolve. Vague references to industry norms are insufficient. Agreements should define how controls will be verified, what data will be exchanged during a breach, how long assurance will be sustained, and which parties carry responsibility for each action. These details create enforceable expectations and reduce the chance of breakdown during critical events.

The role of legal extends into incident response. When a breach, regulatory review, or customer dispute occurs, the legal function must coordinate with cybersecurity, communications, and operations. A well-integrated model ensures that evidence of decision-making, control performance, and policy adherence is available and trustworthy. This reduces liability and strengthens the organization's ability to preserve reputation.

Legal must also help harmonize policy with operations. Rules on acceptable use, data retention, and conduct need to reflect how systems function and how people actually work. When policies are disconnected from practice, they create compliance gaps and erode trust. By aligning policy with reality, legal departments reinforce both assurance and culture.

6.4.3 Embedding risk into value models

Finance holds one of the most powerful levers for embedding assurance at scale, which is capital allocation. Every investment decision, budget approval, and cost optimization initiative is also a decision about risk exposure and resilience capability. Integrated Assurance reframes finance not just as a funder of controls, but as a strategic partner in risk-informed growth.

This begins by recognizing that resilience has a measurable return. Avoided outages, shortened recovery times, reduced legal settlements, and protected customer trust all have economic value. Finance teams should collaborate with security and operations leaders to build recovery ROI models that estimate the cost avoidance achieved through specific assurance investments. These models shift the conversation from cost to value.

Forecasting and scenario planning processes must also evolve. Traditional financial planning often assumes a stable operating environment. But in a world of frequent disruptions, finance must account for risk velocity, vendor fragility, geopolitical shifts, and climate volatility. Integrated Assurance provides the telemetry data necessary to feed these models. Risk-adjusted planning allows finance leaders to see not only potential returns but also the probability and magnitude of disruption.

Finance should also participate in assurance governance. Budget cycles should include risk council reviews that assess how proposed investments align with enterprise assurance priorities. Procurement approvals should be informed by vendor trust scores, not just price and service-level commitments. Capital expenditure models should account for not only build costs but also observability, control testing, and lifecycle assurance.

6.4.4 Trust built into code and infrastructure

Engineering is the heartbeat of digital innovation, and it is where assurance must become ambient. Waiting until after systems are built to assess resilience is no longer viable. Assurance must be integrated directly into design, development, testing, and deployment.

This starts with shift-left security practices. Static and dynamic code analysis, dependency validation, and infrastructure-as-code policy checks must be built into CI/CD pipelines. These controls must provide real-time feedback, not just static reports. Developers should be able to see how their changes affect control integrity, telemetry coverage, and trust thresholds.

Observability is a second assurance pillar. Systems must be instrumented to emit signals that show how controls perform under load, how anomalies manifest, and how recovery unfolds. These signals must feed into shared telemetry platforms that are accessible to security, operations, and product teams. Assurance is not just about identifying vulnerabilities. It is about continuously observing the health and integrity of systems under real conditions.

Postmortems should be used not just to assign blame but to accelerate learning. Blameless reviews, retrospective control mapping, and collaborative incident documentation ensure that each failure becomes a contribution to resilience maturity. These practices build psychological safety and help embed assurance into engineering culture.

6.4.5 Extending trust across the ecosystem

Procurement decisions have far-reaching implications for enterprise trust. Every new vendor introduces new risks. Assurance-aware procurement does not stop at contract signing. It begins with due diligence and continues through ongoing relationship monitoring.

During vendor selection, procurement should assess not only cost and capability, but also control maturity, incident response readiness, regulatory posture, and willingness to participate in shared assurance models. Vendors should be scored based on both technical and behavioral trust factors. This data should inform not only selection but also negotiation. Contracts must include terms for telemetry sharing, breach notification windows, and mutual recovery protocols.

Once relationships are established, procurement must monitor vendor performance through assurance dashboards that include audit participation, incident involvement, and responsiveness to shared assessments. In high-risk categories, procurement leaders should coordinate tabletop exercises with key vendors to ensure readiness. These exercises provide insights that no document review can replicate. Cross-functional collaboration is key. Procurement must work closely with legal to ensure contracts are enforceable. They must work with cybersecurity to validate control claims. They must also work with operations to align vendor capabilities with service delivery requirements.

6.4.6 From policy to culture

This table illustrates how assurance moves from surface-level policy, through operationalized processes, to becoming part of the organizational culture. See Table 6.1: From policy to culture.

This maturity model illustrates that assurance begins as documented policy, but it only delivers value when it matures into operational processes and, ultimately, becomes part of the organizational culture. The real test of resilience is not whether a policy exists, but whether people across HR, Finance, Legal, Engineering, and Procurement act on assurance instinctively in their daily decisions. Feedback loops and cultural signaling are what enable organizations to climb this maturity curve. Once alignment is established at the system level, the next challenge is to integrate assurance into the specific domains where risk materializes.

6.5 FEEDBACK LOOPS AND ASSURANCE MATURITY

Integrated Assurance does not remain effective because it has been written into a policy or documented in governance procedures. It endures because the organization builds the ability to learn from its own experiences. That ability depends on feedback. When feedback is absent, assurance frameworks grow rigid. They become rituals that satisfy audits but fail to protect the business. When feedback is present, assurance adapts, responds, and strengthens with every test it encounters.

Table 6.1 From policy to culture

Domain	*Policy*	*Process*	*Culture*
HR	Security and compliance language is written into employee handbooks and onboarding documents.	Regular risk and resilience training is integrated into performance management cycles.	Employees proactively raise resilience concerns, report anomalies, and embed assurance in daily work without prompts.
Finance	Financial policies reference compliance requirements (e.g., Sarbanes–Oxley Act [SOX], fraud prevention standards).	Automated monitoring for fraud and financial anomalies with defined escalation processes.	Teams instinctively consider financial resilience and fraud risk during decision-making; assurance is tied to stewardship of brand trust.
Legal	Contracts and compliance policies explicitly include security and risk clauses.	Risk reviews are integrated into contract workflows with automated checks against regulatory requirements.	Legal counsel acts as a proactive advisor on resilience, engaging early in business initiatives to shape decisions rather than react to issues.
Engineering/IT	Secure coding policies, change management standards, and system access rules are documented.	Security testing, threat modeling, and risk scoring are integrated directly into DevOps pipelines.	Engineers and IT staff instinctively design for resilience; assurance is seen as enabling speed and innovation, not slowing it down.
Procurement/ Supply Chain	Vendor contracts include baseline security and compliance clauses.	Supplier risk assessments and scoring embedded into procurement workflows before approval.	Teams view supplier assurance as part of enterprise value creation; vendors are selected and managed with resilience as a strategic criterion.

Feedback converts experience into improvement. It links frontline activity with managerial oversight and strategic intent. It shows whether controls stand up under pressure, whether employees act with clarity in difficult circumstances, and whether investments in resilience pay off in real outcomes. Without a feedback structure, assurance loses impact. The organization still produces reports and dashboards, but those artifacts no longer reflect the operational truth.

Modern risk landscapes demand organizations that function as living systems. A living system senses, interprets, and adjusts. A static system continues to apply the same responses even as conditions shift. Many organizations fall into the static category, relying on annual audits, quarterly reviews, and compliance certifications as their evidence of resilience. These practices serve a purpose, but they do not provide the pace of feedback needed to catch emerging threats, track cultural drift, or identify control breakdowns as they happen.

Take the example of a multinational firm investing heavily in cloud services. An annual review of access controls may confirm compliance with regulations. The real challenge occurs when a developer unintentionally leaves a storage bucket exposed. Without a feedback loop that detects the issue, escalates it, and captures the lesson, the same error will occur in other teams and environments. What appears as compliance success in formal reporting becomes an operational weakness in daily practice. Feedback is what closes this gap.

Figure 6.3 Modes of Feedback.

Image created by the author using Gamma.

No single feedback channel is sufficient. A comprehensive assurance system requires feedback across different time horizons. Each mode contributes to a distinct function, and together they form the backbone of resilience. See Figure 6.3: Modes of Feedback.

Real-time feedback functions as the nervous system of assurance. Continuous telemetry streams provide visibility into the health of systems, the behavior of users, and the performance of vendors. These signals allow teams to adjust operations before a disruption escalates. The key is accessibility. If telemetry is limited to a small group of specialists, the organization loses its adaptive capacity. A supply chain director should be able to view vendor reliability indicators just as a finance analyst should be able to see data integrity signals that influence forecasting. Real-time signals democratized across functions prevent assurance from becoming an exclusive domain.

Periodic feedback offers rhythm and perspective. Weekly or monthly reviews allow managers to identify patterns that are invisible in daily activity. Metrics such as mean time to contain incidents, frequency of policy exceptions, or vendor response performance provide a baseline for analysis. These numbers, however, do not speak for themselves. They must be interpreted through dialogue that includes context from the people closest to the work. A rise in policy exceptions could reflect a failing control, but it might also indicate that the policy is unrealistic given current workflows. Without this interpretive layer, metrics risk being misread or misapplied.

Retrospective feedback delivers depth. When disruptions occur, the organization has an opportunity to interrogate both system performance and human decision-making. A post-incident review should map control states before, during, and after the event. It should reconstruct the escalation path and communication flow. It should ask whether employees felt empowered to act, whether thresholds were clear, and whether early signals were overlooked. The goal is not to distribute blame but to transform an incident into institutional learning. Every disruption, whether minor or severe, carries lessons that can strengthen the organization if captured properly.

Cross-functional feedback ensures that insights do not remain siloed. Risk rarely respects organizational boundaries. A vendor issue detected by procurement may have implications for legal contract language. A cultural signal identified by Human Resources may highlight behavioral risks that engineering teams need to address. Without channels for lateral communication, these signals die within their domains. Cross-functional councils, integrated incident reviews, and shared knowledge platforms ensure that one team's lesson prevents another team's failure.

The most advanced telemetry system cannot compensate for a culture that fails to capture human insight. Employees often notice anomalies or weaknesses before they become visible in formal reporting, yet their observations never reach decision-makers. This signal loss is one of the most significant failures in feedback architecture. To address it, organizations must provide multiple, low-friction avenues for surfacing concerns. Pulse surveys, digital suggestion systems, embedded prompts in workflow tools, and informal team debriefs all help create a distributed sensing network. Every employee becomes a contributor to enterprise assurance. A call center representative who notices a suspicious customer pattern, a warehouse supervisor who identifies a process inconsistency, or a software engineer who observes unusual telemetry should all have trusted pathways for sharing their observations.

Once signals are captured, they must be routed appropriately. Not every observation requires executive attention, but no observation should be dismissed without review. A triage system that classifies inputs by relevance, potential impact, and urgency ensures that signals reach the right level of decision-making. This prevents overload while preserving trust that feedback matters.

The quality of feedback loops determines the maturity of assurance. At low maturity, organizations focus on compliance tasks. They produce reports, check boxes, and respond to regulators, but they do not adapt meaningfully when conditions change. Feedback is limited, and lessons are often lost. Moderate maturity emerges when organizations begin to conduct periodic reviews, share insights across departments, and capture lessons in post-incident analyses. At this stage, assurance practices adjust incrementally, but they remain uneven. Some functions learn faster than others, and lessons are not always institutionalized.

High maturity is characterized by continuous, distributed feedback. Signals flow across vertical and horizontal layers. Lessons are documented, integrated into training, and used to refine both systems and behaviors. Employees expect their observations to influence policy. Leaders treat feedback as a core input to strategic decisions. The organization moves from reactive correction to proactive anticipation.

Feedback must be valued as strategic currency. Leaders who consistently ask for lessons in planning sessions, who celebrate employees for raising concerns, and who allocate resources to address surfaced issues create an environment where assurance becomes ingrained. Risk awareness is not a distraction from performance but a contribution to it.

The true measure of maturity is not the number of reports generated but the speed and quality of learning. Organizations that invest in feedback learn faster than their competitors. They recognize blind spots before those blind spots produce crises. They adjust processes while rivals remain anchored in outdated practices. They build resilience not through perfect control but through continuous adaptation.

Consider a global logistics company facing recurring delays due to third-party system outages. In a low-maturity environment, procurement might note the outages, operations might develop temporary workarounds, and finance might track cost overruns. Each function would handle the issue within its own boundaries. The same outage would repeat in the following quarter because no lessons were shared across the organization.

In a higher-maturity model, procurement would escalate the vendor's weaknesses through an assurance council. Legal would review contract terms and adjust breach notification clauses. Finance would revise forecasting models to account for disruption risk. Operations would update contingency plans. These changes would be documented, tracked, and integrated into the assurance maturity model. The outage would not be treated as an isolated inconvenience but as an organizational learning event.

Organizations that succeed in embedding feedback into their assurance systems achieve two important outcomes. First, they develop a culture that treats disruption as a source of growth rather than only a source of loss. Second, they build an assurance capability that evolves in real time, keeping pace with changes in technology, regulation, and threat landscapes.

The path forward requires deliberate design. Feedback must be captured, routed, interpreted, and applied. It must move across time horizons, across organizational layers, and across functions. It must be measured not by volume but by velocity and effectiveness. Above all, it must be treated as essential to performance, not optional.

Integrated Assurance matures when feedback is woven into the daily rhythm of the organization. When lessons are surfaced quickly, acted upon decisively, and reinforced culturally, assurance stops being a compliance exercise. It becomes a dynamic capability that strengthens the organization with every challenge. That is the promise of feedback, and that is the foundation of assurance maturity.

6.6 IAMM AS A BRIDGE ACROSS LEVELS

The connection between governance and culture defines whether assurance functions as strategy or ceremony. The IAMM illustrates how these domains converge to bridge the divide between executive intent and operational behavior. Governance without cultural alignment leaves assurance fragile. When both advance together, assurance becomes a living system that links the boardroom with daily execution.

At Level 1, the divide is absolute. Executives discuss risk in formal meetings while frontline teams work independently. Communication occurs only after incidents. Trust is minimal, and conflicting priorities fragment operations. Assurance remains a paperwork exercise detached from purpose.

Level 2 introduces structure but not cohesion. Governance groups meet and publish policies, yet culture does not internalize them. Employees comply selectively. Leaders assume documentation will drive discipline. Oversight exists, but adoption remains shallow.

Level 3 marks the beginning of coordination. Governance and culture begin to interact. Leaders emphasize shared ownership of assurance outcomes. Middle management translates intent into action, connecting objectives to operations. Communication improves, and assurance begins to matter. Enforcement, however, still depends on individual commitment.

Level 4 reflects integration. Governance structures hold authority, and cultural norms reinforce accountability. Forums act on measurable outcomes. Performance goals include assurance responsibilities, and recognition programs support collaboration. This alignment produces feedback loops that strengthen resilience. New policies are not only approved but also understood and practiced across all levels. Assurance becomes a routine discipline.

At Level 5, the relationship between governance and culture is fully institutionalized. Leaders model the behaviors they expect. Assurance principles appear in decision-making, reviews, and training. Communication is transparent in all directions. Employees see their work as part of organizational resilience and connect daily actions to enterprise success. Trust functions as both structure and habit.

A global logistics company provides an example. At Level 2, executives published governance standards while delivery teams ignored them to maintain speed. At Level 3, training improved awareness, though accountability was unclear. At Level 4, leaders integrated operational managers into governance forums and aligned performance metrics with assurance goals. By Level 5, assurance became instinctive behavior, not an assigned task.

The results of this maturity are measurable. Decision-making accelerates because trust reduces friction. Teams act with confidence, knowing expectations are clear. Governance gains credibility because its outcomes are visible. The organization adapts faster and withstands disruption more effectively.

Assessment criteria reveal the stage of maturity. Governance forums that address behavior and culture signal progress. Assurance responsibilities embedded in performance systems indicate integration. Clear communication across layers confirms alignment. A visible connection between executive direction and frontline practice defines maturity.

IAMM clarifies that governance and culture operate as parts of a single assurance system. Together, they sustain resilience as both structural integrity and shared belief. In a mature organization, assurance is not a compliance task but a collective practice that anchors trust in every decision and action.

6.7 CULTURAL SIGNALING AND LEADERSHIP VISIBILITY

Assurance cannot survive on the strength of policies, frameworks, or technology alone. Its real foundation comes from the culture of the organization. Culture works like the hidden operating system of an organization. It shapes how people behave when conditions are uncertain, how they interpret risk when decisions are hard, and how they protect trust when business outcomes collide with short-term incentives. A governance model may bring structure, and advanced telemetry may deliver visibility, but neither can hold if the cultural signals that surround them are misaligned.

Cultural signals are shaped by what people see and experience every day. Employees take their cues from how leaders show up, how peers behave, and how work actually gets done. These signals are rarely written down, yet they carry more weight than any policy or training module. People watch where leaders focus their time, how managers make trade-offs, and which actions earn recognition or pass without comment. When those patterns consistently support assurance, resilience and trust become part of normal work. When the emphasis stays fixed on speed or cost alone, assurance fades from view.

Leadership visibility makes these signals stronger. The behavior of senior executives is always interpreted as an expression of organizational priorities. When leaders participate in resilience initiatives, speak openly about assurance, and recognize risk-aware contributions, they send a clear message that assurance is not optional. Silence, on the other hand, communicates that other concerns matter more. Employees quickly sense whether trust is truly valued or merely mentioned in passing.

Executives shape culture not only through strategies or control frameworks but also through their presence in key activities. When senior leaders join post-incident reviews, ask about recovery performance, or include control effectiveness alongside growth metrics in planning sessions, they shift the perception of what matters. Their language has lasting power. Leaders who talk about assurance as something that creates value, or who connect resilience to customer trust and brand reputation, change how people see their own responsibility. The work of protecting systems, data, and operations no longer feels like overhead. It feels like part of winning. Assurance becomes something employees take pride in because it is clearly tied to outcomes that matter.

Those beliefs are tested most clearly in moments of stress. When something breaks or fails, employees watch closely. Leaders who are open about gaps, who focus on what was learned, and who call out what has held up under pressure signal that it is safe to raise concerns early. When the response instead centers on deflecting blame, downplaying the issue, or reducing the conversation to dollars lost, the message is just as clear. People learn quickly which behaviors are rewarded and which are better kept quiet.

Middle managers extend these cultural signals into daily practice. They form the bridge between executive vision and frontline execution, and their influence is especially strong because employees interact with them regularly. When a manager integrates assurance into team planning or performance discussions, employees assume that resilience is part of the job. When a manager treats assurance requirements as secondary to speed, that message is absorbed just as quickly. Managers transmit culture through routines. Reviewing assurance indicators in meetings, referencing risk-informed behaviors in evaluations, and recognizing contributions that safeguard trust all build cultural strength. Without those routines, assurance feels peripheral.

Managers face competing pressures such as delivery deadlines, customer expectations, cost control, and now assurance. Without reinforcement through departmental scorecards, time allocation, and budget commitments, assurance is likely to be seen as negotiable. By embedding assurance directly into the performance systems of management, organizations create consistent signals rather than leaving them open to interpretation.

Culture is also shaped through the rituals and routines that define organizational life. Sprint reviews, retrospectives, quarterly planning sessions, and onboarding all offer opportunities to signal priorities. When resilience and assurance are woven into these forums, they become normalized. A new hire who hears stories of employees who prevented incidents will see assurance as a core expectation rather than an abstract idea. An engineering team that evaluates recovery readiness alongside delivery targets will see assurance as part of performance, not an add-on.

Recognition reinforces culture as much as routines. People pay attention to who is celebrated. An employee who is rewarded for raising a concern before it becomes a crisis, or a team recognized for pausing a release to close a resilience gap, sends a message to the entire organization. Recognition should appear in both formal awards and informal acknowledgments, creating signals that reach across layers of the organization.

Stories shape culture in ways policies never will. Most employees will not remember the wording of a control standard, but they will remember the account of a procurement analyst who stopped a risky vendor deal before it damaged the company's reputation. They will remember the frontline operator who raised a concern that prevented an outage no one else could see coming. When leaders share these moments in town halls, internal updates, or training sessions, assurance stops being abstract. It becomes real. Over time, these stories settle into the organization's memory and quietly teach people what is valued and what good judgment looks like.

For this kind of cultural signaling to work, people have to feel safe speaking up. Psychological safety is not a soft concept. It is a prerequisite for effective assurance. When employees worry about blame or retaliation, risks go unreported and early warnings disappear. The organization loses access to its most valuable source of insight. Leaders set the tone by thanking people who raise uncomfortable issues, acknowledging their own blind spots, and responding to mistakes with questions instead of punishment. When that happens, trust grows, silence fades, and meaningful signals move through the organization instead of getting trapped at the edges.

Even the physical and digital environments of an organization send signals. Dashboards in shared spaces, metrics embedded in collaboration platforms, and updates in portals all shape perceptions. These should be designed with clarity and relevance for each audience. Finance teams should see risk-adjusted forecasts. Engineers should see observability indicators and recovery measures. Subtle reinforcement still matters. Visual cues like posters, recognition boards, and short leadership messages can keep trust and assurance visible without turning them into empty slogans. When done right, they remind people of what matters without demanding attention.

Training is where culture either takes hold or falls flat. Too often, it becomes a box to check, something people rush through and quickly forget. More effective programs rely on real scenarios, role-specific simulations, and sessions led by peers who understand the work. That approach helps employees learn how to think, not just what to do. When executives show up for training or reference it in everyday conversations, it signals that assurance is not a side topic. It is something leadership owns and expects others to take seriously. That visibility confirms to employees that assurance is not delegated but held at the highest level.

Culture evolves as markets, technologies, and crises reshape the environment. Signaling and visibility must be continuous rather than occasional. Leaders should track cultural health through surveys, focus groups, and behavioral telemetry. Consistency is vital. Employees notice quickly when leadership words do not match leadership actions. Authenticity requires alignment between what is said, what is done, and what gets reinforced.

The goal is for assurance to become a natural reflex within the organization. Employees should not need reminders to consider resilience, because they should integrate trust instinctively into decisions. Leaders should embody assurance rather than enforce it. Managers should define performance in ways that naturally include resilience.

Reaching this point takes persistence. It requires visible engagement from leaders, reinforcement from managers, stories and recognition that make assurance human, and structures that embed it into operations. When these elements come together, assurance stops being something managed by a small group of specialists and starts becoming part of everyday work. It shows up in how teams make decisions, how partners are chosen, and how commitments to customers are honored. Over time, it turns into a shared expectation rather than a formal initiative. That shared expectation is what gives an organization the ability to absorb disruption without coming apart. In that kind of environment, assurance is no longer theoretical. It is visible, practical, and lived. It is lived, practiced, and trusted.

6.8 CONCLUSION

Integrated Assurance is often treated as something you implement, certify, and then move on from. That view is tempting because it implies a clear finish line. In reality, assurance does not work that way. It has no endpoint. It is not a product deployment or a transformation initiative that wraps up with a final report and a quiet sense of closure. Assurance is a living capability. It grows stronger only through repeated use, honest reflection, and consistent reinforcement. When organizations approach it as a framework to copy or a checklist to complete, they miss the point. Assurance matters only when it changes how people think, how they make decisions, and how they behave, especially when situations become uncertain or uncomfortable.

Most organizations start with the right intentions. They define guiding principles, publish policies, and establish metrics. Those steps are important, but they are not the destination. Assurance may begin with strategy, but it becomes real only when it shows up in everyday behavior. You see it in how leaders set priorities when pressure mounts. You see it in how managers weigh speed against risk. You see it in how employees respond when something feels off, and speaking up is easier said than done. Without that shift in behavior, assurance stays abstract and disconnected from the way the organization actually operates.

One of the biggest challenges lies in how value is measured. Many organizations still point to audit results, certifications, or regulatory filings as evidence that assurance is working. Those artifacts have their place, but they do not define resilience. Real resilience reveals itself during disruption. It shows up when systems stumble and teams adapt without chaos, when decisions are made quickly without sacrificing trust, and when communication stays clear even as conditions evolve. These qualities do not come from static compliance. They come from assurance that is embedded in culture, reinforced by leadership, and practiced as part of the organization's daily operating rhythm.

The most common failure point lies between strategy and execution. Boards may articulate strong expectations around risk, ethics, and resilience. Executives may translate those expectations into initiatives, funding, and roadmaps. Somewhere between the executive layer and the front line, clarity fades. Middle managers often feel pressure to deliver near-term results and may see assurance as a secondary concern. Frontline teams may not understand how their individual choices affect enterprise trust. When intention stops short of execution, the result is a quiet but dangerous gap. Good ideas exist on paper, yet little changes in how work actually gets done.

Closing that gap requires alignment across the organization, not another policy or a carefully worded memo. Priorities become real through everyday decisions. How budgets are allocated, how teams are built, and what leaders choose to discuss in performance reviews all reveal what actually matters. Managers translate those signals into action. They take broad goals and turn them into clear expectations by deciding what gets examined, which issues are raised early, and what kinds of decisions and behaviors are rewarded.

At the front lines, people need to see how their daily work contributes to resilience and operational stability. When that link is obvious, assurance stops feeling like an external requirement and starts to function as part of how the organization runs. When alignment holds, assurance begins to function as a system. Boards focus on recovery and adaptability. Executives invest in observability and testing. Managers review risk signals alongside delivery milestones. Employees raise concerns early because they know it is expected and supported.

Culture is the force that sustains this alignment. Policies do not create culture on their own. People learn what matters by watching leaders, observing what gets recognized, and listening to everyday conversations. A culture of assurance grows when leaders talk openly about risk, when teams share stories of near misses and recoveries, and when vigilance is acknowledged rather than ignored. These signals make assurance tangible. Without them, it remains abstract and easy to sideline.

Feedback is what keeps assurance alive over time. Programs without feedback quickly turn into rituals. Real assurance depends on continuous learning. Telemetry and operational data provide insight into control health and emerging issues. Regular reviews help identify patterns and resource constraints. Post-incident analysis tests assumptions and drives improvement. This feedback must move across functions and levels so lessons are not trapped within a single team. Organizations that treat every disruption, whether major or minor, as a learning opportunity steadily increase their confidence and capability.

Clear decision rights are equally important. Assurance breaks down when people are unsure about what they are allowed to do in moments of risk. Excessive centralization or vague escalation paths slow response and erode trust. Teams need clear lines around who decides what, how far their authority extends, and which trade-offs are acceptable. People should understand when they are expected to act on their own and when they need to slow down and bring others in. Those expectations do not take hold through policy alone. They are built through realistic scenarios, hands-on training, and leadership that models the behavior it expects. When that clarity is in place, fast decisions build confidence and trust instead of creating friction or second-guessing.

Visibility also matters. Polished quarterly reports that smooth over issues create false confidence. Leaders build real credibility when they are open about gaps, share what they have learned, and show steady progress. That kind of transparency makes it clear that assurance is about getting better, not pretending everything is perfect. When people see leaders acknowledge weaknesses and take action, they are far more likely to raise concerns themselves. The same dynamic holds with customers, partners, and regulators. Honest visibility strengthens trust because it replaces polished narratives with observable intent.

Recognition plays an equally important role. When individuals and teams are acknowledged for making decisions that reflect sound judgment and trust awareness, assurance starts to feel like leadership in action rather than administrative overhead. That recognition does not need to be elaborate. Sometimes it shows up in promotions, sometimes in a story shared at a town hall or in a team meeting. What matters is that it happens consistently. Over time, people learn that resilient behavior is noticed and valued. Assurance stops feeling like an obligation and starts to feel like something worth standing behind.

Use this checklist to evaluate whether assurance in your enterprise has moved beyond governance models and policies to become a living, operational capability that is visible in leadership, embedded in daily workflows, and reinforced through culture.

1 Alignment Across Layers

- ☐ Has the board shifted from reviewing static risk reports to asking performance-driven questions about resilience?
- ☐ Do executives allocate budget and mandate assurance as part of growth and innovation initiatives, not just compliance?
- ☐ Are middle managers equipped with practical metrics and tools to integrate assurance into team operations?
- ☐ Do frontline employees understand how their roles influence trust, and do they feel empowered to act when risks emerge?

2 Embedding in Core Functions

- ☐ HR: Are hiring, onboarding, access management, and performance reviews risk-informed and assurance-aware?
- ☐ Finance: Are resilience and recovery ROI models integrated into capital allocation and investment decisions?
- ☐ Legal: Do contracts and policies reflect operational assurance capabilities and enforceable obligations?
- ☐ Engineering: Is resilience designed into pipelines, observability, and code, not added as an afterthought?
- ☐ Procurement: Are vendor selection and monitoring processes based on control maturity, telemetry, and recovery readiness?

3 Feedback and Learning

- ☐ Do you have real-time telemetry available across functions, not just within security teams?
- ☐ Are periodic reviews capturing both quantitative metrics and qualitative lessons from multiple business units?
- ☐ Are post-incident retrospectives inclusive, blameless, and designed to extract learning that improves resilience?
- ☐ Does feedback flow vertically (board ↔ frontline) and horizontally (function ↔ function) across the enterprise?

4 Culture and Visibility

- ☐ Do leaders model assurance behaviors, reference trust metrics, and show up in assurance-related activities?
- ☐ Are assurance-related actions and successes recognized across the organization?
- ☐ Is there a climate of psychological safety that encourages employees to surface anomalies and concerns without fear?
- ☐ Do daily routines (stand-ups, retrospectives, and procurement evaluations) include assurance checkpoints?
- ☐ Are stories of resilience, recovery, and risk-informed decisions shared to reinforce cultural adoption?

5 Practical Enablement

- ☐ Are assurance signals embedded in workflows and tools so that risk-aware decisions are the easiest decisions?
- ☐ Do employees have clear escalation paths and decision rights in moments of uncertainty?
- ☐ Is training scenario-based, continuous, and role-specific, building judgment rather than just compliance awareness?

Executive Action: If you cannot answer "yes" to most of these questions, your assurance program may still be policy-driven rather than behavior-driven. Prioritize embedding assurance into functional workflows, leadership visibility, and cultural reinforcement to ensure it becomes a living capability rather than a governance artifact.

Figure 6.4 Practical Checklist: Embedding Assurance from Boardroom to Break Room. Image created by the author using Gamma.

As assurance matures, it must scale beyond isolated functions. Practices proven in security or IT must extend into finance, human resources, legal, procurement, and engineering. The principles should remain consistent even if their expression differs. Scaling requires shared language, compatible tools, and flexibility in execution. A maturity model can provide structure, but real scale comes from integration across the enterprise.

There is also an external dimension. Organizations that live assurance attract stronger partners, retain customer loyalty, and inspire investor confidence. Stakeholders increasingly expect transparency, ethical conduct, and resilience. Organizations that can demonstrate these qualities through credible practice signal competence, not just compliance. That reputation becomes a strategic advantage.

At its highest level, assurance becomes part of organizational identity. Designers build with resilience in mind. Procurement evaluates vendors for readiness. Human resources treats cultural signals as data. Finance considers resilience in investment decisions. Boards link assurance directly to value creation, and trust becomes everyone's responsibility.

Moving from awareness to action demands commitment and persistence. It requires abandoning the idea that assurance is a constraint and embracing it as an enabler. It calls for leadership that is willing to invest, model the right behaviors, and learn openly. The reward is an organization that navigates disruption with confidence, recovers without panic, and leads through uncertainty with clarity. That is the real discipline of Integrated Assurance. It is the practice of building trust into every role, every process, and every decision. See Figure 6.4: Practical Checklist: Embedding Assurance from Boardroom to Break Room.

Part III

Resilience in the Wild

Use Cases and Outcomes

Chapter 7

Surviving the Surge

7.1 ANATOMY OF A HIGH-STAKES ENTERPRISE INCIDENT

Disruption is the moment when strategy becomes reality. It exposes the true nature of an organization's readiness, not in slide decks or dashboards, but in how people respond when the margin for error disappears. In this chapter, we move beyond theory into the crucible of real-world events. The following use cases reflect high-stakes situations where the principles of Integrated Assurance can be identified as proof points that resilience is measurable, manageable, and, most importantly, achievable.

Each scenario, drawn from sectors as diverse as energy, finance, healthcare, defense, and retail, provides a granular view into how the assurance model can function at the intersection of business operations and risk. From ransomware attacks that strike critical infrastructure, to insider threats during IPO preparations, to AI bias triggering regulatory scrutiny, these are not fictional threats. They represent the real shape of modern risk, which is distributed, persistent, and amplified by interdependencies. What binds them together is not the nature of the threat but the structure of the response. Each organization demonstrates evidence that Integrated Assurance, at the core of an operating model with a focus on the relevant impact of the situation, can transform crisis into control.

The business value, or relevant impact, of the assurance model becomes evident in the outcomes it achieves, such as minimized downtime, preserved brand reputation, streamlined regulatory response, and customer trust reinforced. In one use case, the energy operator who restored production without providing a ransom payment to the attackers saw regulatory goodwill increase and contract renewals accelerate. In another use case, the global retailer whose logistics collapse was resolved in hours, not weeks, avoided brand erosion during peak season. These are strategic business advantages born of operational maturity.

Across these incidents, a clear pattern of cross-functional fluency built on trust and shared telemetry emerges. Legal and HR were involved from the start, taking active roles in coordinating the response. Engineering and security communicated seamlessly, while compliance brought focus instead of friction. Integrated Assurance shows its true power not by eliminating every failure, but by ensuring each one can be contained, understood, and recovered from in proportion to its actual impact on the organization. Instead of isolating assurance within specialized domains, this model extends it across the enterprise so that responsibility for risk is collective rather than confined.

Each use case also uncovers a less visible but equally critical value of the strengthening of organizational muscle. Through retrospective learning, systems were refined, behaviors adjusted, contracts restructured, and governance deepened. The response to the crisis became a catalyst for transformation and not just about recovery. Where organizations had once

DOI: 10.1201/9781003685982-10

struggled with fragmented accountability, they emerged with integrated insight. In this way, the assurance model becomes more than an incident response framework, instead it becomes a lever for cultural, operational, and strategic growth.

These narratives are not simply cautionary tales. They are case-based affirmations that the assurance model can turn disruption into a proving ground for resilience. For enterprise leaders, the lesson is clear: Resilience is no longer just about backup systems and redundant infrastructure. It is about how your people, processes, and partners behave under pressure. The stories that follow demonstrate that the assurance model can be embedded into the DNA of an organization. By measuring risk based on its relevant impact, a crisis doesn't need to become a moment of chaos, it can be a time of coordinated competence.

7.2 RESPONDING TO HIGH-STAKES INCIDENTS WITH INTEGRATED ASSURANCE

The following use cases illustrate the assurance model in action, not as an abstract framework, but as a living, operational advantage. Drawn from real-world scenarios across industries, these narratives demonstrate how resilient organizations detect, contain, and recover from complex threats with speed and clarity.

Note: The use cases in this chapter are fictionalized composites inspired by publicly documented incidents, sector case studies, and cybersecurity advisories. Specific details have been altered for narrative clarity.

7.2.1 Use case: Ransomeware in a multinational energy operator[1]

When a global energy company becomes a target, the stakes extend far beyond technology. Every refinery, pipeline, and terminal is not just an operational asset but a node in the world's economic stability. A ransomware strike in this environment is not a technical glitch, but a geopolitical event. See Figure 7.1: Use Case: Ransomware in a Multinational Energy Operator.

7.2.2 Use case: Supply chain collapse at a global retailer[2]

Retailers live or die by the speed of their supply chain. When customers expect goods at their doorstep within hours, any disruption ripples into lost revenue and reputational harm. A logistics breakdown during peak season is more than an IT outage, it is an existential risk to customer trust. See Figure 7.2: Use Case: Supply Chain Collapse at a Global Retailer.

7.2.3 Use case: Insider data theft in a tech firm[3]

The closer a company gets to an IPO, the more valuable its intellectual property becomes. In this climate, one insider with access to model architectures or proprietary code can inflict damage that competitors or regulators will exploit. The quiet theft of information is often more dangerous than the loudest external attack. See Figure 7.3: Use Case: Insider Data Theft in a Tech Firm.

Figure 7.1 Use Case: Ransomware in a Multinational Energy Operator.

Image created by the author using Gamma.

7.2.4 Use case: Safety failure in an industrial plant[4]

Industrial environments operate under unforgiving conditions. One overlooked fault in a sensor or control loop can escalate into a catastrophe. The difference between safe production and disaster often rests not on machines, but on the awareness and decisions of people under pressure. See Figure 7.4: Use Case: Safety Failure in an Industrial Plant.

7.2.5 Use case: Cloud misconfiguration at a financial services firm[5]

The speed of cloud adoption often outpaces the discipline of governance. For financial services, a single exposed bucket of customer data is more than a compliance issue. It is a direct threat to trust, and trust is the true currency of the sector. See Figure 7.5: Use Case: Cloud Misconfiguration at a Financial Service Firm.

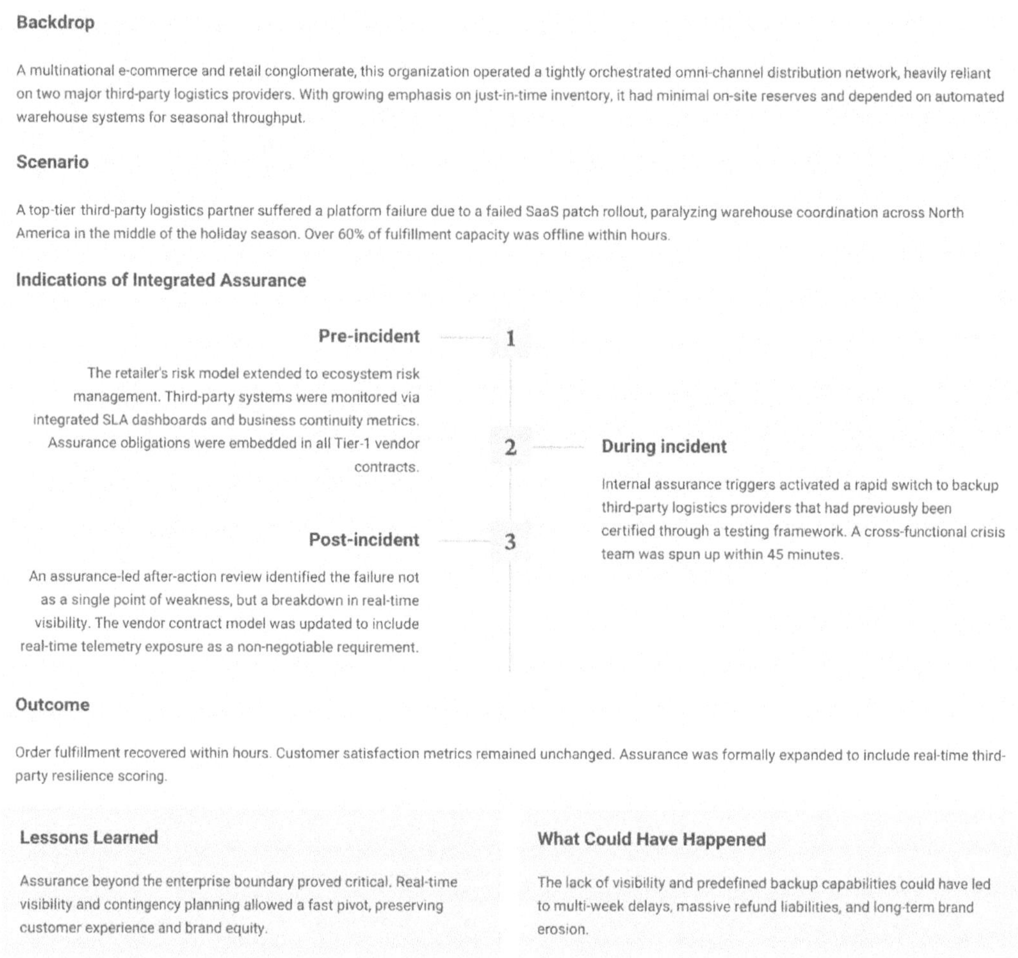

Figure 7.2 Use Case: Supply Chain Collapse at a Global Retailer.

Image created by the author using Gamma.

7.2.6 Use case: Credential stuffing attack on a healthcare provider[6]

Patients expect healthcare providers to protect their most personal information. A surge of fraudulent login attempts against a patient portal may appear as noise, but behind it lies the potential for stolen identities, broken trust, and regulatory exposure. See Figure 7.6: Use Case: Credential Stuffing Attack on a Healthcare Provider.

7.2.7 Use case: Legal exposure from vendor data breach[7]

Law firms are built on confidentiality. When vendors that process discovery data are compromised, the legal exposure can eclipse the technical one. A single breach can undermine decades of earned client trust and jeopardize ongoing litigation. See Figure 7.7: Use Case: Legal Exposure from Vendor Data Breach.

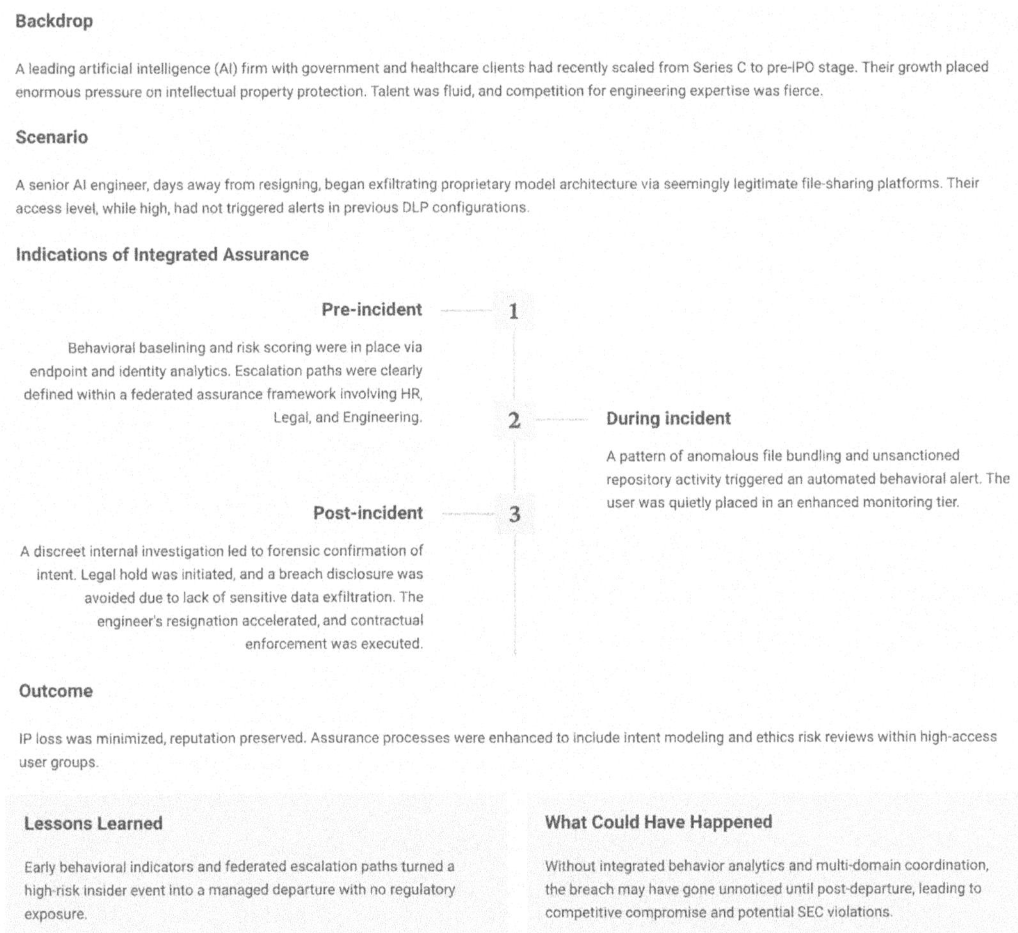

Figure 7.3 Use Case: Insider Data Theft in a Tech Firm.

Image created by the author using Gamma.

7.2.8 Use case: Nation-state phishing campaign at a defense contractor[8]

In defense supply chains, every employee's inbox is a potential entry point for adversaries. A single click can compromise classified work, disrupt alliances, and damage national security. These attacks are about influence and leverage and not stolen passwords. See Figure 7.8: Use Case: Nation-State Phishing Campaign at a Defense Contractor.

7.2.9 Use case: Ethics violation in research and development department[9]

Scientific discovery demands both rigor and integrity. In an environment where milestones drive investment and careers, the temptation to manipulate data is real. When research integrity is compromised, the consequences extend far beyond compliance, threatening credibility and market value. See Figure 7.9: Use Case: Ethics Violation in Research and Development Department.

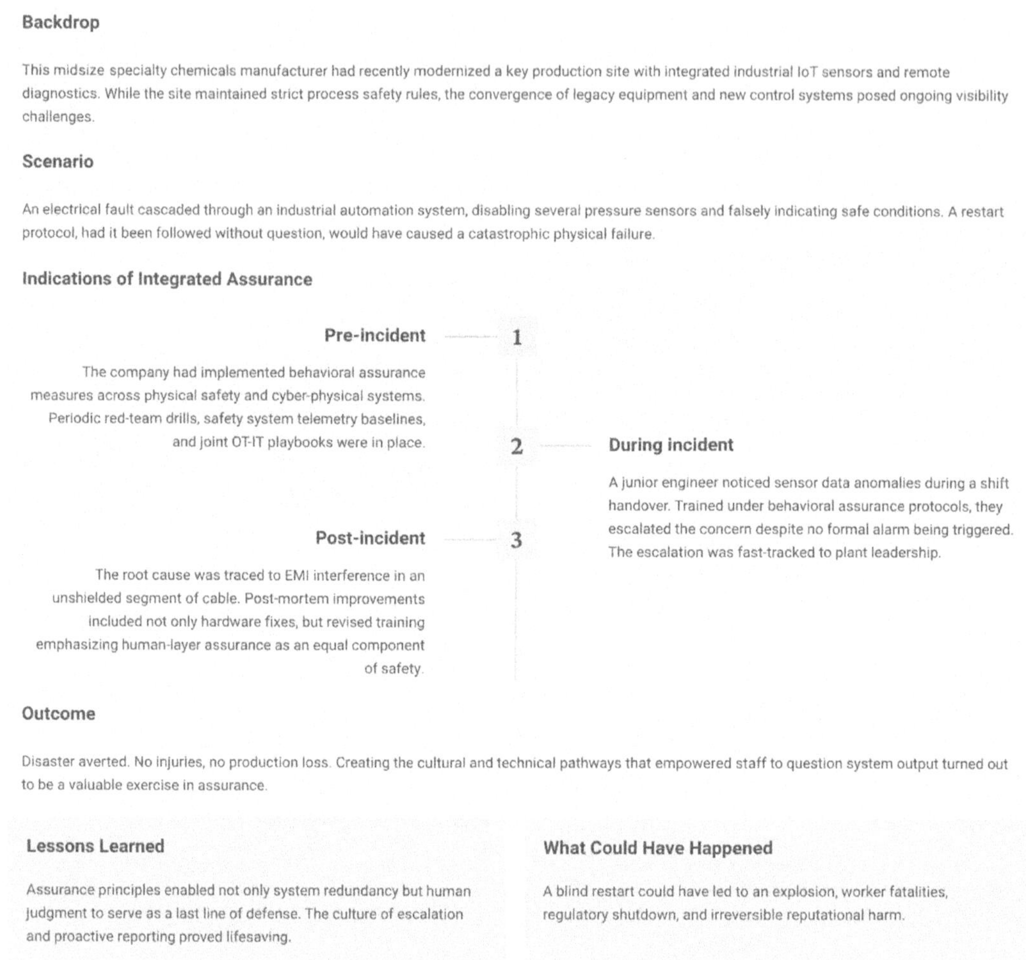

Figure 7.4 Use Case: Safety Failure in an Industrial Plant.

Image created by the author using Gamma.

7.2.10 Use case: Misinformation attack on media organization[10]

For a media organization, credibility is its lifeblood. When attackers weaponize compromised contributor accounts to publish false stories, the result is more than disinformation. It is an attack on public trust and democratic discourse itself. See Figure 7.10: Use Case: Misinformation Attack on Media Organization.

7.2.11 Use case: Executive spear-phishing during merger and acquisition negotiations[11]

During merger and acquisition negotiations, information is power. A single leaked document can shift valuations, trigger insider trading concerns, or collapse a deal. Executives, already moving fast, become prime targets for precision social engineering. See Figure 7.11: Use Case: Executive Spear-Phishing during Merger and Acquisition Negotiations.

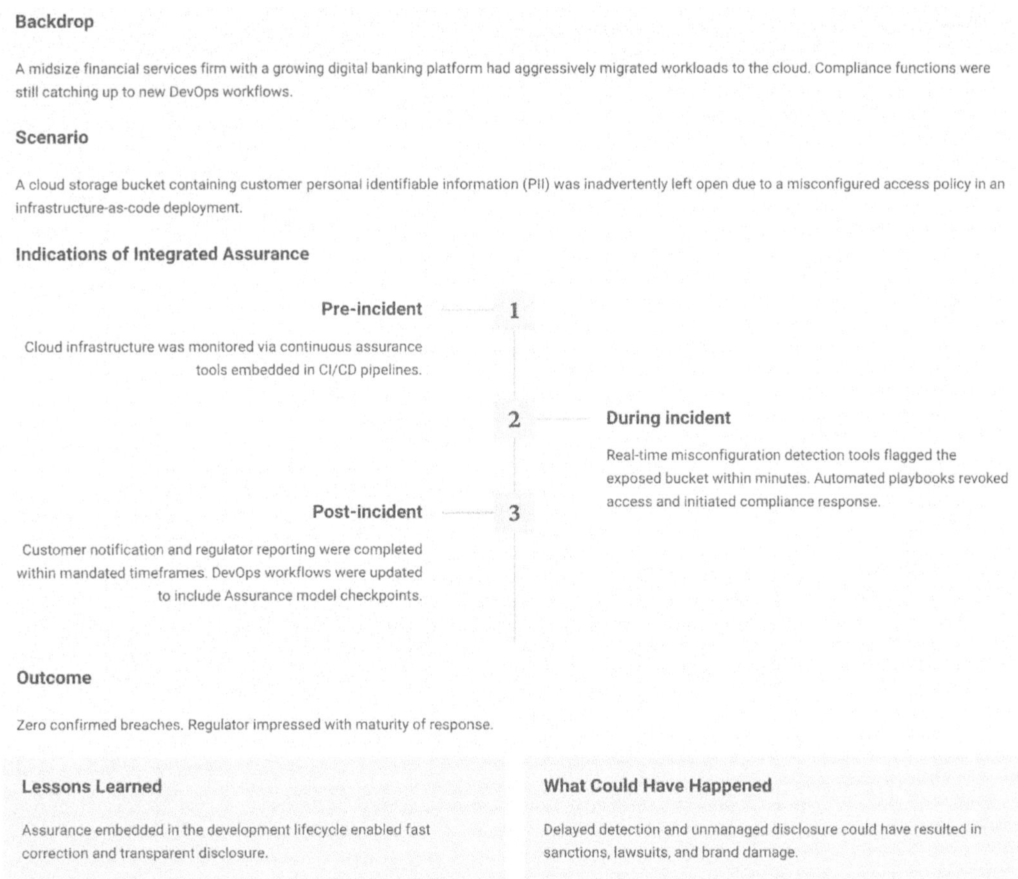

Figure 7.5 Use Case: Cloud Misconfiguration at a Financial Services Firm.
Image created by the author using Gamma.

7.2.12 Use case: AI model bias and regulatory scrutiny[12]

AI models are judged not only on their accuracy but also on their fairness. When bias creeps into automated lending decisions, it ceases to be a technical problem and becomes a regulatory and ethical crisis. In these moments, governance defines survival. See Figure 7.12: Use Case: AI Model Bias and Regulatory Scrutiny.

7.3 CONVERGENCE IN ACTION

During high-pressure incidents, traditional organizational boundaries become liabilities. This section explores how Integrated Assurance drives cross-functional fluency, enabling teams to respond with cohesion, shared telemetry, and aligned decision-making, accelerating outcomes when speed matters most. The use cases in this chapter showcase how the assurance model can be used to transform incident response from a reactive scramble into a structured, confident execution of a cross-functional strategy.

Every second counts in a crisis, but only if you know what's actually happening. The assurance model can make visibility actionable by unifying real-time telemetry across cloud, identity, network, endpoint, and human behavior into a coherent operational picture. In these

Backdrop

A regional healthcare provider had invested significantly in digitizing its patient services, offering online appointment scheduling, test results, and integrated telehealth. However, like many in the healthcare sector, it was balancing legacy IT infrastructure with modern digital interfaces, and its workforce was still maturing in security awareness.

Scenario

Off-hours traffic anomalies emerged on patient portal systems. Initially dismissed as increased usage, deeper analysis revealed a credential stuffing campaign using previously breached credentials from unrelated third-party compromises. The attackers rotated IPs and user agents to evade traditional rate-limit defenses.

Indications of Integrated Assurance

1 **Pre-incident**

Identity telemetry and behavioral analytics were embedded in IAM systems. Continuous monitoring of login attempts, location, and timing baselines enabled deviation detection. Staff had received phishing and access training quarterly.

2 **During incident**

Anomaly detection systems flagged hundreds of failed logins paired with low-entropy password attempts. Bot mitigation controls were auto-triggered, shifting the portal to enforce step-up MFA for all suspicious attempts. SOC analysts were able to correlate signals across identity, network, and cloud layers within 15 minutes.

3 **Post-incident**

A forensics sweep confirmed no unauthorized account access. The organization coordinated threat intelligence sharing with regional healthcare providers and government partners, contributing to a broader industry warning about the attack pattern.

Outcome

No patient health information (PHI) was accessed. The organization's response was cited positively in a follow-up review by state regulators, and the proactive measures increased confidence from health insurers.

Lessons Learned

Modern patient identity systems must treat assurance as continuous, not static. Behavioral baselining was the difference between an event and an exposure.

What Could Have Happened

Dozens to hundreds of patient accounts could have been breached before detection, leading to class-action lawsuits under HIPAA, reputational damage, and potential CMS contract termination.

Figure 7.6 Use Case: Credential Stuffing Attack on a Healthcare Provider.
Image created by the author using Gamma.

cases, leaders didn't make guesses; they made data-informed decisions. This transformed reactive firefighting into a purposeful, measured response.

For instance, the financial services firm's cloud misconfiguration was detected within minutes due to continuous assurance embedded in CI/CD pipelines. The defense contractor's engineers avoided a nation-state breach because anomaly signals across email metadata, user behavior, and spoof detection surfaced quickly. In both cases, telemetry didn't just alert teams, it empowered them to act with precision.

From a business perspective, this visibility translated into fewer delays, more accurate root cause attribution, and higher confidence in post-mortem reviews. Executives had a single version of the truth and weren't left wondering "What happened?" or "How bad is it?". That clarity streamlined regulatory reporting, calmed customers, and supported evidence-based communications with the board. This kind of decision quality is an executive differentiator. In the modern organization, resilience isn't just about detecting threats; it's about

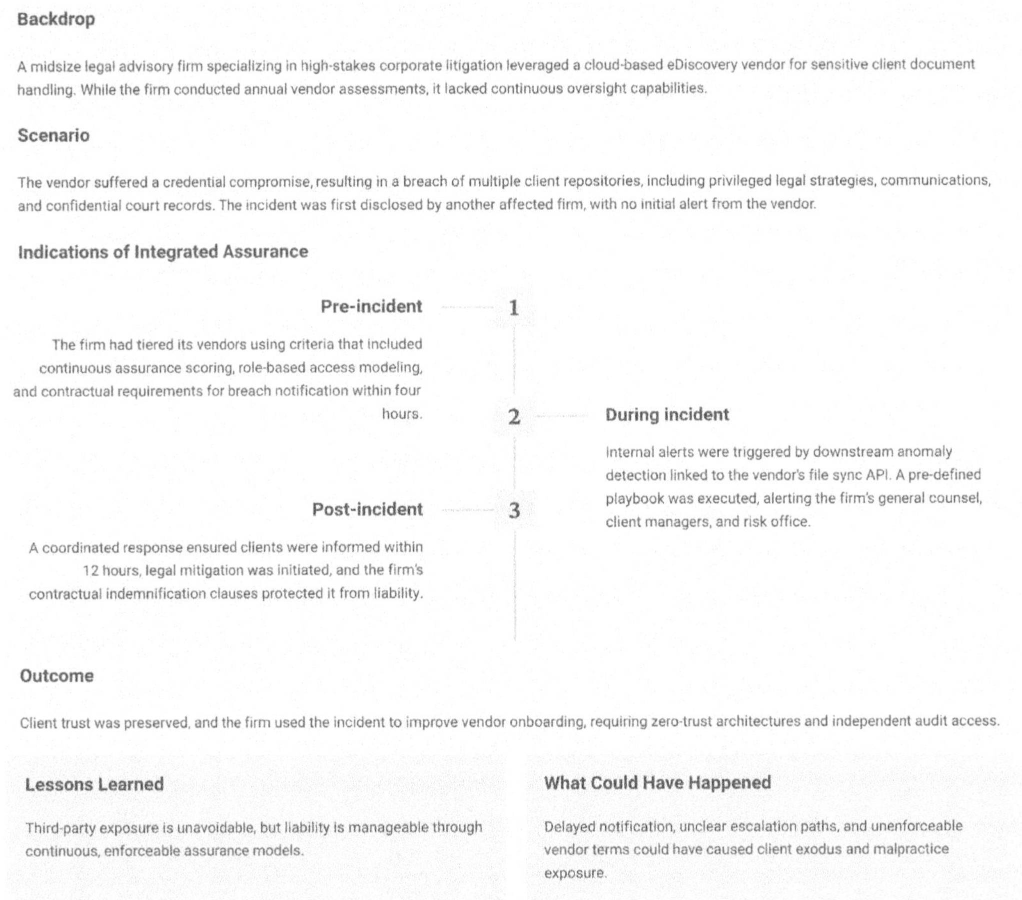

Figure 7.7 Use Case: Legal Exposure from Vendor Data Breach.
Image created by the author using Gamma.

understanding them fast enough to outpace their impact. The assurance model operationalizes this intelligence, making insight not a lucky outcome, but a built-in capability that leaders can depend on.

The most decisive factor in rapid containment across the incidents was not a specific tool or control; it was fluency across business functions. Organizations that had embedded principles of Integrated Assurance into their daily rhythms experienced virtually no jurisdictional delays. Legal teams didn't need to request access to security data, and engineering leaders didn't hesitate to engage HR or compliance. Everyone had trained together, executed tabletop exercises, and operated from the same playbooks. That cohesion became the most powerful accelerant in their response.

In the energy, retail, and legal sectors, we saw coordination compress incident timelines from days to hours. When ransomware hit critical infrastructure or a third-party logistics provider went offline, the ability to execute synchronized response protocols—spanning legal disclosures, technical remediation, and customer communication—avoided chaos and enabled recovery. The cross-functional nature of artificial intelligence reduced reliance on heroic efforts and replaced them with practiced discipline.

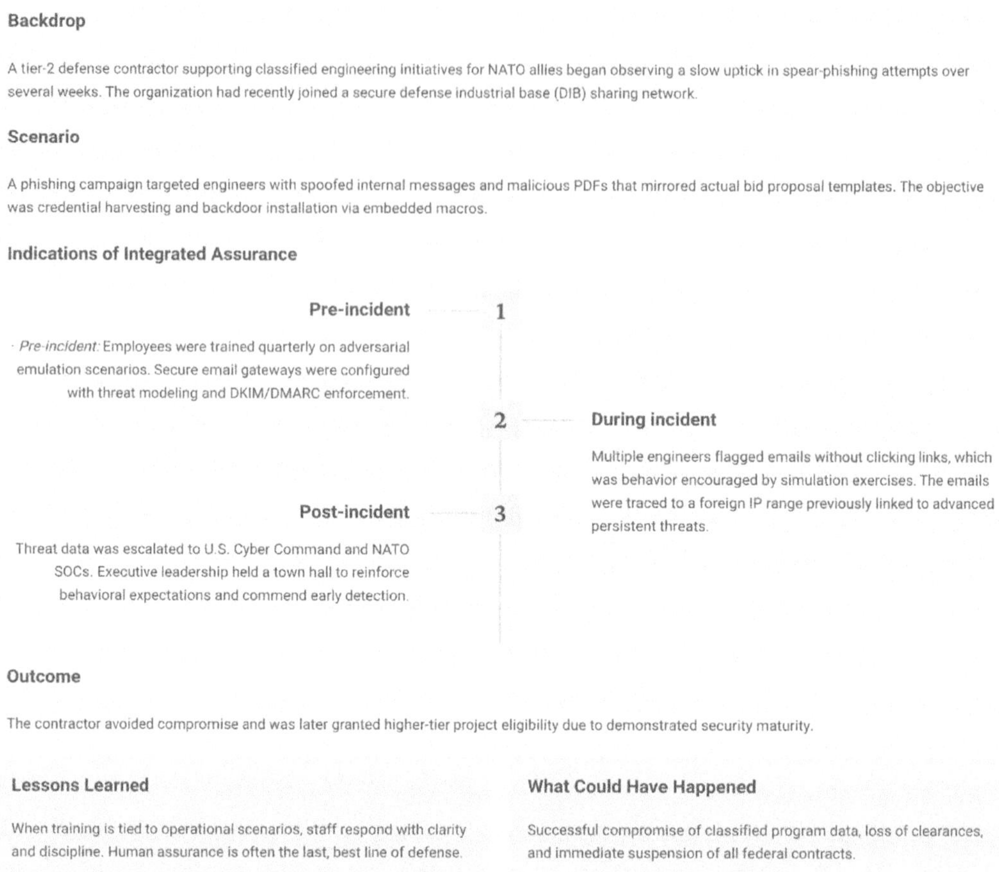

Figure 7.8 Use Case: Nation-State Phishing Campaign at a Defense Contractor.
Image created by the author using Gamma.

The business impact of this level of coordination cannot be overstated. Rapid alignment meant faster time to resolution, minimized regulatory exposure, and reduced customer churn. Executive stakeholders were able to issue informed public statements within hours, backed by verifiable data. More importantly, organizations emerged with internal trust intact, and people across the organization had confidence in one another's roles and responses.

Strategically, this sets a new standard for operational resilience. organizations that function well under stress are more than secure, they are credible. They inspire confidence from regulators, partners, investors, and customers alike. The assurance model doesn't just help organizations respond better, it helps them be perceived as better governed and more trustworthy, even in crisis.

While much focus in security is placed on technical controls, the most impactful interventions in these case studies came from people, junior engineers, security analysts, and finance team members, who acted decisively in the face of ambiguity. What made this possible was an investment in cultural readiness—psychological safety, behavioral baselining, and clear escalation paths.

In the industrial safety failure, a junior technician escalated sensor inconsistencies despite the absence of alarms. In the insider threat scenario, behavioral analytics flagged risky

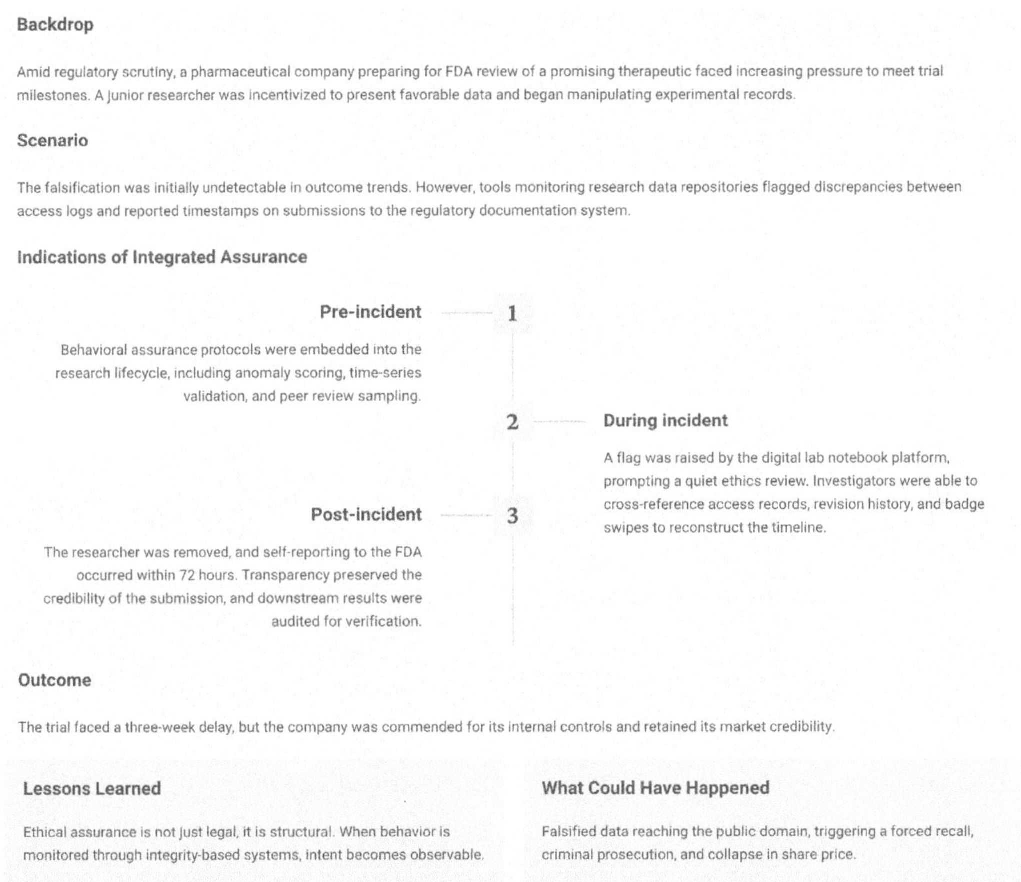

Figure 7.9 Use Case: Ethics Violation in Research and Development Department.
Image created by the author using Gamma.

exfiltration patterns before any sensitive data was leaked. In both situations, it was the human-in-the-loop, trained and empowered, that prevented escalation into catastrophe.

The business value here is profound. Where traditional models rely on compliance checklists and technical guardrails, Integrated Assurance incorporates behavioral assurance to extend security into the domain of decision-making. It equips staff with the confidence to speak up, question systems, and challenge assumptions, which are capabilities that are essential in high-consequence environments.

Culturally, this creates an environment where security isn't feared, it's shared. That cultural posture is a critical advantage when attracting talent, managing change, or navigating public scrutiny. Behavioral intelligence becomes a proactive, strategic layer of assurance that reduces risk in the most complex edge cases.

7.4 LESSONS FROM CYBERATTACKS AND MAJOR OUTAGES

History shows that every organization that faced a major cyberattack or system outage experienced failure at some level. The difference was never about avoiding disruption altogether

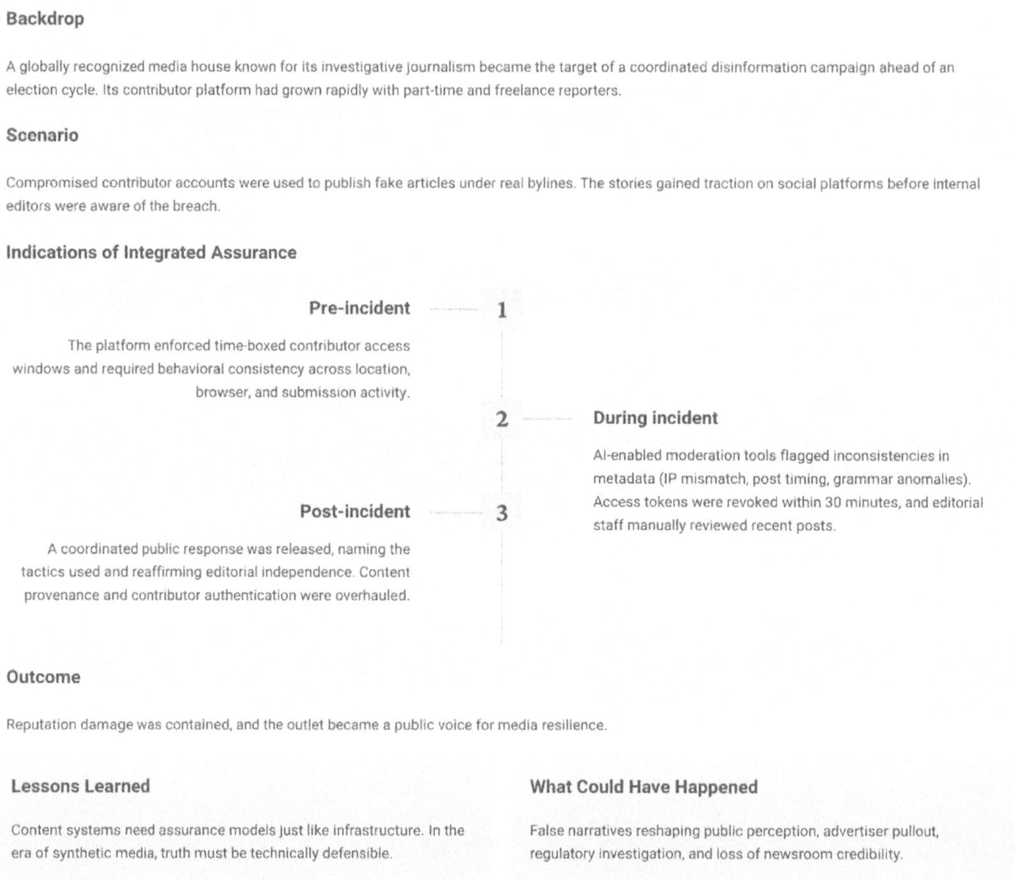

Figure 7.10 Use Case: Misinformation Attack on Media Organization.
Image created by the author using Gamma.

but about how quickly and effectively they met it. The organizations that held their ground had prepared long before the crisis arrived.

Preparation was deliberate and systematic. Playbooks gave teams clear steps for specific incidents. Red team drills tested defenses by simulating real adversaries. Tabletop exercises brought leaders and frontline staff together to rehearse communication, escalation, and decision-making. Some organizations secured backup partners who could take over when primary providers failed. These actions were not isolated events. They were linked to governance processes that captured lessons, clarified responsibilities, and embedded accountability across the enterprise.

Prevention was never absolute. What mattered was containment. Intrusions that could have escalated were isolated. Misconfigurations that threatened operations were corrected quickly. Malicious campaigns that might have forced a shutdown instead produced delays that were disruptive but manageable. These outcomes did not stem from perfect defenses but from a culture of readiness reinforced through practice.

The impact of preparation extended beyond technical containment. A company that controlled a ransomware outbreak without extended downtime preserved customer trust. Another that disclosed a data breach within hours reduced liability and regulatory exposure.

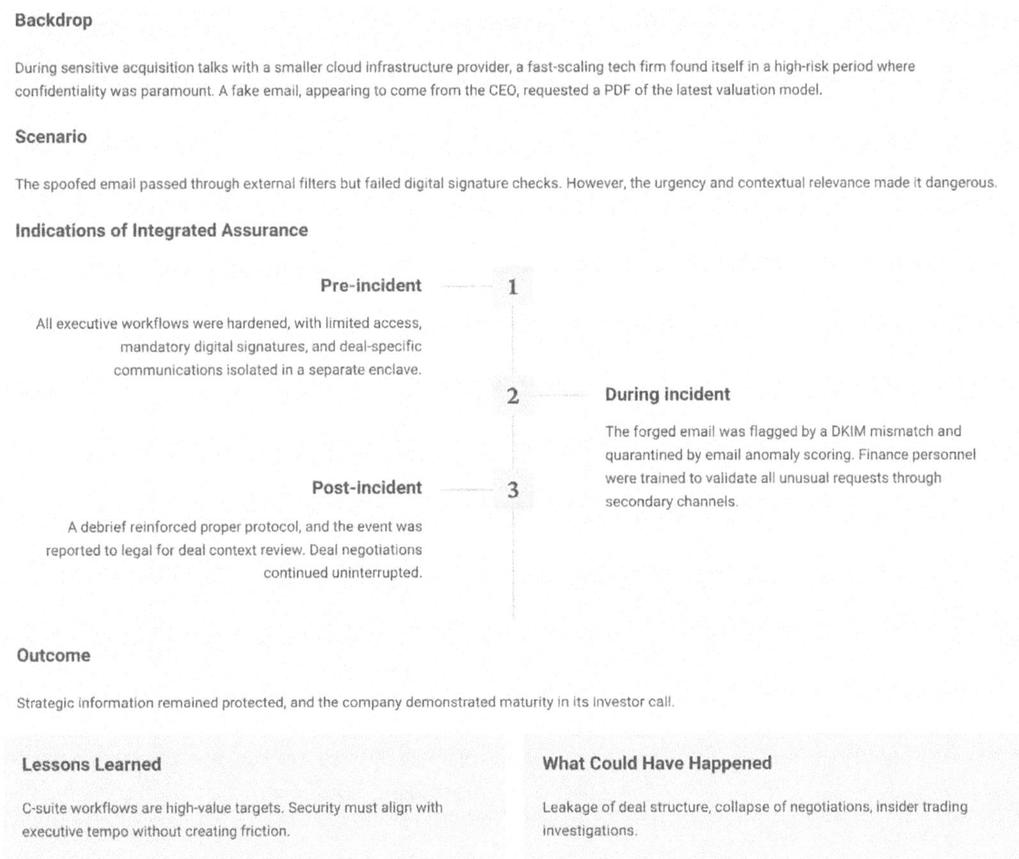

Figure 7.11 Use Case: Executive Spear-Phishing during Merger and Acquisition Negotiations. Image created by the author using Gamma.

Investors gained confidence in organizations that demonstrated faster recovery capability than competitors. What could have been existential threats became temporary challenges.

Resilience proved to be the result of practice, not theory. Tools and policies without rehearsal provided little assurance. True capability came from preparation repeated until it became second nature. A red team exercise may appear as a cost, yet in a real incident, the saved minutes became millions of dollars preserved. A tabletop drill might seem routine, but it created muscle memory that guided executives when a crisis arrived.

Integrated Assurance provides the structure for this preparation. It ensures that resilience is embedded into daily operations instead of being left to isolated teams. Under this model, assurance is not a checklist or an annual event but a cycle of readiness, verification, and improvement. Staff at every level understand expectations and escalation paths. Executives receive operational signals instead of polished reports. The organization operates as a coordinated system able to absorb disruption without losing control.

This perspective also reframes the conversation. Security becomes a matter of capability, not fear or compliance. Success is measured by resilience, which can be designed, rehearsed, and proven. The returns appear in lower downtime, reduced penalties, stronger customer trust, and greater investor confidence.

Backdrop

A fintech startup launched a consumer lending AI model trained on historic financial data. Early success drew the attention of investors and regulators, but outputs soon raised red flags for disparate impact.

Scenario

Audits by a national regulatory agency found the model rejected a disproportionate number of applicants from protected groups. The firm faced the risk of enforcement action for algorithmic discrimination.

Indications of Integrated Assurance

1 **Pre-incident**

Machine Learning lifecycle was developed with fairness testing, explainability audits, and governance checkpoints tied to model retraining.

2 **During incident**

Bias was traced to skewed data in historic defaults from legacy bank portfolios. The AI team triggered a retraining pipeline and rebalanced the dataset using demographic parity adjustments.

3 **Post-incident**

Transparent logs and documented fairness decisions were submitted to the regulator. The firm voluntarily paused approvals and relaunched the model with updated parameters.

Outcome

Regulatory fines were avoided, trust was reestablished, and the company gained reputational capital as a responsible innovator.

Lessons Learned

Assurance isn't just for security; it's for algorithmic accountability. Governance must be built into the entire data and decision pipeline.

What Could Have Happened

Civil rights lawsuits, license revocation, investor retreat, and platform bans from digital marketplaces.

Figure 7.12 Use Case: AI Model Bias and Regulatory Scrutiny.
Image created by the author using Gamma.

Case studies highlight benefits beyond recovery. One company used lessons from an attack to restructure its supply chain, reducing fragility while gaining efficiency. Another identified weak communication channels during a red team drill, and improvements were carried into daily operations. Resilience, once operationalized, became a competitive advantage rather than only a defensive measure.

The assurance model is not another compliance framework. It represents a way of operating where resilience is integrated with business performance. Governance, risk, operations, and security work in alignment. Preparation is distributed across the organization; hence, the response is clear and coordinated.

When rare but severe events occur, organizations following this approach contain the impact. They maintain customer confidence, demonstrate accountability to regulators, and show investors that they remain steady. Over time, these outcomes build trust as a strategic asset.

The essential point is direct. Failure will always come, whether through malicious activity, system fault, or human error. What matters is the ability to withstand and recover without losing identity, credibility, or market position. Integrated Assurance enables this outcome by weaving resilience into the business fabric and making it a practiced, lasting strength.

7.4.1 Supply chain and geopolitical disruption

Supply chain fragility was a consistent theme across industries, from eDiscovery vendors to logistics platforms and remote OT support. Organizations that endured third-party disruption had established continuous, contractual, and measurable vendor assurance.

Telemetry sharing, resilience scoring, and breach notification obligations were written into tier-1 vendor agreements. When incidents struck, escalation paths were already defined, obligations documented, and backup options preapproved. This foresight preserved revenue, legal standing, and customer trust. Instead of crisis meetings and blame, response teams pivoted smoothly to alternatives and minimized disruption. Vendors, under contractual pressure, improved their own standards, raising resilience across the ecosystem.

Third-party assurance was not treated as a checkbox but as a framework of visibility and accountability. Integrated Assurance converted passive dependencies into resilient partnerships.

7.4.2 Recovering faster than competitors

Reputation was shaped by transparency. Organizations that disclosed incidents openly, explained their response, and provided evidence of control strengthened trust. Examples included an energy operator that shared its ransomware recovery process, a law firm that informed clients immediately of a vendor breach, and a fintech that described its AI retraining methods. These were not only responses but demonstrations of maturity. Transparency preserved loyalty, avoided penalties, and reassured investors. Analysts recognized them as credible and resilient. Integrated Assurance supported this transparency by institutionalizing evidence, accountability, and communication pathways.

7.4.3 Security enables innovation, when baked into the build

Digital transformation demanded speed, but governance had to keep pace. Organizations that built Integrated Assurance into the development lifecycle proved that innovation and assurance strengthen each other. Cloud deployments, AI models, and DevOps pipelines carried risk, yet assurance practices converted those risks into manageable conditions. A fintech under regulatory review could retrain and relaunch an AI model because fairness and explainability were embedded from the start. A financial services firm corrected a cloud misconfiguration within minutes because assurance was integrated into its CI/CD process. These outcomes created reputational capital with regulators, customers, and boards.

This is secure-by-design in practice. Safety is not added after the fact but built into the architecture, allowing innovation to scale without uncontrolled exposure. Integrated Assurance makes this possible by aligning resilience with transformation.

7.5 IAMM CASE MAPPING

Ransomware has become one of the clearest indicators of assurance maturity. It reveals whether governance holds authority, whether operations are connected, and whether culture enables a unified response. The IAMM offers a structured way to understand how organizations perform under this kind of stress.

At Level 1, ransomware response is marked by confusion. Ownership is unclear, and communication collapses. Security teams move quickly to contain damage while executives demand constant updates. Legal counsel hesitates to approve outside support, and recovery drags on because escalation paths are undefined. Reports are written after the fact, often to satisfy external parties rather than to guide improvement. The absence of governance and coordinated operations weakens confidence across the organization.

At Level 2, procedures exist but lack force. Incident response plans are documented and rarely tested. Governance committees meet on schedule, yet their influence fades when an attack begins. Teams know their roles in theory but struggle to apply them in practice. Security may isolate systems without notifying operations, which prolongs downtime. Executive communication is uneven, and external messaging appears inconsistent. The delay in coordination leads to longer outages and diminished trust among employees and customers.

Level 3 brings coordination. Incident response playbooks are defined, and tabletop exercises occur regularly. Governance forums review incident reports, and risk managers help with planning. During a real event, escalation paths are known, and collaboration improves. Operations and security work together to restore services by priority. However, much of the process remains manual, and interdependencies are not fully understood. Performance improves, but gaps in timing and information still exist.

Level 4 marks a turning point. Assurance becomes part of daily operations. Playbooks are automated where appropriate, and detection systems integrate threat intelligence. Governance receives live updates, and decisions rely on data. Legal, communications, and technical teams operate through shared dashboards. Metrics such as containment time and recovery duration are tracked and reviewed. The enterprise behaves as a single system, and resilience becomes visible in faster recovery and restored confidence.

At Level 5, resilience is institutionalized. Preparedness is built into the way systems are designed and delivered. Segmentation is standard, backups are immutable, and recovery procedures are continuously tested. Governance treats incident simulation as a board-level priority. Executives understand operational realities and engage in resilience reviews. Culture reinforces accountability in constructive ways. Post-incident analysis focuses on learning rather than blame. This level of maturity transforms response from crisis management into controlled execution.

A comparison illustrates the distinction. Two financial firms experience similar ransomware attacks. The first, operating at Level 2 maturity, spends several days determining which systems are affected. Coordination between IT and security is slow, and executives debate how to communicate externally. The second, operating at Level 4, identifies compromised assets within hours, activates automated containment, and communicates through established governance channels. Its recovery is faster, and public trust remains intact. The outcome reflects discipline and maturity, not fortune.

IAMM demonstrates that ransomware is more than a technical threat. It is an enterprise-wide test of assurance capability. Organizations that see assurance only as compliance remain trapped in reactive cycles. Those that mature through IAMM develop response muscle that aligns speed with purpose.

The application of this model begins with a review. After each incident, organizations can examine how each domain performed. Governance should confirm authority and decision clarity. Operations should assess automation and communication effectiveness. Culture should be evaluated for cooperation and accountability. Metrics should capture recovery performance and trust restoration. These reflections identify the current level of maturity and shape the next phase of improvement.

IAMM reframes ransomware response as a measure of organizational integrity. It exposes whether resilience is designed into the enterprise or improvised when under pressure. In mature organizations, assurance is not an afterthought. It is the structure that sustains trust when everything else is under attack.

7.6 CONCLUSION

When a crisis arrives, theories fade and only capability remains. The examples in this chapter show that resilience is not a fixed condition but a discipline embedded in daily operations. Organizations that practice Integrated Assurance demonstrate that resilience is not an outcome of luck or isolated expertise but the product of preparation and integration. Their success did not stem from avoiding disruption altogether. Ransomware still struck, supply chains still faltered, and misconfigurations still occurred. What set them apart was the ability to detect, interpret, contain, and recover before failures spread across the organization. That ability had been built long before the disruption took place.

Preparedness was the defining characteristic. These organizations had rehearsed their responses in playbooks. They had invested in telemetry that provided meaningful signals. They had written contractual terms that bound third parties to assurance practices. They had reinforced the right behaviors through training, culture, and accountability. None of those measures eliminated disruption, but they transformed its impact. Instead of paralysis, leaders and teams operated with fluency. Instead of fractured responses, they moved with coordination.

Integrated Assurance reframes risk management from a defensive exercise into a source of strategic strength. It replaces fragmented oversight with a working model that safeguards not just systems, but the confidence of customers, partners, and regulators. The impact shows up in measurable ways. Incidents surface sooner. Teams move in step. Recovery happens faster and with less friction. Organizations that performed best did not rely on heroics or centralized control. They invested in a shared understanding of assurance, a consistent operational view grounded in real telemetry, and a federated decision model that allowed action without waiting for permission. Cohesion became their multiplier. Tools played a role, but cohesion proved more valuable than any individual platform.

In moments of disruption, speed matters only when it is guided by clarity. That clarity comes from visibility. In every example, access to a single source of truth distinguished effective responses from chaotic ones. In a healthcare setting, anomalies in credentials were caught before they spread. In a technology company, unusual file movements were contained before they signaled a breach. In an industrial operation, mismatched telemetry pointed to control system tampering and prevented escalation. None of these outcomes depended on perfect foresight. They depended on data that was real-time, complete, and contextual. Assurance turned data into direction.

Visibility, however, is only a foundation. Action is what converts awareness into resilience. The organizations profiled here stood out because they treated assurance as a behavioral discipline as much as a technical one. People were not sidelined as liabilities. They were developed as an assurance surface. Engineers, analysts, and business staff alike were encouraged to observe, question, and report. A finance team could recognize anomalies in vendor invoicing that tied back to credential misuse. A junior engineer could escalate a misaligned code deployment before it reached production. By aligning culture, tools, and trust, organizations transformed their people into guardians of resilience rather than passive participants.

Third parties played a critical role in nearly every narrative. No modern enterprise operates in isolation. Digital supply chains, cloud services, and outsourced operations form the backbone of today's business environment. Yet resilience cannot exceed the strength of the weakest provider. Integrated Assurance changes vendor relationships from transactional service contracts to governed partnerships. Contracts included explicit assurance provisions. Monitoring was continuous rather than episodic. Escalation paths were tested and enforced. When a vendor failed, the organization did not stumble blindly. It executed a plan, absorbing the disruption without losing control of its operations.

Recovery was another defining feature. In an economy where reputational capital equals financial capital, transparency in recovery proved as important as technical containment. Organizations that disclosed quickly, that communicated openly, and that showed how they improved were rewarded by customers and regulators alike. They were not punished for

Use this checklist to test whether your enterprise is prepared to manage and recover from high-stakes disruptions with Integrated Assurance principles.

1

Visibility and Telemetry

- ☐ Do we have real-time visibility across IT, OT, cloud, identity, and human behavior systems?
- ☐ Is our telemetry normalized and shared across functions, avoiding silos?
- ☐ Can leadership access a single version of the truth during crisis situations?

2

Preparedness and Playbooks

- ☐ Have we built and rehearsed cross-functional playbooks for ransomware, supply chain failures, insider threats, and cloud misconfigurations?
- ☐ Are tabletop exercises and red-team drills run regularly to test behavioral and technical readiness?
- ☐ Do we have backup partners and suppliers pre-qualified for rapid substitution during outages?

3

Coordination and Culture

- ☐ Are legal, HR, compliance, engineering, and security fluent in shared response protocols?
- ☐ Does our culture encourage escalation of anomalies even without formal alarms?
- ☐ Have we embedded behavioral assurance that empowers staff to act under ambiguity?

4

Vendor and Third-Party Assurance

- ☐ Do all tier-1 vendor contracts include telemetry sharing, resilience scoring, and breach notification SLAs?
- ☐ Are vendors tested through joint simulations and monitored continuously for assurance posture?
- ☐ Do escalation paths and indemnification clauses protect the enterprise during vendor failures?

5

Recovery and Transparency

- ☐ Are post-incident processes structured to ensure rapid restoration without ransom or regulatory penalties?
- ☐ Do we have clear guidelines for transparent disclosure to regulators, customers, and partners?
- ☐ Can we demonstrate assurance maturity in ways that strengthen reputation and investor confidence?

6

Innovation with Assurance

- ☐ Is assurance embedded into CI/CD pipelines, AI model governance, and digital workflows?
- ☐ Do we have fairness, explainability, and governance checkpoints for AI and ML models?
- ☐ Are transformation projects aligned with secure-by-design principles that enable both speed and safety?

☐ **Executive Action:** If any of the boxes remain unchecked, your organization is at risk of treating disruption as chaos instead of opportunity. Use this checklist to close gaps now, so that resilience becomes not just a defensive posture but a competitive advantage.

Figure 7.13 Practical Checklist: Surviving the Surge.

Image created by the author using Gamma.

experiencing incidents. They were recognized for managing them with discipline and honesty. Transparency became a differentiator. It built trust in markets where silence would have bred suspicion.

Innovation also took on a new dimension. Far from slowing digital ambitions, Integrated Assurance made those ambitions sustainable. By embedding controls in DevOps pipelines, misconfigurations were corrected within minutes rather than weeks. By integrating AI governance into model training, bias was retrained before regulators intervened. By strengthening identity assurance in financial operations, strategic transactions were shielded from impersonation attempts. Assurance enabled innovation to scale without sacrificing control. It proved that growth and governance could move in unison.

What these stories reveal is that Integrated Assurance is not a layer added to existing operations. It is a connective architecture that gives shape and direction to complexity. It does not weigh down the organization. It provides structure. It does not resist change. It channels it. In doing so, assurance shifts from being a perceived cost center to a core business competency. It becomes a source of competitive advantage, enabling organizations to move faster with discipline, to grow in complexity with clarity, and to empower autonomy while preserving accountability.

The test of resilience is not whether disruption arrives. Disruption is inevitable. The test is how an organization responds when it does. Success is not determined by the nature of the threat but by the maturity of the response. The organizations profiled here did not survive by chance. They survived because they had designed for integration. They had built systems where assurance was not an afterthought but a foundation.

When disruption arrived, they did not respond with fragmentation. They responded with fluency. That fluency turned potential crises into recoverable events. It protected operations, preserved trust, and allowed growth to continue even under stress. Integrated Assurance is the reason. It transformed resilience from a slogan into a capability, from a compliance goal into a business imperative.

Organizations that practice this discipline share a common outcome. They remain intact, they recover visibly, and they emerge stronger. Their example proves that resilience is not about being invulnerable. It is about being integrated. That is the true measure of success, and it is the standard toward which all organizations must now move. See Figure 7.13: Practical Checklist: Surviving the Surge.

NOTES

1 Inspired by public reports on the Colonial Pipeline ransomware attack (2021) and Dragos ICS threat briefings.
2 Inspired by public reports on the Amazon/Target fulfillment dependencies; SolarWinds impact on software supply chains, NIST 800–161, Gartner supply chain resilience reports.
3 Inspired by public reports on the Waymo v. Uber, Tesla IP leak incidents; Insider Threat Program guidance from CERT, NIST 800–53 PE & AC controls.
4 Inspired by public reports on the Bayer CropScience and Arkema chemical plant incidents; ISA/IEC 62443 controls; CSB investigation reports, NIST cybersecurity framework for industrial systems.
5 Inspired by public reports on the Capital One AWS misconfiguration breach (2019); OWASP Top 10 for Cloud, CSA Cloud Controls Matrix.
6 Inspired by public reports on the Multiple breaches reported by HHS OCR involving brute force and credential stuffing; Verizon DBIR, HHS guidance on HIPAA and identity risk.
7 Inspired by public reports on the Law firms affected by eDiscovery platform breaches; ABA cybersecurity guidance, ISO 27036–3 on third-party risk.

8 Inspired by public reports on the advanced persistent threat (APT) campaigns like APT29 and attacks on SolarWinds and aerospace vendors; MITRE ATT&CK, CISA threat advisories.
9 Inspired by public reports on the Theranos case and falsified data in drug trials, FDA Good Clinical Practice (GCP), and Institute of Electrical and Electronics Engineers/Association for Computing Machinery ethics in research.
10 Inspired by public reports on the Twitter account hijacks, coordinated disinformation attacks on news outlets; DFRLab case studies, and election security analysis reports.
11 Inspired by public reports on the business email compromise (BEC) targeting executives, FBI IC3 reports, and SANS phishing defense strategies.
12 Inspired by public reports on the Apple Card bias allegation, U.S. Consumer Financial Protection Bureau AI reviews; NIST AI Risk Management Framework, EU AI Act drafts.

Chapter 8

Transformation with Guardrails

8.1 WHY TRANSFORMATION WITHOUT GUARDRAILS CREATES RISK

Transformation is no longer a disruption that arrives on occasion and can be scheduled, managed, and wrapped within the boundaries of a single program. It has become the permanent condition of enterprise life. Organizations now navigate overlapping modernization efforts, technology migrations, and the rapid deployment of AI, all while balancing ongoing operational demands. These forces collide with a speed and scope that most organizations are not prepared to handle with discipline. The outcome is rarely steady progress. More often, it is a fragile cycle of rushed activity, growing risk, and concealed liabilities.

The pace of change has become relentless. Industry studies show that the majority of digital transformation efforts fail to achieve their stated goals. These failures are not explained by inadequate tools or limited budgets. They come from the absence of governance structures designed to match the complexity of modern transformation. Leaders chase efficiency, scale, and competitive edge, but without assurance embedded into the foundation, the race to modernize produces brittle and incomplete results.

The challenge is amplified by how executives continue to frame transformation. In many boardrooms, assurance and governance are treated as slow and obstructive. Sponsors want speed, and checkpoints appear to interfere with momentum. Security reviews, compliance validations, and risk assessments are deferred until late stages, when their influence is weakened. This perception leads to decisions that blur accountability, neglect acceptable risk thresholds, and substitute short-term gains for enduring resilience.

The results show up quickly. As programs scale, weak points emerge in policies, processes, and oversight. Governance models designed for legacy systems no longer fit modern architectures. Monitoring becomes inconsistent. Accountability fragments as teams work in silos. A hidden operating layer takes shape, where undocumented choices, shortcuts, and untracked exceptions accumulate. This shadow layer does not appear in official plans, yet it often becomes the true source of systemic risk.

Risk debt builds in silence. Each missed validation, each shortcut, and each exception adds to the total. A migration that omits observability leaves blind spots that last for months. An AI project that trains on unchecked data brings bias and privacy exposure. A modernization effort that reuses outdated identity structures reintroduces old vulnerabilities. What began as expedience becomes embedded fragility.

These conditions surface as real failures. Breaches, outages, regulatory action, and reputational damage most often occur during periods of change, when leaders assume safeguards are already embedded. When trust fractures at those moments, the impact multiplies. Investors hesitate. Customers pull back. Regulators respond with scrutiny that slows every initiative that follows.

DOI: 10.1201/9781003685982-11

Transformation without guardrails erodes operational confidence. Policy documents alone do not provide protection. Annual compliance exercises do not deliver the visibility required for daily decision-making. Organizations may believe they are moving quickly, but without guardrails, they are simply introducing instability and calling it progress.

AI makes this risk impossible to ignore. Deploying AI systems without assurance transfers authority to models that may be biased, opaque, or insufficiently tested. The fallout extends well beyond technical error. Ethical breaches, financial penalties, and public backlash follow. In finance, healthcare, and logistics, unmonitored models have produced discriminatory decisions, unsafe recommendations, and contract violations. These outcomes were not anomalies. They were the foreseeable result of bypassing assurance.

The same pattern repeats in cloud migrations and modernization programs. Moving workloads without redesigning assurance processes carries forward hidden liabilities. Identity and access controls collapse when stretched across distributed environments. Monitoring becomes fragmented across multiple vendors. Compensating controls built for legacy systems no longer apply. The organization believes it has modernized, but it has only recreated old weaknesses in new settings.

These failures are particularly harmful because they compound. Risk grows faster than linearly when guardrails are absent. Each shortcut invites more shortcuts. Each undocumented exception weakens oversight. Over time, organizations accumulate transformation debt. It rarely shows up on a roadmap. It surfaces later, during an audit, a breach, or a high-pressure incident, when teams discover how much rework sits beneath the surface. By then, recovery costs far exceed what it would have taken to put the right guardrails in place at the start.

Integrated Assurance tackles this head-on. It treats guardrails as practical enablers, not constraints. They set boundaries for acceptable risk, make ownership explicit, and weave controls into the way work actually gets done. Done well, guardrails protect innovation by ensuring that speed does not come at the expense of resilience. When supported by automation, policy expressed in code, and real alignment across teams, they evolve alongside the transformation rather than lagging behind it. They accelerate progress instead of slowing it.

Their value is visible in the prevention of small issues before they become systemic failures. Cloud landing zones that apply consistent security controls remove the need for repeated manual checks. Deployment pipelines that validate compliance prevent costly rollbacks. Registries that track exceptions create transparency and reduce shadow operations. In each case, governance shifts from being a reactive function to an active enabler of safe modernization.

Trust becomes the measure of success. Customers rely on responsible data handling. Investors expect disciplined management of innovation. Regulators demand compliance with law and ethics. Employees need confidence that they can move quickly without causing harm. Guardrails operationalize that trust by embedding assurance into the flow of work rather than leaving it to documents or delayed audits.

The evidence is clear. Transformation without guardrails produces fragile progress that collapses under pressure. Transformation with guardrails creates resilience that compounds over time. Organizations that build guardrails into their approach avoid the cycle of rework and the instability of hidden risks. They achieve scale with integrity and recover from disruption without losing credibility.

Guardrails are not an accessory. They are the architecture of trust. Organizations that recognize this truth can modernize with speed and confidence. Those that ignore it will continue to mistake volatility for progress until the weight of risk debt forces correction. This reality frames the discussion that follows. Organizations face accelerating demands, new technologies, and greater scrutiny from stakeholders. Success belongs to those that embed assurance into every stage of transformation. Only then can innovation, resilience, and trust exist together. See Figure 8.1: Case in Point.

Figure 8.1 Case in Point.

Image created by the author using Gamma.

8.2 IAMM IN ARCHITECTURE AND ENGINEERING

Architecture and engineering determine whether assurance is built into design or applied after the fact. Within the IAMM framework, the Architecture and Engineering domain establishes a pathway from fragmented control implementation to embedded, automated assurance. It defines how every technical choice contributes to resilience.

At Level 1, architectural discipline is missing. Systems are created independently, with each team applying its own conventions. Documentation is partial, and dependencies remain uncertain. Security assessments occur only after deployment, which leads to frequent rework. When incidents arise, tracing causes becomes difficult because design patterns vary across systems. This stage reflects accumulated technical debt in both design and process.

Level 2 introduces structure. Reference architectures are drafted, and change management gains formal processes. Security reviews occur during project phases, though enforcement remains manual. Adherence varies by team, and controls are often bypassed to meet delivery deadlines. Assurance improves but remains superficial, as it is added late rather than embedded.

At Level 3, architecture and engineering begin to align. Secure design patterns are standardized, and reusable templates appear for common services. Threat modeling becomes a design activity. Engineering and security teams collaborate closely, and shared controls enter development pipelines. The organization gains consistency and reduces exposure, yet automation remains limited. Assurance still relies on human enforcement.

Level 4 establishes embedded assurance. Policy-as-code and infrastructure-as-code enforce compliance automatically. Security checks, configuration validation, and resilience testing are integrated into pipelines. Architects produce standardized blueprints that engineers apply directly. Security becomes part of the delivery motion, and new systems are secure by default because the environment enforces it.

Level 5 institutionalizes these capabilities. Continuous validation occurs through telemetry. Deviations trigger alerts automatically. Engineers operate within frameworks that ensure resilience while maintaining speed and innovation. Architecture becomes a guiding function that supports consistency across platforms. At this stage, assurance becomes a design property.

A technology company illustrates this progression. At Level 2, it relied on manual reviews before deployment, which led to late discoveries of vulnerabilities and recurring delays. After adopting policy-as-code and automating checks, the company advanced to Level 4. Pipelines began to block insecure configurations automatically, and deployment cycles accelerated. Assurance evolved from an obstacle to a catalyst. Maturity was achieved not through more controls, but through seamless integration.

IAMM makes clear that progress in architecture and engineering does not come from added documentation. It results from codifying resilience within systems. At higher maturity levels, assurance is no longer a discussion topic. It is an operational condition. Engineers work within environments where protection and proof occur by design. The evolution of this domain turns architecture into a strategic function. Organizations that achieve higher maturity levels can innovate with confidence, knowing their foundations are built on verifiable assurance and sustained trust.

8.3 USING ASSURANCE DURING MODERNIZATION EFFORTS

Modernization is rarely just an IT initiative. It reshapes how the business actually runs. Technology is the most visible change, but the consequences extend into governance, day-to-day processes, customer interactions, and organizational culture. Moving workloads to cloud platforms, paying down technical debt, introducing automation, or reworking large applications each carry their own complexity. When these efforts converge at scale, the risk multiplies. Done well, modernization improves resilience. Done poorly, it hardens fragility into the operating model. The difference comes down to whether assurance is built into the work or treated as an afterthought.

Too often, organizations reduce modernization to a technology upgrade. They track performance, scalability, or licensing gains but fail to align those changes with assurance. Security, privacy, compliance, and operational continuity are then left to chance. Control gaps appear. Risks accumulate without challenge. Recovery capabilities are never validated. The effort remains fragile even when it delivers on technical goals.

Integrated Assurance positions modernization as a chance to realign technology with trust. It shifts the purpose from replicating systems in new platforms to reinforcing outcomes that matter to the organization. The focus moves from platform capability to operational integrity. Modernization becomes less about replacement and more about transforming how the organization designs, delivers, and protects digital services.

A move from a physical data center to a multicloud environment illustrates the challenge. At first, the work seems straightforward: Replicate virtual machines, allocate storage, and spread services across cloud zones. Beneath that surface, assurance pressures emerge. Identity models built for perimeter defense no longer hold. Data governance must handle regional regulation, encryption models, and third-party exposure. Monitoring has to evolve from server logs to event telemetry across providers and geographies.

Without deliberate assurance, trust erodes. Breaches, audit failures, or outages force organizations into reactive investigations. Controls cannot be proven. Dependencies cannot be mapped. Decisions lack evidence. Confidence in the transformation falters.

Integrated Assurance avoids this outcome by building trust into every stage. Architecture work includes threat modeling, dependency mapping, and risk alignment. Design and build phases adopt secure templates and policy-as-code. Deployment relies on change gates that confirm compliance, security, and resilience conditions before release. Operations sustain that trust through continuous monitoring and feedback loops.

This approach does not slow delivery. It accelerates it. Automated validation replaces ad hoc review. Rework after deployment becomes unnecessary. Developers understand their boundaries upfront. Risk teams see where requirements are enforced. Executives receive evidence that change is both rapid and trustworthy.

Threat modeling is one of the most overlooked practices in modernization. Many organizations either skip it or perform it once without follow-through. When applied within an assurance framework, threat modeling connects security to architecture. It anticipates failure conditions, identifies control dependencies, and establishes mitigations rooted in actual business logic. Integrated Assurance elevates it from a tactical checklist to a strategic guide.

Visibility is another critical element. Legacy systems often depend on undocumented workarounds or compensating controls. Modernization resets these assumptions. APIs open to the internet, dependencies move between cloud regions, and logging pipelines get rebuilt. If observability is not deliberately reestablished, situational awareness is lost. Integrated Assurance restores it by standardizing telemetry, mapping data flows, and creating baselines to detect drift or anomalies.

Guardrails anchor this process. They define the conditions for workload movement, enforce permitted configurations, and verify controls before deployment. These guardrails live in code and pipelines, not in static manuals. Landing zones extend this model by providing preconfigured environments with identity, security, and monitoring controls already aligned to enterprise policy. Both reduce the burden of case-by-case review and build repeatability.

Assurance champions provide human reinforcement. They are embedded in engineering teams, trained in assurance principles, and empowered to represent governance in real time. Rather than waiting for central oversight to intervene late, these champions keep assurance active at the point of execution.

Metrics close the loop. Cost savings and delivery speed matter, but they do not tell the full story. Measures such as time to resolve exceptions, adherence rates for controls, and recurrence of incidents track the integrity of modernization. These metrics should be visible across the organization to create shared accountability.

Assurance must also adapt as modernization expands. What works in pilots may not work enterprise-wide. Regulations change. Threats grow in complexity. Guardrails, telemetry standards, and risk thresholds need to evolve without undermining earlier decisions.

Retiring compensating controls is a final step in this cycle. Controls that once addressed legacy limitations can become governance debt if not removed. Integrated Assurance identifies which are still needed, which are obsolete, and which can be eliminated to restore architectural clarity.

Modernization guided by assurance avoids guesswork. It replaces reactive auditing with proactive alignment. It prevents the cycle of deploy, discover, and roll back. It builds confidence among developers, executives, and stakeholders that transformation is not only possible but also sustainable.

Organizations that embed assurance into modernization emerge stronger. They reduce fatigue by preventing rework. They strengthen transparency, which raises confidence. Most importantly, they achieve innovation that can endure because trust has been built into the transformation itself.

8.4 MANAGING AI ADOPTION

AI has moved from the margins into the operating core of modern organizations. It shapes how work gets done, how decisions are reached, and how value is delivered to customers and partners. In call centers, models determine routing and resolution. In plants and logistics networks, predictions drive maintenance and scheduling. These systems are no longer optional enhancements. They are embedded dependencies. The risk frameworks surrounding them have not kept pace.

AI does not behave like conventional software. Once deployed, it changes. It learns from data, adjusts its behavior, and acts with delegated authority. That shift alters the nature of organizational risk. Exposure is no longer limited to system failure or data loss. It includes biased outcomes, regulatory liability, opaque decision paths, and reputational harm that can surface without warning. When AI is placed inside fraud controls, clinical workflows, hiring systems, or credit decisions, these risks stop being theoretical. They become operational realities with direct business consequences.

Integrated Assurance offers a disciplined approach to managing this challenge. It provides a framework to embed trust directly into the AI lifecycle. Rather than treating AI as a black box that produces insights without accountability, Integrated Assurance treats it as a risk-bearing asset. It requires the same discipline used for financial models or contractual obligations. Just as financial controls are embedded in budgeting processes, assurance controls must be built into AI pipelines, tooling, and deployment frameworks.

Visibility is the starting point. Governance breaks down the moment organizations lose sight of how AI systems are built and deployed. Models cannot be governed if their training data, design assumptions, approval paths, and testing results are undocumented or scattered. Auditable lineage matters. It is what allows teams to establish credibility with regulators, business leaders, and external partners when questions arise.

In regulated environments, traceability is not optional. Clinical recommendations must be defensible. Credit decisions must withstand scrutiny under fair lending rules. Hiring systems must be able to show that outcomes are not driven by embedded bias. When traceability is missing, organizations lose the ability to explain decisions or stand behind them under audit, litigation, or public examination. Integrated Assurance treats traceability as a minimum condition, not a maturity goal.

Regulatory frameworks are also advancing quickly. The European Union's AI Act has established the clearest regulatory benchmark so far, and other governments are moving quickly to follow. Across North America, South America, and the Asia-Pacific region, new rules are emerging with familiar expectations. AI use must be defensible. Oversight cannot be optional. Risk has to be understood, documented, and owned.

For leadership teams, this is not an abstract compliance exercise. They are expected to know how their models behave, where controls exist, and how the organization will respond when outcomes go wrong. Being unprepared is no longer a neutral position. It is a governance failure.

Integrated Assurance provides the blueprint for these demands. It begins with categorizing AI systems by impact and sensitivity. High-impact models, such as those that affect medical or legal outcomes, require the highest levels of oversight. They may need human validation, ethical review, and advanced testing. Lower-impact models, such as recommendation engines for media, can follow lighter assurance pathways. This classification ensures oversight is proportional and practical.

Policy-as-code is a vital enabler of this system. Assurance principles must be written into the development pipeline, not left in binders or presentation decks. Automated checks can verify dataset approval, fairness testing, and explainability validation before deployment. Failed checks block promotion to production until remediation occurs. This automation allows assurance to scale alongside development.

Standardization across teams is equally important. Many organizations operate with fragmented platforms and governance methods. Without a unified assurance framework, some models are auditable while others remain opaque, leaving hidden liabilities across the organization. Integrated Assurance establishes consistency, creating shared expectations and boundaries for innovation.

AI presents risks that evolve over time. Models degrade as data shifts, a phenomenon known as drift. A system trained on past patterns may lose accuracy as customer preferences change, economic conditions fluctuate, or adversaries adapt. Drift can silently undermine security or decision-making until significant damage occurs. Integrated Assurance addresses this risk through continuous monitoring, alerting systems, and retraining protocols that keep models reliable.

Third-party AI introduces another set of challenges. Organizations often deploy pretrained systems from vendors without full transparency into training data or decision logic. This lack of visibility can import bias, insecurity, or noncompliance. Integrated Assurance closes this gap by requiring vendors to provide attestation. Vendors must demonstrate bias testing, lineage documentation, incident response plans, and liability terms. AI trustworthiness becomes a vendor responsibility in the same way cybersecurity hygiene already is.

Culture also plays a role. Data science teams often prioritize speed and innovation over governance. Assurance must be introduced without stifling creativity. Embedding assurance champions within these teams helps translate governance into actionable practices. These champions support the creation of models that are both innovative and trustworthy.

Formal governance bodies add another layer of oversight. Model risk committees composed of engineering, compliance, legal, and business leaders can review critical systems before deployment. Their role is to examine accuracy, ethical implications, and alignment with enterprise values. This process elevates deployment from a technical checkpoint to a trust checkpoint.

Explainability is central to this discipline. A system that cannot explain its reasoning cannot be relied upon in sensitive contexts. Integrated Assurance requires organizations to define the appropriate level of explainability by use case. A chatbot recommending products may need little transparency, while a system denying a mortgage must provide a clear explanation of its decision pathway.

Data governance sits at the center of any credible AI program. When training data is biased, incomplete, or gathered without proper consent, those defects surface in outcomes. Models do not correct for poor inputs. They amplify them. Effective assurance treats training data with the same discipline applied to production systems. Quality thresholds are defined. Lineage is traceable. Access and use are controlled. Decisions around retention, reuse, and cross-border movement are made deliberately, not after the fact.

Ethical risk cannot be managed by policy statements alone. It requires clear ownership and escalation when outcomes cause harm. Structured review forums, targeted audits, and direct user feedback create early signals when systems drift in the wrong direction. When harm does occur, organizations need established paths to unwind decisions, correct logic, and address impact. Without that muscle, trust erodes quickly and publicly.

Adaptability matters because the ground is still shifting. Regulations, standards, and expectations will continue to change. Assurance programs that rely on static control sets fail under that pressure. Flexible structures, versioned controls, and clear mappings to new requirements allow organizations to adjust without tearing systems apart. The goal is continuity, not constant reinvention.

AI deployed without assurance becomes a liability. The risk surface stretches from technical failure to regulatory action, ethical breakdowns, and lasting reputational damage. Done properly, assurance does not slow adoption. It makes scale possible. Organizations that embed it early move faster with fewer reversals and less fallout. Over time, the differentiator will not be model capability. It will be the level of trust the organization can sustain.

8.5 OVERCOMING CULTURAL RESISTANCE TO CHANGE

Every meaningful transformation creates friction. New technology is rarely the hard part. The real strain shows up in how people are asked to work differently, how accountability shifts, and how long-standing assumptions are challenged. When assurance practices are introduced into an organization, they rarely arrive in a cultural vacuum. They collide with habits that formed over years, incentives that rewarded speed over discipline, and belief systems shaped by prior transformation efforts. Resistance follows. Not because people oppose resilience or trust, but because they are unsure what those concepts will demand of them.

In most organizations, resistance is not an act of defiance. It is learned behavior. Many teams have lived through initiatives that promised enablement and delivered bureaucracy. They have watched governance programs expand without clear value. They have seen controls applied unevenly or used primarily as tools for blame after something went wrong. Against that backdrop, new assurance structures trigger skepticism. People worry that autonomy will shrink, that creativity will be constrained, or that oversight will return without context. Those concerns are rational. Ignoring them only deepens the divide.

Assurance leaders who treat culture as an obstacle to overcome tend to fail. Culture is not something to be pushed aside. It is the operating system of the organization. It determines how decisions are made when policies are silent, how risk is interpreted under pressure, and how teams behave when deadlines collide with safeguards. Shifting culture requires understanding how values translate into daily behavior. It requires attention to incentives, leadership signals, informal norms, and shared history. Without that understanding, even well-designed controls will be bypassed.

One of the most persistent sources of resistance is the belief that assurance slows progress. Development teams are rewarded for velocity. Product leaders are measured by responsiveness to market signals. Business units are driven by opportunity capture. When assurance is perceived as something that sits outside those objectives, it becomes a tax on momentum. Workarounds appear. Shadow systems emerge. Trust in the transformation effort erodes quietly, long before any formal failure is visible.

The response is not to dilute controls or lower expectations. It is to reposition assurance as a condition for sustainable speed. Teams move faster when they do not have to stop and remediate preventable failures. They scale more confidently when guardrails are predictable and consistent. The key is how those guardrails are introduced. When they are designed as frameworks for safe autonomy rather than checkpoints for approval, behavior changes. A well-designed cloud environment illustrates this clearly. Developers can provision resources quickly, knowing that baseline protections are already in place. The rules exist, but they do not interrupt the flow of work. They shape it.

Leadership plays an outsized role in this shift. Executives often underestimate how closely their actions are watched. Silence is interpreted as indifference. Mixed signals are read as permission to bypass safeguards. Leaders do not need to micromanage assurance, but they must be visible in supporting it. That support shows up in funding decisions, in how trade-offs are resolved, and in how incidents are discussed. When resilience and integrity are consistently reinforced at the top, assurance gains legitimacy across the organization.

Language also matters more than most leaders expect. Terms associated with enforcement or inspection tend to provoke defensiveness. They suggest restriction rather than protection. Language that emphasizes resilience, trust, and reliability reframes governance as something that exists to safeguard outcomes rather than constrain effort. Over time, vocabulary shapes perception. It influences whether controls are seen as external impositions or shared commitments.

Stories reinforce this framing. Every organization has experienced failures tied to weak controls, poor data hygiene, or rushed decisions. When those stories are told constructively, they serve as reminders rather than warnings. They show teams what happens when safeguards are absent or ignored. More importantly, they connect assurance to real consequences rather than abstract policy. Stories of recovery, not just failure, are equally powerful. They demonstrate how preparation reduces impact and shortens disruption.

Incentives must align with this narrative. When delivery teams are rewarded exclusively for speed and assurance teams are rewarded for risk reduction, conflict is inevitable. Each group optimizes for its own success, often at the expense of the other. Shared metrics change that dynamic. Measures such as risk-adjusted delivery, incident-free releases, or successful launches without post-deployment remediation encourage collaboration. People pay attention to what is measured. When success is defined collectively, behavior follows.

Training is another lever, but only when it moves beyond compliance checklists. Assurance spans technical, operational, and business domains. Expecting fluency without context is unrealistic. Workshops, simulations, and cross-functional exercises create shared understanding. They allow teams to experience how controls function under pressure. They also provide safe environments to surface concerns and refine approaches before they are deployed at scale.

Empathy is essential throughout this process. Assurance professionals must understand the constraints under which transformation teams operate. Deadlines, customer expectations, and competitive pressure are real. Controls that ignore those realities will be resisted regardless of intent. When governance reflects how work is actually done, rather than how it looks on paper, it earns credibility. Empathy does not mean lowering standards. It means designing standards that can be sustained.

Peer influence accelerates adoption in ways formal authority cannot. Embedding assurance advocates within development, product, and operations teams normalizes governance. These individuals translate intent into practice. They help teams navigate trade-offs without escalating every decision. Over time, assurance stops feeling external. It becomes part of how the team defines quality.

Feedback mechanisms keep this system healthy. Teams must be able to raise concerns about friction without fear of reprisal. More importantly, those concerns must lead to visible adjustment when justified. An assurance function that listens and adapts signals that governance is alive, not frozen. That responsiveness builds trust and reduces the temptation to work around controls.

Recognition reinforces desired behavior. Avoiding failure is important, but it should not be the only outcome acknowledged. Teams that demonstrate strong assurance practices deserve visibility. Smooth audits, stable launches, and rapid recovery after disruption are achievements. Celebrating them reinforces the idea that governance contributes to success rather than merely preventing disaster.

Not all resistance should be eliminated. Skepticism often highlights real issues with usability, performance, or cost. Engaging with that skepticism improves design. It also shows respect for the people expected to change how they work. Cultural change imposed without dialogue rarely lasts.

Tools play a quiet but decisive role. Controls that add friction, duplicate effort, or interrupt workflows invite avoidance. Controls that integrate seamlessly into existing platforms are far more likely to be accepted. Automation and usability are not luxuries. They are prerequisites for adoption at scale.

The end state is not universal agreement or perfect compliance. It is normalization. Assurance becomes part of how decisions are made and how work is evaluated. Developers consider data protection as they design features. Product leaders account for downstream risk when prioritizing roadmaps. Executives expect transparency and traceability from partners. Responsibility is shared rather than delegated.

Reaching that point takes time. It requires consistent leadership, aligned incentives, thoughtful storytelling, practical training, and trusted feedback loops. When those elements are in place, resistance softens. Ownership emerges. Transformation becomes safer and more resilient without losing momentum. Assurance stops being seen as a drag on progress and starts being recognized for what it is—framework that protects effort, supports ambition, and sustains trust when it matters most.

8.6 MONITORING AND ADAPTING ASSURANCE GUARDRAILS OVER TIME

Assurance guardrails work best when they are treated as part of the organization's day-to-day rhythm, not as fixed controls bolted in place and forgotten. They exist inside a business that is always in motion, shaped by new threats, new technologies, and shifting regulatory expectations. What helps the organization move safely today can just as easily become friction tomorrow if it is not revisited and adjusted to reflect how work is actually getting done. Their value comes from staying grounded in current conditions, not from how well they were designed at a single point in time.

One of the most common failures is treating guardrail implementation as a one-time effort. Controls are put in place, documented, and then left alone until something breaks or an audit forces attention back to them. Over time, this creates quiet risk. Teams change how they operate, platforms evolve, and business priorities shift, while the controls meant to support them remain static. What once enabled progress can start to slow it down or, worse, create false confidence while gaps grow underneath.

Keeping guardrails relevant starts with paying attention to how they behave in the real world. Controls should produce signals that show when they are triggered, under what conditions, who is affected, and what happens next. That operational visibility turns guardrails from abstract policy into something observable and improvable. It is how assurance stays connected to reality instead of drifting into paperwork. Blocked deployments, approved exceptions, and failed validations should all leave evidence behind. This record provides the raw material for understanding whether guardrails are functioning as designed or require adjustment.

Collecting raw data is not enough. It must be interpreted within context. High numbers of exceptions may point to a control that is out of step with operations. Low trigger rates might mean the control is being adopted effectively or that it is too weak to make a difference. Assurance professionals must analyze these signals alongside input from risk, security, operations, product, and compliance. Contextual interpretation turns telemetry into insight.

Structured review mechanisms strengthen this process. Retrospectives are one effective approach. They provide time to assess how guardrails performed during a release, incident, or initiative. These sessions highlight whether controls prevented problems, created friction, or delivered useful metrics for decision-making. Another approach is the periodic health check. Conducted monthly, quarterly, or alongside planning cycles, these reviews determine whether each guardrail still serves its intended purpose. They consider the validity of the control, the strength of its enforcement, the quality of the user experience, and the sufficiency of telemetry. Controls that no longer meet these standards should be redesigned or retired.

Exception patterns also provide important intelligence. When multiple teams request exceptions to the same control, it signals a gap between design and reality. Rather than dismissing these requests as noncompliance, they should be studied for what they reveal about workflow constraints and acceptable risk levels. Aggregating exception data highlights systemic issues that demand redesign.

Shadow systems present another signal. When teams build workarounds, adopt unapproved tools, or bypass official processes, it often reflects that controls have become obstacles. While these behaviors introduce risk, they also provide evidence of where governance has failed to meet operational needs. Examining them openly can reveal opportunities to evolve guardrails so they regain relevance.

Trend analysis deepens understanding by looking at patterns over time. A guardrail that frequently triggers during integration, for example, may expose weaknesses earlier in design. If one business unit generates disproportionate exception requests, it may point to gaps in training or tooling. If certain controls are linked to delayed deployments, they may need refinement to balance assurance with performance. These insights allow the organization to shift from reactive fixes to proactive design.

Adaptation should never be confused with lowering standards. It is the process of evolving standards intelligently. As teams mature, some controls can be made more flexible. As threat conditions intensify, others may need to become more stringent. A rigid approach that applies one model to all situations cannot endure in a complex enterprise. Guardrails must reflect the diversity of risk and operational maturity across the organization. This requires a governance process that can support adjustment without losing control.

Scalability in adaptation is supported through infrastructure-as-code and policy-as-code. Guardrails expressed in code can be versioned, tested, and deployed through established development practices. Updates can be rolled back if necessary, tracked for audit, and aligned with continuous delivery. A guardrail registry strengthens this model by maintaining a central record of all active controls. The registry documents purpose, ownership, enforcement methods, applicable systems, risks, and change history. This transparency supports accountability, regulatory inquiries, and internal reporting.

External change also drives adaptation. Regulatory updates, shifts in industry practice, and advances in technology alter the risk landscape. A control that satisfied compliance last year may no longer suffice. Data localization, supply chain vulnerabilities, and new privacy requirements all introduce pressure to revise guardrails. Integrated Assurance frameworks must absorb these changes while minimizing disruption. Modularity and traceability are essential to this ability.

Not all controls need to exist indefinitely. Some are temporary measures designed to manage transitional risk. When the circumstances that gave rise to a control no longer exist, it should be reconsidered. Leaving outdated controls in place adds friction, slows work, and creates unnecessary complexity. Sunsetting a control deserves the same level of care as introducing one, with clear reasoning, proper documentation, and open communication. In some situations, a control does not need to disappear entirely. It can move from active enforcement to passive monitoring, preserving visibility without getting in the way of day-to-day operations.

Feedback from the people living with these controls is essential. Assurance teams need ongoing conversations with developers, engineers, operators, and business leaders to understand whether a control is actually serving its purpose. Workshops, interviews, and short surveys help surface what works, what does not, and where intent and reality have drifted apart. The aim is simple. The experience of assurance in daily work should match what it was designed to achieve.

Improvement cannot be treated as a side project. Monitoring and adaptation belong to everyone, not just a central assurance function. When teams see themselves as owners of assurance, feedback becomes more honest, and governance becomes more meaningful.

Transparency reinforces this trust by showing how input is used, why decisions are made, and how changes strengthen resilience rather than weaken it.

Pace matters as well. When adjustments take too long, confidence erodes. When changes happen without explanation, trust fades. An effective assurance environment responds quickly, communicates clearly, and behaves consistently.

Done well, the ability to monitor and evolve guardrails shifts assurance from a compliance obligation into a source of strategic advantage. Governance becomes something that supports progress instead of slowing it down. In conditions marked by constant change, resilience depends on how well controls can adapt as quickly as the business they are meant to protect.

8.7 CONCLUSION

Transformation has ceased to be an occasional disruption or a carefully staged initiative tied to a five-year plan. It is now the constant state of modern enterprise. Every organization is adjusting to technological shifts, evolving customer expectations, regulatory pressure, and competitive pressures that refuse to pause. In this environment, governance cannot remain a matter of static policies or one-time controls. Those approaches lack the speed and connection to operational reality. The organization requires assurance mechanisms that move with transformation, shaping its direction in real time. These mechanisms take the form of assurance guardrails.

Guardrails are not barriers to change. They are structural supports that make change safe, scalable, and sustainable. They enable leaders and teams to move with confidence, knowing that boundaries are present, visible, and enforced. Guardrails bring clarity where uncertainty might otherwise slow progress. They allow teams to embrace new technologies, accelerate delivery cycles, and pursue ambitious strategies with fewer unintended consequences. By embedding assurance into transformation, guardrails turn risk into a managed possibility rather than an unmanaged hazard.

The risks of transformation without such mechanisms are well documented. Organizations that operate without guardrails often accumulate transformation debt. Decision-making becomes inconsistent. Incidents occur that could have been prevented. Security functions turn reactive. Compliance becomes retroactive. Trust erodes both internally and externally. Progress may continue, but it produces brittle outcomes that cannot withstand pressure. In this sense, transformation without guardrails is not resilience but fragility disguised as innovation.

Modernization programs illustrate this problem clearly. In the rush to migrate workloads, upgrade platforms, or adopt new architectures, the assurance layer is often neglected. Legacy processes are lifted into modern environments without reconsideration of their risk posture. Architectural assumptions shift, but controls remain unchanged. The result is a landscape filled with hidden exposures. Integrated Assurance responds to this gap by embedding foresight into the modernization process. It places resilience and observability at the center. It ensures that as the technical stack evolves, the governance model evolves alongside it.

AI adds another layer of complexity. These systems learn continuously, behave probabilistically, and operate in ways that influence decisions affecting people's rights, reputations, and outcomes. Traditional IT controls cannot address this reality. New forms of assurance are required, such as traceability of model lineage, alignment with ethical principles, explainability of outputs, and continuous performance validation. At the same time, regulators across industries and jurisdictions are tightening expectations around AI governance. Guardrails provide a structured response. They embed assurance into AI pipelines, create pathways for escalation, and give leaders confidence that AI can be adopted without abandoning responsibility. Integrated Assurance allows AI to become not only powerful but also trustworthy.

The design of guardrails is not a narrow technical exercise. It requires engineering precision, risk awareness, user-centered design, and organizational insight. Guardrails must be enforceable through automation. They must be visible so that people understand the expectations. They must be calibrated to different levels of risk. They should be embedded into the platforms and tools already in use, rather than bolted on as an afterthought. They need clear communication about their purpose, and they must evolve as circumstances shift. When designed in this way, guardrails function as platforms for safe autonomy rather than as obstacles to progress.

Cultural adoption matters as much as technical design. Even well-constructed guardrails fail when the people expected to work within them do not trust their intent. Resistance usually traces back to earlier efforts where governance slowed delivery, added friction, or existed primarily to satisfy oversight rather than improve outcomes. Tightening controls is rarely the solution. What changes the dynamic is reintroducing them with clarity, empathy, and a shared understanding of purpose. When teams see assurance as something that protects their work instead of constraining it, the relationship shifts. Governance stops feeling imposed and starts feeling useful.

That shift does not happen on its own. It requires deliberate leadership. Leaders must explain why guardrails exist and how they support the organization's broader objectives, not just its compliance posture. They must invest in education that makes assurance understandable rather than opaque. Feedback must be encouraged and acted on so that oversight becomes a conversation rather than a verdict. In healthy environments, assurance becomes routine. Teams anticipate it, rely on it, and often contribute to its improvement. Even then, conditions never stand still. Business models evolve. Threats change. Expectations rise. Guardrails that remain static lose relevance. Continuous observation and adjustment are what keep assurance effective over time. Measurement shows what is working. Refinement keeps controls aligned with reality. Together, they ensure assurance remains part of how the organization operates, not a leftover from a prior strategy.

Technology increasingly reinforces this evolution. Practices like infrastructure-as-code and policy-as-code turn guardrails into managed assets rather than manual checkpoints. Controls can be reviewed, tested, versioned, and deployed with the same discipline applied to application changes. This brings assurance into the delivery process instead of leaving it on the sidelines. Oversight becomes visible and collaborative. It moves at the same pace as innovation rather than chasing it after the fact.

The real value of guardrails is the clarity they create. Teams understand what is allowed, what requires additional validation, and where accountability sits. In large or fast-moving transformation efforts, that clarity matters more than rigid enforcement. It reduces dependence on informal knowledge. It limits confusion and unnecessary escalation. It allows decisions to be made closer to the work without sacrificing consistency. That shared understanding is what makes scale possible.

Guardrails also communicate confidence to external stakeholders. Regulators, partners, and customers evaluate an organization by its ability to govern its own complexity. Guardrails provide evidence that the organization can operate at speed without losing control. They signal maturity and trustworthiness in markets where both qualities directly shape competitive advantage.

The outcome of all these efforts is trust velocity. This is the capability that allows organizations to move faster because they continuously understand and manage risk. It enables business leaders to make decisions with assurance rather than hesitation. It accelerates innovation without increasing exposure. It ensures compliance without slowing progress. Trust

This checklist helps leaders determine whether resilience in their enterprise is documented on paper or demonstrated in practice. The goal is to test capability under stress – not just compliance with frameworks.

1

Strategic Alignment

- [ ] Have transformation goals been clearly linked to business strategy and resilience objectives?
- [ ] Is there a defined "risk appetite statement" for the transformation, approved by executives/board?
- [ ] Are performance outcomes balanced between innovation speed, cost, and trust assurance?

2

Governance and Oversight

- [ ] Has a cross-functional steering committee (IT, security, risk, compliance, business units) been established?
- [ ] Are decision rights and escalation paths documented and rehearsed?
- [ ] Is there an independent assurance function monitoring the transformation (not just the delivery team)?

3

Risk and Assurance Integration

- [ ] Have risk assessments been conducted for new technologies (AI, cloud, IoT, automation)?
- [ ] Are risk signals embedded into program dashboards (not separate spreadsheets)?
- [ ] Are third-party/vendor dependencies mapped, scored, and continuously monitored?
- [ ] Has the Integrated Assurance framework (IAMM checkpoints, control mapping) been applied?

4

Regulatory and Compliance Guardrails

- [ ] Have relevant regulations (e.g., GDPR, SEC cyber disclosure, DORA, AI Act) been mapped to transformation initiatives?
- [ ] Are compliance checkpoints automated into workflows (DevOps, procurement, HR systems)?
- [ ] Is regulatory reporting integrated into the program's communication plan?

5

Technical and Operational Guardrails

- [ ] Are resilience-by-design principles embedded (graceful degradation, redundancy, and failover)?
- [ ] Are telemetry and logging systems unified across new and legacy environments?
- [ ] Are AI/automation systems tested for bias, drift, and adversarial manipulation?
- [ ] Is there a "kill switch" or rollback mechanism for new technologies in case of critical failure?

6

Cultural and Workforce Guardrails

- [ ] Are frontline employees trained on new risks and equipped with clear playbooks?
- [ ] Has psychological safety been reinforced so issues can be raised early without blame?
- [ ] Are incentive structures aligned with safe adoption (not just speed of rollout)?
- [ ] Do transformation communications emphasize trust and resilience, not only efficiency?

7

Continuous Monitoring and Feedback

- [ ] Are guardrails reviewed quarterly against evolving threats and regulatory updates?
- [ ] Is telemetry feeding into real-time dashboards available to executives and frontline teams?
- [ ] Are after-action reviews conducted for each milestone or incident, with lessons applied across the program?
- [ ] Is there a mechanism to sunset guardrails once maturity is reached (avoid bureaucracy creep)?

Key Takeaway: Guardrails ensure that transformation programs don't become speed-only efforts and give leaders a quick-reference tool to measure if their modernization initiatives remain safe, compliant, and resilient.

Figure 8.2 Practical Guardrails Checklist for Transformation.
Image created by the author using Gamma.

velocity is the practical result of well-implemented guardrails. It is not an abstract theory but a measurable outcome.

As complexity grows through AI, cloud convergence, regulation, and geopolitical shifts, guardrails will become decisive. They will determine whether the transformation collapses under its own weight or scales in a resilient manner. They will mark the difference between brittle change and lasting evolution. They will anchor aspiration to execution. Assurance, in this role, becomes a catalyst. It turns fear into readiness and fragmentation into coherence. It ensures that progress is not only achieved but sustained.

The essential lesson is that speed is not undermined by control, but by control that is misaligned. Integrated Assurance ensures alignment. It replaces oversight with enablement. It redefines guardrails as the design language of trust. In doing so, it places assurance at the heart of transformation, not as a cost but as the foundation of resilience and growth. See Figure 8.2: Practical Guardrails Checklist for Transformation.

Chapter 9

From Recovery to Relevance

9.1 WHY RECOVERY IS NOT ENOUGH

After a disruption, most organizations focus on getting back on their feet. Systems are restored, customer channels reopen, and leadership communicates that operations have stabilized. There is a strong temptation to treat that moment as the finish line. The incident appears resolved, documentation is completed, and the teams who carried the response finally pause. But stability is not the end of the story. Restoring operations closes only one chapter. What happens next determines whether the organization merely recovers or actually emerges stronger.

Stopping at recovery is dangerous because it addresses only continuity. A patch or fix restores operations, but it does not resolve the doubts that take root among stakeholders. Customers begin to question reliability. Regulators weigh whether oversight was sufficient. Investors examine the strength of governance. Employees who carried the burden may be left fatigued and uncertain about leadership. Trust does not automatically return when systems do. It must be earned again through action that is visible, verifiable, and durable.

Integrated Assurance shifts the way a crisis is understood. Rather than viewing disruption as an interruption to be smoothed over, it reframes the moment as a chance for reinvention. Weaknesses surface but so do possibilities. Leaders are forced to confront assumptions about governance, technology, and culture. They are given an opening to retire outdated practices, strengthen controls, and align the organization with the rising expectations of a trust-driven economy. The true test is whether recovery becomes a foundation for long-term relevance.

Trust is fragile even in steady times. In a crisis, it is often the first to fracture. An outage, breach, or compliance lapse sends the signal that leadership may not have control. Trust rarely returns through words alone. Stakeholders want evidence of improvement. They want to see how safety and accountability are built into daily operations. They want proof that oversight has been strengthened and that the enterprise has grown stronger in the aftermath.

Expectations have sharpened. Customers are more informed, regulators are stricter, and investors watch for signs of governance maturity. Resilience is no longer an internal function. It is a competitive marker. Organizations that embed assurance into their recovery processes regain confidence faster, while those that obscure or delay transparency lose credibility. The severity of the disruption matters less than the quality of the response.

9.1.1 Recovery as a defining moment

Crises are remembered less for the failure itself and more for the conduct that followed. Stakeholders hold on to whether leaders were present, whether information was shared, and whether promised reforms became reality. These actions shape organizational character in memory long after the headlines fade.

DOI: 10.1201/9781003685982-12

For leaders, this reality presents both risk and opportunity. Defensive or opaque responses create permanent blemishes. Proactive and transparent approaches, supported by evidence of reform, turn the same event into a moment of transformation. The difference lies in whether recovery is treated as a closing chapter or as a turning point.

Too many organizations stop at technical closure. They patch a flaw, restore a backup, or reconfigure systems, and then move forward. Operationally, the crisis seems resolved. Yet reputational damage continues. Customers remain uncertain, regulators maintain doubt, and employees question leadership. Technical fixes can create an illusion of completion while leaving the deeper deficit in trust unresolved.

This illusion fuels complacency. Silence is misread as confidence. Doubt festers quietly until it surfaces in contract renewals, audits, or critical market moments. By then, the chance to rebuild credibility has passed. Integrated Assurance addresses this by making trust recovery explicit. It validates reforms, institutionalizes lessons, and provides stakeholders with evidence. Promises turn into proof, and fixes evolve into permanent commitments.

9.1.2 Leadership at the center

Recovery without relevance often points to leadership neglect. Executives may treat a crisis as a technical problem to be delegated. They issue minimal updates and quickly return to business routines. In doing so, they overlook the truth that recovery is a leadership function. Stakeholders look upward for visibility, accountability, and strategic direction. They want to know that senior leadership recognizes the implications and is actively shaping the response.

Visible ownership signals strength. Leaders who take responsibility and communicate openly show that the organization is willing to face scrutiny. Assurance equips them with frameworks and evidence to make these commitments credible.

Containment brings stability. Transformation redefines the organization. The move from one to the other requires deliberate choices. It requires decisions about governance, communication, and culture that shift the crisis from operational disruption to strategic opportunity. Integrated Assurance provides the structure to embed new practices, validate controls, and sustain transparency. It turns the disruption into a proving ground for resilience.

This chapter underscores why recovery is not an end. It distinguishes between remediation and trust restoration. It examines how stakeholders interpret organizational conduct in the aftermath. It presents assurance as the foundation of credibility, transparency, and renewed strength.

The message is that recovery opens the door to the most important work that follows. The path chosen in those weeks and months determines whether the organization is remembered as one that stumbled but survived, or one that stumbled and became stronger. That outcome shapes market confidence, regulatory posture, and employee loyalty.

Every disruption becomes a moment of truth. Integrated Assurance ensures the moment is leveraged rather than lost. It transforms recovery from a technical checkpoint into a catalyst for resilience, credibility, and lasting relevance.

9.2 MODELS OF ASSURANCE REINVENTION

Organizations that emerge stronger from a crisis reinvent rather than react. They use the disruption as a forcing function to reassess assumptions, redesign governance, and realign with stakeholder expectations. While every context is different, a set of distinct models has begun to emerge. These models are not hypothetical frameworks. They are patterns observed in real organizations that use assurance as the core driver of recovery. Each model demonstrates how Integrated Assurance turns disruption into a strategic advantage, and how resilience

1 **The Real-Time Communicator**

- Prioritizes rapid, transparent engagement during crisis
- Uses consistent updates and stakeholder visibility to rebuild trust
- Assurance supports structured messaging with verifiable recovery metrics
- Best for high-visibility industries where timing and transparency shape perception

2 **The Governance Reformer**

- Leverages crisis to overhaul risk governance and control architecture
- Focuses on root causes, systemic misalignments, and policy gaps
- Uses assurance frameworks to redesign processes, validate changes, and mature oversight
- Ideal for organizations needing to rebuild internal alignment and regulatory trust

3 **The Customer-Centric Builder**

- Embeds assurance directly into customer-facing platforms and experiences
- Makes trust observable through transparency tools, consent models, and ethical design
- Turns privacy or data misuse crises into opportunities to build brand loyalty
- Applies especially well in sectors where user trust is easily eroded

4 **The Policy Evangelist**

- Converts recovery into industry leadership and standards influence
- Shares lessons learned through white papers, policy forums, and oversight engagement
- Uses assurance maturity to position the organization as a voice for responsible innovation
- Effective in regulated environments or public sector contexts

5 **The Transparency Leader**

- Rebuilds organizational identity through structural openness and assurance-led culture
- Integrates assurance into architecture, communications, and leadership behavior
- Positions the organization as values-driven and forward-looking, not defined by past failure
- Best suited for organizations facing sustained erosion of trust

Figure 9.1 The Five Patterns of Post-Crisis Recovery.
Image created by the author using Gamma.

becomes a differentiator and not just a defense. See Figure 9.1: The Five Patterns of Post-Crisis Recovery.

9.2.1 The real-time communicator

Some organizations rebuild confidence not by waiting for resolution but by communicating through uncertainty. This model is characterized by rapid public engagement, consistent updates, and a willingness to show work in progress. Assurance plays a critical role by giving these communications structure, metrics, and credibility.

A global financial institution provides a compelling example. After a failed cloud migration caused widespread service outages, the organization did not retreat into silence. Instead, it established a crisis communications cadence that included technical briefings, recovery updates, and public documentation of progress. It also invited third-party validation of new controls, turning assurance from a back-office function into a visible component of its brand. Stakeholders did not respond to perfection; instead, they responded to transparency. Trust began to return not because the systems came back online quickly, but because the organization gave stakeholders something to believe in along the way.

This model works best in high-visibility industries where customer sentiment moves quickly, and regulators demand early disclosure. It demonstrates that trust is not always rebuilt through answers. Sometimes it is rebuilt through presence, clarity, and honesty.

9.2.2 The governance reformer

This model is defined by a deliberate shift from reactive controls to proactive, embedded assurance frameworks. Organizations that follow this pattern take a systemic view of their failure. They examine not just what broke, but why governance failed to prevent, detect, or contain the incident. Recovery becomes an exercise in redesigning how risk is managed across the enterprise.

A global pharmaceutical company exemplified this model after experiencing a targeted ransomware attack. The crisis exposed deep issues in third-party oversight and network segmentation. Instead of isolating the problem, the organization rebuilt its governance from the ground up. It implemented real-time vendor telemetry, redesigned control frameworks, and launched an internal assurance certification program for engineering teams. The changes were documented in a trust recovery roadmap, which became a public artifact of reform and a new foundation for investor engagement.

This approach demonstrates that mature governance is not a prerequisite for trust. It can also be a product of how the organization responds to failure. The Governance Reformer does not seek to restore the old model. It uses disruption to design something more aligned, more resilient, and more transparent.

9.2.3 The customer-centric builder

Some organizations choose to rebuild trust not through policies or internal reforms, but through the customer experience itself. This model emphasizes visible, user-controlled, and ethically designed systems that demonstrate a shift in values. It is especially relevant when the crisis involves privacy violations, data misuse, or ethical concerns.

A large e-commerce platform that suffered a third-party data overreach followed this path. Instead of blaming the vendor or issuing technical explanations, the company redesigned its data transparency interface. It launched real-time dashboards that showed users exactly how their data was being used. It suspended services pending review and created a customer data ethics board with decision-making authority over product design. Assurance metrics were embedded in the product.

This model shows that assurance can be a product feature. When trust is integrated into the experience, it not only helps repair relationships but can become a source of brand loyalty and differentiation. The Customer-Centric Builder turns ethics into usability and makes privacy observable.

9.2.4 The policy evangelist

This model extends beyond the organization itself. It occurs when an enterprise uses its recovery journey to shape public policy, contribute to standards, or lead peer organizations through similar risks. It is rooted in the belief that assurance maturity can be a form of market leadership, especially in highly regulated or public-facing sectors.

A national government agency followed this model after a failed IT upgrade disrupted services and sparked public outcry. Rather than bury the incident, the agency published a full postmortem, created a public dashboard for IT assurance metrics, and participated in industry roundtables to share its lessons. These actions positioned the agency not as a failure, but as a leader in transparency. Its practices were adopted across multiple departments, and it gained political support for increased investment.

The Policy Evangelist treats assurance as more than compliance. It becomes a language of influence. Organizations that take this approach shift from defending their past to shaping the future.

9.2.5 The transparency leader

The most mature model involves not just improving systems or governance but fully rethinking how the organization earns and maintains trust. This model is adopted by organizations that have faced long-term erosion of stakeholder confidence due to opaque practices, overreach, or cultural misalignment. Recovery is not about one incident. It is about starting over with assurance at the center of the new identity.

A global technology company facing scrutiny over algorithmic bias and data harvesting chose this model. It opened its platform architecture, redesigned consent systems, and introduced explainable AI dashboards. Internally, every product had to pass assurance criteria related to fairness and transparency before launch. Externally, these practices were shared with regulators, partners, and the public. Over time, the company repositioned itself as a voice for ethical innovation, not by erasing the past, but by showing how it was building a better future.

The Transparency Leader does not aim to rebuild a tarnished brand. It aims to replace it with something more grounded, more defensible, and more aligned with stakeholder expectations.

9.2.6 The strategic takeaway

These five models demonstrate that there is no single path from recovery to relevance. Each model is a reflection of organizational context, stakeholder pressure, cultural readiness, and leadership intent. What unites them is the use of Integrated Assurance as the foundation for transformation.

Rather than treating disruption as a break in business continuity, these organizations treated it as a moment of truth. They repositioned rather than just respond. In doing so, they showed that assurance is not only a way to manage risk. It is a way to lead.

9.3 COMMUNICATING DURING RECOVERY

When disruption hits, restoring systems is only part of the work. The harder task is restoring confidence. Stakeholders judge leadership less by the speed of recovery than by how the situation is explained and how the next steps are framed. Silence creates doubt. Denial damages credibility. Overly technical explanations signal distance rather than control. In many cases, missteps in communication do more lasting harm than the incident that triggered the response.

Strong executive communication during recovery is defined by plain language, steady messaging, and visible ownership. People need to understand what occurred, what is being done now, and what will change going forward. Messages that shift from one update to the next erode trust quickly. Credibility comes from accuracy and restraint, from acknowledging uncertainty without speculation, and from backing words with observable action.

Update cadence matters. Short, regular communications build more confidence than a single, carefully crafted statement released after the fact. Internal teams need to hear the same core message as external audiences, adjusted only where legal or regulatory limits apply. When that alignment breaks down, confusion spreads. Employees talk to customers, partners, and peers. If they are left guessing, they will fill the gaps themselves, often in ways that are hard to correct.

Tone and timing set the frame for everything that follows. Leaders have to acknowledge disruption without centering themselves in it. An apology on its own creates doubt. Momentum without recognition of impact feels indifferent. Credibility comes from naming the harm plainly and demonstrating that a structured response is already in motion.

Communication cannot be one-size-fits-all. Different audiences are listening for different signals. Investors are assessing exposure, recovery cost, and forward risk. Customers want proof that services are stable and that failures will not repeat. Regulators expect clarity on the cause and evidence that weaknesses are being corrected. Employees want to know the situation is under control and that their work remains grounded. Alignment does not require identical messages. It requires consistency in intent and discipline in delivery.

Transparency is not full disclosure in a single moment. It is accuracy over time. Leaders should be explicit about what is confirmed, what is still being examined, and when updates will follow. Acknowledging uncertainty does not weaken authority when it is paired with visible ownership and follow-through. In complex incidents, trust is built through steadiness, not speed, and through accountability that holds as facts evolve. What they will not accept is the appearance of concealment. Drawing boundaries between verified facts and ongoing inquiry signals discipline and prevents unrealistic expectations.

Values-based framing reinforces credibility. Leaders should link recovery actions to organizational mission and principles. A healthcare provider might emphasize patient safety when explaining a service disruption. A financial institution might frame its remediation plan through its duty of fiduciary responsibility. Anchoring actions in values helps stakeholders interpret recovery as a continuation of purpose rather than a reaction to crisis.

Recovery communication also extends beyond the immediate event. Trust is rebuilt over time, not at the moment systems are restored. Leaders should continue to share progress on root cause analysis, policy updates, assurance safeguards, and cultural adjustments long after headlines fade. Organizations that sustain communication demonstrate maturity. Those that declare closure too soon risk reopening wounds when stakeholders discover deeper issues remain unresolved.

Two-way engagement strengthens recovery communication. Listening to customer forums, employee feedback, and investor sessions provides insight into how recovery is perceived. These signals guide adjustments in tone, content, and frequency. Listening demonstrates accountability and responsiveness, qualities as valuable to stakeholders as technical fixes.

The executive voice during recovery is more than an operational necessity. It is a strategic instrument that can turn a crisis into a demonstration of resilience. Leaders who communicate with clarity, consistency, and credibility shift the narrative from damage control to strength, integrity, and adaptability.

9.3.1 Executive communication framework for recovery

This framework provides leaders with a structured approach to communication during and after a disruption. Its purpose is to prevent silence, confusion, or misalignment from

Table 9.1 Executive communication framework for recovery

Audience	*Primary concerns*	*Messaging priorities*	*Cadence*
Employees	Job security, safety, and the ability to do their work	Acknowledge disruption, share current status, and provide clear role expectations	Daily or as major updates occur
Customers	Service availability, data protection, and continuity	Communicate what is affected, when it will be restored, and what protections are in place	Public updates as needed and no longer than 48 hours between
Investors/ Board	Financial impact, recovery ROI, long-term implications	Provide facts on impact, progress toward containment, and future prevention plans	Initial briefing within 24 hours with regular updates
Regulators	Compliance, root cause, and corrective actions	Show transparency, cooperation, and systemic changes to avoid repeat events	As required, supplemented by voluntary updates
Media/ Public	Narrative framing, brand trust, and reputation	Demonstrate accountability, values-based recovery, and alignment with mission	Initial press statement, followed by measured updates

making the original incident worse. See Table 9.1: Executive communication framework for recovery.

Effective recovery communication starts with a basic truth. Stakeholders do not experience disruption the same way. Executives must adjust delivery without altering facts or intent. Employees worry about stability. Customers worry about the impact. Investors worry about exposure. Regulators worry about control. When messages drift across audiences, trust breaks down. Consistency is not repetition. It is alignment.

Every executive message during disruption must accomplish three outcomes. First, it must acknowledge the disruption directly. Minimizing impact or hiding behind cautious language signals detachment. Stakeholders are not looking for comfort. They are looking for recognition. Second, the message must establish what is happening now and what will follow. Even limited clarity reduces speculation. Silence creates noise. Third, communication must connect recovery to the organization's values and long-term posture. Fixing the issue is not enough. Stakeholders want to see how it will be handled and why that response reflects who the organization claims to be.

Timing determines credibility. Leadership must speak within the first day, even when details are incomplete. Waiting erodes confidence faster than imperfect disclosure. Early communication should establish awareness, containment, and a commitment to transparency. As the situation evolves, updates should be brief and purposeful. Overproduced statements delay trust. Each update should move understanding forward. Once stability is restored, communication must shift. Operational updates give way to accountability, lessons learned, and concrete improvement. At that stage, reflection matters more than technical explanation.

Channels should follow the audience. Employees expect direct communication through internal systems and their managers. Customers look for clear guidance through direct outreach, support channels, and public notices. Investors and board members require structured briefings that explain impact, risk, and mitigation. Regulators expect formal disclosure through established mechanisms. The media and public should hear from controlled sources using consistent facts and restrained language.

Leadership presence cannot be delegated. The chief executive owns the external narrative and frames recovery in terms of purpose and values. Operational leaders provide clarity on progress and constraints. In some situations, board leadership reinforces accountability and governance. Visibility matters more than volume. When leaders disappear, stakeholders assume loss of control regardless of reality.

Recovery communication is not one-directional. Organizations must listen as deliberately as they speak. Feedback from employees, customers, partners, and investors exposes fractures in confidence early. Signals from support channels, media coverage, and public discourse should shape how messaging evolves. Responsiveness demonstrates seriousness.

Recovery follows a clear arc. The initial phase centers on awareness and containment. The next phase focuses on progress, cause, and immediate safeguards. The final phase explains the structural changes and how the organization is better prepared going forward. This progression reinforces that the disruption was not merely survived but used to strengthen the enterprise.

When handled well, executive communication during disruption does more than preserve trust. It reinforces leadership credibility. Recovery becomes a demonstration of accountability, discipline, and resilience rather than a scramble to restore normalcy.

9.4 TURNING RESILIENCE GAINS INTO STRATEGIC BUSINESS VALUE

Resilience is often treated as a cost center. It is built to minimize loss, reduce downtime, and fulfill regulatory requirements. But in organizations that mature beyond defensive postures, resilience becomes a source of competitive strength. When properly designed, measured, and communicated, resilience does more than protect operations; it creates new business value. Integrated Assurance is the mechanism that makes this shift possible. It transforms the gains achieved during crisis recovery into strategic assets that drive market positioning, operational agility, investor confidence, and long-term growth.

The transition from recovery to relevance requires a deliberate reframing of what resilience means. It is not simply the ability to withstand shock or return to baseline after disruption. In a business context, resilience is the ability to adapt under pressure, make better decisions in volatile conditions, and emerge from uncertainty with enhanced capability. These are not theoretical outcomes. They are operational and measurable. The organizations that recognize this create value not despite disruption, but through it.

The first step in turning resilience into business value is measurement. Without quantification, even the most significant improvements remain anecdotal. Leadership cannot advocate for continued investment in resilience unless the returns are visible, evidenced, and aligned with enterprise objectives. Integrated Assurance provides the architecture to capture these returns. It makes resilience visible in terms of control maturity, recovery velocity, process integrity, and stakeholder confidence.

For example, during a recovery, many organizations deploy new automation, improve telemetry, accelerate detection, or redesign governance workflows. These technical enhancements, while born of necessity, often become permanent upgrades. But unless their impact is tracked, their strategic value is not captured. They remain isolated improvements rather than enterprise-wide signals of progress. See Figure 9.2: Case in Point.

Metrics matter not only for internal clarity but also for the signals they provide to the outside world. Boards and investors look for evidence of operational maturity and protection against loss. When assurance teams can present dashboards that track resilience over time, they are in a stronger position to secure resources, shape enterprise priorities, and take part in strategic planning.

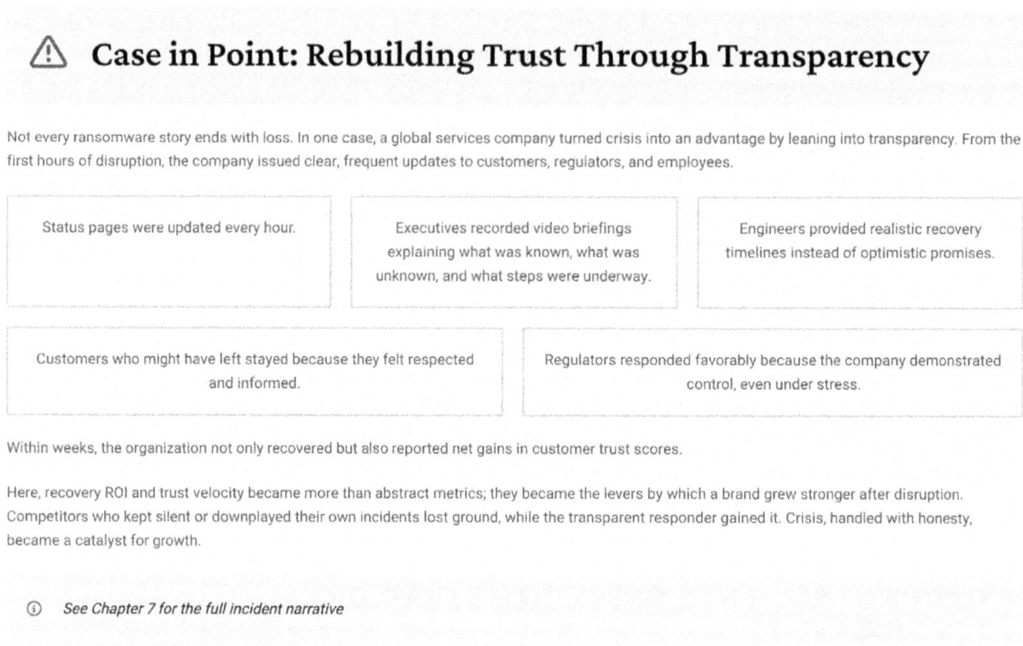

Figure 9.2 Case in Point.

Image created by the author using Gamma.

Resilience maturity also delivers cost benefits. Many organizations find that the controls, platforms, and processes introduced during recovery continue to drive efficiency long after the initial event. A company that deploys automated patch management following a breach usually discovers that overall IT operations run more smoothly. Manual work decreases, vulnerabilities close faster, and audit timelines shorten. Similar advantages appear with stronger access governance or federated identity. These improvements cut administrative workload while improving security.

The financial value of these gains can be measured and linked back to resilience efforts. Integrated Assurance makes that connection visible. Finance and strategy leaders can see how specific investments, such as immutable storage, a zero-trust framework, or real-time monitoring, produced both defensive strength and operational efficiency. This traceability becomes essential when resilience funding must stand alongside revenue-generating projects in transformation roadmaps.

Resilience also brings agility. Enterprises with mature assurance can move into new markets sooner, adopt emerging technologies more quickly, and expand services with less friction. The reason is not just technical readiness but the presence of governance structures, decision authority, and assurance mechanisms that enable fast, confident movement.

An organization that emerged from a regulatory investigation with a redesigned data governance model may have started under compliance pressure, but the outcome can serve as a foundation for growth. With demonstrable data lineage, control enforcement, and consent management, the same enterprise is prepared to expand into jurisdictions with strict privacy laws, such as the European Union or California. What began as regulatory compliance becomes the capability to pursue new markets.

Resilience also underpins innovation. Executive teams are more willing to approve ambitious projects, whether AI pilots, acquisitions, cloud migrations, or global service delivery, when they have confidence that risk can be managed. Integrated Assurance builds that confidence through forward-looking telemetry, structured escalation paths, and scenario modeling. Transformation then advances with safeguards in place, not as a gamble.

The confidence to move fast with precision is a hallmark of resilient organizations. They are not reckless. They are calculated. Their assurance function does not slow them down. It allows them to operate with trust at speed. That trust is internal and external, across partners, customers, regulators, and the broader market ecosystem.

Reputational capital is perhaps the most overlooked asset created during recovery. When stakeholders observe an organization navigating a crisis with integrity, transparency, and competence, their perception of the brand evolves. They no longer see just a service provider or a product vendor. They see a responsible, mature organization capable of leadership during uncertainty. This elevated status can translate into customer loyalty, regulatory goodwill, and investor preference. But reputational gains do not happen automatically. They require intentional storytelling backed by assurance data. Integrated Assurance teams must work alongside communications, investor relations, and customer experience teams to translate recovery metrics into narratives that resonate. For the board, this may mean dashboards tied to risk appetite. For investors, it could be integrated resilience metrics in reports. For customers, it may be service-level transparency reports. Without these efforts, the benefits of resilience maturity remain buried in operational silos.

Sales and procurement functions also benefit from assurance-driven resilience. In many industries, particularly those with strict regulatory or privacy obligations, trustworthiness is a buying criterion. Customers demand proof that vendors can withstand disruption, protect sensitive data, and recover quickly when something goes wrong. Integrated Assurance makes these proof points accessible.

Sales teams equipped with up-to-date assurance documentation, third-party audit results, and real-time risk profiles are better positioned to close deals, especially in competitive scenarios. Procurement teams, likewise, benefit from reduced due diligence overhead when vendors maintain observable and verified assurance postures. This reduces sales friction, speeds onboarding, and enables faster revenue realization.

Some organizations go even further and productize their resilience capabilities. For example, a cybersecurity firm that built advanced detection systems to recover from a past breach may commercialize those capabilities as managed services. A cloud platform that improved deployment rollback automation might repackage that feature into a higher-value service tier. The tools, processes, and practices developed in recovery can become offerings in their own right. Assurance becomes a pathway to innovation monetization.

Resilience also improves strategic alignment across functions. When organizations rebuild using Integrated Assurance, they create governance structures that clarify roles, improve communication, and reduce friction. These changes may be subtle, but they have cascading impacts. Decision rights are clearer. Teams coordinate more easily. Leadership receives better visibility into risk exposure and opportunity windows. These internal dynamics increase execution speed and reduce the likelihood of failure during future transformation efforts.

One effective approach is the alignment of assurance milestones with performance incentives. When resilience goals—such as risk reduction, control integrity, or response coordination—are linked to individual or team performance bonuses, they become part of the operating culture. Assurance moves from being a checkbox function to a value-generating discipline. Teams are incentivized not just to meet deadlines or hit revenue targets, but to build operational structures that are sustainable, scalable, and trustworthy.

Resilience lessons must also be made portable. In large organizations, incidents may occur in one division, region, or business unit, but the lessons should not stay there. Integrated Assurance acts as a knowledge broker across the organization. It captures insights, contextualizes them for relevance, and ensures they are disseminated across peer groups. This lateral transfer of knowledge strengthens enterprise-wide resilience while avoiding duplicated mistakes.

The cumulative impact of these practices is an enterprise that treats resilience not as a temporary requirement, but as a permanent differentiator. It becomes known as a company that does not merely avoid crisis, but that evolves through it. Over time, this identity becomes part of the organization's value proposition. Customers expect reliability. Employees feel empowered. Investors see consistency. Regulators recognize leadership.

The rise of stakeholder capitalism and systemic risk means that resilience is no longer a back-office concept. It is a strategic lever. Organizations that can measure it, communicate it, and grow it will outperform those that view it as a sunk cost.

Integrated Assurance is what makes that leverage possible. It translates the hard-earned gains of recovery into the language of business performance. It connects the technical to the strategic, the operational to the financial, and the resilient to the relevant. In the next section, we will examine how assurance itself can become a visible market differentiation that drives preference, pricing power, and leadership in a competitive, trust-driven economy.

9.5 USING ASSURANCE AS A MARKET DIFFERENTIATOR

Risk exposure, interdependence, and transparency demands define competition. Organizations are no longer judged solely on the basis of their products, services, or pricing. They are judged on how well they manage complexity. In this setting, trust becomes more than a marketing phrase. It functions as business currency, and assurance provides the infrastructure that sustains that currency. When recognized and applied strategically, assurance shifts from being a compliance requirement to a market differentiator that influences customer loyalty, procurement decisions, investor confidence, and overall market share.

Assurance once lived almost entirely in the back office. It was managed by audit teams, compliance staff, and risk managers, often out of public view. The goal was to satisfy regulators, avoid penalties, and clear audit findings. These goals remain important, but they represent only a portion of assurance's value. Modern enterprises can now externalize assurance. They can make it visible, measurable, and directly linked to their business proposition. When handled with discipline, visibility stops being a reporting function and becomes a source of advantage that is difficult for competitors to reproduce.

In sectors where data sensitivity, regulatory pressure, or physical safety are central to operations, trust is scarce by default. Buyers in these environments no longer make decisions on features or price alone. They scrutinize governance behavior, operational resilience, and how organizations absorb disruption without creating downstream risk. Financial services, healthcare, energy, logistics, and cloud infrastructure all show this shift clearly.

That reality rewards organizations that have invested in Integrated Assurance as an operating capability. Instead of asserting that they are secure or compliant, they can show how those conditions are built, measured, and sustained over time. Differentiation comes not from words but from evidence.

One of the most effective strategies is structured transparency. Enterprises that proactively publish trust reports, maintain customer-facing dashboards, issue post-incident summaries, or hold governance briefings establish confidence faster than competitors who remain silent. Structured transparency does not require revealing every detail. It involves providing curated visibility into assurance maturity in ways that are useful to customers, partners, and regulators.

Take the example of a SaaS provider that distributes a quarterly resilience bulletin. This bulletin might present patching metrics, audit results, privacy policy updates, and planned control improvements. When written as a business artifact, it supports customer due diligence by legal, security, and procurement teams. Over time, the regular cadence of these updates becomes part of the customer relationship. Assurance in this context is not a defensive task. It is a relationship asset.

The advantage is most visible during competitive procurement cycles. In regulated markets, procurement teams dig deep into vendor risk. They evaluate whether suppliers pose hidden exposure, whether compliance evidence is readily available, and whether incidents will be managed with integrity. Vendors able to present structured documentation, audit results, and automated assurance data often move ahead of competitors.

Integrated Assurance strengthens this position by making the control environment observable and repeatable. Instead of struggling with one-off questionnaires, organizations can maintain standardized assurance profiles mapped to frameworks like ISO 27001, Security Operations Center (SOC) 2, NIST CSF, or Cloud Security Alliance cloud control model. Security teams reduce administrative burden. Sales teams present trust artifacts with confidence. Legal teams streamline contract terms. The result is faster sales cycles and higher win rates.

Some companies elevate this approach further by branding their assurance posture. A financial technology firm might advertise "audit-ready infrastructure." A logistics provider may market its real-time risk dashboards as a premium service. A digital identity vendor can highlight policy automation as a reason customers scale faster with lower friction. In these cases, assurance is not silent. It is part of the customer promise.

Achieving this level of externalization requires cross-functional alignment. Marketing must translate assurance into messages that customers understand. Legal must ensure disclosures strike the right balance. Product teams must design experiences that reinforce governance maturity. No single team owns assurance. It becomes a shared narrative supported by data.

Language matters in this process. Technical jargon rarely connects with business stakeholders. Translating control concepts into clear business outcomes builds confidence. Least privilege, for example, can be described as a safeguard against misuse of data. Penetration testing can be explained as stress testing that ensures systems are prepared for real threats. Clear communication turns technical maturity into customer assurance.

Clarity also influences pricing power. Customers often pay a premium when they believe a provider is more resilient and accountable than its competitors. Healthcare organizations may prefer cloud providers that offer high-availability architectures backed by live compliance dashboards. Defense contractors may choose vendors that can pass assessments without delay. Trust reduces procurement friction, increases velocity, and protects margin.

The effect reaches beyond the organization itself. Partner ecosystems depend on confidence between parties that do not share control. When assurance is visible and grounded in evidence, oversight becomes lighter and cooperation improves. Clear assurance reduces friction because expectations are understood before problems arise.

Assurance also influences who chooses to work for the organization. In constrained labor markets, experienced professionals pay attention to how seriously leadership treats accountability. When assurance is part of daily operations, it signals discipline and purpose. That signal attracts people who want to work in environments that take responsibility seriously.

External perception shifts over time. Analysts, regulators, investors, and journalists tend to associate consistent transparency with sound governance. Organizations that publish roadmaps, participate in standards bodies, and speak openly about lessons learned are viewed as credible operators rather than reactive ones.

Crisis tolerance is where the difference becomes most visible. Enterprises that have made assurance explicit before a disruption are more likely to retain confidence when something breaks. Stakeholders already understand how risk is managed, how controls are exercised, and how failures are addressed. That familiarity acts as a buffer when pressure is highest.

To achieve this level of differentiation, leaders must invest in substance and story. Substance requires strong controls, processes, and metrics. Story requires communication that stakeholders can understand and believe. One without the other leaves assurance hollow or invisible. Together, they form the basis of a new kind of market leadership.

Integrated Assurance makes this possible. It equips organizations with repeatable, evidence-based mechanisms for demonstrating trust. It shifts assurance from a defensive necessity into a strategic asset that drives confidence, accelerates growth, and strengthens resilience.

9.6 IAMM AND RECOVERY METRICS

Recovery determines whether resilience lives in theory or practice. The IAMM Metrics and Reporting domain provides a structured method for assessing recovery based on impact rather than activity. It draws a line between restoring service and restoring trust.

At Level 1, recovery goes unmeasured. Teams celebrate the return of service without examining the cost, time, or trust implications. Reports rely on anecdotes and lessons-learned sessions that lack structure. Leadership has no clear view of whether recovery investments deliver value.

Level 2 introduces measurement but focuses on basic activity. Metrics capture system restoration time and incident counts. These figures show effort, not effectiveness. Leaders know how long systems were down but not whether customers or regulators regained confidence.

At Level 3, recovery metrics align with business performance. Teams measure downtime costs and recovery time objectives across systems. Service levels are tracked against targets, and reports blend technical and operational insights. This coordination helps leadership prioritize critical systems and improve planning. Yet the organization still struggles to show resilience outcomes.

Level 4 transforms recovery into a measure of trust and return. Metrics expand to include trust velocity and recovery ROI. Trust velocity tracks how quickly confidence returns among customers, employees, and partners. Recovery ROI quantifies whether resilience spending produces proportional benefit. At this stage, recovery becomes an enterprise performance indicator. Leadership can link resilience metrics to revenue retention, brand health, and regulatory confidence.

Level 5 integrates these measures into continuous reporting. Dashboards present live trust indicators and resilience performance. Boards review them with financial reports. Stakeholders see tangible proof that recovery processes sustain confidence. Recovery metrics evolve into part of the organization's market identity, representing dependability and capability.

A regional utility offers a clear example. After a cyberattack causes a prolonged outage, leaders at Level 2 measure only restoration time. Customers grow frustrated, and confidence declines. At Level 4, the same organization measures transparency, communication response, and satisfaction recovery. These insights guide better outreach and justify automation investments. Within months, customer trust recovers, showing that resilience is measured not just by uptime but by renewed credibility.

Barriers to effective recovery measurement arise from limited visibility. Technical teams concentrate on restoring systems, while executives frame recovery in financial terms. IAMM bridges these perspectives by defining metrics that connect technical performance with stakeholder outcomes.

Organizations that apply this structure track trust recovery alongside system restoration. They measure recovery ROI and make resilience metrics visible to boards and customers. Outcomes inform future investments, shifting focus from operational activity to strategic relevance. IAMM shows that recovery maturity extends beyond reducing downtime. It proves the value of resilience to every stakeholder. Enterprises that measure trust recovery secure a lasting advantage because they can demonstrate reliability rather than merely claim it.

9.7 EVOLVING THROUGH POST-CRISIS LEADERSHIP

A brand is no longer built through advertising, product releases, or digital campaigns alone. In a trust-driven economy, it is defined in moments of disruption. A crisis becomes the test that reveals the organization's true character. Spin and surface polish fall away, leaving stakeholders to judge the response itself. In this environment, assurance shifts from a back-office exercise to a visible brand asset. It shapes perception, builds credibility, and reintroduces the enterprise to its markets.

When disruption strikes, whether through a breach, outage, regulatory issue, or controversy, the organization faces a void in the narrative. Stakeholders wait to see who speaks, what message is delivered, and what actions follow. Silence leaves the story to others. Defensive statements raise doubts. Transparent communication, paired with structural change, begins the process of renewal. Assurance provides the backbone for that process, showing that the enterprise is not just reacting but transforming with discipline and permanence.

The first decision in recovery is whether to minimize or to confront. Many organizations fall into the trap of managing perception rather than addressing substance. They release vague updates, assign fault to outside actors, or highlight fast recovery instead of meaningful reform. These approaches may check a compliance box, but they fail to meet modern expectations. Customers, regulators, investors, and employees look for responsibility, visible change, and proof of integration into daily operations. Integrated Assurance gives leadership the ability to present this proof through new controls, governance frameworks, training programs, and stakeholder engagement. These are not slogans. They are systems that speak for themselves.

Reputation begins to turn when the organization stops portraying itself as a casualty and starts leading with evidence of progress. A company known for opacity can shift toward transparency by opening its practices, publishing findings, and inviting independent validation. A business once defined by failure can reshape itself around demonstrable reform. Assurance makes this credible because it anchors the narrative in verified systems and repeatable actions.

The effect extends inside the organization. Employees measure leadership by how it responds under pressure. They stay engaged when they see accountability, humility, and investments in long-term improvement. Motivation comes from action. When staff are brought into recovery efforts, given meaningful roles in rebuilding, and kept informed of progress, morale strengthens. This turns crisis response into a cultural anchor, particularly in technical and risk-heavy functions where retention matters most.

Externally, reputation depends not only on the first statement but on the persistence of follow-through. An apology fades if it is not reinforced. A press release disappears if not backed by visible progress. Enterprises that set a rhythm of updates, publish lessons learned, and maintain open dialogue show maturity. The narrative shifts from one of fragility to one of resilience. What emerges is not perfection but proof, in the form of validated controls, published audits, and engaged stakeholders.

Over time, media, investors, and partners begin to take notice. Journalists who reported the failure may return to cover the transformation if the evidence is there. Investors reward signs of governance maturity with renewed confidence, often treating assurance metrics as indicators of long-term value. Boards highlight recovery milestones in earnings calls. Leadership frames resilience as a competitive advantage. In doing so, the organization demonstrates that it is stronger for having endured the challenge.

Assurance-driven recovery also creates influence. Enterprises that can point to credible transformation often find themselves at the center of industry discussions. They are asked to share lessons, contribute to standards, and mentor others. This influence is difficult to buy with marketing spend, but it comes naturally when trust has been rebuilt through evidence.

Storytelling plays a role, but the story must be grounded in proof. Diagrams of rebuilt systems, metrics from new training programs, and published assurance reports give credibility to the message. Timelines and dashboards help reinforce that recovery is a process, not a moment. In the earliest days, authenticity carries the most weight. Attention is high, and insincerity is easy to detect.

The objective is not to restore the precrisis brand, which may have concealed real weaknesses. The objective is to emerge with a stronger one shaped by pressure and corrective action. Integrated Assurance supports that shift by hardwiring change into governance, operations, and culture rather than treating recovery as a communications exercise.

Organizations that manage this transition well are rarely defined by the incident itself. They are remembered for how leadership responded. Stakeholders recall clarity, follow-through, and visible improvement. Over time, those signals outweigh the failure, and brand equity is rebuilt on proof of resilience and maturity rather than promise.

9.8 EMBEDDING LEARNINGS INTO THE NEXT GENERATION OF ASSURANCE

Every disruption exposes blind spots. It shows the weaknesses in policy, the fragility of design, the gaps in decision-making, and the points where roles are misaligned. The organizations that endure are not those that avoid disruption, but those that capture the lessons and use them to strengthen their operating model. Too often, recovery is treated as the end of the process. The immediate issue is fixed, the audit requirement is met, and operations return to a familiar state. That familiar state is often the environment where the failure began.

Long-term value comes from transforming what has been learned into structural change. This is where Integrated Assurance provides guidance. It moves the enterprise beyond reports and analyses into a framework for reform. The objective is not only recovery. It is the creation of a more trustworthy and capable enterprise.

The first step is codification. Lessons cannot remain in meeting notes or informal conversations. They must be expressed in updated controls, governance protocols, operational playbooks, and training. Integrated Assurance provides the structure that converts reflection into reform. With it, learning becomes systematic.

Each significant incident should trigger a cycle that captures technical, procedural, organizational, and cultural insights. What succeeded, what failed, and what changed must all be recorded. From there, reforms can be designed and implemented. If poor change control contributed to a failure, reforms might include stronger approval gates, automated rollback functions, or improved observability. Each measure must then be validated, monitored, and governed through assurance processes.

Codification should not be episodic. Integrated Assurance ensures that it becomes continuous. Policies are versioned, playbooks updated, and risk registers revised. Metrics are tied to these lessons so that improvement is measured rather than assumed. If access practices are updated, assurance tracks coverage, exception rates, and hygiene scores over time. These measures show whether learning has taken root.

Culture is often where the most serious failures begin. Escalation may be slow, incentives misaligned, or confidence misplaced. Correcting these issues requires leadership that emphasizes systems over individuals. Integrated Assurance brings clarity to cultural issues by framing them in structures that can be examined and corrected.

Governance must also evolve. In the wake of disruption, many enterprises tighten control to reduce risk. This may protect in the short term, but it often leads to stagnation. A better approach is distributed governance, where teams make informed decisions within defined trust boundaries. Integrated Assurance enables this balance by embedding guidance, escalation protocols, and metrics into the daily decision framework.

To support distributed governance, organizations can use enablement tools. These might include policy-as-code engines, health monitors for controls, third-party scoring systems, or deployment guardrails. Such tools give teams the ability to self-govern while keeping the enterprise within its risk tolerance. At the same time, they create feedback loops for central assurance functions without requiring intrusive oversight.

Learning must also travel. Disruptions may occur in one region or one product line, but the insights usually apply elsewhere. Integrated Assurance ensures that those lessons are portable. Centralized knowledge hubs, simulation libraries, and cross-functional forums extend learning across the enterprise.

Simulation strengthens retention. Incidents can be transformed into exercises, continuity drills, or red-team scenarios. These allow leaders and teams to test knowledge, refine responses, and practice decision-making in realistic conditions. Over time, simulations evolve into benchmarks for resilience.

Communities of practice provide another layer of reinforcement. Cross-functional groups that convene to share patterns, review controls, and challenge assumptions accelerate institutional learning. They help organizations refine assurance models as business conditions shift.

Stakeholder engagement deepens the process. After crises, most organizations meet disclosure requirements. Mature organizations extend this further by creating ongoing feedback channels with customers, regulators, and partners. These signals highlight blind spots early and align assurance with external expectations.

Metrics must adapt as well. Traditional measures like audit findings and compliance rates remain useful but do not capture resilience. Advanced metrics such as trust recovery time, control adaptability, or resilience ROI shift the view from compliance to performance. They position assurance as an enterprise driver rather than a narrow control function.

Assurance also needs to broaden its audience. Risks today extend across product design, customer trust, financial management, and human resources. Integrated Assurance treats assurance as a shared enterprise function rather than a specialist responsibility. That means product teams design with resilience in mind, legal teams prepare for evidence in regulatory contexts, finance links control maturity to capital decisions, and HR builds resilience into leadership and performance.

This demands new talent models. Leaders must combine systems thinking with business fluency. Data analysts must connect control telemetry with customer sentiment. Governance professionals must show how decisions influence both risk and reputation.

Technology supports this work. Modern assurance platforms should bring together telemetry, process signals, and stakeholder feedback. They provide visibility, alerting, and workflow automation without overwhelming decision-makers with noise. Most importantly, they present assurance information in a form that executives and operators can act on.

Culture anchors the transformation. An organization that values reflection, transparency, and progress over perfection will embed learning more effectively. Leaders must be willing to share failures and reward improvement. Teams must see assurance not as interference but as an enabler of clarity and confidence.

Organizations that reach this level treat assurance as a living capability. They no longer wait for disruption to reveal weaknesses. They simulate, test, and refine continuously. Each event becomes fuel for progress. The result is a more agile, coordinated, and credible enterprise. Assurance moves from a compliance function to a driver of performance, signaling leadership and reinforcing trust.

9.9 CONCLUSION

Organizations often declare victory once operations are restored. Servers are back online, employees return to their routines, customers regain access to services, and leaders declare that the crisis has passed. Yet this sense of closure is misleading. Returning to baseline is only the beginning. The true test is whether the enterprise builds lasting credibility and remains relevant in the eyes of its stakeholders.

Recovery represents a technical accomplishment. Relevance represents a leadership accomplishment. Restoring a database or patching a system does not rebuild confidence on its own. What strengthens confidence is the visible demonstration that lessons have been absorbed and improvements have been embedded. Stakeholders want to see that the enterprise has reduced the likelihood of recurrence and that its leaders recognize the weight of the disruption.

Many executives assume that stability alone will restore trust. Smooth operations do not erase memory. Customers recall the outage that interrupted their experience. Regulators recall the oversight gaps. Investors recall the financial impact. Employees recall the stress of working under strain. These recollections influence reputation long after systems return to normal.

The period of silence after recovery is often the most dangerous. If leaders fail to explain what has been learned and how it has been applied, stakeholders will assume reforms are superficial. Doubt lingers quietly and begins to shape decisions about loyalty, compliance, and investment.

Trust today requires evidence. Stakeholders expect data that shows reforms are real. They want reports, dashboards, independent validation, and ongoing visibility. Words alone are dismissed as public relations. Assurance provides the structure to produce and communicate this proof. It ties reforms to measurable outcomes, maps them to governance, and shows resilience in a way that can be observed rather than assumed.

Moving from recovery to relevance requires visible leadership. Executives must signal that the crisis is not treated as a passing event but as a turning point for lasting improvement. When leaders acknowledge responsibility, explain actions, and invite accountability, credibility begins to rebuild. Without this presence, even the most effective technical recovery is weakened.

The most important work begins once headlines fade. Reforms must be institutionalized and embedded in governance and culture. Temporary measures may address short-term concerns, but only tested and reinforced controls create lasting resilience. Integrated Assurance keeps reforms active by linking them to risk registers, resilience indicators, and executive reporting. It ensures they are visible to employees, regulators, investors, and customers alike.

Organizations that embed assurance gain advantages beyond stability. They attract investors who value transparency. They appeal to customers who prioritize reliability. They earn respect in regulatory discussions and industry partnerships. This is not a passive outcome. It is created by leaders who convert resilience into strategic value, measure improvements, and communicate results as part of their narrative.

At the highest level of maturity, assurance becomes an identity. The enterprise is recognized not only for its products or services but also for its transparency and reliability. Disruption

Use this checklist as a discussion guide with your team to turn recovery into lasting relevance. Treat each question as a prompt for action, not a box to tick.

1

Rebuilding Trust Post-Crisis

- ☐ Have we distinguished between technical recovery (systems back online) and trust recovery (stakeholder confidence)?
- ☐ Did we conduct transparent and blame-free post-incident reviews that reinforce shared risk ownership?
- ☐ Are corrective actions validated, documented, and communicated as proof of change rather than just fixes?

2

Applying Assurance Models

- ☐ Which of the five models (Real-Time Communicator, Governance Reformer, Customer-Centric Builder, Policy Evangelist, Transparency Leader) best aligns with our organization's context and culture?
- ☐ Do we have the governance and cultural readiness to adopt that model, or should we adapt elements from several?

3

Executive Communication

- ☐ Are our communication strategies built around clarity, consistency, and credibility?
- ☐ Do we segment messaging for employees, customers, investors, regulators, and the public with aligned but tailored priorities?
- ☐ Is leadership visibly present and accountable during recovery, not hidden behind technical teams?

4

Turning Resilience into Business Value

- ☐ Do we measure resilience gains (e.g., recovery velocity, control integrity, resilience ROI) and tie them to enterprise strategy?
- ☐ Have we identified efficiency gains (automation, reduced audit cycles, improved operations) and quantified their financial impact?
- ☐ Are resilience investments being linked to agility, innovation confidence, and market readiness?

5

Using Assurance as a Market Differentiator

- ☐ Do we externalize assurance through trust reports, dashboards, or transparency summaries?
- ☐ Are assurance achievements communicated in business language that resonates with customers, partners, and investors?
- ☐ Have we considered productizing resilience or assurance capabilities as part of our value proposition?

6

Evolving Brand and Reputation

- ☐ Is our post-crisis narrative backed by evidence (audit trails, new controls, training metrics), not just words?
- ☐ Do employees feel included in recovery and see visible signs of accountability and change?
- ☐ Are we sustaining communication beyond the initial crisis, reinforcing our brand as trustworthy and adaptable?

7

Embedding Learnings

- ☐ Have lessons from disruption been codified into policies, runbooks, governance protocols, and training?
- ☐ Do we have mechanisms (simulations, knowledge hubs, or communities of practice) to share lessons across the enterprise?
- ☐ Are new assurance metrics (trust recovery time, stakeholder confidence velocity) part of ongoing performance management?

8

Leadership Reflection

- ☐ Can we demonstrate that recovery actions have become systemic improvements, not temporary fixes?
- ☐ Are we positioning resilience as a permanent differentiator and assurance as an enabler of relevance?
- ☐ Most importantly: can we prove to boards, regulators, customers, and employees that we do not just recover from disruption—we grow stronger because of it?

☐ **Executive Action:** Recovery is only the midpoint. Executives must ensure that lessons learned are codified, trust is visibly rebuilt, and resilience is leveraged as a strategic advantage. The mandate is clear: Turn every disruption into evidence of maturity, transparency, and relevance.

Figure 9.3 Practical Checklist: From Recovery to Relevance.

Image created by the author using Gamma.

becomes a moment to reinforce that identity, and every assurance practice becomes proof of it. For this to work, assurance must be cultural. Employees need to see it as part of their daily role. Leaders must provide tools that make assurance actionable. Governance must integrate assurance metrics into decisions. Only then does assurance move from the back office to the front line of enterprise character.

Success after a crisis is not measured by survival. It is measured by whether the enterprise has emerged stronger. Evidence of reduced likelihood, stronger governance, and renewed confidence must be visible. The organizations that achieve this are remembered for their resilience, not for the incident itself. Leaders must recognize that recovery is not the finish line. It is the moment when the real work begins. Weaknesses have already been exposed. The responsibility now is to address them directly and to institutionalize improvements through Integrated Assurance. This is not the role of compliance or technology teams alone. It is a leadership responsibility that demands enterprise-wide commitment.

Recovery stabilizes. Relevance elevates. Between these two outcomes lies the opportunity to redefine the enterprise. Disruption will come again. The only question is whether the next event will reveal fragility or demonstrate resilience. Leaders who embed assurance ensure that the next crisis becomes proof of strength. Recovery is fleeting. Relevance endures. The organizations that understand this turn trust into a permanent source of value, influence, and leadership. See Figure 9.3: Practical Checklist: From Recovery to Relevance.

Part IV

Designing for Endurance

Chapter 10

Futureproofing with Integrated Assurance

10.1 FUTUREPROOFING WITH INTEGRATED ASSURANCE

The future does not wait for the enterprise to be ready. Breaches unfold in minutes, not months. New regulations arrive faster than policy libraries can be updated. Business models pivot with little warning. Competitors exploit speed as their advantage, while attackers use automation and AI to outpace defenses. In this environment, organizations that continue to rely on static assurance models will not simply fall behind. They will be left exposed in ways that are both measurable and visible to stakeholders.

The danger of static assurance is not theoretical. Consider the enterprise that secures a major cloud provider contract based on a year-old vendor assessment. The provider introduces a new feature powered by generative AI, but the change slips through unnoticed because the review cycle has not yet reached its next checkpoint. Within weeks, customer data is processed under conditions the enterprise neither anticipated nor approved. When regulators demand answers, the organization can only produce outdated documents. Trust evaporates instantly.

Examples like this illustrate why the old belief that "structure equals security" no longer holds. For decades, organizations equated detailed policies, layered approval processes, and expansive checklists with maturity. That mindset belonged to an earlier era when technology evolved slowly and risk moved along predictable paths. Today, the speed of deployment, the distributed nature of architectures, and the porous boundaries of data ecosystems demand something different. They require assurance that behaves more like a living system than a static report.

Living assurance is the defining concept of futureproof resilience. It is an assurance designed to sense change, adapt posture, and maintain trust in real time. Unlike static models, which freeze controls in policy binders or compliance calendars, living assurance draws its strength from continuous observability and embedded decision points. It connects directly to the systems it governs, learns from feedback, and responds without waiting for quarterly reviews. It is less about preventing every failure and more about ensuring that the enterprise detects, contains, and recovers before damage becomes existential.

This chapter examines why futureproofing is not about technology alone. The enterprise can migrate workloads to the cloud, deploy container platforms, adopt AI pipelines, or automate delivery cycles, but none of those investments guarantee resilience if the assurance framework remains anchored to outdated assumptions. Tools without adaptive trust mechanisms introduce fragility. They accelerate business change while leaving governance stranded in the past. The result is an expanding attack surface paired with shrinking visibility.

The argument begins with the limits of static assurance. Rigid frameworks once offered comfort by imposing order, but they now operate too slowly for environments defined by microservices, ephemeral infrastructure, and distributed identities. By the time an audit

DOI: 10.1201/9781003685982-14

identifies a risk, it may already be in production, visible to customers, or exploited by adversaries. Even when controls appear to be in place, they are often misaligned with reality, creating a false sense of confidence. Assurance becomes documentation rather than defense.

The second theme is integration. Assurance cannot be an add-on that appears at the end of a project. It must be woven into enterprise architecture, pipelines, and operations from the start. When embedded into blueprints and design patterns, assurance becomes as natural as cost optimization or performance tuning. It guides decisions at the point of action, ensuring that trust is not a later concern but a structural property of the system itself.

The third theme is anticipation. Threats evolve in ways that outpace checklists. Deepfakes, poisoned data, adversarial AI, and supply chain manipulation are not captured well in static questionnaires or annual vendor reviews. Futureproof assurance depends on the ability to detect the unknown, interpret its meaning, and respond before risk turns into impact. That requires telemetry, scenario testing, and the cultural discipline to treat risk as a shared responsibility.

Finally, the chapter explores evolution. Assurance that stands still becomes irrelevant. The organization must treat it as a capability that matures over time, not a project with a start and end date. That means using feedback loops, scorecards, and experimentation to ensure controls remain effective. It means learning from every incident, no matter how small, and codifying that learning into processes and tools that can scale across the enterprise. Evolution is not optional. It is the only way to ensure that assurance keeps pace with both technology and business expectations.

Living assurance binds these themes together. It functions less like a gatekeeper and more like an immune system. It detects anomalies as they emerge, responds proportionally, and grows stronger through exposure. It connects to enterprise telemetry, adapts through automation, and scales with architecture. It is supported by people who understand that resilience is measured not only by technical defenses but also by clarity of accountability and cultural alignment.

Futureproofing, therefore, is not about building systems that never fail. It is about building systems that know how to recover quickly, prove their integrity under scrutiny, and sustain trust even in turbulence. It is about shifting assurance from a static artifact that reacts to yesterday's conditions into a living capability that evolves with tomorrow's reality.

This chapter makes the case that Integrated Assurance is the only credible path forward. By embedding assurance into design, pipelines, and governance, organizations create trust as an input rather than an afterthought. By embracing living assurance systems, they build resilience that is both adaptive and measurable. By committing to continuous evolution, they transform assurance from compliance theater into a strategic advantage.

Readers should approach the material with two guiding questions. First, is the assurance function in their enterprise keeping pace with the velocity of change? Second, can they demonstrate trust not only through documents but also through live, observable evidence? The answers to these questions will reveal whether their current posture is capable of protecting not only technology but also brand, reputation, and long-term strategic value.

The following sections will explore these questions in detail. We begin by confronting the weaknesses of static assurance models and why they collapse under the pressure of modern enterprise speed. We then examine how embedding assurance into architecture and pipelines transforms it from a reactive checkpoint into an enabler of safe innovation. Next, we look ahead to emerging threats that static models cannot anticipate, and we outline how Integrated Assurance prepares organizations for the unknown. From there, we turn to the principles of building living assurance systems that adapt in real time, and we conclude with strategies for ensuring assurance capabilities continue to evolve alongside business needs.

Futureproofing with Integrated Assurance is not a slogan. It is a practical requirement. The organizations that survive disruption will be those that treat trust as a designed property, not a side effect. They will not rely on last year's assessments to defend against tomorrow's adversaries. They will operate with living assurance systems that measure, adapt, and prove trust continuously. That is the new baseline for resilience.

10.2 INTEGRATING ASSURANCE INTO ENTERPRISE ARCHITECTURE

Assurance cannot operate effectively as something added after the fact. In an enterprise defined by scale, complexity, and constant change, lasting trust can only be achieved when it is built into the very structure of the organization. That structure begins with enterprise architecture.

Architecture is far more than a system map. It is the translation of business strategy into technology capabilities. It determines how systems connect, how decisions are made, how data flows, and how resilience is established. If assurance is not embedded in this translation, it becomes reactive. It ends up downstream of design, disconnected from context, chasing problems it had no opportunity to prevent.

Integrating assurance into architecture requires changing its place in the enterprise. It cannot exist only in a policy library or on a compliance calendar. It must be present in reference models, solution design templates, and the systems of record used by architects and engineers to make decisions. This is not about oversight. It is about positioning. Assurance must be at the blueprinting table, not simply waiting at the approval gate.

Many architecture frameworks, such as The Open Group Architecture Framework (TOGAF), Zachman, and Sherwood Applied Business Security Architecture (SABSA), provide room for security and governance. In practice, however, these considerations are often abstracted or placed in silos. Assurance is treated as a nonfunctional requirement, secondary to performance or scalability. This is a critical misstep. Trust is not an optional feature. It is a core property of a well-architected system. Like performance or cost optimization, it must be engineered from the outset.

The process begins with patterns. Architecture benefits from repeatable models, and assurance should follow the same principle. Develop architectural patterns that include embedded trust capabilities such as preconfigured access models, observability scaffolding, service-level boundaries, and encryption by default. These patterns should be version-controlled, auditable, and context-aware. They are anchors of assurance.

From there, attention must turn to decision points. Every architectural choice introduces or mitigates risk. The selection of a cloud region, the choice of a data platform, and the method of federating identity all carry risk implications. These decisions should be made with assurance as a source of clarity rather than as a blocker. Key questions include what risk the architecture introduces, what compensating controls are assumed, and what telemetry will indicate that the system is behaving outside expected norms.

Integrated Assurance provides the language and tools to address these questions without slowing momentum. It allows architects to discuss risk in architectural terms such as control coverage, attack surface, and dependency integrity rather than relying solely on compliance terminology. It enables assurance teams to participate in architecture review boards not as gatekeepers but as trusted advisors.

The practical benefits of this alignment are significant. When assurance is built into architecture, it scales naturally. There is no need to manually inspect every implementation because the architecture enforces baseline controls. Governance does not have to be retroactively applied to each project because the framework already guides compliant design. Assurance becomes part of the environment, operating automatically and consistently.

This integration is especially important in environments undergoing change. Digital transformations, cloud migrations, and platform consolidations all introduce volatility. Without assurance embedded in the design fabric, every change triggers a governance scramble. Teams are forced to improvise controls, exceptions multiply, and risk escalates.

When assurance is integrated into the architecture discipline, change becomes safer. New initiatives can follow preapproved trust patterns. Deviations are visible by design. Trade-offs are documented and accountable. Assurance grows with transformation instead of being sidelined by it.

There is also a visibility advantage. Integrated Assurance has access to upstream telemetry. Architecture knows what systems exist, how they interconnect, and what dependencies they carry. This information enables real-time control coverage analysis, dependency risk mapping, and predictive failure modeling. These are not theoretical gains but foundational capabilities for proactive assurance.

Integration also shortens the time-to-trust for new products and services. Instead of requiring lengthy bespoke assurance reviews, these offerings inherit their trust posture from the architecture they are built on. A service deployed using a secure-by-design pattern with validated telemetry pipelines does not need weeks of review. It simply needs confirmation that the approved pattern was followed, reducing friction without reducing rigor.

Embedding assurance in architecture also changes how engineering teams work. It becomes part of their design thinking rather than a compliance afterthought. Instead of asking whether security has been added, they ask which assurance pattern should be applied. This transforms assurance from a reactive checklist into a design-time decision.

Effective integration requires the right tools. Architecture repositories must support assurance metadata. Design tools should link to control catalogs. Continuous integration and delivery pipelines should validate that patterns are correctly applied. Documentation must present assurance obligations in clear, accessible language. Without these tools, integration can be burdensome. With them, it becomes routine.

Leadership support is essential. Architecture functions must have the authority to prioritize trust. This means resisting the temptation to cut corners for speed. It means ensuring architects have a voice in product governance as well as technical delivery. It elevates architecture to the level of a strategic enabler, not merely a delivery function.

Some organizations create an Assurance Architecture Board to formalize this commitment. This cross-functional group of enterprise architects, security leaders, compliance experts, and business sponsors is responsible for evolving trust patterns, reviewing deviations, and aligning assurance architecture with emerging risks and opportunities. Such a body ensures assurance remains current and relevant.

This group can also serve as a strategic foresight mechanism. Because architecture spans all transformations, it can identify systemic risks before they cause harm. It can detect where legacy systems create control gaps, where technical debt undermines resilience, and where governance is falling behind technological change. When assurance is integrated, these observations lead to timely action.

This forward-looking posture is essential in a volatile business environment. Regulations, threat vectors, and business models shift rapidly. A static architecture, no matter how technically sound, will eventually become fragile. A reactive assurance program, no matter how thorough, will become outdated. Alignment between architecture and assurance creates adaptability and the capacity to absorb disruption without losing integrity.

There is also a storytelling advantage. Organizations that can clearly show how trust is built into their systems gain credibility. They can demonstrate to regulators, investors, and partners that assurance is a design principle rather than an afterthought. It is visible in architectural diagrams, embedded in templates, and measurable through telemetry. This credibility changes the conversation. It reduces audit fatigue, accelerates procurement, strengthens stakeholder confidence, and positions the organization as one that actively designs for risk management rather than simply reacting to it.

This approach is not theoretical. Leading organizations already embed assurance into their architecture, treat trust as a cross-cutting concern alongside performance and scalability, and define resilience as an architectural property. They achieve levels of assurance maturity that static checklists and compliance frameworks alone cannot deliver. To truly futureproof assurance, it must be built into the point where systems are conceived. That means placing it in the hands of architects, embedding it in the blueprints of platforms, and integrating it into the strategic conversations that determine how the organization operates.

10.3 EMBEDDING ASSURANCE INTO ENGINEERING AND AI PIPELINES

Assurance delivers little value if it arrives too late. Once code is running in production, models are actively used, or features are exposed to customers, any security or compliance flaw becomes more costly to correct and harder to justify. The future of assurance is not found in post-mortems or audit reports. It lives within the pipelines that shape how systems are built, tested, and deployed. The closer assurance is embedded into these processes, particularly for intelligent systems driven by AI, the stronger the organization's resilience becomes.

Modern engineering operates in continuous delivery cycles. Ideas can reach production in days or even hours. Feature flags, short-lived environments, and containerized microservices now define the operating landscape. Assurance practices that rely on tickets, manual approvals, or isolated reviews will be bypassed or ignored, not due to negligence, but because they cannot keep pace.

Embedding assurance requires a shift from traditional policy enforcement to workflow integration. Controls need to be expressed in code, validated automatically, and tailored to the systems they protect. Static documents and checklists are no longer adequate. Assurance must be built into the tools already in use, such as version control, build automation, deployment orchestration, and monitoring platforms.

The best place to embed assurance is at the creation point. Policy-as-code frameworks allow developers to encode security, compliance, and reliability requirements into the same toolchains used for infrastructure and application logic. Every code commit should be checked not only for technical correctness but also for assurance compliance. Are secrets stored securely? Are dependencies current? Are permissions properly scoped?

These checks must occur during the commit or merge process, not after deployment. Code that fails assurance criteria should be rejected with clear feedback. This early detection reinforces good practices and gradually builds a culture where developers naturally design with assurance in mind.

CI/CD pipelines are the logical enforcement point for assurance guardrails. They offer automation, consistency, and clear evidence. Pipeline stages can run security scans, confirm license compliance, and verify configurations against approved baselines. Assurance becomes a transparent, continuous process, with logs serving as proof of compliance.

Automation allows assurance to scale. Manual reviews may work for a few monthly releases, but they collapse under modern deployment volumes. Embedding assurance into pipelines enables consistent enforcement across hundreds of releases without slowing delivery or increasing headcount.

Automation, however, must be applied with context. Not every service requires the same level of review. Low-risk services can pass through fully automated checks, while critical systems handling sensitive data may require additional gates, such as dynamic testing, peer reviews, or formal sign-off. This risk-based approach preserves speed while maintaining rigor.

AI systems add complexity. Unlike traditional software, they operate on probabilistic models that rely heavily on data quality. Assurance must be embedded throughout the AI lifecycle, from data ingestion to ongoing monitoring. Training data must be sourced ethically, handled securely, and validated for accuracy and relevance. This includes verifying lineage, ensuring consent, and documenting representativeness.

Model validation should include fairness testing, robustness assessments, and explainability thresholds. These measures can be integrated into the same pipelines used for functional testing. If a model fails to meet defined standards, it does not go live.

After deployment, assurance must watch for model drift, bias, and anomalous behavior. Real-time monitoring should track performance across different contexts and trigger alerts when deviations exceed acceptable thresholds. This transforms assurance from a static review into an active governance function.

AI governance also requires clear accountability. Responsibility for model outputs must be defined. Escalation procedures and audit trails should be in place for every stage of the model lifecycle. Without this clarity, organizations risk both regulatory penalties and erosion of trust.

Creating AI assurance playbooks helps standardize safe development. These living, version-controlled guides should define how to design, validate, and deploy models under a unified governance framework. They provide code snippets, templates, and escalation protocols so that teams know what safe and compliant delivery looks like.

To support all this, pipelines need strong telemetry. They must record not only build successes or failures but also control enforcement results, granted exceptions, and corrective actions. This data should feed dashboards that provide real-time visibility for engineering leaders, risk managers, and executives.

Embedding assurance also has a cultural dimension. New tools, checks, and expectations must be accompanied by education. Engineers need to understand not just how to comply but why these measures strengthen resilience, protect customers, and accelerate delivery when applied effectively.

Wins should be recognized. If a risky deployment is stopped by a pipeline control, it is not a failure but evidence that the system is working. When a team automates a new safeguard or improves its assurance posture, these achievements should be shared across the organization. Over time, this builds a culture where assurance is not a hurdle but a valued capability. Teams come to expect it, depend on it, and contribute to improving it.

The results deliver tangible results, such as faster delivery, fewer exceptions, shorter audit cycles, stronger control integrity, and greater stakeholder confidence in the organization's ability to innovate without adding unnecessary risk.

For leaders, this creates agility rooted in trust rather than just speed. Market opportunities can be pursued with confidence. Regulatory engagement becomes easier. Assurance shifts from being viewed as a cost to being recognized as a strategic asset.

In many ways, pipelines are the circulation system of a digital enterprise. If assurance is not present in this flow, it remains disconnected from the lifeblood of the organization. When assurance is embedded at every stage, from commit to deployment, it becomes adaptive, responsive, and continuously learning. See Figure 10.1: AI Pipeline Assurance Model.

Figure 10.1 AI Pipeline Assurance Model.

Image created by the author using Gamma.

10.4 PREPARING FOR EMERGING THREATS

Organizations rarely plan to be unprepared, yet many find themselves in that position. The threats that cause the most harm are often absent from risk registers. They emerge in ways that move faster than planning cycles, sidestep established controls, or grow out of unexpected interactions among technology, human behavior, and scale. Future assurance will not be secured by cataloging the risks of today. It depends on anticipating how tomorrow's threats will outpace current defenses.

Traditional security models were built around familiar attack types such as malware signatures, phishing attempts, and unauthorized access. The environment has shifted dramatically. Attackers now rely on automation, AI, complex supply chains, and legitimate tools that allow them to remain hidden. Any assurance program that depends on historic data alone will always trail the reality of modern risk.

Many emerging threats are systemic rather than purely technical. Adversarial AI can poison machine learning models or conduct inference attacks that never trigger a traditional alert. The effect is corrupted decisions, weakened trust, and new regulatory exposures. Static assurance programs are not designed to capture events like these.

Complexity itself has become a form of risk. Modern enterprises operate thousands of interconnected services across multiple clouds, often managed by different teams and updated continuously. Misconfigurations, privilege sprawl, and cascading failures are unavoidable. Something as simple as an API change can lead to a major service disruption.

Addressing this reality requires assurance that can detect, interpret, and respond to unfamiliar conditions. The focus must shift toward resilience, visibility, and adaptability. A purely defensive stance is no longer sufficient.

Future-ready threat modeling takes a continuous, data-driven, and multidisciplinary approach. It goes beyond known attack categories and builds a living view of blind spots, failed assumptions, and unintended system interactions. These models must evolve with the environment and extend into nontechnical domains such as shifting regulations, geopolitical instability, economic volatility, insider threats, and reputational risks.

Supply chain exposure remains one of the most underestimated factors. Enterprises may depend on hundreds or even thousands of vendors, contractors, and open-source components. Each one adds surface area for attack. Vendor oversight cannot be reduced to procurement tasks. It is an essential part of security. Dependency hijacking, poisoned packages, compromised firmware, and impersonated services require behavioral analysis, zero-trust approaches, and verification of software origins.

AI presents a dual challenge. Threat actors now use generative models to craft persuasive phishing campaigns, automate reconnaissance, and build polymorphic malware. At the same time, enterprises integrate AI into decision systems, customer interactions, and critical infrastructure. Assurance must address both the hostile use of AI and the risks introduced by internal adoption. That includes monitoring for model drift, testing for bias, simulating adversarial manipulation, and assessing exposure of AI assets.

Insider activity must also be taken seriously. In remote and distributed environments, barriers to exfiltrating large datasets are lower. Employees may misuse data, train external models with sensitive material, or attempt to sell intellectual property. Strong detection requires behavioral monitoring, anomaly analysis, and a workforce trained to understand its responsibilities.

Governance failures remain a high-risk issue. Policies can exist on paper while being ignored in practice. Responsibilities may be unclear, or rapid development cycles may leave oversight behind. Sensitive services can reach production without a single review. Integrated Assurance helps reduce this exposure by embedding governance into workflows so that deviations surface immediately.

Synthetic media has also expanded beyond social platforms. Threat actors now use deepfakes, synthetic voices, and fabricated identities for fraud, impersonation, and manipulation of trust systems. Enterprises must enforce verification for critical communications and prepare employees to recognize social engineering that exploits these tools.

The human element remains central to readiness. Technology shifts quickly, but human decisions determine outcomes. Assurance must strengthen workforce literacy, clarify decision authority, and enable practical scenario planning. Realistic exercises, including wargames and cross-functional drills, can reveal gaps that formal documents never expose.

Detection is only half the equation. Response matters just as much. Playbooks should be dynamic and tied directly into operational systems. They must guide containment, communication, escalation, and legal review in ways that adjust as conditions change.

Regulatory change has become a moving target. Requirements around privacy, AI, cybersecurity, and data sovereignty change continuously, often without clean transition periods. Compliance that is defensible today can become inadequate with little warning. Integrated Assurance addresses this by preserving traceability across data movement, control design, and access decisions, so compliance can be demonstrated at any point rather than reconstructed under pressure.

Organizations that succeed in this environment treat readiness as a standing capability. Assurance signals inform business decisions in real time. Incentives reinforce resilience instead of short-term optimization. Incidents and near misses are examined for what they reveal, not buried once operations resume.

The organizations that will lead over the next decade will not be defined by policy volume or tool spend. They will be defined by their ability to recognize change early, understand its impact, and adjust controls before risk turns into loss. See Figure 10.2: AI as a Threat Vector.

10.5 BUILDING ADAPTIVE, LIVING ASSURANCE SYSTEMS

The assurance models of the past were static, relying on fixed controls, annual reviews, and checklist compliance. The assurance models of the future must be fundamentally different. They must be living systems that evolve alongside the environments they protect, respond to emerging risks in real time, and learn continuously. Anything less will be unable to keep pace with the speed and complexity of modern enterprise operations.

This is not a philosophical change. It is an operational necessity. Today's enterprise systems change constantly. Cloud resources expand and contract within hours. AI models retrain themselves using new data. Business logic is deployed through automated pipelines. Identities are dynamic, federated, and influenced by behavioral patterns. The attack surface is in constant motion. Assurance that cannot adapt in step with these changes loses its relevance.

A living assurance system is more than real-time monitoring. It is reflexive. It recognizes when its own assumptions are outdated, and it adjusts based on context, current risk conditions, and feedback. It knows when a control is healthy, when it is weakened, and when it is being circumvented. It does not wait for an audit cycle to identify weaknesses. It detects and reacts as conditions shift.

To create such a system, organizations must first make assurance observable. This means linking every key control, whether technical or procedural, to telemetry. The system must be able to answer critical questions in real time. Is the control active? Is it being exercised? Is it producing the intended results? Without this signal layer, assurance operates in the dark.

These signals must be collected, analyzed, and interpreted as they happen. The focus should be on the health of assurance, not just operational statistics. Questions such as whether encryption is applied across all data stores, whether administrative accounts are using MFA, or whether models are performing within approved parameters should be answered with live data, not static documentation.

The next requirement is a functioning feedback loop. A living system senses, decides, and adapts. It requires defined thresholds for deviation, automated triggers for escalation, and

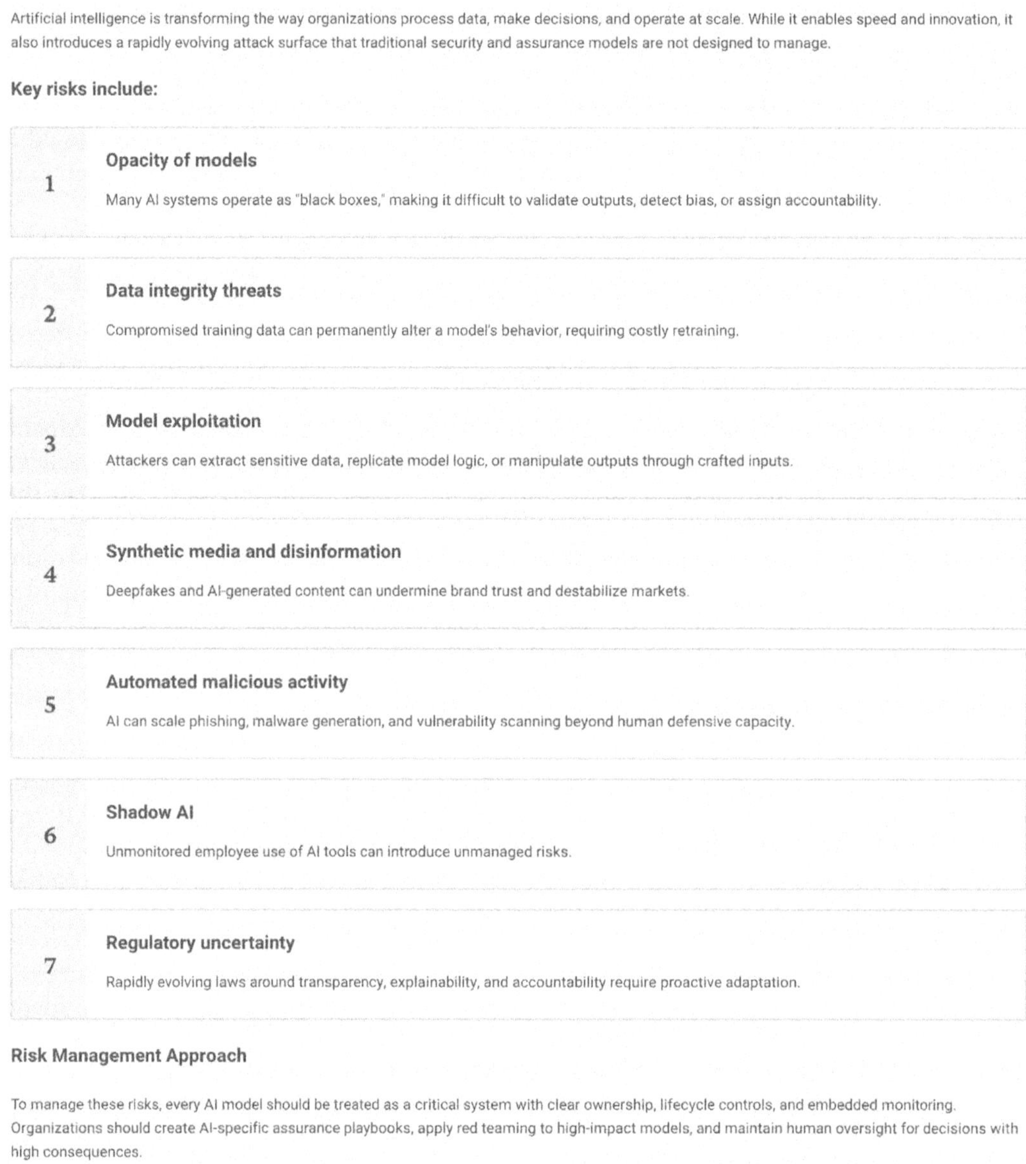

Figure 10.2 AI as a Threat Vector.

Image created by the author using Gamma.

delegated authority to act. For example, if anomaly detection flags irregular data access, the system might immediately reduce access privileges, alert security, and initiate a case review.

To operate at this scale, responses must be codified as policy-as-code. Manual intervention cannot handle the signal volume in a modern enterprise. Assurance must act as an automated decision layer that enforces controls, adjusts security posture, and issues alerts without requiring constant human approval.

Humans, however, must remain engaged strategically. Assurance teams refine the logic driving automated actions, review exceptions, analyze patterns, and improve the quality of policy over time. Automation performs the enforcement, but humans provide the learning and adaptation.

The architecture must also be built for adaptability. Controls should be flexible, able to operate with parameters, dynamic inputs, and conditional logic. For example, access control policies may need to adjust based on location, behavioral context, or time of day. The assurance system should interpret these factors and apply the right policies at the moment of use.

Context awareness is a critical enabler. Traditional controls work in isolation, checking whether a port is closed, a patch is applied, or a policy is acknowledged. Context-aware controls understand intent and can detect when a system is being used outside expected patterns, even if no single action appears to violate policy. This requires correlating identity, behavior, configuration, and network data to create a real-time picture of normal operations.

This intelligence allows assurance systems to detect drift not only in technical configurations but also in business processes. For example, if a financial reconciliation process suddenly involves a new data flow or a different user role, it should be flagged as a change in the trust boundary. This may not be malicious, but it signals a risk condition that requires review.

Adaptivity also relies on risk scoring. Every system, process, or change should carry a dynamic score based on its criticality, exposure, and operational history. This score determines the depth of assurance enforcement. A low-risk service may pass through with minimal oversight, while a high-risk change may require deeper review. These scores must be recalculated continuously. If a new vulnerability affects a key dependency, the risk score for all affected systems should increase immediately. If a critical control is disabled, the trust posture should degrade. Such updates drive access decisions, prioritization, and response actions.

Institutional memory is another requirement. The system must retain a complete history of decisions, exceptions, and incidents, recording why actions were taken and what outcomes followed. This record serves not only for compliance purposes but also as a learning resource. Living assurance protects the present while training for the future. These records should feed analytic models that detect patterns, forecast failures, and improve policies. For example, if a pipeline repeatedly fails the same control, the system can suggest architectural changes. If incidents recur, it can highlight remediation gaps. This approach makes assurance cumulative and self-improving.

Living assurance must also integrate directly with developer workflows. Developers are often the first to introduce changes. They need immediate feedback when a control fails, clear guidance within their tools, and actionable instructions on how to correct issues. In this way, assurance shifts from being a gatekeeper to an enabler. Instead of only blocking risky changes, it helps teams make safe changes faster. This can be achieved through reusable policy-as-code libraries, preapproved infrastructure templates, and real-time checks that teach while protecting.

Governance for a living assurance system must be distributed. Ownership of cloud platforms, data systems, identity services, and AI pipelines will be spread across the organization. The assurance model must enable each team to manage its risks within enterprise-defined boundaries. This requires a combination of global policy definitions, localized enforcement, and shared observability. It is a trust contract. Teams retain autonomy to innovate while honoring the safeguards.

Such a model changes the relationship between assurance and compliance. In a living system, compliance emerges naturally from well-structured operations. Controls are tested continuously, evidence is gathered automatically, and regulators can be shown live dashboards rather than static reports from months earlier. It also creates strategic agility. When a new requirement appears, the assurance system can integrate it quickly. Updated controls can be pushed into policy-as-code repositories, pipelines can adopt them automatically, and dashboards can display the new posture without interrupting delivery.

Creating such a capability requires investment and collaboration across architecture, engineering, risk, and operations. It is not a security side-project. Once implemented, it becomes an adaptive trust layer that spans the enterprise, continuously enforcing and proving trust.

Organizations that operate with living assurance gain measurable advantages. They can move at speed without creating silent risks, detect drift before it becomes a failure, learn from incidents, and present trust data rather than just trust claims. This is what Integrated Assurance looks like when it is fully realized. It is not a static artifact or a periodic report. It is a system that understands, adapts, and grows, treating trust as a living function of enterprise design.

10.6 CONTINUOUS EVOLUTION OF ASSURANCE CAPABILITIES

Adapting assurance once is not enough. To remain relevant and effective, it must evolve continually. The systems we protect are in constant motion. Threats, regulations, customer expectations, and the pressures of business transformation change alongside them. Any assurance capability that cannot keep pace will drift toward irrelevance. The decline may not be sudden or dramatic, but the function will quietly lose its impact until it no longer matters.

The most dangerous point for an assurance program is not during a visible failure but when everything seems to be operating smoothly. Green dashboards, clean audits, and the absence of open findings are often seen as signs of success. In a dynamic organization, those same indicators can mask stagnation. A capability that is not producing fresh insights is not learning. One that is not identifying new risks is not looking closely enough.

Sustained evolution begins with viewing assurance as an enterprise capability, not as a project. Projects have an endpoint. Capabilities grow and mature. Projects are measured by scope. Capabilities are measured by their long-term impact. Assurance cannot be treated as a compliance initiative that ends when controls are implemented. It must be an operational discipline embedded into governance, staffing, architecture, and budgeting so that it matures over time.

Assurance teams should operate with the mindset of a product team. They need to maintain a backlog, prioritize improvements, iterate on feedback, and deliver measurable value to stakeholders. This may include expanding telemetry coverage, reducing the time to detect control failures, or integrating seamlessly with the engineering toolchains used across the enterprise. As with any product, the capability must remain responsive to user needs and earn its place within day-to-day workflows.

Relying on legacy tools or a few subject matter experts creates fragility. If key personnel depart or the tools become misaligned with current systems, the effectiveness of the program can collapse. To avoid this, assurance must be portable. Knowledge should be codified in automation, captured in documentation, and distributed across shared platforms that survive changes in personnel or technology.

Feedback is another essential driver of evolution. Effective assurance systems must both generate and absorb feedback at all levels of the enterprise. When a control fails, the system must record the failure and the conditions that allowed it. Exceptions must be tracked, reviewed, and understood. Lessons from incidents must be fed back into architecture, design, and organizational culture so that they improve the system as a whole.

Insights from assurance must also be shared widely. Product teams can use them to refine design patterns. Risk teams can use them to adjust posture scores. Executives can apply them to guide strategic investment. Assurance cannot thrive in isolation. It must be part of a broader organizational learning engine.

This learning engine must be powered by the right metrics. Counting open tickets or policy violations measures activity, not progress. Evolution depends on insights such as how quickly changes in trust posture are detected, how many controls are validated through telemetry, and how often new risks are discovered before they materialize.

Leading organizations create assurance scorecards that track maturity across automation coverage, feedback cycle speed, decision latency, exception trends, and business alignment. These scorecards are designed for leadership visibility, not just for regulatory compliance. They answer the strategic question of whether the assurance capability is becoming more valuable and trusted over time.

External awareness is just as important. Threat intelligence must be mapped to control frameworks. Regulatory changes need to be translated into updated policies. Emerging technologies, whether new AI models, distributed ledgers, or quantum-resilient encryption methods, must be assessed for assurance implications. This requires a formal horizon-scanning function responsible for identifying tomorrow's blind spots before they impact the organization.

An externally aware assurance program strengthens resilience. If regulatory shifts are anticipated, preparation can occur before enforcement begins. If new supply chain risks are spotted in related sectors, the organization can assess and respond without waiting for a crisis. Proactive movement before the trigger is what defines continuous evolution.

Experimentation is also essential. Assurance capabilities should regularly test new approaches, just as engineering teams test new features. This might mean replacing manual reviews with AI-driven control validation, using synthetic data to test edge cases, or simulating system failures to validate response processes. Without experimentation, assurance becomes rigid. Without calculated risk-taking, it cannot grow.

These experiments should be quick to run and safe to evaluate. Failures should yield insights that refine future designs. This iterative cycle of building, measuring, and learning aligns assurance with the operational tempo of modern organizations.

Rotation strengthens the capability further. Moving assurance leaders into product, engineering, operations, or customer-facing roles spreads knowledge and builds stronger interdepartmental connections. In turn, bringing in external perspectives helps refresh the program's thinking and methods.

A clear operating model supports this adaptability. Roles and responsibilities must be transparent, escalation paths tested, and connections with other functions clearly defined. This structure allows the capability to scale and absorb change without breaking under pressure.

Cultural evolution is equally critical. Assurance must be seen as an enabler, not a gatekeeper. This requires intentional storytelling. Leaders should highlight where assurance accelerated a launch, prevented a risk from materializing, or guided the design of a better solution. These stories shape the organization's perception and encourage collaboration.

Training should be integrated into the workflow rather than relegated to annual modules. Real impact comes from just-in-time guidance, decision support embedded in control gates, and tools such as risk calculators that help teams self-assess before building. Assurance must meet teams where they work, in the moments where decisions shape outcomes.

Technology can help democratize assurance. Platforms that provide self-service control mapping, real-time monitoring, and collaborative policy development make trust a shared responsibility. Participation, not passive compliance, is what drives sustained evolution.

Intentional retrospection is the final key element. Assurance teams should hold learning reviews regularly, not just after incidents. These sessions should focus on identifying what worked, what slowed the business, and what failed to detect an issue in time. They must be candid, structured, and blame-free, with the sole aim of improvement.

When these practices are applied consistently, they form a self-reinforcing loop. Insights drive change, change leads to learning, and learning produces stronger insights. Over time, small improvements compound into significant organizational strength. This is the core promise of Integrated Assurance. It is not a one-time redesign, but a durable capability that evolves as quickly as the systems it protects. It serves as a compass for navigating risk, enabling the enterprise to operate with speed, confidence, and trust.

The business environment will not slow down for our processes. Threats will not become simpler, and customers will not lower their expectations. The only viable approach is to maintain assurance that evolves continually, deliberately, and at the pace of relevance. This is how organizations remain resilient during crises, through recovery, and in whatever challenges come next.

10.7 IAMM AS LIVING ASSURANCE

Resilience has long been viewed as a project that ends once objectives are met. The IAMM redefines it as a living system that evolves with the organization. At its highest level, maturity is not a destination but a continuous state of adaptation. Enterprises that reach this level function as ecosystems where assurance shapes design, operations, governance, and culture. This is the state IAMM calls living assurance.

At Level 1, risk and resilience are fragmented. Governance lacks coherence, architecture lacks structure, and culture lacks engagement. Controls are applied inconsistently and often by hand. Each team protects its own space without coordination or shared direction. Assurance exists only in scattered parts, not as a unified practice.

At Level 2, order begins to form. Frameworks are introduced, documentation expands, and compliance audits record progress. Policies become visible, yet most activities still look backward. Assurance follows a schedule rather than responding to real conditions. It operates as an event rather than a living system.

By Level 3, coordination takes shape. Governance structures meet regularly, architectural patterns stabilize, and operations start to align. Metrics begin to reflect performance rather than activity. The system depends on people, and its rhythm falters when leadership changes or priorities shift. The framework exists, but consistency remains fragile.

Level 4 transforms this coordination into automation. Assurance becomes part of the enterprise's digital fabric. Controls operate automatically, and telemetry connects systems across domains. Governance, operations, and architecture gain shared visibility of health and risk. Feedback loops close the distance between event and response. The enterprise now runs assurance as part of its operating system rather than as a compliance exercise.

Level 5 achieves self-reinforcement. Controls evolve as threats change, governance adjusts dynamically, and metrics verify themselves through constant validation. Culture sustains accountability, and leadership treats assurance as a component of growth. Resilience becomes indistinguishable from business execution. The organization learns, adapts, and improves as a trusted ecosystem.

Consider a global logistics provider serving hundreds of regions. At Level 2, it follows policies and conducts annual audits, but disruptions expose its rigidity. Controls remain static, and recovery depends on manual intervention. By Level 4, assurance is woven into its digital twin. Cyber telemetry, operational data, and financial performance feed a unified model. When storms or supply disruptions occur, decisions are made with real-time insight. At Level 5, predictive systems anticipate these disruptions and adjust routes automatically. The enterprise shifts from reaction to anticipation.

The shift from compliance to living assurance demands both discipline and humility. Discipline maintains alignment among governance, architecture, and operations. Humility accepts that assurance must evolve with its environment. Level 5 organizations thrive because they treat assurance as a constant process of learning and refinement rather than a static claim of success.

IAMM sustains this growth by guiding leaders through continual self-assessment. It calls for validation of control adaptability, verification of feedback systems, and alignment between metrics and outcomes. Cultural reinforcement becomes measurable through consistent accountability. These checks ensure that improvement remains permanent.

Living assurance changes how organizations communicate trust. Instead of static reports, they present continuous data that demonstrates performance in motion. Regulators observe active control evidence. Customers see reliability expressed in outcomes. Investors witness governance that operates with transparency and sustainability. Assurance evolves from internal oversight to a visible expression of credibility.

The idea of living assurance breaks with the past. It replaces the notion of resilience as a one-time goal with a practice that must be refreshed and proven each day. IAMM operationalizes this concept by connecting technology, people, and processes into an adaptive system that grows stronger through use. In doing so, it turns resilience from a milestone into a living discipline.

10.8 CONCLUSION

Futureproofing is not the pursuit of systems that never break. It is the practice of preparing the enterprise so that when systems shift, fail, or evolve, trust remains intact. Every technology will reach a point where it needs to be replaced. Every control will require adjustment. Every threat will change faster than a policy can be updated. The organizations that remain resilient are not those that cling to stability but those that embed assurance as a living capability—one that moves as quickly as the world around them.

Throughout this chapter, we have seen how static assurance models collapse when pressure mounts. They create snapshots that comfort leadership without equipping them to face reality. Annual reviews, rigid policies, and oversight mechanisms that operate on delay deliver paperwork instead of protection. By the time problems surface in those models, the damage has already spread into lost revenue, reputational harm, or noncompliance. These programs do not safeguard the present. They memorialize the past.

The alternative is integration. When assurance is integrated, it no longer sits outside of the business, waiting to be consulted after decisions are made. It becomes a property of the enterprise itself. By designing trust into architecture, pipelines, and governance, organizations shift assurance from a check-the-box function into an operational muscle. This alignment changes how strategies are executed. It turns resilience into an enabler of innovation, giving enterprises credibility when they take risks and confidence when they move into new markets.

The threat environment shows why this transformation is not optional. The speed and complexity of new risks outpace yesterday's controls. Deepfakes erode the boundary between fact and fabrication. Adversarial AI manipulates models that were once trusted to inform critical decisions. Supply chains, once seen as linear and predictable, now hide poisoned components that can bring entire industries to a halt. Governance failures at systemic levels reveal how fragile global interconnections have become. None of these challenges can be met with outdated playbooks. They demand readiness, anticipation, and the ability to respond before exposure becomes impact.

Integrated Assurance provides that readiness. It aligns decision rights so that responsibility does not vanish into silos. It embeds observability so that signals are captured the moment they arise. It prepares systems to respond in a way that is measured, proportional, and timely. With these qualities, assurance ceases to be an afterthought. It becomes a foundation of the enterprise's immune system.

Apply this checklist as a quarterly leadership review tool. Each question should spark a discussion across architecture, engineering, risk, and executive stakeholders. Treat gaps as opportunities for building assurance maturity and resilience.

1 Assess Current Assurance Model

- ☐ Have we identified where static, checklist-driven assurance practices still dominate your organization?
- ☐ Are we measuring real-time trust posture, or relying on outdated audit cycles?

2 Embed Assurance in Architecture

- ☐ Is assurance present in reference models, design patterns, and solution templates?
- ☐ Do architects and assurance leaders collaborate at the blueprint stage rather than at approval gates?

3 Integrate Assurance into Engineering and AI Pipelines

- ☐ Are policies expressed as code and validated automatically in CI/CD pipelines?
- ☐ Do AI models undergo bias, drift, and robustness testing as part of deployment, with monitoring for changes post-launch?

4 Strengthen Emerging Threat Readiness

- ☐ Have we conducted continuous threat modeling that includes systemic and AI-driven risks?
- ☐ Are supply chain, insider threats, and deepfake risks accounted for with living playbooks and detection protocols?

5 Build Living Assurance Systems

- ☐ Are controls observable, contextual, and adaptive rather than static?
- ☐ Do we maintain feedback loops and policy-as-code to enforce, learn, and evolve continuously?

6 Drive Continuous Evolution

- ☐ Is assurance treated as a capability with a backlog, metrics, and iterative improvements?
- ☐ Do we maintain horizon scanning for regulatory, technological, and systemic changes?

7 Embed Trust as a Design Principle

- ☐ Are decisions guided by trust as an input, not a byproduct?
- ☐ Do teams see assurance as an enabler of speed and resilience, not a blocker?

Executive Action: Futureproofing requires assurance that never stops evolving. Make trust an input to every design, pipeline, and decision, so that resilience becomes a continuous capability, not a static deliverable.

Figure 10.3 Practical Checklist: Futureproofing with Integrated Assurance.
Image created by the author using Gamma.

Living assurance ties these qualities together. It is continuous rather than episodic. It evolves rather than remaining fixed. It learns from each disruption and adjusts in ways that make the enterprise stronger. Like a biological system, it senses abnormal conditions, adapts, and strengthens itself through feedback. It operates in the bloodstream of the organization, measuring trust in real time rather than assuming it exists because a report once said so.

Evolution is the final requirement. No enterprise can treat assurance as a finished project. If it is not growing, it is fading. Lessons from incidents must be absorbed. Shifts in regulation must be anticipated and incorporated. New approaches must be tested before they are needed in full production. Enterprises that treat assurance as a static deliverable will watch it drift into irrelevance. Enterprises that recognize assurance as a discipline that must be cultivated will see it become a source of advantage.

The outcome of assurance is not a binder of policies or a completed audit. It is trust. Trust that the organization can move at speed without stumbling blindly. Trust that regulators will see tangible evidence rather than vague promises. Trust that customers will remain loyal even when disruption occurs. Trust means that resilience is more than aspiration, that it is operationalized and visible in how the enterprise behaves.

Futureproofing through Integrated Assurance requires design and intent. Leaders must recognize assurance as a system that lives within operations rather than a compliance artifact to be archived. Architects must embed trust into the blueprints that guide development. Engineers must treat controls as code, updating them with the same rigor and velocity as any other element of the pipeline. Executives must evaluate assurance not by the absence of findings but by the demonstrated ability of their organizations to adapt under stress.

Enterprises that commit to this path will stand apart. They will act with confidence in environments defined by volatility. They will adapt faster than adversaries. They will show integrity when competitors struggle to explain failures. Most importantly, they will earn and sustain the one resource that outlasts every disruption, which is trust.

The closing point is straightforward. Trust is not built in quarterly reviews, nor is it preserved in audit findings. It is built every time a disruption is met with competence. It is preserved every time resilience proves stronger than uncertainty. Integrated Assurance turns that truth into practice by embedding assurance as a living discipline. In doing so, it gives the enterprise the ability to face the future with confidence, no matter how fast the ground shifts beneath it. See Figure 10.3: Practical Checklist: Futureproofing with Integrated Assurance.

Chapter 11

Federated Assurance at Global Scale

11.1 THE CHALLENGE OF GLOBAL AND FEDERATED ASSURANCE

In theory, scaling assurance through policy seems straightforward. In practice, it rarely works as intended. This is the core tension facing global enterprises today. As organizations expand across continents, navigate diverse legal jurisdictions, and operate within distinct cultural environments, the assurance strategies that once delivered stability begin to strain. A centralized model that once ensured consistent controls can become rigid and unresponsive. A federated model that offers flexibility risks losing cohesion. Between these extremes lies the challenge of maintaining trust, compliance, and resilience in a landscape where no single operating model applies to every market.

At the center of this challenge is the assumption of control. Many executive teams believe that deploying a unified governance framework will naturally cascade across all global operations. They expect that standards created at headquarters will be interpreted consistently from Southeast Asia to Western Europe. They anticipate that reporting structures and control obligations will align without friction across time zones and functions. Reality tells a different story. On the ground, drift occurs.

Control interpretations shift between teams. Risk tolerance shifts between business units. Operational practices shift between borders. What begins as strategic consistency evolves into local improvisation. This is not a symptom of poor intent. It is a consequence of operating at scale in an environment where speed, local context, and market relevance dictate execution. When assurance is not designed for these realities, it becomes a reactive function, constantly addressing gaps, reconciling inconsistencies, and responding to avoidable breakdowns.

In a federated organization, local entities carry a dual responsibility. They must deliver outcomes tailored to their markets, customers, and regulatory obligations while also meeting global control expectations that may not reflect their local realities. This is not just a logistical issue. It is a design issue. It reveals a structural misalignment in how risk, accountability, and trust are distributed across the enterprise.

11.1.1 When misalignment becomes visible

Misalignment between global governance and local execution often remains hidden until pressure exposes it. When a security incident occurs in one region, the ripple effects are immediate. Global teams demand visibility into the event. Legal teams seek clarity on breach reporting obligations. The board wants to understand which safeguards failed and whether the outcome could have been avoided. If assurance is not structurally embedded into both global design and local execution, the result is confusion. Reporting slows. Controls are misrepresented. Response efforts lose coordination. Even worse, the root cause may remain obscured under layers of regional abstraction.

DOI: 10.1201/9781003685982-15

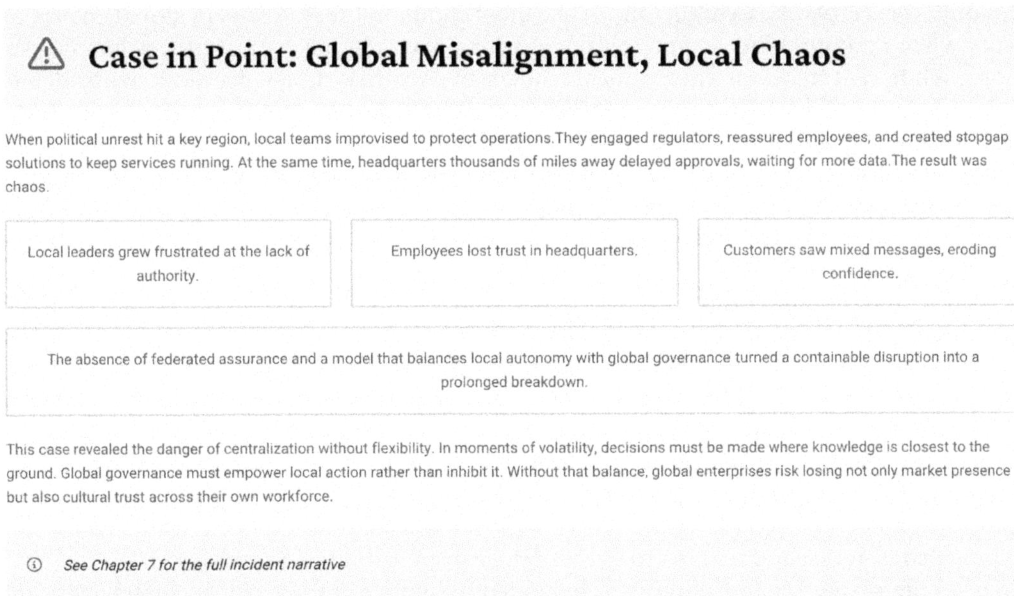

Figure 11.1 Case in Point.

Image created by the author using Gamma.

This breakdown is not confined to crisis events. It appears during audits, regulatory inquiries, technology deployments, and mergers or acquisitions. Any event requiring cross-border risk coordination becomes either a proving ground or a point of failure for federated assurance. Traditional models tend to falter because they rely on central command without enabling local capability. They issue policies without providing operational pathways. They define global standards without building the bridges necessary for local adoption.

To succeed, assurance must be built for both reach and adaptability. It must account for the differences in market conditions, regulatory frameworks, and cultural contexts, while maintaining the global integrity that protects the enterprise's reputation and resilience. See Figure 11.1: Case in Point.

11.1.2 Assurance must adapt

To operate effectively across federated structures, assurance can no longer function as a simple broadcast from headquarters. A model that relies on central teams issuing standards and waiting for compliance reports will not scale in the current global business environment. Instead, assurance must operate as an ecosystem where trust, telemetry, and accountability are distributed, but where coordination remains intentional and deliberate.

This requires an architecture that reflects geopolitical realities, respects local context, and embeds risk management into day-to-day operations without weakening global coherence. There is no single blueprint for achieving this, but there are principles that consistently hold.

First, federated assurance starts with visibility, not control. Regional teams need room to operate in ways that fit their environment, but the signals that describe risk, performance, and control health must roll up into a shared global view. That visibility cannot depend on spreadsheets or periodic reporting. It has to come from live telemetry, integrated views, and shared governance mechanisms. Without that foundation, trust rests on assumption rather than evidence.

Second, role clarity is essential. One of the most common breakdowns in global enterprises occurs when accountability is unclear. Local teams may assume central offices handle escalations, while central teams expect local leaders to own risk. Clear decision rights, defined escalation paths, and shared risk ownership frameworks ensure that every geography knows its responsibilities and how it contributes to the broader assurance structure.

Third, the model must allow for variation without sacrificing core standards. Different markets face different regulatory requirements, privacy laws, and third-party risk profiles. Controls must be modular and adaptable at the local level while still verifiable and consistent with enterprise objectives.

Fourth, effective communication is key. Assurance cannot succeed if it is delivered only in the headquarters' terminology or language. Risk concepts, compliance requirements, and trust expectations must be translated into terms that resonate with local teams and align with cultural norms. Without this, assurance efforts risk becoming procedural rather than substantive.

Fifth, structural enablers—such as training, integrated platforms, peer networks, and shared metrics—are necessary to hold the model together. These investments build the distributed capability needed for assurance to work across geographies. Local leaders must have the knowledge, tools, and forums to execute their responsibilities effectively.

When enterprises expand without a federated assurance framework to match, they create an operational gap. The business structure evolves, but the risk management model lags behind. Integrated Assurance provides the connection between global expectations and local execution. It decentralizes risk ownership while centralizing insight, enabling global organizations to move quickly without losing control of their trust environment.

11.2 DESIGNING FEDERATED ASSURANCE MODELS

Designing a federated assurance model is not an administrative shuffle of oversight responsibilities. It is a strategic redesign of how trust is created, how risk is distributed, and how assurance is executed within a multinational enterprise. Traditional governance, with its reliance on centrally imposed policies and rigid audit cycles, struggles to withstand the complexity of distributed operations. Enterprises that span multiple regions cannot depend solely on command-and-control models. They must adopt an approach that extends laterally, strengthens local capabilities, and preserves coherence across the enterprise.

A federated assurance model succeeds only when it achieves balance. Autonomy at the regional level cannot come at the expense of consistency at the enterprise level. To achieve this balance, the model must be constructed on foundational elements that provide shared identity, structural integrity, and a system of trust that adapts to diverse operating environments.

The first element of a federated model is assurance anchoring. Every region within the enterprise must operate with freedom to interpret its environment, yet boundaries must remain unambiguous. Anchors are those nonnegotiable principles that define what trustworthy operations look like. They take the form of minimum risk thresholds, core control objectives, and enterprise-wide threat models. Anchors are expressed through policies, architectural reference models, onboarding practices, and contractual terms with partners and suppliers.

Anchors are not intended to restrict initiative. Their purpose is to prevent drift from enterprise-wide standards while granting distributed units space to innovate. They provide clarity so that local teams know the limits within which they can make independent decisions without jeopardizing collective resilience.

The second element is control modularity. Global enterprises must respect local variation without creating fragmentation. Regulations, cultural norms, and business models differ across markets, yet all must be reconciled with enterprise objectives. By designing controls as modular components, the organization gains flexibility. Data retention, privacy enforcement, or access management may need adjustment to meet local obligations, but every variant still integrates with a shared control catalog and reporting infrastructure.

This modular approach allows the enterprise to maintain one system of record for assurance while recognizing that enforcement may look different in Tokyo than it does in Toronto. The result is variation without chaos, a federation of control practices bound together by enterprise objectives.

The third element is distributed telemetry and assurance instrumentation. Centralized reporting often arrives late, stripped of operational context. To avoid blind spots, assurance data must be generated at the point of activity. This requires embedding instrumentation into systems, processes, and workflows so that they automatically emit assurance signals. Control verification, audit logging, and risk posture indicators are created as part of the work itself rather than as an afterthought.

When assurance signals flow from the edge inward, central teams gain real-time visibility into conditions across the enterprise. Local teams benefit as well, since they see the immediate effect of their actions and can correct missteps before they propagate. Distributed telemetry transforms assurance from a delayed report into a live operational feed.

The fourth element is role specialization. Federated assurance depends on clearly defined responsibilities and a fabric of accountability. Local assurance leads act within their regional context to interpret global standards, adapt controls, and manage compliance. Central assurance architects oversee the design of the enterprise assurance framework, ensure integrity across adaptations, and refine architectural models.

Federated risk councils draw representatives from across geographies to address incidents, harmonize regulatory responses, and guide cross-border strategy. These councils strengthen alignment not by enforcing hierarchy, but by fostering transparency, escalation paths, and joint decision-making. Each role complements the others, creating a distributed network of expertise bound by common purpose.

The fifth element is adaptive governance. Governance in a federated model cannot remain static. It must evolve based on insights generated by assurance telemetry. Deviations from global standards must be reviewed, risk-assessed, and interpreted in context. Sometimes, these deviations expose vulnerabilities. Other times, they reveal opportunities for modernization. Adaptive governance absorbs these lessons and turns them into refinements, making the system stronger with each cycle.

The ability to learn distinguishes federated governance from its centralized predecessor. Rather than treating variation as failure, it is treated as data. The enterprise becomes capable of improving not only its compliance record but also its overall assurance maturity.

The sixth element is lifecycle integration. Assurance must be designed into every phase of enterprise activity, not added as an afterthought. It belongs in procurement negotiations, system design reviews, product launches, and workforce onboarding. Vendor due diligence, technology deployment, and contract renewal all become opportunities to embed assurance controls.

This integration ensures that assurance does not emerge only during audits or crisis response. It becomes a living part of how the enterprise operates, continually shaping choices and reducing the likelihood of systemic surprises.

The seventh element is the adoption of shared metrics and outcomes. Federated assurance cannot be assessed region by region in isolation. It requires enterprise-wide measures that capture both technical effectiveness and business impact. Meaningful measures might include resilience performance by region, trust movement between business units, containment speed during incidents, and compliance maturity within each function.

When those measures are defined the same way across the enterprise, performance can be compared without debate. Weak spots surface quickly. Progress can be tracked without reinterpretation. Shared metrics also change behavior. They create collective responsibility and pull assurance out of narrow compliance teams and into normal operational ownership.

When alignment holds, the outcome goes beyond governance structure. It shapes how the organization operates. Local realities are respected, but they do not dilute identity or standards. Trust and resilience become embedded in routines, decisions, and system design rather than being treated as abstract goals.

A federated assurance approach built on clear anchors, modular controls, distributed visibility, defined accountability, adaptive oversight, lifecycle integration, and shared measurement gives global organizations the structure they need to operate with confidence. It supports speed without eroding control and resilience without centralizing everything.

Integrated Assurance is what holds this together. It connects global expectations to local execution and allows scale without fragmentation. In a federated model, assurance stops acting as friction and starts acting as an enabler of reliable operations and sustained trust across every region where the enterprise operates.

11.3 BALANCING LOCAL AUTONOMY WITH GLOBAL GOVERNANCE

Organizations that operate across regions, industries, or regulatory regimes live with constant tension. What works well in one environment often breaks down in another. A directive that feels sensible at headquarters can struggle when it meets local regulations, customer expectations, labor markets, or infrastructure realities. When this friction is ignored or oversimplified, it does real damage. Controls drift. Reporting fragments. Accountability blurs. Over time, the organization becomes harder to govern and easier to surprise. The challenge is not choosing between global governance and local autonomy. It is designing them to reinforce each other.

Local teams are where relevance lives. They understand how regulators interpret rules, how customers behave under stress, and where operational shortcuts quietly exist. That proximity gives them speed and judgment that centralized teams cannot replicate. It also gives them credibility inside the business. When regional leaders have room to make decisions that fit their environment, execution improves. Ownership increases. Problems surface earlier. Autonomy, when used well, is a source of resilience.

But autonomy without structure does not scale. Left unconstrained, regional teams can slowly diverge from enterprise standards. They adopt different tools, interpret controls differently, and optimize for local performance at the expense of systemic risk. These deviations are rarely malicious. They are usually practical responses to pressure. Over time, however, they accumulate into inconsistencies that weaken the organization's ability to see itself clearly. Risk reporting becomes uneven. Incident response varies by geography. Control effectiveness depends more on location than intent. At that point, resilience becomes uneven and trust erodes.

Global governance exists to prevent this outcome. At its best, it establishes a shared foundation of expectations. It defines what must be protected, what cannot be compromised, and what behavior is unacceptable regardless of market or margin. It ensures that the organization speaks a common language when describing risk, assurance, and accountability. This consistency matters. Regulators expect it. Investors assume it. Customers rely on it, even if they never see it directly.

Yet governance can easily overreach. When rules become overly prescriptive, they slow decision-making and breed quiet resistance. Headquarters often underestimates the constraints faced by regional teams, whether those are staffing shortages, technology limitations, or legal barriers. When global mandates ignore local reality, regional leaders comply in form while adapting in practice. Controls look intact on paper, but trust deteriorates beneath the surface. The organization becomes compliant without being controlled.

The answer is not a compromise for its own sake. Balance comes from design. Specifically, it comes from being explicit about where authority sits, how flexibility is exercised, and how disagreements are resolved. Several design choices consistently separate organizations that manage this tension well from those that struggle.

First, control objectives must be global, even if implementation is local. The enterprise cannot tolerate variation in what it considers essential. If protecting customer data, detecting malicious behavior, or ensuring regulatory reporting are nonnegotiable, those expectations must be uniform. How those outcomes are achieved, however, should remain in the hands of local teams. A global requirement might state that endpoints must support behavioral monitoring and rapid containment. Regional teams then decide which tools to deploy, how to staff them, and how to operate within local constraints. This preserves consistency without forcing uniformity.

Second, exceptions must be visible and managed, not hidden or stigmatized. In a complex organization, exceptions are inevitable. Laws differ. Technologies are unavailable. Budgets fluctuate. What matters is how exceptions are handled. A clear process for requesting, approving, and reviewing exceptions keeps them transparent. More importantly, exceptions become data. They reveal where global assumptions no longer hold or where additional investment is needed. Treated properly, they strengthen governance rather than undermining it.

Third, leadership needs comparable information across regions. That requires normalization. If one region measures incident containment in hours and another in days, or if risk severity means different things in different places, enterprise visibility collapses. Establishing common definitions and reporting structures allows information to move upward without distortion. Executives gain a reliable view of exposure. Regional teams gain clarity on expectations. Decisions improve on both sides.

Fourth, governance must operate on a living cadence. Annual reviews and static audits are no longer sufficient. Risk changes too quickly. Effective federated models rely on rhythm. Regular reviews with regional assurance leads, short-cycle updates driven by telemetry, and governance forums that include both central and local voices keep oversight connected to reality. Governance becomes a conversation rather than a decree.

Fifth, capability differences must be acknowledged openly. Not every region operates at the same level of maturity. Assuming otherwise leads to mandates that cannot be executed. Mapping local capabilities before introducing new requirements allows the organization to sequence change intelligently. Training, tooling, and staffing can be aligned to actual needs. This avoids creating control debt that looks compliant but fails under stress.

Sixth, assurance platforms must reflect the same balance that the organization is trying to achieve. Fully centralized systems optimize reporting but strip local teams of flexibility. Fully localized systems preserve autonomy but fracture visibility. A federated platform does both. It allows headquarters to see risk and performance across the enterprise while giving regional teams control over configuration and operation. This structure reinforces the idea that governance and autonomy are complementary, not competing.

At the center of all of this sits trust. Global leaders must trust that regional teams will act in good faith and uphold shared standards. Regional teams must trust that global guidance reflects real constraints, not abstract ideals. That trust is built through transparency, collaboration, and shared outcomes. Each successful cycle of governance and local execution reinforces confidence in the model.

When designed with clarity and discipline, federated governance delivers more than compliance. It produces resilience that scales. Local teams move quickly and act decisively in their environments. Global leadership maintains confidence that risks are visible, controls are coherent, and accountability holds. Governance stops being a brake on performance and becomes a system that allows the enterprise to move faster without losing control.

11.4 IAMM IN FEDERATED GOVERNANCE

Global enterprises operate within a constant tension between consistency and autonomy. They must preserve unified assurance standards while allowing regions to make decisions that fit their realities. The Governance and Culture domains of the IAMM resolve this tension through federated governance, where oversight strengthens resilience instead of restricting it.

At Level 1, global operations move independently. Regional teams define their own controls and frameworks without coordination. Headquarters receives uneven reports, and compliance is interpreted differently across regions. Fragmentation takes hold, and in moments of disruption, coordination breaks down. Regional leaders act alone, and the organization loses trust because it cannot respond as one.

Level 2 introduces central authority but often in a rigid form. Headquarters issues uniform standards and procedures with little room for context. Policies are written at the top and handed down for enforcement. Local leaders comply to meet requirements rather than strengthen assurance. Fragmentation gives way to uniformity, yet collaboration remains absent.

By Level 3, the conversation begins to shift. Regional and global teams start to coordinate and exchange context. Shared templates, training sessions, and reporting structures appear. Governance evolves into a collaborative process. Headquarters defines principles, while regional teams interpret and apply them. This balance begins to build trust, replacing fatigue with participation.

Level 4 achieves the balance that defines federated governance. Global councils set direction, and local entities adapt those standards within clear boundaries. Common risk language and shared metrics unify decision-making. Governance aligns corporate strategy with execution on the ground. A culture of cooperation sustains this balance, keeping oversight and local action in motion together. At this stage, assurance reaches scale without losing its relevance to local conditions.

Level 5 represents maturity. Governance frameworks are embedded throughout the enterprise, and cultural alignment is natural. Local teams provide transparent reporting, while global oversight translates those insights into strategic direction. This cycle of feedback allows governance to evolve with growth, preserving agility and preventing the rigidity often found in centralized systems.

A practical illustration can be seen in global financial institutions. At Level 2, corporate offices enforce uniform compliance rules, which delay operations and frustrate local teams. By Level 4, federated risk committees emerge. Local branches adapt global standards to regional regulation, and reporting remains consistent. Corporate offices gain visibility without direct control over every decision. The result is assurance that scales with nuance and coordination that respects context.

Federated governance in the IAMM framework is about coherence rather than control. It builds a shared system of trust that crosses borders, laws, and languages. Governance becomes scalable because it invites participation rather than enforcing compliance. Progress through the model depends on the inclusiveness of governance. Local leaders contribute directly to forums that shape direction. Global standards allow for contextual interpretation. Risk and compliance data are unified across all regions. Information moves freely between leadership and the field. When these conditions exist, governance is shared rather than imposed.

Federated governance strengthens resilience by enabling distributed response. When disruption affects one region, others can provide immediate support through shared processes and common metrics. This cohesion turns distributed competence into organizational strength. IAMM makes clear that global assurance is not defined by uniformity. It succeeds through unity of purpose, transparency of data, and accountability that moves in both directions. Enterprises that reach Level 5 maturity in federated governance can scale trust at the same pace they scale their operations.

11.5 MAINTAINING GLOBAL STANDARDS WITH LOCAL FLEXIBILITY

Global standards are what hold a large enterprise together. They create a shared definition of acceptable risk, reliable performance, and accountability, regardless of where work is done. When standards are weak or uneven, organizations begin to fragment. Risk becomes a matter of opinion. Assurance depends on who is asked and when. Trust between regions erodes quietly, often long before leadership notices.

At the same time, rigid uniformity can be just as damaging. Federated enterprises do not operate in identical conditions. Legal environments differ. Labor models vary. Infrastructure maturity is uneven. A control that works cleanly in one country may be impractical, prohibitively expensive, or even unlawful in another. When global standards ignore these realities, local teams either fail outright or comply in ways that look acceptable on paper while weakening real-world resilience.

The challenge is not choosing between consistency and flexibility. It is learning how to design standards that protect the enterprise's integrity while allowing local operations to function effectively. That balance starts with how standards are written.

Prescriptive policies that dictate exactly how something must be implemented rarely scale. They assume stable conditions and uniform capabilities, neither of which exists in a global organization. A more durable approach is to define standards around outcomes rather than methods. Instead of mandating a specific technology or process, the standard describes what must be achieved and why it matters.

For example, a global identity standard might require continuous verification that adapts to risk and context, rather than specifying a single authentication method. This preserves the security objective while giving regional teams the freedom to select tools that fit local regulation, workforce realities, and technical constraints. The enterprise stays aligned on intent while avoiding unnecessary friction at the point of execution.

Outcome-based standards work best when they are supported by a clear control catalog that anticipates variation. High-level principles alone leave too much room for interpretation. A control catalog bridges the gap by offering approved implementation patterns designed for different environments. It might include one approach optimized for highly regulated markets, another for cloud-native teams, and a third for regions with limited resources or legacy systems.

Each option meets the same enterprise requirement, but each acknowledges a different operational reality. This reduces improvisation, shortens implementation cycles, and gives local teams confidence that their choices are supported rather than merely tolerated.

Validation is another area where balance matters. Centralized audit models struggle at a global scale. They create bottlenecks, delay insight, and often reduce assurance to periodic snapshots that are out of date before reports are delivered. At the other extreme, fully decentralized self-attestation can erode trust if evidence is inconsistent or incomplete.

A more effective model distributes responsibility without abandoning oversight. Local teams assess their own implementations using enterprise-defined criteria. They collect evidence as part of normal operations rather than as a special exercise. Global assurance functions then validate selectively, using targeted audits and continuous telemetry to confirm accuracy. This approach reinforces accountability at the local level while preserving enterprise-wide visibility.

Measurement also needs to evolve beyond simple pass or fail assessments. Binary compliance hides important differences. A team that barely meets a requirement and one that continuously improves control effectiveness both appear compliant, yet their risk profiles are not the same. More nuanced measurement looks at maturity, effectiveness, responsiveness, cost efficiency, and impact on risk reduction.

When metrics are consistent across regions, comparison becomes meaningful. High-performing teams stand out. Weak spots become visible without debate. Best practices can be shared based on evidence rather than opinion. Over time, shared metrics reshape behavior by creating collective responsibility rather than isolated compliance ownership.

The way standards are created matters as much as their content. Too often, policies are written centrally and delivered as finished products. This approach assumes understanding and buy-in that rarely exist. Involving regional teams early changes the outcome. Co-designing standards surfaces constraints before they become blockers. Piloting requirements in multiple geographies reveals unintended consequences. Feedback loops allow refinement before broad rollout.

This process does more than improve implementation. It builds credibility. When local leaders see their realities reflected in standards, compliance feels less like enforcement and more like participation in a shared system.

Flexibility, however, only works if local teams are equipped to use it well. That means investing in regional assurance capability. Training cannot be generic or optional. It must be tailored to local roles and risks. Tooling must be accessible, not reserved for headquarters. Performance objectives must reinforce resilience, not just delivery speed or cost reduction.

When local leaders are rewarded solely for short-term output, assurance will always feel like a tax. When resilience and reliability are recognized as contributors to business performance, assurance becomes part of how success is defined.

Visibility is what allows this model to function at scale. Static policies and periodic audits cannot reveal whether standards are actually working. Live telemetry provides that insight. Dashboards that show control performance, exception trends, and incident patterns allow both local and global leaders to see reality as it unfolds. Problems surface earlier. Intervention becomes targeted rather than reactive. Flexibility can be distinguished from drift.

Exception management deserves particular discipline. Exceptions are inevitable in a federated enterprise, but unmanaged exceptions quietly undermine standards. Every deviation should have a clear justification, documented risk acceptance, defined compensating measures, and a time limit. Exceptions that never expire are no longer exceptions. They are unacknowledged changes to the standard.

Aggregated exception data is especially valuable. Patterns often reveal where standards no longer reflect operational reality or where specific regions lack the necessary capability. Used well, exception analysis becomes a feedback mechanism for improving the system rather than a source of blame.

Cultural integration is the final, often overlooked element. Standards do not live in documents. They live in how people interpret expectations and make decisions under pressure. Policies written in the language of one legal system or cultural context will struggle elsewhere. Translation is not enough. Framing matters. Examples must resonate. The intent behind the standard must be clear to those responsible for executing it.

When teams recognize themselves in the standards, compliance becomes a shared commitment rather than external enforcement. Trust grows because expectations feel legitimate, not imposed.

None of this is static. Global standards must evolve as the business evolves. New regulations, acquisitions, technologies, and incidents all test existing assumptions. Each change is an opportunity to reassess whether standards still serve their purpose. Integrated Assurance treats governance as a living system, one that adapts without losing coherence.

When global standards and local flexibility are designed together, they do not pull the organization in opposite directions. They reinforce one another. The result is an assurance model that scales, absorbs change, and maintains trust across regions without sacrificing operational reality.

11.6 ASSURANCE IN CROSS-BORDER REGULATORY ENVIRONMENTS

For global organizations, regulation is no longer something that sits quietly in the background. It has become a core design factor that shapes decisions across strategy, technology, vendor management, and the flow of information. Expanding into a new geography, moving into a regulated sector, or adopting a new technology architecture all require a careful accounting of the rules that apply. The requirements differ not just by country, but also by industry, use case, and the type of data being processed.

The challenge comes from both conflict and variation. One jurisdiction's requirements can contradict those of another. Data localization laws may force changes to infrastructure that slow down efficiency. Export restrictions on encryption can limit technical design choices. Cybersecurity certification schemes may demand overlapping but inconsistent forms of evidence. What satisfies one regulator can create exposure in another market. Organizations that treat regulation as a box-checking activity quickly find themselves paralyzed. The only viable path is to treat regulatory alignment as an active capability that sits inside operations, not as a periodic compliance review.

The starting point is the creation of a regulatory intelligence layer. This is not a static register of laws stored in a binder or database. It is a living system that continuously tracks new legislation, revisions, and enforcement practices in every jurisdiction where the organization operates. Legal, compliance, and assurance teams should collaborate to translate requirements into operational terms. Each entry should be tagged by geography, business process, system boundary, and data classification. This mapping creates a clear line of sight from regulation to control, and it allows for rapid updates when laws shift.

A regulatory intelligence layer that functions as a shared operational system makes compliance practical at scale. When a data protection law changes in one market, affected systems and processes can be flagged immediately, with updates cascaded to the relevant teams. Without this, enterprises risk discovering gaps only after a regulator has acted.

Once obligations are mapped, the next step is harmonization. Regulations overlap, but they are rarely written in identical terms. A harmonization engine identifies where a single control can satisfy multiple requirements. For example, if access logs are designed and retained correctly, they may meet general data protection regulation transparency requirements, the privacy provisions of California law, and record-keeping mandates in the Asia Pacific. By identifying these intersections, organizations avoid the waste of parallel compliance programs and reduce the burden on technical teams.

Harmonization also creates consistency. If the same assurance framework serves multiple regulators, updates flow through a single channel rather than a tangle of disconnected compliance projects. This reduces duplication and strengthens the enterprise's ability to defend its practices during audits or investigations.

Each jurisdiction should have an assurance profile. These profiles gather all relevant obligations for a region into a practical playbook. They include breach notification timelines, sovereignty rules, local enforcement practices, and technology restrictions. They are not legal summaries written for lawyers, but operational guides designed for business leaders and architects.

When architecture teams plan a new product launch or infrastructure build, the relevant profile should inform decisions before commitments are made. For example, if a country requires that encryption keys never leave its borders, this rule must be visible to technical teams before they design the key management system. Profiles turn abstract regulation into real design constraints that prevent costly rework.

Trying to manage global compliance with static reports does not work anymore. Things change too fast. Regulations move, systems evolve, and incidents do not wait for quarterly reviews. What leaders actually need is a live view of how controls are performing in each jurisdiction. If the law says a breach must be reported within 72 hours, the organization has to know the moment something happens, not days later. It needs a clear timestamp, a reliable record of actions taken, and confidence that nothing is being pieced together after the fact. Local teams need to see their own posture in real time. Global teams need to spot patterns that suggest something is starting to slip. When visibility is continuous, compliance stops being reactive and starts to feel manageable.

When an incident does occur, regulation quickly becomes part of the response. Different countries have very different rules about who must be notified and when. In some places, regulators come first. In others, public disclosure follows a specific sequence. These details matter, and they are not things you want to figure out under pressure. The only way to handle this well is to plan for it ahead of time. That means having regional legal counsel already lined up, communication templates reviewed and approved, and clear escalation paths that reflect local expectations. When that preparation is in place, teams can focus on responding instead of scrambling to interpret rules.

Data movement across borders is another area where good intentions are no longer enough. Regulators increasingly want proof, not promises. They want to see where data lives, how it moves, and what controls are in place to prevent misuse. Mature organizations track data flows continuously, identify regulated data automatically, and enforce geographic restrictions through technology, not policy statements. When something moves where it should not, alerts fire immediately. That allows teams to intervene early and explain what happened with confidence. It also reassures customers who want transparency about how their information is handled.

Third parties remain one of the most common sources of regulatory trouble. Many organizations learn this the hard way. In many jurisdictions, responsibility does not end with the contract. If a vendor fails, the enterprise is still accountable. That makes vendor due diligence more than just a checklist exercise. It means understanding how suppliers handle encryption, how they report incidents, whether they rely on subcontractors, and how they communicate with regulators. Contracts need to reflect local legal obligations and include real audit and escalation rights. Without that foundation, vendor issues have a way of becoming enterprise crises very quickly.

No single function can handle regulatory response alone. Legal teams understand the rules, but they do not run systems. Security teams understand the technology, but they are not responsible for regulatory dialogue. Customer and communications teams see the impact firsthand. The organizations that handle incidents well bring these groups together before something happens. They practice real scenarios based on local rules. Over time, that practice builds muscle memory. When pressure is high, people know their role and trust one another. That confidence shows, especially to regulators.

Regulation also needs to be part of the conversation much earlier in major initiatives. Too many transformation projects run into trouble because compliance is addressed late. Whether the effort involves AI, cloud platforms, supply chain systems, or operational technology, regulatory impact should be assessed at the design stage. Doing this early surfaces constraints while there is still room to adjust. It saves time, reduces rework, and prevents projects from stalling under last-minute scrutiny.

Handled the right way, regulatory assurance does not have to feel like a constant drag. Organizations that invest in visibility, preparation, and clear ownership earn credibility over time. Regulators see an enterprise that knows its environment. Customers see transparency instead of excuses. Partners see reliability. Integrated Assurance supports this by weaving regulatory requirements into daily operations rather than treating them as separate obligations. The organizations that succeed across borders are usually the ones that stay adaptable, remain consistent without being rigid, and treat compliance as a way to build trust instead of something to get through.

11.7 COORDINATING ACROSS TIME ZONES, CULTURES, AND GEOGRAPHIES

Technology allows organizations to scale at a remarkable speed, yet people do not move at the same pace. That difference lies at the center of global assurance challenges. A multinational enterprise may have systems that run 24 hours a day, but the individuals responsible for governance, compliance, and operational continuity remain subject to local time zones, cultural norms, language differences, and workplace rhythms. Global assurance cannot be reduced to tool deployment or policy publication. It requires a design that accounts for how humans coordinate across distance, interpret risk, and respond when pressure mounts.

The first difficulty comes from temporal dispersion. Teams distributed across geographies rarely share the same working hours. An incident in Singapore may require urgent attention from legal advisors in New York, regulators in Brussels, and technology vendors in Bangalore. Unless the organization has a structure for deliberate handoff, hours will be lost waiting for calendars to align. Lost time is not an inconvenience. It introduces real exposure in the form of delayed containment, regulatory breaches, or extended operational disruption. Enterprises counter this risk by creating relay structures that function like a baton handoff in a race. Responsibility transfers smoothly between regions through overlapping shifts, structured briefings, documented alternates, and shared workspaces. When designed well, the work continues without interruption as the clock turns.

Asynchronous decision frameworks reinforce this handoff approach. Not every decision requires a meeting, and not every meeting must be synchronous. When approval criteria, escalation thresholds, and authority limits are clearly defined, regional teams can act on events that fit established parameters. These frameworks prevent bottlenecks that arise when a decision must wait for leadership on another continent. They keep operations aligned to the urgency of the task rather than the timing of a meeting slot.

The second challenge is cultural variation in risk perception. Cultural norms shape how people report, escalate, and remediate incidents. In some regions, addressing problems directly signals strength. In others, direct confrontation may be read as disrespect. These variations influence the speed of incident reporting, the clarity of control deficiency communication, and the order in which issues are prioritized. Enterprises must localize their assurance training to account for this. Training content should use regional examples, be delivered in local languages, and employ culturally resonant framing so that enterprise standards are not just acknowledged but fully understood in daily practice.

Localization benefits further from the presence of regional assurance champions. These individuals operate as advocates for global standards while representing local concerns to central leadership. Their role is not ceremonial. Champions need operational credibility, the ability to navigate cultural nuance, and the trust of both the regional teams they represent and the global executives they report to. With these qualities in place, they become the connective tissue that translates intent into consistent action.

Language fragmentation presents another barrier. Even when English functions as the corporate standard, assurance materials often contain technical language that loses accuracy when translated. Misunderstanding the definition of a "material breach" or misinterpreting a "critical control" requirement can result in missed obligations. Enterprises avoid this risk by establishing a controlled vocabulary of assurance terms. This vocabulary is defined centrally, translated professionally, validated against local regulations, and embedded into policies, dashboards, and workflow systems across the enterprise. Shared definitions reduce the chance of error and preserve the precision needed for compliance.

Governance asymmetry adds complexity. Some regions may enjoy greater autonomy because of their maturity or lower regulatory obligations, while others remain tightly directed from headquarters. The result can be inconsistent decision speed, fragmented accountability, and unequal authority. A structured solution involves tiered autonomy based on measurable performance. Criteria such as maturity level, incident history, and data reliability determine the level of discretion granted to a region. These tiers should be dynamic, reviewed regularly, and adjusted as performance improves or deteriorates.

Technology inconsistency across regions also undermines coordination. A headquarters may operate with an integrated governance, risk, and compliance platform, while a newly acquired subsidiary continues to manage assurance with spreadsheets. This breaks data continuity and prevents meaningful comparisons. The path forward lies in platform federation. Different systems can interoperate through secure interfaces, normalize data into shared formats, and present a unified view of assurance posture across the organization. Standardization is less about enforcing identical tools and more about ensuring interoperability and comparability.

Stakeholder relationships create another asymmetry. Regulators, auditors, and key vendors prefer to work with local contacts, but those contacts often lack the authority or information needed to represent the enterprise. Delays and credibility loss follow. The solution is to appoint regional interlocutors with the authority, resources, and training to respond directly to external stakeholders. These interlocutors remain fully connected to the global assurance function, ensuring that the local presence reflects the global standard.

Incident management highlights how inconsistent behavior across geographies creates further friction. In one location, a breach may be escalated to senior leadership within minutes. In another, local staff may attempt to manage the situation until further evidence emerges. This disparity extends dwell time and creates confusion about responsibility. Organizations address this through assurance choreography. Predefined response structures and role assignments dictate who acts, how information flows, and when global coordination is triggered. Everyone understands the script before the incident occurs, leaving less room for hesitation or improvisation.

Time zone fatigue also threatens performance. Teams that are continually expected to work late nights or early mornings for global calls experience declining morale. To counteract this, enterprises rotate meeting times so the inconvenience is distributed evenly, design decisions for asynchronous review when possible, and delegate authority to local leaders within defined guardrails. This reduces overreliance on central leadership and protects team well-being.

Integration of new acquisitions adds further complexity. A newly acquired business may bring its own systems, cultural assumptions, and assurance maturity levels. Imposing enterprise standards too quickly breeds resistance. A phased onboarding approach works better. It maps existing practices to enterprise requirements, identifies gaps, and sets a realistic timeline for integration. This gradual alignment respects local culture while driving toward common standards.

Beneath all these measures lies the role of leadership. Tools and policies provide structure, but leadership brings coherence. Leaders build relationships across borders, invest in trust, and understand both technical controls and cultural nuance. Integrated Assurance succeeds when people, not just systems, are aligned. When designed thoughtfully, global dispersion can become an advantage. Regional strengths combine with centralized direction to create a model where assurance is continuous, resilient, and responsive to the pace of global operations.

11.8 CONCLUSION

Global enterprises rely on their ability to sustain trust across regions, partners, and customers. This trust is not confined to geography. It stretches into digital borders, regulatory landscapes, and cultural expectations. Maintaining it requires more than compliance or a framework designed at headquarters. Trust at scale must operate as a living system, able to evolve with markets, adapt to new rules, and keep pace with the rapid movement of technology. Federated assurance offers the structure for this kind of system when it is built on clear standards, shared accountability, and recognition that risk is experienced differently across every part of the enterprise.

The limits of traditional assurance models show most clearly during disruption. A central command structure may appear to deliver control, yet it responds too slowly to the speed of modern threats. Audit cycles review history, not the present. Compliance reports present a single interpretation of control effectiveness that rarely fits every region or market. This produces the illusion of security, one that collapses when regulators investigate or attackers exploit unseen gaps. Federated assurance replaces this illusion with a distributed capability that is transparent, connected, and responsive.

The strength of federated assurance comes from its ability to align local agility with global integrity. Regional teams sit closest to customers, regulators, and suppliers. They are the ones who understand the local realities of risk, culture, and implementation. Their daily choices decide whether a control succeeds or fails in practice. At the same time, the enterprise cannot afford to let each market define its own understanding of risk. Global standards must provide the anchor, while regional teams adapt those standards into workable practices that make sense within their environment. This balance preserves speed while maintaining consistency across the enterprise.

Trust gains real weight when federated assurance operates with live telemetry rather than paper records. Continuous monitoring of control performance, risk exposure, and incident response replaces speculation with evidence. Executives and boards gain visibility into conditions as they stand, not as they once were. This allows leaders to act with confidence. The idea of trust velocity, the speed at which confidence can be restored after a disruption, becomes more than a concept. It becomes a metric that can be measured and managed across the enterprise. By tracking velocity across regions, leaders gain both an early warning mechanism and a way to benchmark resilience.

Culture determines whether assurance can take root. A global model that ignores language, customs, and leadership styles will not succeed. Federated assurance works when standards are translated into the terms that resonate locally while preserving their original intent. Regional assurance leaders serve as both translators and integrators. They carry global priorities to local teams while explaining local realities back to global leadership. This human bridge ensures assurance is lived through practice rather than left on a page.

The resilience of assurance will be tested by the rise of AI, the expansion of digital supply chains, and the control of cross-border data. Regulations are diverging across regions. Governments are asserting sovereignty over digital assets. Customers are increasingly unwilling to grant trust without evidence of security. Centralized control will not meet these demands, nor will fragmented experimentation. A federated model distributes responsibility to those closest to the risk while retaining a shared foundation of visibility. This combination creates the balance that allows enterprises to show both agility and accountability.

Metrics become the common language of this model. When every region contributes to a shared framework of resilience scores, compliance maturity, and recovery outcomes, the enterprise gains the ability to compare performance fairly. High-performing regions provide examples that others can follow. Regions that lag behind can be supported before weaknesses escalate into failures. These metrics supply evidence that regulators demand and assurance that investors expect. They turn trust into a measurable asset that can be proven rather than claimed.

The long-term strength of federated assurance depends on integration into everyday work. It should not only appear during audits or incident reviews. It must be present in product design, procurement discussions, supplier negotiations, and customer commitments. When assurance is built into the natural flow of business, it becomes a capability that supports confidence rather than a constraint that slows progress. Leaders then begin to view it as an advantage, enabling faster and more reliable decision-making.

Resilience also requires a feedback loop. Lessons from incidents, results from audits, and deviations discovered at the local level must flow back into the global framework. This feedback keeps the system alive. Without it, assurance becomes brittle, locked in a cycle of outdated checklists. Organizations that treat assurance as a living framework position themselves to adapt faster than adversaries and anticipate regulatory changes rather than simply respond after they arrive.

Scaling trust without losing control is not a compromise. It is a deliberate act of design. Federated assurance places responsibility where it is most effective, close to execution, while protecting global integrity. It recognizes the importance of local conditions while refusing to dilute the enterprise standard. It distributes authority yet unites accountability. It turns compliance into a strength that not only defends the organization but also advances its competitiveness.

Enterprises that embrace this model strengthen their ability to manage risk, but the benefits extend further. They turn trust into a differentiator in the marketplace. They enter new regions with confidence. They adopt new technologies with fewer surprises. They recover

Use this checklist at the close of your planning, review, or strategy sessions to ensure your federated assurance model balances global governance with local autonomy. Each item is meant to spark a quick review and confirm that the principles outlined in this chapter are applied in practice.

1

Strategic Alignment

- [ ] Have we clearly defined the assurance anchors (minimum risk posture, control objectives, enterprise threat models) that are understood globally?
- [ ] Are global standards framed as principle-based outcomes rather than prescriptive rules?
- [ ] Do our federated assurance models support both speed of local execution and enterprise-wide resilience?

2

Governance and Accountability

- [ ] Are roles and responsibilities (local leads, central architects, and risk councils) explicitly documented and understood across geographies?
- [ ] Do we have tiered governance autonomy tied to assurance maturity and performance?
- [ ] Is there a transparent escalation and exception process with risk-based approvals?

3

Controls and Telemetry

- [ ] Are controls designed for modularity, allowing local adaptation without fragmenting enterprise oversight?
- [ ] Do we collect live telemetry and assurance signals at both local and global levels?
- [ ] Is assurance data normalized into a common schema for comparability across regions?

4

Strengthen Emerging Threat Readiness

- [ ] Have we conducted continuous threat modeling that includes systemic and AI-driven risks?
- [ ] Are supply chain, insider threats, and deepfake risks accounted for with living playbooks and detection protocols?

5

Regulatory Alignment

- [ ] Do we maintain an active regulatory intelligence layer with jurisdictional profiles for every market?
- [ ] Have we built a policy harmonization engine to reduce redundant compliance efforts?
- [ ] Are cross-border data flows, vendor risks, and jurisdiction-specific incident paths actively governed?

6

Human and Cultural Factors

- [ ] Have we embedded localized training and cultural adaptation into assurance programs?
- [ ] Do regional assurance champions/interlocutors represent local needs and global expectations effectively?
- [ ] Are time zones, languages, and work rhythms accounted for in handoffs, decision protocols, and coordination models?

7

Continuous Assurance

- [ ] Are assurance metrics (resilience scores, trust velocity, and control maturity) tracked enterprise-wide?
- [ ] Is assurance integrated into the business and technology lifecycle (procurement, development, onboarding, and vendor management)?
- [ ] Do we have a process for continuous improvement, feeding lessons from incidents, audits, and exceptions back into the model?

- [ ] **Executive Action:** Ensure that federated assurance connects global standards with local execution by embedding clarity, modularity, telemetry, and cultural adaptation into every aspect of governance. Trust must be continuously visible, measurable, and reinforced across all geographies.

Figure 11.2 Practical Checklist: Federated Assurance at Global Scale.

Image created by the author using Gamma.

from disruptions with greater speed. In a world where customers and regulators demand transparency, federated assurance provides the architecture that makes transparency credible.

Scaling trust in this way defines the maturity of a global enterprise. It signals to regulators, customers, and partners that the organization is not only capable of managing risk but also committed to resilience as a business principle. Federated assurance is not just a governance approach. It is a strategic capability that secures credibility and sustains growth in a world where trust is the most valuable form of capital. See Figure 11.2: Practical Checklist: Federated Assurance at Global Scale.

Chapter 12

Leading through Disruption

12.1 LEADERSHIP IN THE AGE OF CONSTANT DISRUPTION

Leadership used to be defined by an ability to steer an organization through periods of relative calm, punctuated by occasional crises. Plans were built around predictable cycles. Disruption was treated as an interruption rather than a condition. When something broke, leaders stepped in, stabilized the situation, and returned the organization to a known state. That model no longer reflects reality.

Today, disruption is not episodic. It is continuous. Enterprises operate inside an environment shaped by overlapping pressures that rarely slow down. Geopolitical instability affects supply chains overnight. Economic signals shift without warning. Cyber incidents unfold at machine speed. Regulatory expectations change while organizations are still adapting to the last mandate. There is no meaningful concept of "back to normal" because normal is in constant motion.

This reality forces a fundamental change in how leadership works. The old assumption that leaders can remain largely removed from operational volatility until something escalates no longer holds. When disruption is persistent, leadership cannot be reactive. It has to be structural. It must be embedded into how decisions are made, how information moves, and how accountability is reinforced long before visible pressure arrives.

Many organizations still rely on an event-driven leadership model, even if they do not describe it that way. Leaders mobilize when incidents reach a certain threshold. Escalation paths are activated. Committees assemble. Authority concentrates at the top. This approach assumes that disruption is temporary and containable. It also assumes that central control can keep pace with complexity. In modern enterprises, neither assumption is consistently true.

A system-driven leadership model responds to a different set of conditions. Instead of waiting for events, it operates continuously. Resilience is designed into the organization's operating model rather than layered on through crisis playbooks. Decision rights are clarified in advance. Communication norms are established before stress distorts behavior. Trust is treated as an operational requirement rather than a cultural aspiration.

This shift changes how resilience is understood. Resilience is often discussed in abstract terms, as if it were an outcome or a capability that can be activated on demand. In practice, resilience is expressed through daily behavior. It shows up in whether teams understand who can decide and when, and in how openly leaders communicate trade-offs and uncertainty. It shows up in whether people feel safe acting within intent rather than waiting for permission.

Every organization reveals its true resilience posture under pressure. Decisions made in ambiguous moments either reinforce confidence or expose fragility. Silence creates anxiety. Inconsistent messaging erodes trust. Overcentralization slows response. Leaders may believe they are maintaining control, but what they are often doing is creating hesitation. Over time,

DOI: 10.1201/9781003685982-16

teams learn that initiative carries risk while waiting feels safer. That is not resilience. It is dependency.

For resilience to be sustained, it cannot live only within specialized teams or formal continuity plans. Those structures are necessary, but they are insufficient on their own. Resilience must be practiced as a leadership discipline. Leaders who appear only when disruption becomes visible unintentionally signal that preparedness is optional. Leaders who model steady presence and clear accountability during ordinary operations send a different message. They normalize readiness. They make resilience part of the organization's rhythm rather than an exception.

Authority itself takes on a different meaning in this environment. Positional authority still matters, but it carries less weight when conditions change faster than directives can travel. What replaces it is coherence. Teams watch closely for alignment between what leaders say, what they do, and what they tolerate. Perfect decisions are not required. Consistency is.

People will forgive mistakes when leaders explain their reasoning and adjust transparently. They will not forgive unexplained reversals or shifting standards. When priorities change without context, teams lose their sense of orientation. When rules apply differently depending on circumstance or seniority, trust deteriorates. Coherence provides stability even when outcomes are uncertain. It gives people confidence that leadership behavior will remain predictable even if the environment does not.

The skills that define effective leadership under constant disruption extend beyond traditional measures of strategy and execution. Emotional intelligence becomes practical rather than theoretical. Leaders must sense when teams are overloaded, confused, or hesitant, and respond before performance degrades. Situational awareness becomes critical. Not all information is equally relevant, and leaders must help organizations focus on what matters without oversimplifying reality.

Decision-making under ambiguity becomes a daily requirement rather than a rare test. Leaders cannot wait for complete information. They must act with partial insight, explain their intent, and be willing to adapt. Communication shifts from providing certainty to providing orientation. People do not expect leaders to eliminate uncertainty. They expect leaders to help them navigate it.

This reality demands a change in how leadership is developed. Many leadership programs still emphasize executive presence, financial acumen, and strategic planning in stable conditions. Those skills remain important, but they are no longer sufficient. Modern leadership development must include exposure to ambiguity, cross-functional tension, and sustained pressure. Crisis simulations, scenario-based decision-making, and collaboration across silos are no longer optional exercises. They are essential preparation.

Progress must be measured not only by outcomes, but by observable behaviors. How do leaders communicate when information is incomplete? *How do they distribute authority under pressure? How do they respond when plans fail?* Readiness is no longer demonstrated by performance after stability returns. It is demonstrated by the ability to sustain direction when stability never arrives.

This redefinition of leadership cannot stop at the executive level. Disruption does not respect hierarchy, and leadership cannot be confined to the top of the organization. Frontline managers shape the first response to uncertainty. They translate intent into action. Mid-level leaders coordinate across teams and maintain continuity when signals conflict. Senior leaders set the tone by modeling coherence and accountability that cascade throughout the enterprise.

Organizations that endure are not necessarily those with the most advanced technology or the largest budgets. They are the ones that distribute leadership, institutionalize trust, and treat resilience as a shared responsibility. Their systems are designed to function under stress without sacrificing integrity. They do not depend on heroics. They depend on clarity.

Leadership in the age of constant disruption is not about restoring stability. It is about operating effectively without relying on it. It is the capacity to sustain trust, direction, and performance even when certainty is unavailable. That is the measure of leadership today.

12.2 TRAITS OF RESILIENT LEADERS

In high-pressure environments, leadership is not measured by job title or polished presentation. It is measured by the ability to create stability in uncertainty, maintain trust under scrutiny, and sustain direction when conditions are shifting. Resilient leaders do not eliminate disruption. They create the conditions that allow the organization to move through it without losing cohesion, confidence, or clarity. Their influence is not situational. It is embedded into the operational fabric of the enterprise.

Resilience is not simply a personal quality. It is a leadership discipline. While some associate resilience with individual toughness or endurance, enterprise resilience depends on how leaders behave, communicate, and decide in moments of ambiguity. These behaviors can be observed, taught, reinforced, and modeled. To institutionalize them, organizations must redefine what leadership excellence means. See Figure 12.1: Case in Point.

Most current leadership models prioritize business execution, strategic vision, and team development. These are necessary but incomplete. In the reality of continuous disruption, three domains of leadership competence must become central: Trust architecture, adaptive clarity, and emotional credibility. Each of these domains contains distinct traits that make resilient leadership scalable across the enterprise. See Table 12.1: Leadership traits to behaviors.

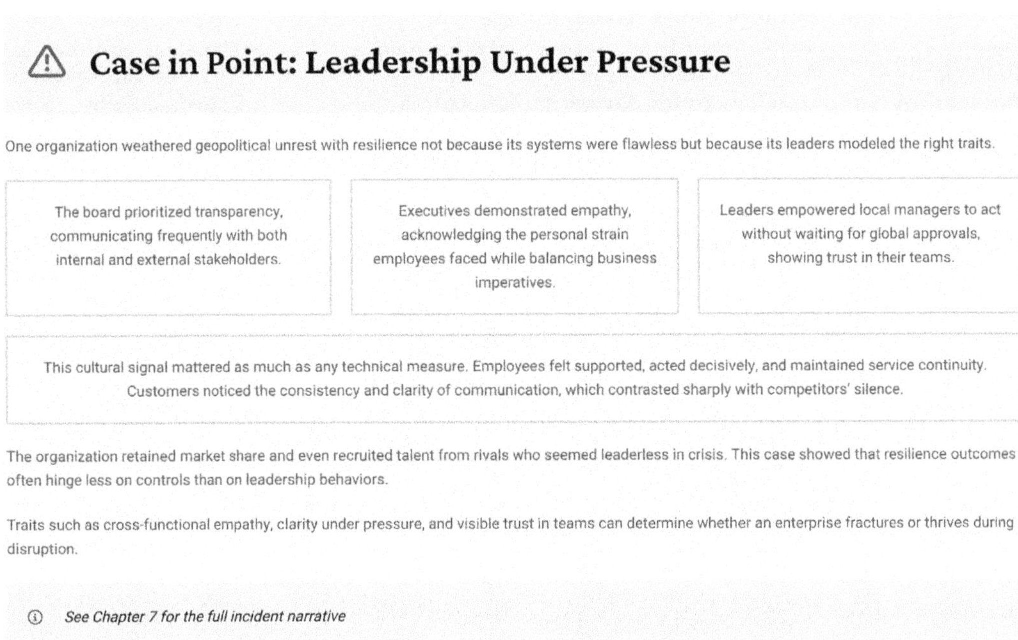

Figure 12.1 Case in Point.

Image created by the author using Gamma.

Table 12.1 Leadership traits to behaviors

Trait	*Observable behaviors during disruption*	*Organizational impact*
Empathy	• Practices *active cross-functional listening* in crisis briefings. • Acknowledges stress, uncertainty, and individual contributions in communications. • Ensures frontline perspectives are heard before final decisions.	• Builds trust across levels. • Increases psychological safety. • Reduces rumor-driven fear.
Adaptability	• Quickly recalibrates priorities when conditions shift. • Models flexibility by changing course without defensiveness. • Encourages experimentation with fallback strategies.	• Enables faster organizational pivots. • Minimizes paralysis. • Preserves momentum.
Decisiveness	• Makes timely calls with available data, avoiding analysis paralysis. • Uses clear escalation paths and defined decision rights. • Communicates decisions with rationale, even when information is incomplete.	• Provides clarity in uncertainty. • Reduces confusion. • Accelerates coordinated response.
Transparency	• Shares accurate, timely updates with all stakeholders. • Admits unknowns or gaps instead of overpromising. • Uses consistent messaging across channels (board, employees, and customers).	• Strengthens credibility. • Prevents erosion of trust. • Improves alignment.
Resilience	• Demonstrates calm under visible stress. • Frames disruption as an opportunity for growth rather than only loss. • Shows persistence by staying engaged throughout the recovery phase.	• Inspires confidence. • Normalizes endurance. • Sustains energy during prolonged crises.
Cross-Functional Awareness	• Invites input from diverse functions before decisions are finalized. • Uses Integrated Assurance dashboards to balance perspectives. • Encourages shared accountability over siloed blame.	• Enhances coordination. • Reduces silo conflicts. • Speeds holistic decision-making.
Cultural Sensitivity	• Adapts communication styles to different geographies and teams. • Avoids imposing one-size-fits-all playbooks in global contexts. • Seeks local insights when disruption affects specific markets.	• Improves global team cohesion. • Reduces cultural friction. • Aligns federated operations.
Strategic Foresight	• Scans for second- and third-order impacts of disruption. • Uses scenario planning to test recovery options. • Aligns immediate responses with long-term organizational goals.	• Prevents short-term fixes from creating long-term risks. • Preserves enterprise value.
Integrity	• Models ethical behavior in high-pressure trade-offs. • Rejects "cover-up" instinct when errors occur. • Upholds commitments made to customers, regulators, and employees.	• Preserves reputation. • Reinforces trust as currency. • Sets ethical tone.
Empowerment	• Delegates authority to frontline teams for rapid response. • Recognizes and rewards initiative shown under pressure. • Creates space for independent action within defined guardrails.	• Accelerates local decision-making. • Boosts morale. • Reduces executive bottlenecks.

12.2.1 Trust architecture

Resilient leaders understand that trust is not a soft skill. It is a structural asset that determines how quickly teams act, how reliably information flows, and how effectively the organization recovers from setbacks. In the absence of trust, systems fail, communication slows, and collaboration breaks down.

Trust begins with consistency. Teams do not expect leaders to have all the answers, but they expect predictability in how leaders respond. Shifting tone, changing priorities without explanation, or adjusting expectations under pressure erodes trust. Consistent leaders provide stability. Their standards are steady. Their reactions are measured. Their words and actions align over time and across situations.

The second trait is transparency. Resilient leaders do not conceal uncertainty. They acknowledge it. They share what is known, admit what is unknown, and explain how decisions will be made. Transparency does not require full disclosure of every detail. It requires credible assurance that leaders are not withholding critical information.

The third trait is ownership. Leaders who take responsibility, even when results are unfavorable, strengthen trust through accountability. Ownership is not about assigning blame. It is about being present, accepting scrutiny, and standing with the team when pressure is high. It includes being able to say, "We did not get this right, and here is how we will address it," and following through.

The fourth trait is signal management. Leaders must be aware of the messages they send through their actions, tone, and presence. Every choice, from how they respond to escalation to how they prioritize issues, sends a signal. Consistent and aligned signals accelerate trust. Conflicting signals undermine it.

12.2.2 Adaptive clarity

Disruption redefines the meaning of clarity. In stable environments, clarity often means delivering definitive answers and fixed plans. In dynamic environments, that approach can create false expectations and misdirected effort. Resilient leaders provide clarity that adapts as conditions change.

The first trait in this domain is pattern recognition. Leaders identify and connect signals across technology, operations, finance, risk, and culture. They detect early indicators of trouble, recognize systemic drift, and understand the implications before problems fully materialize.

The second trait is scenario fluency. This is the ability to operate effectively across multiple possible futures without losing momentum. Leaders who wait for the "right" scenario before acting are often too late. Those who assume their first plan is correct fail to pivot when needed. Scenario-fluent leaders outline several potential outcomes, take actions that fit multiple paths, and adjust when one becomes more likely.

The third trait is decision velocity. Timely decision-making under ambiguity prevents confusion, limits risk exposure, and sustains operational momentum. This does not mean rushing. It means knowing when a decision is necessary, acting decisively, and being accountable for the trade-offs. It also includes the ability to reverse a decision when conditions change and to communicate that reversal without undermining credibility.

The fourth trait is narrative alignment. Leaders explain why decisions are made, how they connect to the mission, and what they mean for the team. This alignment maintains morale and purpose even under stress.

12.2.3 Emotional credibility

Resilient leaders are emotionally consistent. They are not emotionally detached, but they manage their presence with discipline and empathy. They do not avoid the experiences of others. They navigate them in a way that strengthens the organization.

The first trait is emotional regulation. Disruption creates tension and fear. Leaders who react with volatility, whether anger, withdrawal, or defensiveness, erode trust even if their decisions are correct. Emotional regulation is the ability to stay grounded, respond deliberately, and reduce rather than amplify stress.

The second trait is situational empathy. Leaders recognize that different teams experience disruption in different ways. Product teams facing delays may need decisiveness. Finance teams facing unexpected costs may need reassurance. Operations teams dealing with customer issues may need a visible presence. Situational empathy is the ability to adjust leadership style to meet these needs.

The third trait is psychological safety leadership. In high-stakes situations, teams often hesitate to raise concerns or admit mistakes. Resilient leaders create conditions where this hesitation is reduced by responding constructively when issues are surfaced.

The fourth trait is authentic presence. Leaders remain visible and engaged, particularly in difficult moments. They do not delegate challenging communication. They are honest about what they know, clear about what they are doing, and physically or virtually present when it matters most.

These traits are not theoretical. They can be applied in every meeting, decision, and response. Resilient leaders integrate them into routine operations, retrospectives, and simulations. They build them into feedback processes. They view trust, clarity, and emotional consistency as leadership capabilities that require continuous development.

Resilient leadership does not protect teams from stress entirely. It equips them to navigate it productively. It is not about projecting strength for appearance. It is about creating an environment where others can act with confidence. Leaders who practice these traits become multipliers of trust and performance across the enterprise.

To sustain this model, leadership development must evolve. Promotion decisions should be based not only on business results but also on demonstrated resilience behaviors. Talent identification should highlight individuals who show situational empathy, clarity under pressure, and the ability to connect priorities across functions. Coaching and development programs should include exercises in pattern recognition, decision-making under ambiguity, and trust-building under scrutiny.

In an increasingly complex operating environment, the organizations that will endure are those led by individuals who view disruption as the normal setting for leadership. These traits are not reserved for the executive level. They are necessary for every leader at every tier who makes decisions that influence others. When these behaviors are distributed across the enterprise, resilience becomes scalable and sustainable.

12.3 IAMM AND LEADERSHIP CULTURE

Leadership represents the visible form of assurance culture. In the IAMM, the Culture and Collaboration domain measures whether leadership drives resilience through behavior or only through endorsement. Maturity in this domain defines whether assurance is procedural or behavioral.

At Level 1, leadership involvement is limited. Executives approve budgets and compliance programs without direct participation. Messaging is delegated to communications or risk teams, creating a visible gap between leadership intent and action. That distance weakens credibility and discourages accountability across teams.

Level 2 brings visibility but little engagement. Leaders mention assurance in town halls and strategy meetings, expressing public support without behavioral follow-through. The message that assurance matters reaches the organization, but it feels detached from leadership practice. Employees still view it as an external obligation rather than a shared value.

At Level 3, leadership begins to participate. Executives sponsor cross-functional initiatives and attend resilience simulations. Middle managers start connecting enterprise priorities with daily operations. Communication between leaders and staff improves, and assurance begins to feel practical. These efforts often rely on individual initiative instead of systemic expectation.

Level 4 defines leadership as an active architect of assurance. Resilience becomes part of strategic planning and performance management. Leaders participate in after-action reviews and model transparency during disruption. They own outcomes, fostering a culture of trust and learning. Assurance becomes a lived discipline rather than a statement of intent.

Level 5 establishes assurance as an integral part of leadership identity. Executives treat resilience as a performance metric equal to financial and operational results. Leadership pipelines are built with assurance competencies, and future leaders are evaluated on collaboration, accountability, and adaptive decision-making. Assurance becomes inseparable from leadership practice.

A global energy firm illustrates this progression. At Level 2, executives fund programs but remain detached from operations. During an incident, communication failures slow response and heighten confusion. By Level 4, those same leaders participate in exercises, debriefs, and strategy revisions. Response times improve, and trust strengthens across teams. At Level 5, assurance becomes part of leadership training. Executives understand resilience metrics, communicate them externally, and mentor others on assurance-driven behavior.

IAMM defines leadership maturity through behavior rather than statements. Mature leaders create space for reflection and accountability, treating assurance as a shared discipline. They model steadiness under pressure and consistency in communication. Leadership culture amplifies the full assurance ecosystem. Governance provides structure, operations build capability, and culture sustains continuity. Leadership aligns them all. When leaders embody assurance, the enterprise operates with confidence, clarity, and consistency in every circumstance.

12.4 FOSTERING CROSS-FUNCTIONAL EMPATHY AND TRUST

Resilient organizations are not built from isolated excellence. They are built from coordinated action. When disruption occurs, it does not confine itself to one department or domain. It moves laterally, crossing boundaries between cybersecurity, finance, engineering, operations, legal, marketing, and human resources. The speed and effectiveness of the response depend on how well those boundaries are bridged. In that moment, the difference between recovery and fragmentation often comes down to one factor, which is trust across functions.

Cross-functional trust is not a byproduct of collaboration. It is a condition that must be cultivated intentionally. Most organizations recognize the need for collaboration. They encourage cross-functional projects, establish steering committees, and hold town halls. But they often overlook the core ingredient that determines whether these initiatives succeed. That ingredient is empathy. Not surface-level agreement, but the structured ability to understand another function's pressures, priorities, and constraints and to act accordingly.

Empathy is not sentimentality. In a business context, it is a strategic asset. When leaders and teams understand the context in which others operate, they make better decisions, escalate more effectively, and interpret behavior with greater precision. Empathy enables fluency. It allows a cybersecurity leader to understand why a product team is hesitant to delay a release. It allows a finance leader to recognize why the procurement cycle needs to change to accommodate faster onboarding of secure vendors. Without empathy, these discussions become adversarial. With it, they become strategic.

Trust across functions is not achieved through shared goals alone. Many organizations assume that alignment on business outcomes will produce collaboration. In practice, shared goals often mask divergent incentives. One team may be measured by speed, another by compliance. While one team may prioritize innovation, another may prioritize continuity. These underlying tensions do not disappear because a slide deck says the enterprise is aligned. They must be surfaced, examined, and reconciled through relational effort.

The first step in building cross-functional empathy is role mirroring. This practice involves structured exercises where teams articulate the challenges, constraints, and success metrics of adjacent functions. For example, an engineering team participates in a tabletop where they must act as the risk function. They experience what it means to review an exception request, interpret a regulatory clause, or navigate a third-party control failure. Likewise, the risk function experiences what it means to triage a production outage, meet a customer SLA, or resolve an integration blocker.

These exercises create insight. They move empathy from concept to experience. They shift the conversation from "Why are they slowing us down?" to "I see the trade-off they are managing." This reframing is powerful. It does not eliminate conflict, but it reduces the attribution of malice. People stop assuming bad intent and start asking better questions.

The second step is shared learning across domains. Cross-functional trust grows when teams develop a mutual language. This begins with creating shared mental models. For instance, incident response does not look the same to legal, security, communications, or engineering. Yet all are involved. When each function learns how the others define criticality, escalate decisions, and interpret risk, coordination improves. Learning modules should include real-world scenarios, not just theory. They must reflect how decisions are made under pressure.

Organizations that invest in cross-functional education often see improved clarity in response coordination, fewer delays in decision-making, and more consistent control application. These improvements are not the result of process redesign alone. They are the result of empathy becoming operational.

The third step is trust cadence through structured coordination rituals. These rituals create rhythm. They include cross-functional standups, joint retrospectives, integrated planning sessions, and assurance-steering forums. Each ritual has a specific purpose. Standups ensure awareness. Retrospectives create shared learning. Planning sessions align trade-offs. Steering forums review performance against cross-functional metrics.

These rituals are not added as extras. They are embedded in the operational calendar. They are designed to be efficient, data-informed, and relationship-building. Most importantly, they are consistent. Trust is not built through occasional alignment. It is built through repeated interaction under predictable conditions.

The fourth step is signal reconciliation. Each function interprets risk differently. Legal looks for liability. Security looks for exposure. Finance looks for cost. Operations looks for continuity. When a new initiative is proposed, each function brings its own lens. If these perspectives are not reconciled, the result is friction. One team proceeds while another raises objections. One function approves a control, while another questions the data.

Signal reconciliation requires structured dialogue. It means surfacing assumptions, reviewing metrics together, and understanding where data interpretation diverges. Assurance teams must lead these efforts. They must serve as translators, helping each function understand how risk signals affect others. This coordination ensures that decisions reflect enterprise context, not siloed analysis.

The fifth step is psychological safety across functions. Many cross-functional failures are not technical. They are relational. A security team may know there is a vulnerability but hesitate to report it if the product team is known to react defensively. A finance leader may see a budget gap but avoid surfacing it if past feedback has been ignored. A compliance analyst may question a vendor, but fear slowing down operations.

Psychological safety means creating conditions where people can raise concerns without fear of retribution, embarrassment, or being labeled obstructive. This is not created by declaring safety. It is created by how leaders respond when concerns are raised. It is reinforced when people see that hard truths are respected, not punished.

Cross-functional psychological safety is modeled at the leadership level. If executive teams engage in visible blame, silo protection, or performative alignment, that behavior cascades downward. If they instead demonstrate respect across functions, elevate dissenting voices, and share credit across teams, trust spreads.

The sixth step is resilience-informed performance metrics. Trust deteriorates when teams are held to conflicting metrics. If one team is rewarded for speed, while another is punished for risk, they will view each other as obstacles. Over time, collaboration becomes conditional. Teams help each other only when it benefits their scorecard.

To prevent this, performance metrics must reflect shared accountability. Joint objectives and key results, cross-functional KPIs, and outcome-based rewards all reinforce that success is interdependent. Security is not just a security function. Resilience is not just an operations function. Risk reduction, trust velocity, customer protection, and system continuity are shared outcomes. Teams must be evaluated not only by what they deliver, but by how well they coordinate with others in doing so.

The seventh step is cross-functional incident retrospectives. Most post-incident reviews are conducted within functions. Engineering meets with engineering. Legal meets with legal. This limits learning. It isolates root cause analysis to one perspective. Cross-functional retrospectives create shared visibility into what happened, why it happened, and how signals could have been surfaced earlier.

These sessions are not about assigning blame. They are about reconstructing decision flows, identifying friction points, and improving communication channels. The most resilient enterprises use incident reviews as trust-building exercises. They reinforce shared ownership. They highlight coordination breakdowns as system failures, not personal ones. This practice improves operational alignment and strengthens trust under pressure.

The eighth step is integrated escalation models. In high-stakes scenarios, escalation must move across functions, not just upward. A control failure identified by IT must be visible to compliance. A customer incident escalated by legal must include cybersecurity. A service outage involving a third-party vendor must engage procurement, engineering, and public relations.

This requires predefined escalation matrices that specify cross-functional involvement. Escalation is not a chain. It is a network. Teams must know who needs to be informed, who has authority, and how decisions will be validated. These models must be tested, not assumed. Simulations and tabletop exercises help ensure that the network functions under stress.

The final step is co-ownership of assurance structures. Assurance cannot be relegated to a single function. Each domain must own a portion of the enterprise's trust posture. This includes control implementation, signal integrity, telemetry accuracy, and escalation readiness. Ownership creates accountability. When ownership is distributed with empathy, trust increases. Teams recognize that they are not alone. They are part of an interdependent system where resilience is everyone's responsibility.

Empathy and trust are not soft skills. In federated assurance models, they are strategic imperatives. The speed, integrity, and success of the enterprise depend on how well its parts understand and support one another. This cannot be achieved through policy alone. It must be led, modeled, and operationalized by leaders who see coordination not as overhead, but as a core element of resilience.

12.5 LEADING CULTURALLY DIVERSE TEAMS THROUGH DISRUPTION

Disruption within an enterprise does not stop at national borders. It moves through regions, cultures, and systems of belief. Sustaining resilience in a global organization depends as much on aligning people as it does on maintaining secure architecture or reliable controls. Leading culturally diverse teams in these conditions introduces a level of complexity that extends beyond differences in language or time zone. It demands trust, clarity in communication, and a sense of psychological safety that accounts for local behaviors, leadership expectations, and team norms.

Disruption is experienced differently across cultures. Some view decisiveness and speed as hallmarks of strength. Others value collective agreement and deference to authority. What signals credibility in one region may appear uncertain or inexperienced in another. Leaders who overlook these differences risk misinterpreting behavior and reading silence as agreement, urgency as panic, or compliance as commitment.

Cultural diversity, when managed intentionally, becomes a strategic asset. Leadership in this environment cannot rely on assumptions that alignment will occur naturally. It must be constructed through careful coordination and the creation of bridges across perception and communication. The goal is not uniformity but fluency, the capacity to work with authenticity in varied contexts.

Resilient leaders begin with awareness rooted in curiosity rather than assumption. They understand that culture shapes communication, decision-making, and the expression of authority. This awareness grows through direct engagement, not through training slides or policy documents. It comes from conversations, observation, and listening that reveal how a team defines disagreement, risk, and success.

Leadership presence must also adapt to local realities. Headquarters-driven messaging can create distance when it reflects only one cultural lens. Announcements, updates, and crisis communications delivered in a single tone or language often fail to resonate elsewhere. Strong leaders give regional voices agency, tailor messages to local conditions, and ensure that engagement reflects regional sensitivities. A cyber incident in one country should be addressed with language and dialogue that respect that country's norms, not through a single global script.

Adaptability in communication is essential. Tone, phrasing, and silence convey meaning differently across regions. Direct speech may be efficient in one culture but disruptive in another. Silence can represent reflection or disagreement depending on where it occurs. A leader's task is to deliver messages that retain the enterprise's integrity while being understood locally. Layered communication works well in these moments: A clear sequence of what happened, why it matters, what will occur next, and how each region contributes to the response.

Fairness in collaboration must follow. Disruption often shifts work rapidly across time zones, and without careful coordination, some teams become overburdened while others disengage. Equitable scheduling, shared accountability, and transparent recognition preserve trust. Inclusion in planning must equal inclusion in execution.

Psychological safety remains the foundation of effective multicultural leadership. Open dialogue cannot thrive without cultural awareness. In certain regions, challenging authority is rare. While in others, admitting an error carries stigma. A resilient leader encourages disclosure without penalty and listens without interruption. Appreciation for those who surface concerns reinforces a culture where speaking up represents commitment, not defiance. Anonymous channels can provide a secure path for input when public dialogue is difficult.

Respect for regional pacing and risk tolerance is another component. Some teams deliberate and seek consensus before acting. While others move immediately to a decision. A balanced leader establishes checkpoints and escalation thresholds that maintain pace without undermining autonomy. Local discretion in execution strengthens ownership and reduces resistance.

Governance must also reflect cultural inclusion. Global resilience cannot operate as a centralized directive. Regional insights should shape retrospectives, policy formation, and assurance oversight. This ensures that global standards remain connected to the realities of data protection, legal boundaries, and ethical expectations in each area.

Integrated Assurance strengthens this model by embedding cultural awareness into the operating fabric of the enterprise. It treats cultural fluency as part of assurance maturity, aligning trust measures to geography, adapting standards to local interpretation, and holding leadership accountable for both technical outcomes and cultural stewardship.

Enterprises that excel through global disruption are not those that erase difference but those that convert difference into capability. They sustain coherence while respecting variation. They recognize that trust, when cultivated across cultures, is not only an ethical achievement but also one of the strongest assets of organizational resilience.

12.6 BALANCING STABILITY WITH ADAPTIVE LEADERSHIP

Resilience cannot depend on the presence of a few exceptional leaders. It must be sustained through a deliberate system that grows, strengthens, and renews leadership capacity. As enterprises evolve, their leadership pipelines must evolve as well. The skills required to guide, protect, and govern organizations through persistent disruption differ greatly from those emphasized in traditional succession models. The leaders who carry enterprises forward must not only manage operations but also embed assurance into how those operations function and adapt under pressure.

Leadership pipelines are often managed as HR initiatives. Programs identify high-potential individuals, assign mentors, rotate them through business units, and provide executive education. These efforts build managerial competence but rarely produce assurance literacy or risk fluency. Resilience behaviors remain secondary to performance metrics. As assurance becomes central to enterprise strategy, leadership development must be restructured to prioritize these competencies.

Redefining readiness is essential. Future assurance-aligned leaders will not be measured only by profit, efficiency, or satisfaction scores. Their effectiveness will rest on their ability to sustain trust across systems, anticipate risks across functions, and make choices that maintain stability without slowing execution. They must think clearly in uncertain environments, connect insights across disciplines, and lead teams through complex change cycles.

12.6.1 Five foundational elements of the assurance leadership pipeline

A resilient enterprise does not produce strong leaders by accident. It does so through structured preparation and consistent reinforcement of behaviors that protect trust and operational integrity. The assurance leadership pipeline depends on five foundational elements designed to cultivate leaders capable of safeguarding the enterprise while advancing its goals.

- Assurance fluency as a core competency.
  Leaders must understand risk signals, interpret control performance, and engage in assurance discussions with confidence. They do not need to become auditors, but they must have a working knowledge of assurance systems, regulatory obligations, and operational indicators that show whether resilience is holding. This foundation should

be established early. Rotational programs should include exposure to risk, compliance, security, and governance. Simulations should present failure scenarios and force alignment with stakeholder expectations. Assurance fluency grows through repeated exposure, reflection, and mentoring from senior leaders who model its importance.

- Structured exposure to disruption.
  Resilience cannot be learned from theory. Leaders must experience environments defined by ambiguity, competing priorities, and rapid change. Development programs should normalize disruption as a condition of leadership. Crisis exercises, transformation assignments, and leadership roles during mergers, upgrades, or regulatory shifts build the capacity to stay composed under pressure. These experiences teach decision-making when information is incomplete and control is limited.
- Cross-functional trust assignments.
  Leaders in resilient organizations must navigate boundaries across disciplines such as engineering, compliance, finance, and operations. Trust develops through presence, listening, and translation of priorities into shared outcomes. Development programs should move leaders into roles outside their expertise. A technology lead may drive a compliance initiative, and a regional director may oversee governance modernization. These assignments expand empathy, expose hidden risks, and reinforce the shared ownership of assurance.
- Behavioral reinforcement through incentive design.
  Leadership behavior is sustained by what the organization rewards. If recognition focuses only on speed, cost, or margins, resilience will erode. Incentives must encourage assurance-minded behavior. Early identification of emerging risks should be recognized. Team performance under stress should influence evaluations. Collaboration with assurance functions should be tied to advancement. Senior leaders must model these standards consistently, as any tolerance of shortcuts weakens the message. Culture follows the pattern of rewards and consequences.
- Succession planning with assurance readiness.
  Preparing future leaders must include evaluating how they operate under uncertainty, build cross-functional trust, align controls with strategy, and maintain performance during disruption. Assessment centers, 360-degree feedback, and executive sponsorship programs should measure these capabilities directly. In regulated or complex industries, assurance readiness often predicts long-term leadership success more accurately than conventional metrics.

Embedding these elements ensures that leadership development becomes a resilience function, not just a talent program. It creates decision-makers who preserve trust, manage complexity, and maintain clarity through continuous disruption. In such systems, stability is not static. It is adaptive, learned, and renewed with every generation of leadership. See Figure 12.2: Five Foundational Elements of the Assurance Leadership Pipeline.

12.6.2 Building and sustaining the pipeline

Establishing a leadership pipeline for assurance requires coordinated effort across the enterprise. Human resources, assurance teams, business units, and executive sponsors must share a common vision of what resilient leadership means and how it will be developed over time.

Key steps include:

- Integrated leadership frameworks that merge core management competencies with assurance-driven behaviors.

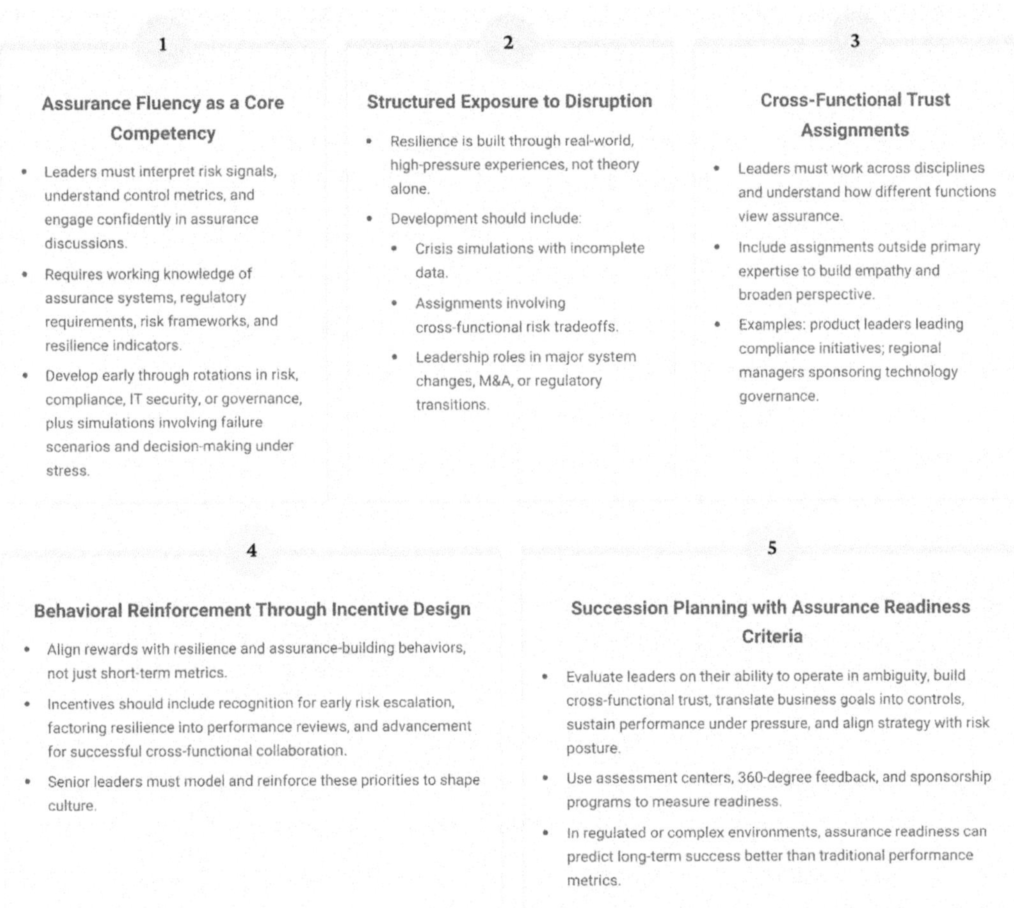

Figure 12.2 Five Foundational Elements of the Assurance Leadership Pipeline.
Image created by the author using Gamma.

- Shared language to describe leadership effectiveness in the context of disruption and recovery.
- Cross-functional cohorts that move through leadership development together, reinforcing trust and collaboration.
- Mentorship by resilient leaders who serve as culture carriers and practical examples of composure under stress.
- Governance participation to give emerging leaders early visibility into assurance-based decision-making.
- Performance reviews with contextual data that measure outcomes alongside the integrity of how those outcomes were achieved.

Leadership gaps often reveal themselves during disruption, not because talent is absent but because preparation is incomplete. Programs built around operational performance alone produce capable managers who struggle in uncertainty. The absence of assurance-oriented training causes hesitation when clarity is needed most. Teams lose alignment, confidence weakens, and response efforts slow.

An assurance-focused leadership pipeline resolves this weakness. It develops leaders who see risk as a natural part of their function and who strengthen the enterprise's foundation of trust through every decision. These leaders carry both the authority to act and the judgment to protect continuity.

Resilience is more than endurance through a crisis. It is the ability to reduce the damage, shorten the surprise, and diminish the long-term impact of what comes next. Assurance-aligned leadership delivers this outcome by investing in preparation rather than prediction.

Traditional leadership models were built for steady markets and stable operations. Modern organizations face volatility that tests both competence and character. The leaders of the future must not only deliver performance but also preserve trust. Those who learn to balance both will define the enterprises that thrive in the years ahead. See Figure 12.3, Leadership Reflection Exercise: Preparing to Lead through Disruption.

Use the following prompts as a self-assessment or discussion guide with your executive team. The goal is to evaluate your readiness not just to manage disruption, but to lead your organization through it with resilience and trust.

1 Personal Leadership Check

- When was the last time I made a decision under pressure that balanced stability with adaptability?
- Do my teams see me as a source of calm and clarity during disruption, or do they wait for me to react?
- How do I personally model resilience in my communication, priorities, and actions?

2 Organizational Trust Building

- In the last disruption, how did my leadership team reinforce trust with employees, customers, and stakeholders?
- Have I created an environment where teams feel safe raising concerns and surfacing early warning signals?
- Do we measure trust explicitly, or do we assume it exists until it is broken?

3 Cross-Functional Collaboration

- How often do I engage directly with functions outside my primary domain (e.g., operations, HR, cybersecurity, and finance) during strategic reviews?
- What mechanisms exist today to break down silos during crisis response?
- Am I empowering leaders at every level to act, or am I unintentionally centralizing authority during high-pressure moments?

4 Future Leadership Readiness

- Who on my team is being prepared to lead through the next disruption?
- Have I invested in leadership development that includes scenario-based training and stress testing?
- If I stepped away tomorrow, could my leadership bench guide the organization through a major disruption without hesitation?

Action Step

Write down three commitments you will make to strengthen your leadership resilience over the next 90 days. Share these commitments with your leadership team to build accountability and model transparency.

Figure 12.3 Leadership Reflection Exercise: Preparing to Lead through Disruption.
Image created by the author using Gamma.

12.7 CONCLUSION

The success of an enterprise in a disruption-saturated world depends on how it is led. Processes, technologies, and budgets provide leverage, but they do not determine whether an organization holds together under stress. Leadership does. Resilience is not accidental. It is created deliberately, moment by moment, by those who have influence. Leaders decide whether disruption becomes a source of confusion or a proving ground for confidence. They determine whether volatility fractures trust or reinforces it.

Use these questions and actions to evaluate your leadership approach and your organization's readiness. The goal is to transform the insights from this chapter into measurable leadership behaviors that build trust, adaptability, and resilience in practice.

1

Leadership Traits and Behaviors

- ☐ Have I demonstrated consistency between what I say, what I do, and what I allow?
- ☐ Do I show transparency by sharing what is known, admitting what is unknown, and providing clear rationale for decisions?
- ☐ Am I modeling emotional regulation and calm presence under visible stress?
- ☐ Do I actively practice situational empathy across teams, functions, and geographies?
- ☐ Have I created psychological safety that enables people to raise concerns without fear of blame?

2

Cross-Functional Trust and Collaboration

- ☐ Have I built structures for role mirroring or exercises where teams experience the tradeoffs of other functions?
- ☐ Are there shared learning modules or joint retrospectives to surface insights across domains?
- ☐ Do we have a clear trust cadence (regular stand-ups, planning sessions, and steering forums) that reinforce alignment?
- ☐ Are performance metrics aligned across functions to avoid conflicting incentives?
- ☐ Have we tested and validated integrated escalation models that cross boundaries instead of moving only upward?

3

Leading Culturally Diverse Teams

- ☐ Do I adjust my communication style to reflect cultural norms without losing enterprise clarity?
- ☐ Are regional voices empowered to adapt enterprise messaging and response to local realities?
- ☐ Have I established fair collaboration structures that distribute workload equitably across time zones?
- ☐ Do I ensure cultural inclusion in retrospectives, governance forums, and policy development?

4

Building the Assurance Leadership Pipeline

- ☐ Am I reinforcing assurance fluency as a core leadership competency in my teams?
- ☐ Have I provided structured exposure to disruption (simulations, transformations, crisis assignments) in development programs?
- ☐ Are leaders given cross-functional trust assignments that place them outside their home discipline?
- ☐ Do incentive systems reward early risk raising, collaboration, and resilience behaviors, not just short-term outcomes?
- ☐ Does succession planning include assurance readiness criteria such as decision-making under uncertainty and trust-building under pressure?

☐ **Executive Action:** Commit to embedding resilience as a daily leadership discipline. Align leadership development, cross-functional collaboration, and cultural inclusion with assurance practices so your organization can thrive in disruption rather than merely survive it.

Figure 12.4 Practical Checklist: Leading through Disruption.

Image created by the author using Gamma.

The habits of leadership matter more than any single decision. When leaders communicate consistently, trust accelerates. When they take ownership during failure, credibility strengthens. When they model calm in uncertainty, teams mirror that behavior and sustain direction. When they provide clarity without promising certainty, they create alignment without illusion. These patterns of behavior become the true infrastructure of resilience. They are more influential than frameworks or tools because they shape how people interpret, respond, and act when the environment refuses to stabilize.

The outdated belief that leadership is about having the answers has lost relevance. In the current era, the true value of leadership lies in interpreting complexity and providing direction when clarity is limited. Authority is no longer granted by position alone. It is maintained through the alignment of words and actions. Teams will follow leaders who demonstrate coherence even when conditions do not. They will trust those who admit uncertainty but commit to principled decisions. They will respect those who take responsibility and share accountability.

Resilient organizations are distinguished not by the absence of disruption but by the presence of leaders who make disruption survivable. These organizations design leadership development to reinforce behaviors that protect trust and sustain clarity. They evaluate leaders not only on results but also on how those results are achieved. They prepare successors who understand that resilience is a leadership obligation, not a technical function. They build systems that spread these capabilities across levels, functions, and geographies. The outcome is a culture where resilience is scalable and sustainable.

The benefits extend beyond immediate crisis response. Teams that trust their leaders raise risks earlier, act with greater confidence, and recover more quickly. Organizations that see empathy modeled collaborate more effectively under pressure. Cultures that take responsibility for failure learn faster and adapt better. In such organizations, disruption does not define the enterprise. Leadership does. That distinction determines whether the next crisis becomes a collapse or a catalyst for strength.

As enterprises prepare for the future, the challenge is not whether disruption will continue. It will. The challenge is whether leadership will evolve fast enough to meet it. Resilient leadership is the most scalable control an organization possesses. It is more adaptive than technology, more enduring than process, and more decisive than policy. It is the capacity that turns uncertainty into alignment and volatility into progress. The question facing every organization is, when disruption arrives, will your leadership hold? See Figure 12.4: Practical Checklist: Leading through Disruption.

Chapter 13

The New Currency of Trust

13.1 TRUST AS THE CORE METRIC OF RESILIENT ENTERPRISES

In the current business environment, speed, complexity, and volatility are not passing trends. They are structural conditions that shape the competitive landscape and redefine what it means to succeed. Within this context, trust has undergone a fundamental transformation. It has shifted from being a soft, reputational concept to becoming a concrete, measurable performance metric that drives enterprise viability. No longer is trust something that organizations can hope to gain through marketing, brand familiarity, or positive sentiment alone. It is now the deciding factor in whether customers choose to engage, whether regulators provide approval, whether partners commit capital, and whether employees dedicate themselves to the mission of the organization.

This shift is not theoretical. It is playing out every day in competitive decisions, in regulatory rulings, and in market responses to both opportunity and crisis. Trust is now earned through demonstrable resilience and delivered through operations that are secure, reliable, and accountable. In the modern enterprise, operational reliability is inseparable from the quality and integration of assurance. If assurance is not deeply embedded in systems, decision-making processes, and day-to-day behaviors, trust will remain fragile and easily eroded.

Trust is not a byproduct of public relations or brand storytelling. It is the first lens through which risk is perceived by customers, partners, regulators, and investors. A company can withstand a data breach, absorb a regulatory fine, or recover from a failed product launch if it can prove that these events do not reveal systemic weaknesses in governance or security. However, what many organizations fail to survive is the permanent erosion of stakeholder confidence that occurs when they are seen as unable to manage risk with integrity and foresight.

The measurement of trust is becoming as structured as the measurement of financial performance. Indicators such as operational uptime, control performance reliability, breach response times, stakeholder confidence indices, and even stock market valuation can reflect an enterprise's trust posture. The implication is that trust must be managed as both an input and an output of enterprise operations. It is not simply a reputational result of success, but a foundational driver of it.

Too many organizations continue to mistake compliance for trust. Compliance is necessary, but it is not sufficient. It represents the minimum acceptable threshold for operating within regulatory or contractual boundaries. It communicates that an organization has met formal requirements, checked the necessary boxes, and passed certain inspections. Trust, on the other hand, requires a higher standard. It must be proven through proactive controls that anticipate risk, through governance that is transparent and consistent, and through a continuous feedback loop that links emerging risk signals to business decision-making.

DOI: 10.1201/9781003685982-17

This means trust must be designed into the enterprise architecture itself. It should be visible in system design, evident in operational performance, and reflected in leadership conduct. Integrated Assurance is the operational mechanism that enables this. By unifying cybersecurity, IT operations, compliance, and governance into a single operational fabric, the assurance model translates the concept of trust into actionable frameworks. It builds the conditions for systems to perform predictably under stress. It ensures that controls function as intended in real time, not just during scheduled audits. And it allows leaders to see the relationship between organizational actions and the promises made to stakeholders.

Enterprises that embrace this model no longer view security and resilience as cost centers to be minimized. They view them as the infrastructure of trust. This change in perspective affects how performance is measured, how investment decisions are made, and how business cases are evaluated. Executives begin to ask new types of questions. Instead of asking only whether systems are secure, they ask whether the business is trustworthy. Instead of focusing solely on risk mitigation, they ask whether stakeholders are confident in the organization's ability to anticipate, adapt, and respond effectively.

These changes can be measured. An enterprise's trust velocity, which is the rate at which it gains or loses trust during a crisis, can be modeled in relation to its Integrated Assurance maturity. Control integrity, which is the consistency with which controls behave as designed under real-world conditions, can be validated in live operational scenarios, not just in controlled audit environments. Recovery ROI is the degree to which recovery actions restore stakeholder confidence and can be benchmarked across industries. These metrics are strategic assets because they tie operational performance directly to market confidence.

There is also a necessary cultural shift. In traditional organizations, trust was often seen as the domain of marketing or corporate communications. Brand managers would be tasked with protecting reputation, while technical teams operated independently. In a resilient enterprise, trust is the responsibility of everyone. Engineers build trust through secure, reliable design. Product teams build trust by making ethical choices in development and delivery. Security teams build trust by anticipating threats before they cause disruption. Leaders build trust through transparent decision-making and visible accountability. This shared ownership is only possible when assurance is integrated at the architectural level and aligned across all functions.

Organizations are expanding their trust metrics to include control predictability, stakeholder confidence, and governance agility. They treat trust as an asset that can grow and compound over time, creating strategic advantage, or erode quickly when neglected. In this framing, trust becomes the core metric of enterprise resilience. It is not simply a marker of reputation. It is a measurable business performance indicator, a leadership principle, and a competitive differentiator.

If trust is the currency of resilience, Integrated Assurance is the means by which that currency is minted and maintained. It produces trust through operations that are consistent, validated, and explainable. It supports the systems and processes that allow organizations to keep their commitments to stakeholders under both normal and adverse conditions. This is how resilience is transformed from an abstract aspiration into an operational discipline that can be monitored, measured, and improved continuously.

The enterprise that treats trust in this way will do more than survive in a challenging threat landscape. It will lead. It will attract customers who value reliability and accountability. It will engage partners who require transparency in their business relationships. It will gain regulatory goodwill by demonstrating integrity and responsiveness. It will retain talent by creating a culture of clarity, purpose, and stability. In an era marked by persistent uncertainty, the enterprise that is consistently trusted becomes a point of orientation for the market.

Trust, in this view, becomes the ultimate output of enterprise design. It is the result of deliberate architectural choices, disciplined governance, and continuous operational alignment. Like any other strategic asset, it must be actively developed, rigorously monitored, and protected from erosion. The assurance model provides the structural and operational foundation to deliver trust at scale. It does not represent the creation of a new function. Rather, it is the integration and alignment of existing capabilities into a coherent and measurable trust infrastructure.

The organizations that take this approach will not only meet today's challenges but will also position themselves to thrive in what comes next. They will have the capacity to move faster without sacrificing integrity. They will have the credibility to enter new markets with confidence. They will have the operational stability to navigate disruptions without losing stakeholder support. And perhaps most importantly, they will have established trust as a tangible, measurable, and renewable enterprise resource.

Trust is no longer an intangible quality to be hoped for or taken for granted. It is a measurable, operational outcome that reflects the enterprise's ability to deliver on its promises. Integrated Assurance is the architecture that makes this possible. It is the system by which resilience is not only maintained but also scaled. For leaders who understand the competitive value of trust, the decision is clear: Build it deliberately, measure it rigorously, and protect it relentlessly. Everything else in the enterprise depends on it.

13.2 THE VALUE CHAIN OF CONFIDENCE

Trust is often described as something abstract, yet in practice it is concrete, measurable, and tied directly to the economics of an enterprise. When trust is strong, valuation grows, customers remain loyal, and brands sustain a premium in the marketplace. When it erodes, value declines. Share prices slip, customer relationships fracture, and recovery is slow even when technical issues have been resolved. Trust is not only cultural capital. It is also financial capital.

Capital markets show this clearly. Investors reward predictability, transparency, and resilience. Enterprises that display these qualities trade at higher multiples and borrow at lower costs because markets perceive them as less risky. During disruption, their share prices recover faster because confidence in their ability to respond remains intact. In mergers and acquisitions, firms with established trust profiles command higher valuations. Their reliability becomes a form of leverage. When resilience and transparency are proven, market confidence compounds their worth.

The same pattern appears with customers. Organizations often invest heavily in acquisition campaigns while overlooking the economic efficiency of retention. In reality, keeping existing customers is far less expensive than replacing them. Trust anchors that relationship. In sectors where reliability and data protection define reputation, transparent communication during a breach often preserves most of the customer base. Concealment or delay accelerates loss. The expense of replacing that revenue far exceeds the cost of maintaining trust from the start. Retention becomes a reflection of how well trust holds under stress.

Brand equity represents the most visible expression of this principle. Customers consistently pay more for brands that demonstrate care for their safety, data, and experience. When products converge in quality and price, trust separates leaders from competitors. The premium paid to trusted brands is not a function of features. It is a reflection of credibility. Enterprises that honor their promises convert that credibility into a measurable market advantage. Those that betray it seldom regain their former standing. Once confidence is lost, reputation rarely returns to its prior strength.

The economic dimension of trust extends throughout the enterprise. Employees stay longer in organizations where leadership is transparent and credible. Supply chain partners align more willingly with companies that act with integrity. Regulators treat open and accountable firms with greater confidence and less scrutiny. Each of these outcomes carries financial weight. Lower turnover reduces hiring costs. Reliable partners improve efficiency. Constructive regulatory relationships reduce the likelihood of fines or investigations. Every benefit links to the depth of trust the enterprise sustains.

For leadership, the meaning is clear. Trust must be managed as an economic driver, not as a symbolic value. It belongs beside growth, margin, and market share on executive dashboards. Metrics such as recovery ROI, trust velocity, and customer confidence must be treated as forward indicators of enterprise health. When boards and leadership teams measure them consistently, trust becomes integrated into strategic planning, capital allocation, and brand management.

The progression from assurance to trust to economic value is now direct. Integrated Assurance establishes operational confidence. Operational confidence builds stakeholder trust. Stakeholder trust produces tangible economic gains in valuation, retention, and brand strength. This cycle is visible in every resilient organization that outperforms competitors during a crisis, in every brand that emerges stronger after disruption, and in every enterprise that converts credibility into growth. Trust has become the currency through which resilient enterprises secure their future.

13.3 FROM ASSURANCE TO TRUST INFRASTRUCTURE

Assurance has long existed as a network of independent control functions. Audits, compliance reviews, cybersecurity safeguards, policy enforcement, and risk reports formed the traditional model. These activities verified adherence to defined standards and identified deviations when they occurred. They were necessary for accountability but operated in silos—reactive to events and detached from the organization's strategic direction. They validated outcomes rather than influencing them.

That structure no longer fits the modern enterprise. In an economy driven by digital interdependence, trust has become the measure of market relevance. Assurance can no longer look backward at evidence of compliance. It must look forward and provide confidence that decisions, systems, and behaviors align with organizational intent. It must become a living capability that enables opportunity, manages exposure, and sustains stakeholder confidence.

Trust infrastructure represents this transformation. It is not theoretical. It functions as an operational system composed of interdependent people, processes, data flows, and platforms that continuously demonstrate integrity and reliability. It integrates architecture, engineering, compliance, product development, vendor oversight, and leadership behavior. Its objective is to make trust measurable and repeatable. Trust infrastructure is built into operations from inception, rather than applied as a corrective layer after the fact.

Integration marks the starting point. Many enterprises remain fragmented. Security monitors technical risk. Compliance manages regulatory duties. Audit tests control design and effectiveness. Risk management compiles reports for governance committees. These groups rarely share continuous data or synchronize planning cycles. The result is duplication, latency, and inconsistent interpretation of control evidence. Fragmentation prevents leaders from seeing the full picture when a crisis arises.

Integrated Assurance replaces this disorder with a connected function. It establishes a shared language across assurance disciplines and ties control objectives directly to business results. Governance becomes continuous rather than episodic. Accountability remains distributed but coordinated under a single operating model. This alignment enables assurance to expand at the same pace as the enterprise. It minimizes friction, reduces bottlenecks, and supports rapid, evidence-based decision-making.

The infrastructure model introduces continuous validation. In the old model, trust was tested through periodic audits or incident reviews. That approach cannot sustain relevance in a world of continuous deployment, evolving threats, and distributed systems. Trust infrastructure, by contrast, collects and correlates live data from across environments. It observes access activity, control performance, policy adherence, and anomaly patterns. Analytics and automation interpret this telemetry and respond to shifts in real time.

Within this model, assurance functions like any other critical enterprise service. It operates continuously, is embedded into every process, and scales with complexity. When it performs well, it is seamless to the user, but when it fails, the disruption is immediate and visible. For that reason, assurance requires the same investment, leadership, and modernization focus given to other infrastructure services. It must be measured, maintained, and evolved as the enterprise grows.

The advantages extend beyond compliance. Integrated Assurance enables faster innovation. New products, services, and markets can be validated without long review cycles. Governance supports rather than restricts. Reporting becomes an inherent output of well-governed operations instead of a separate exercise in evidence gathering. The organization gains the ability to act confidently at speed.

For global enterprises, structure is essential. Trust infrastructure combines centralized governance with federated execution. Centralization establishes architecture, standards, and metrics. Federation ensures that accountability and decision authority remain close to the operational context. This balance provides consistency without restricting adaptability. It embeds assurance throughout the enterprise rather than concentrating it in a few departments or regions.

Cultural change reinforces the transition. Assurance teams must evolve from enforcement to enablement. They become partners in delivery, not gatekeepers. Engineering, operations, and product teams must treat assurance as a design input that supports safe innovation. Executives must view it as a driver of growth that lowers uncertainty and improves resilience. This change begins by embedding trust principles in design, defining metrics that align with business performance, and rewarding collaboration across functional lines.

Technology gives the infrastructure its reach. Observability, automation, and intelligent analytics are central to its operation. Systems must correlate signals across domains, detect anomalies in context, and adjust controls dynamically. AI strengthens predictive and adaptive capacity by identifying control weaknesses and modeling the trust impacts of change. Technology alone, however, cannot create trust infrastructure. It must operate under disciplined governance and within a culture that values sustained integrity.

An enterprise that completes this transition behaves differently. Trust becomes visible in every transaction and workflow. It shapes vendor engagement, software pipelines, and incident communications. Leadership dashboards display trust indicators beside financial metrics. Teams make decisions with assurance data at hand. Customers experience reliability as part of the brand. Investors recognize the organization's credibility as a competitive advantage.

Integrated Assurance provides the blueprint. It defines the architecture, roles, and data relationships that sustain trust at scale. It converts assurance from an afterthought into a foundation for continuous growth and innovation. It aligns security, governance, and operations within a single operating rhythm that reflects the speed of business.

The cost of inaction is measurable. Enterprises that remain in fragmented assurance models face repeated breaches, audit fatigue, and reputational decline. They spend more on remediation and litigation. They struggle to meet evolving regulatory expectations. They also lose the confidence of both customers and employees. Building trust infrastructure is now a strategic imperative. It links governance to innovation, converts resilience into measurable performance, and positions assurance as a source of lasting value. In this environment, assurance becomes not a safeguard of the past but a platform for the future.

13.4 THE COMPETITIVE ADVANTAGE OF TRUSTED ENTERPRISES

Organizations today are judged on more than what they sell or how efficiently they operate. They are evaluated on how they behave when things go wrong, how clearly they govern themselves, and how well their systems hold up under pressure. In that reality, trust has become one of the most valuable assets an enterprise can hold, and one of the easiest to lose. It shapes customer loyalty, regulatory relationships, investor confidence, and even a company's access to certain markets.

When trust is built intentionally into the enterprise, it stops being a side effect of success and becomes something far more powerful. It turns into a capability that influences how decisions are made, how risks are handled, and how growth is pursued. Brand awareness can be created through messaging. Trust cannot. It is earned through consistent behavior, visible controls, and outcomes that stand up to scrutiny. It is practical, observable, and increasingly decisive.

For years, organizations optimized for speed, efficiency, and cost. Those goals still matter, but they no longer protect a business on their own. A company that moves fast but cuts corners will eventually be slowed by scrutiny. A low-cost provider that mishandles data will pay for it in reputation and customer churn. Even strong products struggle when they are supported by weak governance. Trust changes the math. It amplifies the value of operational excellence and innovation rather than replacing them.

Enterprises that treat trust as part of their operating model see it reflected across their ecosystem. Customers are more willing to adopt new services and share sensitive information when security and governance are visible, not assumed. Regulators engage more constructively with organizations that demonstrate discipline before an incident forces it. Partners commit more deeply when confidence comes from how the business operates day to day, not just what is written into contracts. Internally, employees show up differently when they believe the organization does what it says it will do.

Trust that is designed into systems and processes compounds over time. It reduces the frequency and impact of breaches, compliance failures, and governance breakdowns. Organizations spend less energy repairing damage and more time building what comes next. They attract better talent, enter partnerships from a position of strength, and recover faster when disruption hits. When pressure arrives, their communications carry weight, and their relationships hold.

The absence of trust produces the opposite outcome. Organizations that fail to recognize its value fall into reactive cycles. Their assurance programs fragment, visibility into risk weakens, and communications lose credibility. They may operate successfully for a time, but the first major incident reveals the fragility beneath the surface. The resulting damage reaches far beyond technology. It diminishes brand equity, erodes customer confidence, and weakens shareholder trust. The cost of distrust appears in financial losses, credit downgrades, penalties, and lost opportunities.

Operationalizing trust through Integrated Assurance shifts this trajectory. Assurance becomes a generator of value rather than a compliance exercise. It aligns the enterprise's risk posture with its strategic intent, allowing leaders to act with confidence. An organization with a mature trust posture can enter new markets with fewer delays, launch digital platforms with faster adoption, and integrate acquisitions without losing control integrity. These advantages emerge from deliberate design and disciplined execution.

Trust reinforces authenticity. In an era of overstated claims and superficial commitments, credibility depends on proof. The organizations that stand apart are those that can demonstrate their integrity through consistent evidence. Trust is not declared in marketing statements but verified through measurable performance. The assurance model creates the structure to make this visible. Policy enforcement, third-party attestations, performance metrics, and transparent leadership actions all contribute to a clear view of organizational reliability. When that visibility remains consistent, stakeholder confidence grows.

Internally, trust fosters alignment across business and technical functions. Shared vocabulary around assurance simplifies communication and decision-making. Leaders act decisively because they have confidence in the accuracy of information and the reliability of controls. When disruptions occur, teams respond quickly because responsibilities are clear and reporting is credible. The reduction in operational friction strengthens both resilience and productivity.

In governance, trust has become a board-level concern. Directors no longer accept general assurances that risk is under control. They expect trust to be measurable. They seek data that confirms whether control environments adapt in real time and whether assurance supports business objectives. Organizations that provide these insights earn credibility with their boards, enabling faster, more informed oversight.

Capital markets are also recognizing the correlation between trust and value. Investors now evaluate resilience alongside financial performance. ESG frameworks already reflect elements of operational trust, and disclosure requirements are evolving toward greater transparency in governance and control. Enterprises with measurable trust metrics and Integrated Assurance models secure better financing, lower insurance costs, and stronger reputational standing. Trust is not treated as overhead but as a multiplier of enterprise value.

In product and service design, trust determines adoption. When assurance is integrated into the development lifecycle, reliability becomes intrinsic to every release. Customers experience security and transparency as natural extensions of product quality. These attributes reinforce loyalty because they reduce uncertainty without introducing friction. Trusted systems deliver both protection and ease of use, turning dependability into a market advantage.

In the connected digital economy, trust functions as a condition of participation. As ecosystems merge through APIs, data exchanges, and automation, inclusion depends on verifiable assurance. Enterprises that demonstrate control maturity are invited into federated networks, trusted to manage sensitive processes, and chosen for collaborative innovation. Access to these environments cannot be purchased. It must be earned and sustained through consistent evidence of reliability.

Trust as a competitive advantage is not theoretical. It represents the outcome of sound design, disciplined governance, and a culture of accountability. Integrated Assurance provides the structure to turn trust into an operational system rather than an aspirational goal. It forms the basis for credibility across every relationship, transaction, and initiative.

Organizations that adopt this perspective make stronger choices. They treat assurance as enterprise infrastructure. They embed it across functions, measure trust continuously, and integrate it into strategic planning. They rise above competitors through reliability and clarity of purpose. Over time, they earn and sustain the confidence of every stakeholder, turning trust into both a currency and an engine of growth.

13.5 LEADING THE MARKET WITH TRUSTED OPERATIONS

Enterprises that lead through trust do more than manage risk effectively. They redefine markets. They establish performance expectations that others follow. They shape how regulations evolve and attract ecosystems of customers, partners, and investors who prize credibility over convenience. In these organizations, trusted operations are not the outcome of compliance or brand positioning. They are the foundation on which enduring leadership is built. Companies that recognize this shift no longer focus on surviving disruption. They become the stabilizing force that helps entire markets navigate through it.

Operational trust is built on reliability, transparency, and accountability. It takes shape when systems perform as intended, when issues are disclosed without delay, and when recovery is swift and verifiable. These outcomes are not coincidental. They result from deliberate architectural design, disciplined governance, and a unified assurance model that places trust at the center of every operational layer. In mature enterprises, trust is not a consequence of strategic planning. It defines the strategy itself.

The evolution of dominant technology platforms illustrates this truth. Market leaders are not distinguished by speed or price alone. They prevail because of their consistent performance, secure data stewardship, reliable delivery, and adherence to ethical governance. This reputation attracts customers and regulators alike. It gives confidence to partners whose growth depends on predictable integration. Such trust cannot be assembled after the fact. It must be constructed through infrastructure designed for continuity, repeatable processes, and governance that reinforces integrity.

Sustaining operational trust requires precision in accountability. Fragmented control environments cannot produce dependable assurance. When information flow is uneven and decision-making is misaligned, the signal of instability becomes visible to all stakeholders. Customers experience inconsistency. Regulators detect control drift. Employees sense confusion in priorities. The solution lies in federated assurance, where governance roles are clear, decision rights are transparent, and every participant understands how their actions affect enterprise integrity.

Resilient organizations show their strength through clarity in adversity. They do not hide during incidents. They communicate facts. They act quickly to contain risk and restore continuity. Their control environments provide visibility into conditions, enabling leaders to make measured, transparent decisions. The ability to recover with composure earns lasting credibility. Markets interpret this as competence, not damage control. Investors and partners respond with confidence, reinforcing the organization's long-term position.

Trusted operations also transform culture. Once teams internalize the organization's commitments to stakeholders, those commitments shape how they design, build, and serve. Engineers prioritize resilience. Product leaders emphasize transparency in communication. Customer-facing teams resolve issues with the understanding that every action reinforces confidence. Over time, trust becomes embedded in the organization's vocabulary and workflows. It transitions from a compliance mandate to a shared behavioral norm.

From an architectural perspective, trust-driven operations share identifiable characteristics. Continuous validation ensures that controls function as intended. Governance informed by telemetry keeps leadership decisions grounded in real data. Live visibility into risk enables agility without undermining stability. These features allow trust to scale. When new markets or product lines emerge, they are absorbed into a framework already proven to maintain consistency and integrity.

The most advanced enterprises make their trust posture observable. They publish transparency reports that include challenges as well as achievements. They welcome independent verification. They build explainable systems so that decisions can be traced and justified. They measure their control performance against both internal objectives and industry benchmarks. In environments where competitors rely on claims, this visibility becomes a differentiating asset that strengthens both reputation and compliance posture.

Trust leadership extends beyond organizational boundaries. Enterprises that operationalize trust influence the evolution of policy, standards, and best practices. Their maturity gives them authority in shaping secure supply chain models, ethical AI governance, and cross-border data integrity frameworks. This influence enhances their role in the broader economy of trust and demonstrates that resilience can serve as a public good as well as a private advantage.

Leadership through trust does not imply flawlessness. It is grounded in transparency and accountability. Organizations that acknowledge their weaknesses and demonstrate measurable improvement cultivate more confidence than those that conceal imperfections. Trust grows through consistency and through the ability to adapt under pressure. A willingness to reveal and repair strengthens credibility far more than the illusion of perfection.

The advantages of operational trust extend across sectors. Whether in financial services, energy, manufacturing, healthcare, or public administration, the capacity to deliver reliable, transparent, and secure outcomes defines resilience. Trust bridges industries that would otherwise be separated by incompatible risk appetites or governance requirements. It becomes the connective tissue that enables collaboration and innovation at scale.

Financial results validate this approach. Enterprises that maintain trusted operations experience lower exposure to risk, stronger customer loyalty, and higher investor assurance. Their cash flows are more stable, and their valuations reflect the market's recognition of governance maturity. In transactions or partnerships, the presence of a tested assurance model often determines the outcome of negotiations.

In time, trusted operations become indistinguishable from the enterprise identity. They define how the market perceives leadership, how regulators assess reliability, and how customers decide loyalty. Organizations that build this foundation are directing change. They set the standards for what responsible growth and ethical innovation look like in a volatile economy. Integrated Assurance provides the structure that allows this consistency. It aligns architecture, operations, and governance into one cohesive system that sustains trust at enterprise scale.

As markets evolve, trust will remain the measure that endures. It will not depend on campaigns or product cycles. It will be reaffirmed through every reliable transaction, every transparent communication, and every predictable recovery. The enterprises that master this discipline will define the next era of leadership. They will not claim trust through words but demonstrate it through the evidence of performance that stands up under scrutiny every day.

13.6 EVOLVING ASSURANCE AS A STRATEGIC ASSET

As transformation accelerates and disruption becomes constant, the enterprises that endure will not be those that react the fastest or recover the easiest. They will be the ones that build with intent, creating systems where trust, resilience, and adaptability are part of the foundation. In this environment, assurance cannot remain a background function. It must stand as a strategic capability that strengthens performance, reinforces market confidence, and sustains relevance. This shift requires a new way of thinking about control, governance, and accountability. It calls for assurance to operate as a driver of enterprise value rather than a reporter of compliance.

Strategic assets create lasting strength. They are designed to evolve, scale, and reinforce themselves over time. Traditional assurance functions were not built with this mindset. They existed to verify compliance, conduct audits, and confirm adherence to standards. Those tasks remain important, but they are no longer enough. The threat landscape changes daily, regulations expand without pause, and stakeholders expect clarity that reaches far beyond policy adherence. These pressures demand assurance that is integrated, predictive, and directly supportive of business innovation. Strategic assurance enables speed while maintaining control. It protects and projects trust as a visible, measurable asset.

Building assurance into enterprise planning begins before any investment is made. It is not a matter of review after approval. It means placing assurance professionals at the strategy table when plans are being formed. Whether the focus is AI, multicloud migration, market entry, or supply chain redesign, assurance must be present from inception. When assurance participates early, control design aligns naturally with business objectives. Integrity is maintained without slowing progress.

This level of integration depends on leadership support. Boards and executives must position assurance with authority that reaches beyond compliance reporting. Many enterprises accomplish this through Integrated Assurance councils or similar governance structures. These bodies must influence investment priorities, risk decisions, and policy formation. Their oversight should extend to technology, behavior, ethics, and operations. When this occurs, assurance becomes an instrument of enterprise architecture rather than an audit of past behavior.

An evolved assurance function also requires new capabilities. The professionals leading it will act as strategists who understand both risk and performance. They will interpret how governance shapes growth and how technology decisions influence trust. They will design control environments that align with business intent and explain those relationships in terms the board understands. Assurance at this level operates as a system of coordination rather than a series of independent checks.

To sustain this vision, organizations must invest in tools and infrastructure that enable real-time visibility. Automation, telemetry, and advanced analytics form the foundation for this transformation. Unified control libraries eliminate duplication and reduce friction. Assurance data becomes part of executive dashboards, sitting beside financial and operational metrics. Trust posture is monitored continuously, and decisions are guided by current evidence rather than delayed reports.

Measurement defines progress. Traditional key risk indicators still matter, but they do not capture the full story. Modern enterprises need assurance metrics that describe performance under pressure. Trust velocity, recovery ROI, control integrity, and governance responsiveness form a more complete picture. These measures reflect the organization's ability to anticipate disruption, maintain confidence, and adapt responsibly. When assurance is evaluated in business terms, it earns strategic recognition equal to other enterprise assets.

Culture must reinforce these principles. Trust should not exist as a slogan or a compliance statement. It must become part of identity. Engineers build secure designs because it represents quality. Legal teams draft agreements that reflect the same intent. Communications and marketing present truthfully what the organization stands for. Every employee contributes to the stewardship of trust. Strategic assurance, therefore, operates through culture as much as through controls.

This cultural grounding requires development. Training programs should teach ethical reasoning, risk awareness, and resilience as core competencies. Leadership programs should include assurance maturity as a measure of readiness. Performance reviews should recognize contributions that strengthen control environments and reinforce accountability. Stewardship of trust must become an organizational expectation, not a specialist's concern.

Technology amplifies this effort. As AI, automation, and distributed systems redefine operations, assurance must evolve to match their speed. AI-driven validation tools can detect control drift in real time. Digital twins can model trust scenarios before deployment. Embedded controls can evolve alongside applications within development pipelines. Strategic assurance becomes intelligent, adaptive, and inseparable from daily operations.

Scalability defines its sustainability. Expansion into new markets or business models should not weaken control effectiveness. Modularity in design, consistency in governance, and clarity in accountability make this possible. Assurance functions must operate independently of geography or structure. They must retain fidelity to purpose across every boundary.

This maturity also creates a competitive advantage. Companies that can demonstrate advanced, Integrated Assurance frameworks gain trust in ways that competitors cannot easily replicate. Customers, partners, and investors assess trust as a signal of reliability. The strength of an organization's assurance model increasingly determines its access to opportunity. In this way, assurance influences not only operational performance but also market position.

Enterprises that internalize these principles will not wait for failure to reveal their weaknesses. They will test continuously, adapt immediately, and validate effectiveness in motion. Assurance will live within the rhythm of operations, guiding design, execution, and recovery. Trust will become measurable, tangible, and inseparable from enterprise value.

Integrated Assurance provides the model for this transformation. It unites governance, risk, and operations into a continuous capability that scales trust across every function. It converts assurance from a static report into a living system that supports resilience, transparency, and sustainable growth. The organizations that embrace it will not only withstand disruption but also use it to strengthen their position in an unpredictable world.

13.7 IAMM AND THE CURRENCY OF TRUST

Trust grows through consistent assurance. It is not purchased, mandated, or claimed. It is earned through proof of integrity across systems, people, and decisions. The IAMM defines trust as a measurable outcome. Maturity reflects how well an enterprise can prove reliability, accountability, and adaptability across time.

At Level 1, trust happens by accident. Customers, regulators, and partners extend confidence only until the next disruption. Communication is reactive, and transparency is rare. The organization may deliver strong products or services, but it struggles to show consistent dependability. When incidents occur, explanations differ and accountability is uncertain. Trust fades because integrity cannot be demonstrated.

Level 2 introduces structure, though still defensive in nature. Policies and compliance reports appear to reassure stakeholders. Risk statements exist for auditors, and metrics are selected to satisfy expectations. These gestures improve the image but not the substance. Trust remains conditional, dependent on documents rather than lived performance.

At Level 3, reliability becomes measurable. Governance, culture, and operations align around assurance principles. Metrics expand to include recovery time, audit closure cycles, and control performance. Customers notice steadier delivery, and regulators observe fewer exceptions. Yet trust remains procedural. Stakeholders recognize progress but remain unsure how the enterprise will respond under pressure.

Level 4 transforms trust into a behavioral outcome. The enterprise manages trust velocity, recovery ROI, and the integrity of evidence. Boards review trust data besides financial metrics. Employees understand that daily actions affect reputation. Incidents are addressed openly, and communication is timely. Trust strengthens because the organization demonstrates learning and self-awareness.

Level 5 treats trust as a strategic asset. The organization operates with complete visibility into assurance performance. Customers, regulators, and partners can verify resilience through transparent metrics. Governance reinforces accountability, culture sustains consistency, and leadership models openness. Trust becomes a measure of enterprise health, visible in every interaction from service quality to ethical judgment.

A clear example comes from the technology sector. A cloud provider at Level 2 maturity advertises compliance certifications yet hides outage details. Customers appreciate polished transparency but doubt operational honesty. By Level 4, the provider releases live dashboards, incident reports, and remediation progress. At Level 5, customer feedback becomes part of the assurance process itself. Trust becomes quantifiable, and the enterprise gains lasting distinction.

IAMM establishes that trust is proof of predictable and responsible behavior rather than reputation. Enterprises with higher maturity levels understand that trust drives market advantage. Regulators collaborate rather than penalize. Investors value consistency. Customers remain loyal because dependability is visible.

Mature organizations define and track trust metrics. They disclose incidents and recovery performance with clarity. They share lessons learned both internally and externally. Leadership accepts accountability for sustaining trust across every stakeholder group. These practices turn trust from occasional success into operational discipline. At its highest levels, IAMM reframes assurance as the stewardship of trust capital. Every decision, control, and communication contributes to that capital. The organization's ability to maintain and grow defines long-term relevance and resilience.

13.8 CALL TO ACTION FOR EXECUTIVES AND ENTERPRISE LEADERS

Things have changed, and everyone feels it. Technology moves faster than most organizations can keep up with. Disruption is no longer something you plan around. It is part of daily life. And people are paying closer attention than they ever have. They are not just looking at products or growth charts anymore. They are watching how a company shows up when things get hard, and how leaders act when there is pressure, uncertainty, or real risk on the table.

In that environment, leadership is not just about performance. Growth and innovation still matter, but they are no longer enough. They are simply expected. What truly separates leaders now is trust. Trust that systems were built with care, not convenience. Trust that risks were considered before they became crises. Trust that the organization will respond with discipline and honesty when something breaks. This kind of trust is not claimed. It is proven, quietly and repeatedly, through the choices leaders make when no one is asking them to. True resilience is not a claim made through marketing. It is earned through evidence and repeated performance.

For executives, this represents a permanent shift in strategic focus. Trust now stands beside revenue, market share, and innovation as a core priority. To make trust operational, assurance must be transformed. It cannot survive as a static compliance exercise hidden in the back office. It must become an enterprise-wide capability that is continuous, measurable, and tied directly to performance outcomes.

This is a responsibility that resides with leadership. It cannot be delegated entirely to compliance, security, or risk teams. The tone must begin at the top. Boards and C-suites must treat the enterprise's trust posture with the same rigor as financial performance. Ownership of trust involves visibility, oversight, and accountability. It depends on facts rather than promises, on real data rather than impressions.

Visibility is the foundation of this ownership. Leaders cannot control what they cannot see, and many organizations still operate with fragmented or outdated assurance information. Executives must insist on continuous, unified visibility rather than quarterly summaries. They must demand real-time validation of control performance and interdependencies. This level of visibility requires investment in observability platforms, telemetry, and integrated data systems that provide a continuous picture of enterprise trust. The shift is from isolated audit records to ongoing validation of behavior under real conditions.

Alignment between trust and business strategy begins with visibility. Assurance cannot sit on the sidelines while organizations pursue growth and transformation. Every major initiative, whether it is a cloud migration, an expansion into a new market, or an acquisition, needs assurance built into its design from the start. This approach does not slow momentum. It prevents rework, protects confidence, and allows innovation and trust to mature together. Integrated Assurance offers a practical way to make this real by turning governance intent and risk appetite into day-to-day operational confidence.

Strong cross-functional governance reinforces that alignment. Trust is not owned by a single team or function. It cuts across cybersecurity, compliance, engineering, product, finance, human resources, and customer experience. Governance structures must reflect that reality. Decision forums should consistently include assurance perspectives and clearly define roles, accountability, and incentives tied to trust outcomes. When assurance becomes shared work, it stops feeling like a control function and starts operating as a core principle of how the organization runs.

Trust cannot stop at the edge of the organization. Most companies now depend on vendors, service providers, and sprawling digital supply chains to operate day to day. If those relationships fail, trust fails with them. Assurance has to move with those dependencies. That starts by being explicit about what trust actually means in external relationships and how it will be proven over time. Contracts and partnership agreements should spell out clear, observable standards, not vague promises. And oversight cannot be treated as a checkbox at onboarding or something revisited once a year. It has to stay active for as long as the relationship exists.

What keeps trust alive over time is culture. The way leaders talk about assurance determines whether it becomes part of how people work or just something discussed after an incident. When trust only shows up during audits or breach reviews, it will always feel reactive. When it shows up in planning conversations, performance expectations, and how people are recognized, it starts to shape daily decisions. Leaders reinforce this by being transparent, by asking for evidence instead of reassurance, and by aligning their actions with their words. Culture is built through what people see every day, and it endures when commitment is visible and consistent.

A trust-centric enterprise also depends on sustained investment in people. The individuals who operationalize assurance bring together technical depth, business judgment, and ethical clarity. They are the ones who turn complexity into confidence. Executives have to be deliberate about finding and growing this kind of talent, and about tying excellence in assurance to real leadership paths and compensation. When assurance roles are recognized as strategic work rather than back-office functions, the right people stay. The organization keeps hard-won knowledge, context, and judgment that cannot be replaced by reports or tools.

Measurement is what turns good intentions into real maturity. Counting audits completed or incidents closed only tells you what already went wrong. Resilient organizations look ahead instead. They track how quickly emerging threats are spotted, how often control weaknesses are stopped before they cause damage, and whether products and services consistently ship with assurance built in from the start. Just as important, they watch how trust evolves. Customer confidence, regulator posture, and partner expectations all leave signals over time.

Taken together, these measures define not just resilience but whether the organization will remain relevant in the long run.

Technology underpins all of this. Assurance should be woven directly into the systems that run the business. Modern assurance platforms bring operational data together, validate controls continuously, and support adaptive governance at scale. These capabilities are no longer optional. They are essential for demonstrating reliability to regulators, customers, and investors. As such, they deserve the same level of funding, oversight, and executive attention as any other core business system.

External pressure adds urgency. Regulators are introducing new operational resilience mandates. Customers expect transparency in data protection and risk management. Investors examine disclosures that reflect trust performance alongside financials. Enterprises that act now can define the standards of their industries rather than be defined by them. Delay invites regulation and erodes confidence.

Symbolism is no longer enough. Trust must be embedded into architecture, culture, and execution. This requires conviction from leadership and willingness to invest over time. The organizations that make this commitment will not only withstand volatility but will shape markets through credibility and reliability. Those that hesitate will struggle to regain ground once trust is lost.

Integrated Assurance provides the model for this transformation. It unites fragmented functions and connects assurance to business value. It removes inefficiency, improves decision quality, and embeds accountability into every layer of the enterprise. It is not bureaucracy. It is the operating framework for sustained trust.

The window for action is open now. Every industry faces disruption. Threats evolve with intelligence and speed. Stakeholders demand clarity and proof, not claims or slogans. The organizations that lead with trust will command attention, strengthen loyalty, and define the benchmarks that others must follow. The rest will remain in recovery mode, explaining rather than leading.

Trust is no longer a marketing statement. It is a measurable condition of performance and a direct reflection of enterprise integrity. It determines which organizations endure and which fade. Every decision made today writes that story. The leaders who choose to anchor their enterprises in trust will secure not only resilience but enduring relevance. See Figure 13.1– Five Questions Every Executive Should Ask About Trust.

13.9 CONCLUSION

Trust is no longer abstract or elusive. It has evolved from a quality that leaders hope to inspire or marketers attempt to shape into a defined and measurable attribute of enterprise performance. In the modern operating environment, trust is designed, managed, and proven. It does not emerge from advertising or engagement campaigns. It arises from disciplined architecture, transparent governance, and a culture that behaves consistently with its stated values. For organizations that intend to thrive amid continuous disruption, trust must serve as the primary design principle behind every system, product, and relationship.

The purpose of this work has been clear. Resilience must be understood differently. It cannot remain a tactic for recovery after disruption. It must function as a strategic advantage that separates adaptable enterprises from those that depend on reaction and repair. This shift cannot occur through disconnected controls or outdated compliance routines. It demands an operational model that integrates assurance across business functions and aligns risk management with enterprise strategy. Integrated Assurance represents that model. It embeds trust

1 **Do we measure trust as rigorously as we measure revenue and cost?**

If trust is a form of capital, it deserves its own metrics, including customer confidence, recovery ROI, trust velocity, and control integrity under stress.

2 **Is trust embedded into every decision, or is it treated as an afterthought?**

Review whether major business moves, including acquisitions, product launches, AI adoption—are evaluated not just for compliance, but for their impact on stakeholder trust.

3 **How do we prove resilience beyond compliance?**

Ask whether your organization can demonstrate tested, repeatable recovery capabilities in real scenarios, not just in policy binders or audit reports.

4 **Do our people feel safe raising concerns before they become failures?**

Trust thrives where psychological safety exists. Ensure cultural mechanisms encourage transparency, learning from mistakes, and collective accountability.

5 **Are we using trust as a competitive differentiator?**

Consider how trust strengthens brand equity, accelerates market adoption, and shapes valuation. The most resilient organizations don't just preserve trust – they leverage it as their strongest market advantage.

Executives who can confidently answer these questions are not just protecting their enterprises. They are building the foundation for relevance, resilience, and leadership in a world where trust is the most valuable currency.

Figure 13.1 Five Questions Every Executive Should Ask About Trust.
Image created by the author using Gamma.

within every decision, process, and system, ensuring that the organization performs with both confidence and coherence.

Throughout these pages, the framework has been examined as both a philosophy and a practice. Integrated Assurance changes how technology services are delivered and how cybersecurity is engineered. It alters the way governance and compliance operate by uniting oversight with agility. It influences architecture, design, and data protection, and it strengthens vendor oversight and enterprise culture. It connects functions that once worked in isolation and builds the structure required for sustained resilience. It provides a maturity model that enables organizations to measure progress against the accelerating risks of AI, modernization, and global interdependence.

Within this model, trust becomes the defining measure of resilience. It is not a secondary result of control effectiveness or compliance scores. It becomes the leading indicator of whether an enterprise can perform under pressure. Metrics such as trust velocity, control integrity, and recovery ROI express this concept in measurable form. They define how trust operates as a tangible outcome that influences reputation, regulation, and market access. In this sense, trust determines who leads and who follows, who remains relevant and who fades from view.

Trust must be cultivated intentionally. It requires design discipline, governance consistency, and leadership that treats stewardship as a continuous responsibility. It must be measured, managed, and evolved to match technological and societal change. Integrated Assurance supplies the framework for this responsibility. It positions resilience as a shared enterprise function rather than a departmental activity. Governance becomes a mechanism for transparency instead of a constraint on innovation. Security becomes a continuous source of credibility and assurance.

Across industries, the shift toward Integrated Assurance has begun. Enterprises are leaving static defense postures behind and adopting continuous, adaptive models. Risk, audit, compliance, and cybersecurity are no longer isolated disciplines but parts of unified governance

This checklist is designed to move trust from an abstract concept into daily executive practice. Use it as a quick reference to evaluate whether your enterprise is embedding trust into its architecture, operations, and culture.

1 Trust as a Strategic Asset

- ☐ Have we elevated trust to the same level of importance as financial capital in executive discussions?
- ☐ Do our dashboards and board reports include trust metrics (e.g., trust velocity, recovery ROI, control integrity)?
- ☐ Are trust outcomes explicitly tied to growth, investment, and innovation decisions?

2 Integrated Assurance as Infrastructure

- ☐ Is assurance unified across cybersecurity, IT operations, compliance, and governance rather than fragmented?
- ☐ Do we operate with continuous validation of controls, not just periodic audits?
- ☐ Are real-time risk and trust signals visible at the leadership level?

3 Culture and Accountability

- ☐ Is trust framed as everyone's responsibility, not just the domain of security or marketing?
- ☐ Do leaders model transparency, accountability, and integrity in decision-making?
- ☐ Are incentives and recognition tied to trust-building behaviors across teams?

4 External Relationships and Ecosystems

- ☐ Do we embed trust requirements into supplier contracts, partnerships, and joint ventures?
- ☐ Are customer and regulator communications built on openness and evidence, not spin?
- ☐ Can we demonstrate trustworthiness with verifiable metrics, attestations, and transparency reports?

5 Future Readiness

- ☐ Is trust designed into our enterprise architecture, product lifecycles, and digital platforms from the outset?
- ☐ Are we equipping our people with assurance-aligned skills (risk literacy, resilience awareness, ethical reasoning)?
- ☐ Can our assurance model scale across geographies, markets, and emerging technologies (AI, multi-cloud, and decentralized systems)?

Executive Action: Make trust measurable, visible, and actionable. Embed it into systems, decisions, and culture as deliberately as you manage financial capital. Everything that matters next depends on it.

Figure 13.2 Practical Checklist: Operationalizing the Currency of Trust.
Image created by the author using Gamma.

structures that respond in real time. Assurance principles are now being embedded into product design, procurement, and AI deployment. These changes are driven not only by regulation but also by stakeholder demand for verifiable trust.

Integrated Assurance is not a final destination. It forms the operational foundation for future capability. As enterprises confront AI integration, geopolitical volatility, and environmental or economic instability, trust will determine who adapts first. Those grounded in trust will move faster, coordinate better, and recover stronger. They will interpret risk signals with clarity and transform them into performance outcomes. They will demonstrate integrity through evidence rather than declarations.

The call to leadership is unambiguous. Risk awareness must give way to resilience as a deliberate operating stance. Assurance must evolve from a reporting activity to a structural component of enterprise design. Fragmented defense models must yield to unified governance and measurable impact. Organizations that make this transition will not only manage crises but also define what strength and continuity mean in the modern economy.

Trust is not proven by an absence of failure. It is demonstrated through integrity, accountability, and transparency when conditions deteriorate. It is visible when an enterprise can explain its decisions, stand behind its actions, and meet its commitments despite adversity. Such trust cannot be borrowed or reconstructed. It must be embedded from the start, sustained through practice, and protected through vigilance. Integrated Assurance makes this possible by turning trust into infrastructure rather than intention.

The organizations that prevail will be those that operate at the speed of trust, scale resilience as a built-in function, and embed assurance into every dimension of their operations. Trust has become the operating currency of leadership. It must be earned, maintained, and applied with discipline. Trust should be managed as carefully as capital. It should be invested in systems, processes, and people that preserve reliability and reinforce integrity. It should be monitored through meaningful indicators that reveal both performance and perception. It should be protected through transparency, ethics, and proactive governance.

Every significant outcome now depends on it. Market access, customer loyalty, investment confidence, regulatory alignment, and innovation leadership are all reflections of an organization's trust posture. Enterprises that understand this will no longer treat trust as a message. They will treat it as a measurable condition of performance.

The moment for action has arrived. The framework exists. The methods are proven. What remains is the commitment to lead through trust as both a discipline and a differentiator. Organizations that do so will not only achieve resilience but also create enduring competitive strength.

Trust must be built with intention, invested with purpose, and protected with resolve. Everything that follows will depend on it. See Figure 13.2: Practical Checklist: Operationalizing the Currency of Trust.

Appendix I

How to Use This Appendix

This appendix is designed as a practical guide for applying the Integrated Assurance Maturity Model (IAMM) inside a real organization. It is not intended to be read cover to cover in a single sitting. It is meant to be used. Leaders, architects, and practitioners should approach it as a working reference that supports decision-making, pilot execution, and maturity growth over time.

IAMM is not a diagnostic to complete once and file away. It is a lens for understanding how assurance actually operates across the enterprise and a roadmap for strengthening resilience, trust, and execution under pressure.

WHO THIS APPENDIX IS FOR

This appendix supports multiple audiences, each with different entry points.

- Executives and board-level leaders should use it to understand how assurance maturity affects readiness, recovery, and confidence in decision-making. The maturity levels and heat map interpretation provide a shared language for discussing resilience without technical abstraction.
- Security, risk, and IT leaders should use it to align fragmented programs into a single operating model. The maturity domains, self-assessment, and improvement planning sections are designed to expose gaps between policy, technology, and behavior.
- Architects, engineers, and operations leaders should use it to embed assurance into daily workflows. The 90-day implementation guide translates maturity into concrete operating practices that can be tested and refined.
- Program and transformation leaders should use it as a structuring mechanism for pilots, modernization efforts, AI governance initiatives, and post-incident recovery programs.

HOW THE SECTIONS FIT TOGETHER

Each section of this appendix serves a distinct purpose and builds on the others.

The IAMM maturity model defines what good looks like at different stages of assurance development. It establishes a common reference point for evaluating the current state and setting realistic expectations for improvement.

The 90-day implementation guide explains how to move from assessment to action. It provides a time-bound, low-risk approach for proving Integrated Assurance in practice before scaling.

The self-assessment questionnaire reveals how assurance actually functions today across governance, architecture, operations, risk, metrics, and culture. Its primary value is the conversation it creates, not the score it produces.

The heat map and interpretation guidance turn assessment results into shared visibility. They allow leaders to see imbalance, dependency, and trajectory at a glance.

Improvement planning and sustaining maturity sections explain how to translate insight into deliberate progress and how to keep assurance alive once early momentum fades.

RECOMMENDED STARTING POINTS

Readers should begin based on their role and organizational context.

- If you are an executive or board member, start with the maturity levels and the section titled *What Success Looks Like After 90 Days*. This will help you understand what changes you should expect to see and how to evaluate progress.
- If you lead security, risk, IT, or operations, begin with the self-assessment and heat map sections. Use them to establish a shared view of the current state before committing to investment or structural change.
- If you are responsible for implementation, start with the 90-day guide. Select a pilot that matters, follow the phased approach, and use the maturity model to measure whether capability is actually improving.
- If your organization is responding to a recent incident, regulatory pressure, or major transformation, treat this appendix as a stabilizing framework. Focus first on alignment, ownership, and visibility before attempting broad maturity advancement.

HOW NOT TO USE THIS APPENDIX

This appendix should not be used as a compliance checklist, a benchmarking contest, or a marketing artifact. IAMM is not designed to produce perfect scores or universal maturity across all domains at once.

- Do not attempt to jump multiple maturity levels in a single cycle. Sustainable progress comes from strengthening foundational behaviors before scaling complexity.
- Do not delegate IAMM entirely to a single function. Assurance maturity only holds when ownership is shared across business, technology, and leadership.
- Do not treat the assessment as work. It reveals reality. Work begins afterward.

A FINAL NOTE ON INTENT

IAMM exists to help organizations operate with clarity under uncertainty. Its purpose is not to eliminate risk, but to ensure that when risk appears, the enterprise can see it, decide together, and act with confidence.

Used properly, this appendix becomes a practical companion. It helps leaders replace assumptions with evidence, coordination with collaboration, and compliance with capability.

Appendix 2

How to Navigate This Appendix

This appendix is not meant to be read in order. It is designed to be entered based on pressure, role, and readiness. Use the following guide to find the right starting point quickly and avoid overscoping or misusing the Integrated Assurance Maturity Model (IAMM).

1. IF YOU ARE NEW TO IAMM OR ALIGNMENT IS STILL FORMING

Start Here

- Appendix 1: How to Use This Appendix
- Appendix 6: IAMM Quick Start

Why

- You need orientation, not assessment
- Skepticism or confusion exists
- Leadership intent is still forming

What You Will Get

- Shared understanding of purpose
- Clarity on where to begin
- A low-risk way to engage without committing to a full program

What to Avoid

- Full assessments
- Enterprise-wide rollout
- Treating IAMM as a framework to adopt rather than a capability to test

2. IF YOU ARE AN EXECUTIVE, BOARD MEMBER, OR EXECUTIVE SPONSOR

Start Here

- Appendix 3: Understanding IAMM
- Appendix 5: Role-Based Entry Paths
- Appendix 7: 90-Day Implementation Guide (Executive View)

Why

- You need confidence that assurance improves decision-making
- You want proof, not reports
- You must judge readiness and trajectory

What You Will Get

- A clear mental model of maturity
- Visibility into what should change in 90 days
- A defensible way to sponsor without overreaching

What to Avoid

- Treating IAMM as a scorecard
- Asking for maturity levels without evidence of operational change

3. IF YOUR ORGANIZATION IS UNDER PRESSURE RIGHT NOW

Pressure Type and Entry Path

- **Post-Incident or Near-Miss**
  - Start with Appendix 4: Entry Path 1
  - Then refer to Appendix 7
- **Audit, Regulatory, or Board Pressure**
  - Start with Appendix 4: Entry Path 2
  - Then refer to Appendix 8 (Minimum Viable IAMM)
- **Digital, Cloud, or AI Transformation Risk**
  - Start with Appendix 4: Entry Path 3
  - Then refer to Appendix 7 (Pilot Focus)
- **Silo Fatigue or Decision Paralysis**
  - Start with Appendix 4: Entry Path 4
  - Then refer to Appendix 8 (Heat Map Interpretation)

What You Will Get

- A realistic starting point
- Focused credibility under pressure
- Reduced noise and faster decision clarity

What to Avoid

- Trying to fix culture first
- Launching IAMM everywhere at once

4. IF YOU LEAD SECURITY, IT, RISK, OR OPERATIONS

Start Here

- Appendix 6: IAMM Quick Start
- Appendix 8: Minimum Viable IAMM
- Appendix 7: 90-Day Implementation Guide

Why

- You need to expose gaps between policy and reality
- You are accountable for execution, not theory
- You need proof that assurance can work in daily operations

What You Will Get

- A credible baseline
- Shared visibility across teams
- Practical operating changes within 90 days

What to Avoid

- Treating IAMM as another framework
- Overscoping the first pilot

5. IF YOU ARE READY FOR MEASUREMENT AND IMPROVEMENT

Start Here

- Appendix 8: Comprehensive IAMM Self-Assessment
- Heat Map Interpretation
- Developing Improvement Plans

Why

- Integrated Assurance already has sponsorship
- You need a defensible maturity narrative
- You are ready to manage assurance as an enterprise capability

What You Will Get

- Honest maturity visibility
- Clear imbalance and dependency signals
- A structured path for sustained improvement

What to Avoid

- Optimizing for scores
- Attempting to jump multiple maturity levels at once

IF YOU ONLY REMEMBER ONE THING

Do not start with the appendix section that looks most impressive. Start with the one that reflects your current pressure and authority. IAMM works when it meets reality first. Everything else follows.

Appendix 3

Understanding IAMM

Throughout *Relevant Impact*, the focus has been on outcomes: Resilience as a lived capability, trust as an operational currency, and assurance as a cultural force. Behind these outcomes is a structured foundation. The Integrated Assurance Maturity Model (IAMM) provides the lens through which leaders can evaluate their organization's current position and chart the path forward.

This appendix is not meant to reteach the framework introduced in *Integrated Assurance: Unified Risk Strategy*. Instead, it offers a resource, accessible to executives and practitioners alike, that connects the ideas in this book to a practical roadmap.

IAMM is more than a scoring mechanism. It is a way of seeing resilience development in stages. It helps leaders understand what is possible at different levels of maturity, why some organizations stall, and how the most resilient enterprises distinguish themselves.

THE FIVE LEVELS OF MATURITY

IAMM defines five levels of maturity, each representing a deeper integration of assurance into enterprise DNA. Moving up these levels is not about compliance milestones. Treat it as being about operational effectiveness, cultural adoption, and trust performance. See Table A3.1: The five levels of maturity.

IAMM maturity is assessed across six domains. These domains represent the foundation of assurance as a living system. See Figure A3.1—Integrated Assurance Maturity Model (IAMM).

Together, these domains create a holistic view. An organization may be strong in governance but weak in culture. Or it may have robust engineering practices without executive alignment. IAMM exposes these imbalances and provides a map for growth.

NOTE ON ESTABLISHED FRAMEWORKS

IAMM exists to unify, not to replace. Established frameworks like NIST CSF, ISO/IEC 27001, COBIT, and COSO ERM remain the structural foundations of sound governance and risk management. What IAMM adds is coherence across them. It transforms these frameworks from reference models into active systems that work together.

Each IAMM domain draws from these standards while emphasizing execution. The Governance domain aligns naturally with COBIT and COSO ERM, providing oversight and accountability mechanisms that ensure decisions reflect risk appetite and strategic intent. The Architecture and Engineering domain reflects the intent of ISO/IEC 27001, embedding control thinking into design rather than inspection. The IT and Operations domain finds its

Table A3.1 The five levels of maturity

Level	*Description*	*Characteristics*	*Risks*
Level 1: Fragmented	Assurance functions are siloed, compliance-driven, and reactive.	Multiple frameworks used in isolation, reliance on documentation, and minimal collaboration.	False sense of readiness, slow response under stress, and high duplication of effort.
Level 2: Coordinated	Teams begin to align on shared processes and reporting.	Some cross-functional communication, limited telemetry, and pockets of collaboration.	Inconsistent execution, uneven trust across business units.
Level 3: Unified	Cybersecurity, IT operations, and risk converge into a single framework.	Integrated Assurance framework adopted, governance structures established, metrics linked to business outcomes.	Cultural inertia, risk of reverting to a compliance mindset.
Level 4: Embedded	Assurance is embedded across functions and operations.	IAMM informs decision-making across HR, finance, and engineering; trust velocity and recovery ROI are measured.	Requires strong leadership to sustain; high visibility of failures.
Level 5: Resilient by Design	Assurance is a living capability and cultural norm.	Continuous adaptation, federated assurance models, AI governance integrated, trust as the currency of the enterprise.	Complexity of maintaining global, distributed consistency.

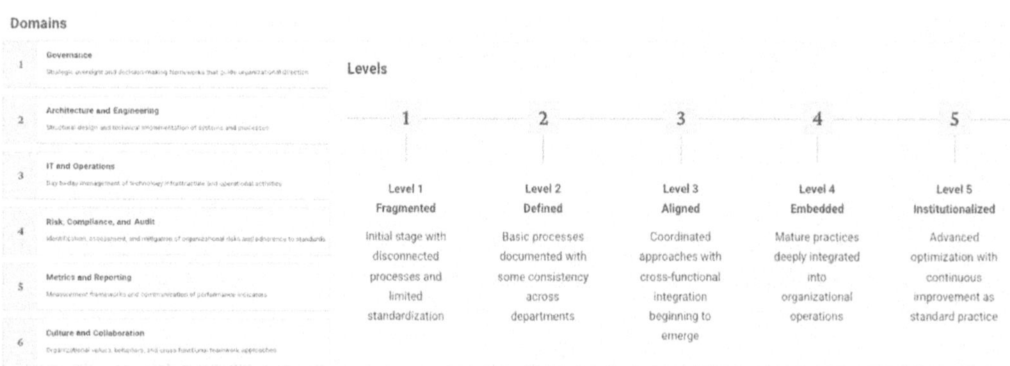

Figure A3.1 Integrated Assurance Maturity Model (IAMM).

Image created by the author using Gamma.

roots in the operational resilience principles of NIST CSF and ITIL, connecting technical controls to business outcomes. MITRE ATT&CK informs how validation and continuous testing become operational disciplines rather than isolated red team exercises.

By integrating these references, IAMM helps enterprises maintain compliance while maturing agility. A compliance audit may confirm adherence to policy, but IAMM reveals whether those policies create real resilience. The difference is in how these frameworks are lived.

Executives should view IAMM as the connective tissue that gives these standards practical form. It provides a shared language for translating governance expectations into engineering design, for connecting risk registers to metrics, and for linking technical validation to cultural behavior. In this sense, IAMM does not compete with other frameworks. It operationalizes them, turning reference into rhythm and structure into strategy.

SUSTAINING MATURITY

Reaching maturity is an accomplishment; sustaining it is leadership. Assurance does not remain stable on its own. It decays under pressure, distraction, and turnover. To keep maturity alive, it must become part of how the enterprise measures itself, the same way it tracks financial performance or operational capacity.

Sustaining maturity begins with cadence. Reviews should occur on a predictable schedule, ideally aligned with strategic and operational planning cycles. Each review examines whether controls are functioning, whether collaboration remains intact, and whether leadership engagement has remained visible. These moments serve as both a checkpoint and a recalibration.

Culture is the next sustaining force. When assurance behaviors are celebrated, reinforced, and tied to performance expectations, they persist through leadership transitions. Leaders who tell the story of assurance success keep the narrative alive. This story should not be about avoiding loss but about enabling confident action in uncertain moments.

Technology will continue to evolve, and so will the threat landscape. Mature organizations treat these changes as triggers for recalibration rather than disruption. They revisit IAMM assessments annually to verify whether the current level still represents reality. When automation, AI governance, or new digital dependencies emerge, the model expands to include them. In this way, maturity remains adaptive, not static.

Finally, sustaining maturity requires sponsorship. Executives must remain visibly engaged in assurance conversations, not as auditors, but as participants. Their attention signals importance, and their curiosity sustains accountability. When boards and leadership teams treat IAMM reviews as seriously as financial results, assurance ceases to be an initiative and becomes an enterprise function.

True maturity is not an endpoint. It is a state of awareness, maintained through curiosity, discipline, and commitment. When organizations learn to treat assurance this way, they transform from being compliant to being resilient, from being reactive to being ready. IAMM becomes more than a model; it becomes the operating fabric that holds the enterprise together.

Appendix 4

Entry Paths Based on Organizational Reality

Organizations rarely arrive at Integrated Assurance from a clean starting line. Most begin in response to pressure: a disruption exposed fragility, a regulator asked harder questions, or a transformation initiative moved faster than governance could follow. The Integrated Assurance Maturity Model (IAMM) is designed to meet organizations where they actually are, not where frameworks assume they should be.

The purpose of this section is to help leaders choose a realistic entry path. The wrong entry point creates fatigue and resistance. The right one creates momentum and credibility.

Below are common entry realities and guidance on how to begin without overreaching.

ENTRY PATH 1: POST-INCIDENT OR NEAR-MISS

Some organizations arrive here after a breach, outage, ransomware event, or public failure. Others arrive after a near-miss that revealed how close the enterprise came to serious impact. Emotions may be high. Trust may be strained. There is often urgency to "fix everything." This is not the moment for broad transformation.

The correct starting point is clarity. Leaders should focus first on governance, IT and operations, and metrics. The goal is to understand how decisions were made under pressure, where visibility broke down, and how long it took to regain control. Begin with a targeted IAMM self-assessment centered on incident response, escalation paths, telemetry, and recovery readiness.

The 90-day guide should be applied narrowly, using the incident itself as the pilot context. Playbooks, decision rights, and dashboards should be rebuilt around the failure that just occurred. Cultural improvement comes later. At this stage, restoring confidence through repeatable execution matters more than philosophical alignment.

A common mistake in this entry path is launching sweeping cultural programs or new tools immediately. Doing so often masks the real problem: Unclear ownership and slow decision-making.

ENTRY PATH 2: REGULATORY, AUDIT, OR BOARD PRESSURE

Some organizations encounter IAMM when oversight increases. A regulator questions control effectiveness. Audit fatigue sets in. The board asks whether risk reports reflect reality or merely a compliance posture. This entry path requires restraint. The instinct is often to add more reporting or expand audit scope. That rarely improves assurance.

Instead, begin with the Risk, Compliance, and Audit domain alongside Governance. Use IAMM to rationalize frameworks, clarify risk ownership, and expose duplication. The self-assessment should be used to reveal where controls exist on paper but fail operationally.

The early objective is coherence. Leaders should aim to produce a single, defensible view of risk that aligns business priorities with control effectiveness. Metrics and reporting become critical, but only after rationalization. The 90-day pilot should focus on continuous control validation and exception handling, not wholesale process redesign.

The most common failure in this path is treating IAMM as another reporting layer. Its value comes from reducing noise, not adding it.

ENTRY PATH 3: DIGITAL, CLOUD, OR AI TRANSFORMATION

Many organizations encounter assurance gaps during transformation. Cloud migration accelerates faster than governance. AI systems are deployed before accountability is clear. Product teams move quickly while risk functions lag behind.

This entry path benefits from starting in Architecture and Engineering and IT and Operations. The immediate risk is not malicious activity alone. It is a loss of control through complexity.

Begin by using IAMM to assess whether secure-by-design and resilient-by-default principles are actually embedded in delivery workflows. Focus on policy-as-code, reference architectures, and shared telemetry. Assurance must be present at design time, not retrofitted after deployment.

The 90-day guide should center on a transformation program already underway. Use it to embed assurance into pipelines, change processes, and incident response tied to new technology. Avoid slowing delivery. The goal is guardrails, not gates.

A frequent mistake here is assuming advanced technology equals maturity. IAMM exposes whether speed is supported by discipline or dependent on heroics.

ENTRY PATH 4: FRAGMENTATION AND SILO FATIGUE

Some organizations are not reacting to a single event. They are simply tired. Security, IT, risk, compliance, and business teams operate in parallel with limited trust. Meetings multiply. Decisions stall. Everyone feels busy, but no one feels confident. This is a cultural entry path, but culture should not be addressed directly at first.

Start with governance and metrics. Use the IAMM self-assessment to make fragmentation visible without assigning blame. The heat map becomes a neutral artifact that shows imbalance across domains.

The 90-day pilot should focus on shared visibility and decision forums. The objective is not immediate performance improvement, but shared understanding. Once teams see the same data and participate in the same decisions, trust begins to form naturally.

The most common error in this scenario is launching collaboration initiatives without structural change. IAMM works because it aligns structure, behavior, and accountability together.

CHOOSING THE RIGHT PATH

Organizations may recognize themselves in more than one entry path. That is normal. The key is to choose the one that reflects the greatest current pressure and start there. Integrated

Assurance does not reward ambition without discipline. Starting in the right place builds credibility. Credibility builds momentum. Momentum makes maturity sustainable. IAMM meets organizations where they are, but it expects honesty in return.

If you only do three things at this stage, do these:

- Be honest about why IAMM is being considered now. Whether the pressure comes from an incident, regulatory scrutiny, transformation risk, or organizational fatigue matters more than your current maturity score. Starting in the wrong place creates resistance and false progress.
- Choose a single entry path that reflects the greatest current pressure. Do not attempt to address every issue at once. Focus creates credibility, and credibility is what allows Integrated Assurance to take hold.
- Resist the urge to fix culture first. Use structure, visibility, and decision clarity to create the conditions where trust can form naturally. Culture follows behavior, not the other way around.

Appendix 5

Role-Based Entry Paths to IAMM

The following tables are designed to help readers quickly determine where to begin, what to focus on, and what outcomes to expect. Integrated Assurance Maturity Model (IAMM) is intentionally flexible, but successful adoption depends on starting in the right place. See Tables A5.1–A5.6.

Table A5.1 Executive leadership and board members

If you are...	*Start here*	*Focus on*	*What you should expect*	*What to avoid*
CEO, COO, CIO, CFO, Board Member	Understanding IAMM and What Success Looks Like After 90 Days	Decision clarity, ownership, and readiness under pressure	Clear visibility into how risk decisions are made and acted on	Treating IAMM as a scorecard or compliance artifact
Executive Sponsor	Entry Paths Based on Organizational Reality	Selecting the right starting pressure point	Confidence that the organization is improving its capability, not just reporting	Launching IAMM enterprise-wide before proof exists

Table A5.2 Security, risk, and it leadership

If you are...	*Start here*	*Focus on*	*What you should expect*	*What to avoid*
CISO, CIO, CRO, Head of IT or Risk	Minimum Viable IAMM → 90-Day Implementation Guide	Exposing gaps between policy, operations, and behavior	Alignment across teams and early operational proof	Overscoping the pilot or treating IAMM as another framework
Assurance Program Owner	Comprehensive Self-Assessment	Honest scoring and cross-functional dialogue	A realistic maturity baseline and visible imbalance	Forcing consensus too early

Table A5.3 Architects, engineers, and operations leaders

If you are...	*Start here*	*Focus on*	*What you should expect*	*What to avoid*
Enterprise Architect, Engineering Leader, Ops Leader	90-Day Implementation Guide—Phase 2	Embedding assurance into workflows	Reduced friction during incidents and changes	Treating assurance as documentation or review gates
DevSecOps or Platform Teams	Architecture and Engineering Domain	Secure-by-design and resilient-by-default practices	Earlier risk visibility and fewer downstream surprises	Assuming tooling equals maturity

Table A5.4 Program, transformation, and change leaders

If you are. . .	*Start here*	*Focus on*	*What you should expect*	*What to avoid*
Transformation Lead, PMO, AI Program Owner	Entry Path 3: Digital, Cloud, or AI Transformation	Guardrails that scale with speed	Fewer last-minute risk escalations	Bolting assurance on after delivery
Modernization Program Manager	90-Day Guide (Pilot Selection)	Choosing a meaningful pilot	Practical evidence that assurance can coexist with velocity	Treating IAMM as governance overhead

Table A5.5 Organizations under pressure (incident, audit, or trust breakdown)

If your organization is. . .	*Start here*	*Focus on*	*What you should expect*	*What to avoid*
Recovering from an incident	Entry Path 1: Post-Incident or Near-Miss	Decision flow, visibility, recovery readiness	Faster stabilization and restored confidence	Culture programs before structural clarity
Facing audit or regulatory pressure	Entry Path 2: Regulatory, Audit, or Board Pressure	Framework rationalization and control reality	Less noise, more defensible risk posture	Adding more reporting layers
Experiencing silo fatigue	Entry Path 4: Fragmentation and Silo Fatigue	Shared visibility and decision forums	Reduced friction and clearer accountability	Collaboration initiatives without authority

Table A5.6 First-time iamm users or skeptical organizations

If you are. . .	*Start here*	*Focus on*	*What you should expect*	*What to avoid*
New to IAMM	Minimum Viable IAMM	Orientation and shared understanding	A credible snapshot of assurance reality	Debating scores instead of discussing gaps
Skeptical Stakeholder	Heat Map Interpretation	Seeing imbalance without blame	Evidence-based conversations	Turning maturity into competition

HOW TO USE THESE TABLES

These entry paths are not exclusive. Most organizations will recognize themselves in more than one role or situation. The goal is not to follow every path, but to choose the one that reflects current pressure and begin there. Starting in the right place builds credibility. Credibility builds momentum. Momentum makes maturity sustainable.

If you only do three things based on your role, do these:

- Start where you have authority, not where you have interest. IAMM works when leaders begin in the areas they can actually influence and model, not where the problems feel abstract or distant.

- Align expectations before assessing maturity. Make it clear that IAMM is about understanding reality, not assigning grades. When people believe the process is safe, the data becomes useful.
- Avoid launching IAMM enterprise-wide. Use a focused entry point to prove value in real operations before asking the organization to change how it works.

Appendix 6

IAMM Quick Start

Integrated Assurance does not begin with a full assessment or a transformation mandate. It begins with orientation. The purpose of this Quick Start is to help leaders and teams enter Integrated Assurance Maturity Model (IAMM) deliberately, without overscoping, overengineering, or overpromising. Most organizations do not struggle because they lack frameworks. They struggle because assurance efforts start in the wrong place. This guide exists to prevent that.

STEP 1: IDENTIFY YOUR ENTRY REALITY

Before scoring maturity or selecting metrics, determine why IAMM is being considered now. The entry point matters more than the initial score.

Organizations typically enter IAMM through one of the following realities:

- A recent incident or near-miss exposed decision delays or unclear ownership
- Regulatory, audit, or board pressure raised questions about control effectiveness
- A digital, cloud, or AI initiative outpaced governance and risk visibility
- Fragmentation and silo fatigue slowed decisions and eroded trust
- Leadership seeks a clearer view of readiness and resilience without technical abstraction

If more than one applies, select the one creating the greatest current pressure. IAMM is most effective when it responds to lived reality, not abstract ambition.

STEP 2: CHOOSE THE RIGHT STARTING DEPTH

IAMM does not require a full maturity assessment on day one. Starting depth should match organizational readiness.

Use the following guidance to decide how far to go initially:

- Use the IAMM Quick Start only if alignment is still forming or skepticism is high
- Proceed directly to Minimum Viable IAMM if leadership wants a fast, credible snapshot to guide next steps
- Move into the full IAMM self-assessment if Integrated Assurance is already sponsored and resourced

Starting lighter is not a failure. It is often the reason IAMM succeeds.

STEP 3: SELECT A MEANINGFUL PILOT CONTEXT

IAMM works best when applied to something real. Before any scoring begins, identify where assurance will be tested, not just discussed.

A strong pilot candidate has three traits:

- It supports a business service or capability that matters
- Failure would have a visible impact, but learning is still safe
- The teams involved are close enough to daily operations to expose the truth

This could be incident response, cloud operations, a product platform, a high-risk vendor relationship, or a regulated process. The pilot does not need to be large. It needs to be honest.

STEP 4: ALIGN ON INTENT, NOT SCORES

IAMM assessments are not about achieving high numbers. They are about creating shared understanding.

Before beginning Minimum Viable IAMM, align on three principles:

- Scores are directional, not definitive
- Differences in perspective are signals, not problems
- The conversation matters more than the average

When teams understand this, assessment becomes a tool for clarity rather than debate.

STEP 5: COMMIT TO ACTION WITHIN 90 DAYS

IAMM is not designed to produce insight without movement. If the organization is not prepared to act within a 90-day window, pause.

Action does not mean enterprise transformation. It means:

- Testing new decision paths
- Making assurance visible in daily work
- Running at least one exercise or simulation
- Reviewing evidence, not opinions

Momentum matters. Even small, visible change builds confidence that Integrated Assurance is more than a framework.

WHAT THIS QUICK START IS NOT

This Quick Start is not a checklist, a compliance shortcut, or a maturity certification process. It is not designed to rank teams or compare organizations. Its purpose is to help leaders begin Integrated Assurance in a way that reflects reality and builds credibility.

WHERE TO GO NEXT

If this Quick Start reflects your current situation, proceed to Minimum Viable IAMM in the section on Conducting a Self-Assessment. Use it to establish shared visibility and decide whether deeper assessment and sustained investment are warranted. If alignment is already strong and leadership commitment is explicit, you may move directly to the full IAMM self-assessment. Either path is valid. What matters is starting with intent, honesty, and focus.

If you only do three things to begin IAMM, do these:

- Identify your entry reality clearly and agree on it as a leadership team. IAMM succeeds when it responds to lived experience, not abstract ambition.
- Start lighter than you think you should. Minimum Viable IAMM exists to create alignment and momentum, not to prove sophistication. Starting small increases the chance that you will start at all.
- Commit to visible action within 90 days. Even modest changes in decision flow, visibility, or response behavior build confidence that Integrated Assurance is more than a framework.

Appendix 7

90-Day Implementation Guide for IAMM

Integrated Assurance is not something a leadership team flips on with a single decision or launches across every department in one motion. It is more like learning a craft. The first attempts are often rough. Coordination feels unfamiliar. People hesitate. Old habits surface. That is why the best place to begin is not everywhere. It is somewhere specific. The organizations that succeed do not start by declaring a full transformation. They start with a focused experiment and a clock.

A 90-day pilot gives you exactly that. Long enough to build momentum. Short enough to stay urgent. Instead of redesigning the entire enterprise, you choose a smaller slice of the business where failure would hurt, but learning would matter more. This could be your cloud operations team, your core payment or manufacturing service, your incident response function, or a high-risk vendor process. What matters is not how large it is, but how real it is. A pilot is only useful if it touches daily work and exposes the gaps between policy, technology, and human behavior.

When I have worked with teams that tried to launch Integrated Assurance across all business units at once, they rarely made it past the first steering committee. The scope was too large. Every meeting turned into a debate about ownership. Every department saw it as additional work rather than a better way to work. In contrast, when leaders committed to a small, time-bound pilot, everything changed. Decisions were made faster. Obstacles appeared earlier. Results were visible. Most importantly, the organization saw that Integrated Assurance was not another framework. It was an operating model that could actually function in the real world.

What I have provided is a 90-day guide to help you start that way. It is not a master plan. It is a starting plan. It is written for executives, architects, and operational leaders who are ready to test Integrated Assurance, not as theory, but as practice. The goal over the next 90 days is not perfection. It is proof. Proof that governance can inform decisions when time is short. Proof that technology and business teams can make risk decisions together without waiting for a crisis. Proof that trust can be measured, not assumed.

You begin by aligning a small group of leaders around purpose and scope. You choose the business service or team where the pilot will run. You establish who owns what, how decisions will be made, and how progress will be measured. Then you move. You embed assurance into daily workflows. You measure trust, containment, and recovery, not just compliance. You run simulations that stress people, not just systems. By the end of the 90 days, you will know if this model works in your culture, with your tools, and with your people.

Integrated Assurance is built in stages. This is the first one. Start small. Move with intention. Prove capability. Then scale. The journey is structured in three phases.

PHASE 1 (DAYS 0–30): GETTING ALIGNED AND READY TO MOVE

The first month is about building clarity and commitment. Nothing in Integrated Assurance works unless the leadership team agrees on why this matters and what it will take to do it well. This is where expectations get set, responsibilities become real, and the organization shifts from discussing resilience to building it.

It starts in the executive room. The chief executive officer (CEO), chief operating officer (COO), chief information officer (CIO), chief information security officer (CISO), and the leaders who carry real influence over operations, finance, risk, and technology sit down and answer one question together. Why now? If that answer is vague or fragmented, everything that follows will be slow, misunderstood, or ignored. When the answer becomes consistent and owned, the work can begin. The outcome of this step is written in a short charter that explains why the company is committing to Integrated Assurance and how success will be judged. Nothing complicated, just honest and clear enough to be useful.

With direction established, the next step is choosing who will lead the effort. Not a task force that disappears when the meeting ends, but a cross-functional group that carries real responsibility. I often call it the Integrated Assurance Leadership Team. It includes security and risk, operations, IT, finance, HR, and one or two business unit leaders who actually run revenue-generating functions. Titles matter less than authority. Each person must have the ability to influence decisions in their area. This team defines how decisions will be made, who has the right to approve, who needs to be informed, and who is responsible when something fails.

Once people are aligned, we need to know where we really are. That means conducting a baseline assessment using the Integrated Assurance Maturity Model. We are not collecting paperwork to make someone look good. We are identifying truth. How do we govern risk today? How fast can we detect and contain disruption? Do teams trust each other enough to act on incomplete information? Can our systems recover before customers notice? The output is a heatmap that makes it impossible to avoid reality. It shows gaps we have ignored and strengths we can build on.

At the same time, we identify the business services that cannot fail without consequence. These are not just servers or applications. They are revenue engines, customer-facing platforms, core manufacturing systems, logistics networks, financial transaction systems, or public safety functions. Knowing where failure matters most allows us to focus our effort instead of spreading it evenly across everything.

Before this first month ends, we choose where to start. Not across the entire enterprise. That is the fastest way to stall. Instead, we select a few pilot teams that are ready for change and close enough to critical business services to matter. This could be the security operations center (SOC), IT operations, product engineering, or procurement if the supply chain is where risk concentrates. What matters is that these teams are willing to test new ways of working and have leadership support behind them.

By the end of the first 30 days, we are not resilient yet. But we are no longer pretending. The organization knows why this matters, who is responsible, how decisions will flow, where we stand today, and where we will begin. That is the foundation. If you try to skip it, the rest of the journey becomes theater. See Figure A7.1: Phase 1: Core Activities.

PHASE 2 (DAYS 31–60): MAKING ASSURANCE REAL IN DAILY WORK

The second month is where the work becomes visible. The conversations from Phase 1 now have to turn into operating behavior. This is the point where Integrated Assurance moves

Phase 1 (Days 0–30): Getting Aligned and Ready to Move

Core Activities

1 **Executive Alignment and Charter**

- Convene the CEO, COO, CIO, CISO, CRO, and key business leaders.
- Agree on why Integrated Assurance is being adopted, what it must achieve, and how success will be measured.
- Document this alignment in an executive charter.

2 **Create the Integrated Assurance Leadership Team (IALT)**

- Appoint a cross-functional leadership group from security, operations, risk, finance, HR, and business units.
- Define roles and decision rights using a RACI model.
- Assign a single accountable leader. This is often the CISO or Chief Risk Officer.

3 **Establish Governance and Decision Structures**

- Define governance cadence: weekly operational syncs, monthly steering reviews.
- Clarify escalation and approval pathways for risk decisions.

4 **Conduct an IAMM Baseline Assessment**

- Evaluate current maturity across the six IAMM domains: Governance, Risk, Operations, Technology/Architecture, Metrics, and Culture.
- Produce a heat map showing current performance and desired target states.

5 **Identify Critical Business Services**

- List the essential services and processes that cannot fail without significant financial, operational, or reputational impact.
- Examples include payment platforms, core manufacturing lines, cloud infrastructure, supply chain operations, customer-facing systems.

6 **Select Pilot Teams**

- Choose two to three business or technical teams to pilot Integrated Assurance practices.
- Candidates often include IT operations, cloud engineering, SOC or security operations, procurement, or product development.

Outcome of Phase 1

Executive charter approved	IAMM maturity heat map completed	Governance structure documented	Critical systems and pilot teams selected

Figure A7.1 Phase 1: Core Activities.

Image created by the author using Gamma.

from intention to practice. If Phase 1 is about alignment, this phase is about contact with reality.

We begin by defining how the organization will actually operate under Integrated Assurance. Not another policy document that gets filed away. This is a working model that explains how risk information moves, how decisions are made, and how teams interact when something goes wrong. It shows who owns the decision, who supports it, and who needs to know when it happens. It connects executive expectations to frontline execution. It becomes the backbone for how teams respond when uncertainty arrives.

With that model in place, we start embedding assurance into the places where work already happens. Not as another layer of oversight, but into the systems and routines that teams already use. Change management reviews begin to include risk-based reasoning. Incident response stops being an IT-only function and now includes communications, legal, and business leadership in the same conversation. Vendor onboarding begins to consider dependency risk before contracts are signed. Product teams start asking threat-focused questions while they are still building, not after something has shipped. The goal is simple. Assurance becomes something people do during the work, not something added at the end.

By this stage, we also begin measuring performance in ways that show whether resilience is improving or not. The first Integrated Assurance dashboard comes to life, even if it is rough. The metrics are not chosen for compliance reports. They are chosen because they explain how well the organization can sense, respond, and recover—time to detect, time to contain, control integrity under stress, trust velocity, and recovery ROI. None of these is theoretical. They expose how quickly the organization can make a confident decision when pressure appears.

People also need shared visibility. It is not enough for security or operations to have their own dashboards. SOC, NOC, cloud teams, business continuity, procurement, and risk teams need to see the same truth. For the first time, security events, system failures, vendor issues, and business impact begin to sit side by side. That is how trust starts to form between teams.

We then test what we think we have built. Not in a tabletop script where everyone knows their part, but in an exercise that introduces friction. A ransomware scenario that forces legal, communications, technology, and finance to interact before they are comfortable. A cloud outage that triggers uncomfortable trade-offs. A third-party failure that affects revenue. The job of this exercise is not to show success. It is to expose delay, hesitation, lack of clarity, or absence of authority. Every one of those failures is an opportunity to refine the model.

By the end of the second month, the organization has felt the weight of this shift. Integrated Assurance is no longer a slide deck or an idea. Leaders have made decisions differently. Teams have seen new metrics appear on dashboards. Business functions have participated in risk decisions instead of observing them from the outside. Some resistance has surfaced. That is normal. It means people are taking it seriously.

We are not finished. But the work is no longer hypothetical. Assurance has entered the rhythm of daily operations. And once it gets into the rhythm, it becomes hard to remove. That is how you know progress is real. See Figure A7.2: Phase 2: Core Activities.

PHASE 3 (DAYS 61–90): PROVING IT WORKS AND PREPARING TO SCALE

The third month is where the organization proves whether Integrated Assurance is becoming a real capability or remains an experiment. By now, the structure exists, the workflows are shifting, and metrics have started to reveal truths people used to ignore. This final phase is about testing what has been built, extending it beyond pilot teams, and securing the commitment to carry it forward.

We begin by turning individual actions into repeatable behavior. That means writing the playbooks for how the organization responds to the events that matter most. Not for the sake of documentation, but so people know what to do without waiting for permission. A ransomware outbreak. A cloud service failure. A vendor outage that halts operations. A breach that requires legal disclosure. A data corruption event inside an AI system that no one understands at first. Each playbook explains who makes the call, what resources they control, who

Phase 2 (Days 31–60): Making Assurance Real in Daily Work

Core Activities

1. **Build the Integrated Assurance Operating Model**
   - Document how risks, decisions, and incident information flow across teams.
   - Define touch points between IT Operations, Security, Business Continuity, Procurement, Legal, and Communications.

2. **Embed Assurance into Existing Processes**
   - Change Advisory Boards include formal risk-impact reviews.
   - Procurement workflows trigger third-party risk scoring before vendor approval.
   - Incident response expands to include executive communication, legal guidance, and operational recovery.
   - DevOps teams integrate threat modeling and control checks into development sprints.

3. **Launch the First Operational Dashboard**
   - Mean Time to Detect (MTTD)
   - Mean Time to Contain (MTTC)
   - Control Integrity Under Stress
   - Trust Velocity (how quickly decisions can be made with confidence)
   - Recovery ROI (financial value of downtime avoided)

4. **Connect Operational Telemetry**
   - Create shared communication channels between SOC, NOC, Cloud/Ops, and Risk.
   - Begin linking SIEM, ITSM, and ticketing tools to provide a unified view of disruption and response.

5. **Conduct First Simulation Exercise**
   - Stage a realistic event (ransomware attack, vendor outage, cloud failure).
   - Include both technical and non-technical stakeholders.
   - Capture gaps in escalation, communication, and decision ownership.
   - Document after-action improvements.

Outcome of Phase 2

First operational model published	Assurance-infused workflows active in pilot areas	Live dashboard prototype established	First resilience exercise completed and reviewed

Figure A7.2 Phase 2: Core Activities.

Image created by the author using Gamma.

must be notified, and what thresholds trigger escalation. When a crisis hits, confusion costs time. A good playbook prevents hesitation.

At this point, we also begin to harden expectations around ownership. If assurance is going to last, it has to exist outside of security and risk teams. It has to live in engineering, finance, procurement, operations, and anywhere decisions carry consequences. That requires updates to performance expectations. Leaders begin to see metrics such as time to contain, communication clarity, and recovery readiness reflected in their scorecards. When something is measured, it becomes part of the culture. When it affects evaluation and reward, it becomes part of behavior.

Next, we expand the work beyond the initial pilot teams. Not across the whole company at once, but into two or three additional business areas that have influence and urgency. Sometimes that means manufacturing. Sometimes product development. Sometimes finance or customer support. The pilot teams become the teachers. They show what worked, where they failed, and how to adapt the model instead of forcing it.

Then we test again. This time with more pressure. The second simulation introduces stress that does not follow the script. Leadership receives incomplete information. Communications

Phase 3 (Days 61–90): Proving It Works and Preparing to Scale

Core Activities

1 Develop Standardized Playbooks

Create integrated playbooks for high-risk scenarios:

- Ransomware or data breach
- Cloud or data center outage
- Third-party vendor failure
- Insider threat or fraud
- AI failure or model manipulation event

Each playbook defines:

- Roles and responsibilities
- Business impact thresholds
- Communication procedures
- Required technologies and dependencies

2 Integrate Assurance into Performance Systems

- Work with HR and Finance to include resilience behaviors in leadership performance reviews.
- Establish metrics for time-to-containment, cross-functional collaboration, and trust scores.

3 Expand to Additional Business Units

- Extend assurance practices to two to three more teams (e.g., engineering, manufacturing, finance, and customer support).
- Use the pilot teams as internal mentors or "assurance champions."

4 Conduct Second Simulation

- Increase realism suc as incomplete information, media pressure, executive decision windows.
- Include customer response and regulatory notification timing.

5 Executive Review and Future Roadmap

- Evaluate progress against goals set in Phase 1.
- Identify budget, tooling, and staffing requirements for the next 12 months.
- Publish the Year 1 Assurance Roadmap.

Outcome of Phase 3

Assurance adopted beyond pilot teams	Playbooks standardized and in use	Leadership validates progress and funds future growth	Roadmap approved for next maturity phase

Figure A7.3 Phase 3: Core Activities.

Image created by the author using Gamma.

must respond before legal feels comfortable. Operations must act before risk has full certainty. External pressure is added. Customers are asking questions. News outlets are calling. The purpose is not to create chaos, but to help teams learn how to function inside it. Real resilience looks less like control and more like composed adaptability.

As the 90 days come to a close, one final task remains. The leadership team meets again. The first meeting was about belief and commitment. This meeting is about evidence and continuation. They review what has changed. They evaluate where the organization is stronger and where it is still weak. They look at data, not opinion. They decide whether Integrated Assurance has proven enough value to invest further. If the answer is yes, they approve the roadmap for the next year. That roadmap includes maturing Integrated Assurance Maturity Model (IAMM) levels, expanding assurance across business units, investing in automation, and evolving the metrics as the system matures.

By day 90, the organization is not fully transformed. But it is different. Risk is no longer spoken of only during audits. Trust is no longer an abstract virtue. It is something measured and practiced. Operations, finance, security, legal, and technology are beginning to operate from the same picture. Most importantly, resilience is no longer something written in a policy. It is something people have felt, tested, and taken ownership of.

This is how assurance becomes real. Not through a perfect plan. Through practice, pressure, and commitment to keep going. See Figure A7.3: Phase 3: Core Activities.

If you only do three things during the first 90 days, do these:

- Select a pilot that matters. Choose a business service or function where failure would be felt, but learning can occur without existential risk. Assurance only becomes real when it touches daily work.
- Embed assurance into existing workflows instead of creating new ones. If Integrated Assurance feels like an additional process, it will stall. If it improves how decisions are made, it will spread.
- Measure what changes under pressure. Track detection speed, containment time, decision clarity, and recovery readiness. These metrics reveal whether resilience is actually improving or merely being discussed.

Appendix 8

Conducting an IAMM Self-Assessment

A self-assessment is not an administrative exercise. It is an act of organizational honesty. The goal is to reveal how assurance operates today, not how leaders wish it did. When done well, it brings together multiple perspectives and converts abstract maturity levels into shared understanding. What follows are two approaches for conducting an Integrated Assurance Maturity Model (IAMM) self-assessment.

MINIMUM VIABLE IAMM: A FAST-START ASSESSMENT

Not every organization is ready to complete a full IAMM assessment on the first pass. Time constraints, limited alignment, or early skepticism can make a comprehensive evaluation feel premature. That does not mean assurance maturity cannot be explored. It means the entry point should be lighter.

The Minimum Viable IAMM is designed as a fast-start option. It provides a credible snapshot of how assurance operates today using a small number of high-signal questions. Its purpose is not precision. It is orientation. When used properly, it creates enough shared visibility to decide whether deeper assessment and investment are warranted. This assessment can typically be completed in a single working session.

WHEN TO USE THE MINIMUM VIABLE IAMM

This option is appropriate when:

- Leadership alignment is still forming
- An organization is under time pressure and needs directional insight
- Assurance discussions have stalled due to scope or complexity
- A pilot needs to be justified before committing to a full assessment

It should not replace the full IAMM assessment once Integrated Assurance becomes an active program. It exists to create momentum, not to declare maturity.

HOW TO USE IT

The Minimum Viable IAMM should be completed by a small cross-functional group. Ideally, this includes security or risk leadership, IT or operations, and at least one business leader.

Each participant should score independently before the discussion begins. Scores are less important than divergence. Differences in perspective signal where assurance breaks down under pressure.

MINIMUM VIABLE IAMM QUESTIONS

Rate each question on a scale of 1 to 5, where:

- 1 means the capability is largely absent or ad hoc
- 3 means it exists but is inconsistently applied
- 5 means it is embedded, repeatable, and trusted

See Table A8.1: Minimum viable IAMM questions.

INTERPRETING THE RESULTS

A consistent score of 1 or 2 indicates assurance is largely reactive and fragmented. Improvement should focus on governance clarity and shared visibility before expanding scope.

- Scores clustered around 3 suggest coordination exists but breaks down under pressure. This is a strong signal that a 90-day pilot would produce value.
- Scores of 4 or higher across most questions indicate readiness for a full IAMM assessment and deliberate maturity advancement.

Table A8.1 Minimum viable IAMM questions

Domain	*Assessment question*	*Rating*
Governance and Decision-Making	When a high-impact risk or incident emerges, it is clear who has the authority to make decisions, and those decisions are acted on quickly.	
Architecture and Design Discipline	Security and resilience considerations are built into system and product design before implementation, not added after problems appear.	
Operational Visibility	Security, IT, and business leaders share a common view of operational health, risk signals, and system dependencies.	
Incident and Disruption Response	When something breaks, teams across technology, legal, communications, and business respond together using known playbooks.	
Risk Ownership	Material risks have named owners beyond security or compliance functions, who are accountable for outcomes.	
Metrics That Matter	Leaders review metrics that reflect detection speed, containment, recovery, and business impact, not just compliance status.	
Cross-Functional Trust	Teams are willing to act on incomplete information and escalate issues without fear of blame or delay.	
Learning and Adaptation	After incidents or exercises, the organization makes visible improvements to processes, playbooks, or controls.	

More important than the average score is the variance. Large gaps between participants indicate misalignment that IAMM is specifically designed to address.

WHAT TO DO NEXT

The Minimum Viable IAMM is not an endpoint. It is a decision aid. If the conversation it creates reveals confusion, dependency, or distrust, proceed directly to the 90-day implementation guide and select a focused pilot. If alignment already exists and leadership wants deeper insight, move into the full IAMM self-assessment that follows. If resistance or skepticism dominates, pause. Use the results to clarify purpose, not to force progress.

The goal of this exercise is simple. Replace assumption with shared understanding. Once that exists, Integrated Assurance can begin in earnest.

If you only do three things with the Minimum Viable IAMM, do these:

- Score independently before discussing results. Differences in perspective are not problems to be resolved. They are signals that reveal where assurance breaks down.
- Focus on variance, not averages. Wide gaps between responses matter more than the overall score and should guide where to act first.
- Use the results to decide whether to move, not to debate maturity. The Minimum Viable IAMM is a decision aid, not a certification exercise.

COMPREHENSIVE IAMM SELF-ASSESSMENT

The process begins with assembling representatives from every core function. Security, operations, risk, finance, HR, and business leadership all contribute their view of how assurance actually works within their domain. Each team completes the IAMM questionnaire independently before discussion begins. The intention is to surface authentic perceptions rather than align to consensus too early.

Once individual assessments are complete, the group gathers to discuss the results. This is where the real value begins. Differences in scoring open conversations about why a process works in one area but falters in another. Patterns emerge that show how decisions travel, where data becomes siloed, and where collaboration breaks down. The goal is not to assign blame but to understand dependency.

During these sessions, maturity becomes more than a number. It becomes a narrative. Teams begin to describe what "Level 3" means in their daily reality, what keeps them from reaching "Level 4," and what success would look like if assurance were embedded into their workflows. Leaders start to see that maturity is not uniform across the enterprise, and that this imbalance is itself a signal. A domain that depends on heroics or manual oversight is not mature, even if outcomes appear strong.

The most important outcome of a self-assessment is not the score itself. It is the conversation it creates. When leaders and practitioners see the same picture, strategy becomes grounded in truth. This process sets the foundation for every decision that follows, from investment priorities to cultural interventions. Maturity cannot be managed if it cannot be seen, and a good self-assessment ensures that everyone is finally looking at the same map.

If you only do three things after completing a full self-assessment, do these:

- Treat the results as a narrative, not a number. The story the scores tell about decision-making, visibility, and ownership is more important than the level itself.

- Select improvement targets that deliver business value, not cosmetic maturity gains. Strengthen the domains that reduce disruption, delay, or confusion first.
- Review progress on a predictable cadence. Maturity improves when it becomes part of the operational rhythm, not a one-time exercise.

IAMM SELF-ASSESSMENT QUESTIONNAIRE

Instructions:

Rate the current state in each area on a scale of 1 to 5, where:

1—Not Present/Fragmented
2—Defined but Siloed
3—Coordinated and Aligned
4—Embedded and Operationalized
5—Institutionalized and Strategic

Add comments or examples where applicable to support context and future planning. See Table A8.2: IAMM self-assessment questionnaire.

Table A8.2 IAMM self-assessment questionaire

Section	*Category*	*Sub-category*	*Rating (1–5)*	*Comments/ evidence*
Governance	Are there formal cross-functional forums that govern assurance-related decisions?	How often do these forums meet, and what is their mandate?		
		Are decisions documented and followed through operationally?		
		Do representatives from all key business and technical units participate?		
	Do security, IT, compliance, and business teams jointly prioritize risks and manage exceptions?	Is there a shared risk taxonomy across teams?		
		Are exception processes transparent and time-bound?		
		Do all teams contribute data to the risk prioritization process?		
	Is there a federated model for assigning and managing risk ownership across the enterprise?	Are roles and responsibilities clearly defined and documented?		
		Is there accountability for residual risks at the line-of-business level?		
		Are federated decisions escalated appropriately when needed?		

(*Continued*)

Table A8.2 (Continued)

Section	*Category*	*Sub-category*	*Rating (1–5)*	*Comments/ evidence*
	Does executive leadership visibly sponsor and engage in assurance initiatives?	Do executives receive regular briefings on assurance posture?		
		Are leaders involved in incident response or control failures?		
		Are sponsorships linked to strategic investments?		
	Are assurance principles integrated into enterprise strategy and business planning?	Is assurance discussed during annual planning and budget cycles?		
		Are strategic programs assessed for assurance risks?		
		Are business leaders evaluated on assurance-related objectives?		
Architecture and Engineering	Are "secure by design" and "resilient by default" principles embedded into enterprise architecture?	Are threat models used during early architecture phases?		
		Is resilience part of capacity and availability planning?		
		Are these principles codified in architecture governance?		
	Do reference architectures and templates include standardized security controls?	Are templates routinely updated to reflect new threats or tech stacks?		
		Are they used consistently across projects and platforms?		
		Are control requirements traceable to policy?		
	Are policy-as-code and infrastructure-as-code practices used to enforce controls in development pipelines?	Are these controls version-controlled and peer-reviewed?		
		Are code changes tested against policy gates automatically?		
		Are deviations logged and escalated?		
	Are security architects engaged early during solution design and modernization planning?	Are security reviews part of the solution intake process?		
		Do architects participate in backlog grooming or epic reviews?		
		Are nonfunctional requirements for security enforced?		
	Is architectural risk regularly assessed and tracked throughout implementation?	Are architectural risks documented as part of project risk logs?		
		Are risk mitigations embedded in design choices?		
		Is risk reassessed when solutions pivot?		

Table A8.2 (Continued)

Section	*Category*	*Sub-category*	*Rating (1–5)*	*Comments/ evidence*
IT and Engineering Operations	Are assurance controls embedded in ITIL or daily operational workflows?	Are change, incident, and problem workflows mapped to controls?		
		Are control failures logged as operational incidents?		
		Are approvals gated by assurance criteria?		
	Are systems validated against hardened baselines with drift detection in place?	Are baselines reviewed and updated periodically?		
		Is deviation automatically detected and alerted?		
		Are exceptions managed through a formal process?		
	Is telemetry from IT and security systems shared for unified risk monitoring?	Are logging formats standardized across domains?		
		Are security information and event managements (SIEMs) or observability platforms fed from IT and SecOps?		
		Is telemetry used for performance and security equally?		
	Are resilience and recovery practices documented and operationally tested?	Are backup and recovery tests automated and scheduled?		
		Are recovery time objectives (RTOs) validated?		
		Are lessons learned from tests used to improve runbooks?		
	Do delivery teams contribute to risk remediation and mitigation planning?	Are developers and engineers involved in root cause reviews?		
		Is risk mitigation logged as part of the user story backlog?		
		Do teams have key performance indicators (KPIs) tied to reduced exposure?		
Risk, Compliance, and Audit	Are control frameworks aligned to avoid duplication and audit fatigue?	Is there a single source of truth for control mapping?		
		Are frameworks rationalized (e.g., NIST to ISO crosswalks)?		
		Is audit scheduling coordinated across teams?		
	Are controls continuously monitored and validated in operational settings?	Are automated control checks part of daily operations?		
		Are failures triaged and resolved quickly?		
		Is validation evidence stored centrally?		

(Continued)

Table A8.2 (Continued)

Section	*Category*	*Sub-category*	*Rating (1–5)*	*Comments/ evidence*
	Is operational risk ownership clearly defined and assigned?	Are risks mapped to the responsible department head?		
		Are risk acceptances logged and justified?		
		Is there a process to reassess ownership when teams shift?		
	Are risk registers actively maintained and tied to business priorities?	Are registers updated in real time or periodically?		
		Are risks categorized by business function or impact?		
		Do leaders use these registers to drive prioritization?		
	Are audit findings resolved through root cause analysis and cross-team collaboration?	Is RCA documented and linked to the finding?		
		Are systemic gaps tracked and remediated beyond symptoms?		
		Are findings presented to and reviewed by multidisciplinary teams?		
Metrics and Reporting	Do assurance metrics measure control effectiveness and business impact—not just coverage?	Are metrics based on real events, not just compliance checkboxes?		
		Are outcomes (e.g., reduced fraud, downtime) included?		
		Are metrics periodically challenged for relevance?		
	Are dashboards tailored for executive, operational, and technical audiences?	Are different levels of abstraction used per audience?		
		Are visuals actionable or just informational?		
		Are dashboards used in regular reporting cadences?		
	Do KPIs and KRIs influence strategic decisions like funding and risk acceptance?	Are performance indicators tied to budget cycles?		
		Are risk thresholds formally defined?		
		Are these indicators referenced in investment cases?		
	Are metrics used to track convergence and collaboration across functions?	Are shared metrics used across departments?		
		Are friction points flagged through trend analysis?		
		Are cross-functional remediations tracked over time?		

Table A8.2 (Continued)

Section	*Category*	*Sub-category*	*Rating (1–5)*	*Comments/ evidence*
	Is assurance performance reviewed regularly by leadership teams?	Are metrics part of board or C-level reviews? Are corrective actions owned and tracked? Is assurance maturity discussed as a KPI?		
Culture and Collaboration	Is assurance widely understood as a shared organizational responsibility?	Are there awareness campaigns or leadership messaging? Are responsibilities reflected in team charters? Are shared failures and successes debriefed together?		
	Are assurance roles embedded within both business and technical teams?	Are business units accountable for specific controls? Are security champions or liaisons designated? Are embedded roles part of organizational charts or job descriptions?		
	Do employees receive role-specific training on assurance expectations?	Is training targeted (e.g., DevSecOps for engineers)? Is onboarding mapped to assurance role requirements? Are there refresher or just-in-time learning modules?		
	Are assurance behaviors encouraged through incentives or performance reviews?	Are positive behaviors recognized informally and formally? Are control failures addressed in performance feedback? Are there gamified or competitive assurance initiatives?		
	Are working groups established to address cross-functional control, risk, or security concerns?	Are these groups empowered with decision rights? Are their charters aligned to the risk strategy? Do they report out to leadership or governance boards?		

The following scoring and interpretation for the IAMM self-Assessment can be found in Table A8.3.

Table A8.3 Scoring and interpretation

Total score range	*Maturity level*
30—59	Level 1–2: Fragmented/Defined
60—89	Level 3: Aligned
90—114	Level 4: Embedded
115—150	Level 5: Institutionalized

Table A8.4 IAMM heat map

Domain	*Level 1*	*Level 2*	*Level 3*	*Level 4*	*Level 5*
Governance					
Architecture and Engineering					
IT and Operations					
Risk, Compliance and Audit					
Metrics and Reporting					
Culture and Collaboration					

Interpreting the heat map

A heat map turns conversation into clarity. When the scores from each domain are plotted visually, it becomes impossible to hide uneven progress. Green boxes show where assurance is thriving. Yellow or red boxes mark where dependency on manual effort or isolated ownership still dominates. The pattern tells a story about how the organization works under pressure.

Leaders should view the heat map as a diagnostic instrument rather than a report card. A domain sitting at Level 2 is not a failure; it is a signal that foundational capabilities need attention before scaling. The objective is not to paint the map green, but to ensure each color reflects deliberate awareness and focused improvement.

When reviewed as a team, the map becomes a common language for prioritization. Executives can see at a glance where governance is mature but culture lags, or where technology advances faster than organizational readiness. This view prevents the common mistake of investing in tools while neglecting behaviors. It also helps leaders explain progress to boards and regulators without resorting to jargon.

Over time, the heat map evolves into a living artifact. Quarterly updates reveal how maturity shifts as initiatives take hold. Some areas will improve rapidly as new controls, playbooks, or governance routines mature. Others may regress if ownership changes or leadership attention drifts. These fluctuations are valuable. They show that assurance is dynamic and that vigilance must remain constant.

To interpret the map effectively, leaders should focus on the trajectory. A steady climb across several domains indicates alignment and cultural adoption. A flat line or regression may point to structural issues, such as a lack of authority or competing priorities. In every review, the map should invite reflection: What changed? Why? What must we do next to sustain progress? When the organization learns to read its own heat map this way, it begins to operate with greater self-awareness and accountability. See Table A8.4: IAMM heat map.

Developing improvement plans

Once the current state is visible, the next step is deliberate improvement. The mistake many organizations make is trying to leap multiple maturity levels at once. IAMM was designed to be evolutionary, not revolutionary. Moving from one level to the next builds stability and prevents fatigue.

Improvement planning begins by selecting specific domains that will deliver the greatest business value if strengthened. For example, an organization that struggles with incident coordination might focus first on the IT and Operations domain. One that faces audit fatigue might begin in the Risk, Compliance, and Audit domain to rationalize overlapping frameworks. Each plan should be anchored in a clear objective: What will be different once this level is achieved?

For each chosen domain, leaders define ownership, outcomes, and measurement. Ownership identifies who carries the responsibility for change. Outcomes describe the tangible behaviors or systems that should exist once the improvement is realized. Measurement provides the evidence that progress is real. This may include new metrics, playbooks, or patterns of collaboration visible in daily work.

Progress should be reviewed in cycles that mirror business cadence, typically quarterly. This keeps maturity integrated into performance conversations rather than treated as a special project. When teams present their progress, they should show how improvements affected resilience outcomes such as containment time, recovery readiness, or trust velocity. These results connect maturity to value.

Every improvement plan must also consider dependencies. Raising maturity in one domain often requires reinforcement in another. A governance improvement will not hold if culture remains weak. A metrics overhaul will fail if operations cannot produce reliable data. By sequencing plans in logical order and ensuring each builds upon the previous, organizations create a sustainable climb instead of a series of disconnected efforts.

When these plans are executed with patience and visibility, maturity shifts from aspiration to evidence. Teams begin to recognize that improvement is possible, measurable, and meaningful. That realization strengthens confidence across the enterprise and fuels the momentum to continue.

Index

For Product Safety Concerns and Information please contact our EU
representative GPSR@taylorandfrancis.com
Taylor & Francis Verlag GmbH, Kaufingerstraße 24, 80331 München, Germany

www.ingramcontent.com/pod-product-compliance
Ingram Content Group UK Ltd.
Pitfield, Milton Keynes, MK11 3LW, UK
UKHW051930240926
475702UK00036B/1104
* 9 7 8 1 0 4 1 1 6 7 0 0 6 *